COMMUNITY RESEARCH

EDITORS AND CONTRIBUTORS AND THEIR AFFILIATIONS

Editors:

Edwin C. Susskind	University of Maryland Baltimore County
Donald C. Klein	Union for Experimenting Colleges and Universities

Contributors:

John W. Lounsbury	The University of Tennessee
Michael P. Cook	Appalachian State University
Dianne S. Leader	The University of Tennessee
Elizabeth P. Meares	The University of Tennessee
James H. Dalton	Bloomsbury University of Pennsylvania
Maurice J. Elias	Rutgers University
George W. Howe	George Peabody College of Vanderbilt University
Glenn Shippee	University of Missouri
Stefan E. Hormuth	Universität Heidelberg
Nancy M. Fitzgerald	Northwestern University
Thomas D. Cook	Northwestern University
Slobodan B. Petrovich	University of Maryland Baltimore County
Eckhard H. Hess	The University of Chicago
Edison J. Trickett	University of Maryland
James G. Kelly	University of Illinois at Chicago
Trudy A. Vincent	University of Maryland
Rolf von Eckartsberg	Duquesne University
Raymond W. Novaco	University of California, Irvine
Alan Vaux	Southern Illinois University
Thomas D'Aunno	University of Michigan

tm

COMMUNITY RESEARCH

Methods, Paradigms, and Applications

Edited by

Edwin C. Susskind
and Donald C. Klein

PRAEGER

PRAEGER SPECIAL STUDIES • PRAEGER SCIENTIFIC

New York • Philadelphia • Eastbourne, UK
Toronto • Hong Kong • Tokyo • Sydney

Library of Congress Cataloging in Publication Data
Main entry under title:

Community research.

   Includes bibliographies and index.
   1. Community psychology--Research. 2. Community
psychology. I. Susskind, Edwin C. II. Klein, Donald C.
RA790.C681224 1984   362.2'042'072   84-17921
ISBN 0-03-070644-0 (alk. paper)

To Our Families

Nava, Yifat, Hadar, Ari Benjamin and Coby

Lola, Stefan, Jonathan, Alan and Jeremy

Published in 1985 by Praeger Publishers
CBS Educational and Professional Publishing
a Division of CBS Inc.
521 Fifth Avenue, New York, NY 10175 USA

© 1985 by Praeger Publishers

56789 052 987654321

Printed in the United States of America
on acid-free paper

Foreword

John C. Glidewell

This book makes a highly significant contribution to community psychology and to community research in general. It provides an impressive variety of approaches and orientations. As Editor of the <u>American Journal of Community Psychology</u> I am frequently reminded of the tendency within psychology to think that the way of the true experiment is the only way to gather valid and useful information. Unfortunately, any other approach to knowledge building in community settings is seen all too often as an <u>alternative</u> to experimentation, an alternative that, however unavoidable under the circumstances, is to be regretted, and therefore abandoned as soon as circumstances permit.

One of the most important things that could happen to community psychology--and, indeed, to the community research enterprise in general--is the recognition that there are many useful alternative routes to the exploration of community phenomena. Only one of those alternatives is the true experiment. The unique strength of this volume is that it presents a wide variety of approaches, not as alternatives to the experimental ideal but rather as useful and appropriate tools from which to select depending on the nature of the phenomena to be studied and the circumstances under which the research is being carried out.

I especially recommend this book to any person concerned about confidence in research discoveries. In essence, this is a book about confidence. Research enables one both to create ideas and to find out how confident one can be in the usefulness of those ideas. Recently I have been more deeply involved than I really wanted to be in trying to articulate clearly a sensible answer to the question, "<u>Just what is superb scholarship?</u>" I was discussing the matter with colleagues who were scholars, professional practitioners, or both. We agreed that <u>scholarship was a search for important, dependable knowledge</u>. We disagreed about how successful that search had to be in order to call it superb scholarship.

After much argument, we decided that there were two issues: the <u>importance</u> of a discovery and the <u>confidence</u>

one had in the means of the pursuit of that discovery. Privately, I thought that judgments of importance were necessarily more time limited than judgments of confidence. Confidence usually depends on method, and that is why I see this as a book about confidence. The methods of scholarship presented herein are means of ensuring as much confidence as possible in what one discovers. That discovery may, in the end, turn out to be more or less important as one's discipline or practice gains perspective, but <u>a scholar actively regulates methods to ensure an enduring confidence in the process of discovery itself</u>.

The authors of the chapters in this book give most of their attention to methods that enhance confidence in discoveries. Most of the many ways of enhancing confidence are given clear exposition here.

Like any book on method, this one is grounded in a set of dialectic considerations. Though allowed to remain implicit by the authors, the theses and the antitheses are evident. Confidence requires that:

- Research design be complex; research design be simple.
- Data be observation; data be self-reported experience.
- Analysis be quantitative; analysis be qualitative.
- Phenomena be measured; phenomena be sensed.
- Variables be under the control of the researcher; variables be under the control of nature.

These dialectic avenues to confidence are well explored in this volume. Complexity is, on the one hand, decomposed to simple connections, as by Dalton and his colleagues; simplicity, on the other hand, is arranged and organized into complex systems, as by Petrovich and Hess. Some data are disciplined observations, as specified by Lounsbury and his colleagues; some data are insightful self-reports of vital experiences, as noted by von Eckartsberg. Some analyses are quantitative, whether truly experimental (Shippee specifies the virtues) or quasi-experimental (Hormuth and his colleagues evaluate the approaches).

Some analyses are <u>quantitative</u>, counting or measuring units of behaviors, motives, feelings, skills, beliefs—units having vague boundaries and ambiguous forms. Other analyses are <u>qualitative</u>, questions of "what kind" rather than of "how much." The quality of community life is found in both: for example, the quantity of the number of pounds of bread and the quality of the kinds of affection, issues given special meaning by Novaco and Vaux. Some arguments form a linear series of connections, such as the causal modes of connections between stress, support, coping, and illness. Other arguments reflect the ecological spirit of Trickett, Kelly, and Vincent and deal with networks of associations, such as patterns of social support and friendship structures in a neighborhood. Some phenomena are counted or measured, for example, employment, income, family size, or intensity of attitude. Other phenomena are sensed, felt, or firmly known, without scales, yardsticks, or estimations of magnitude. These latter form the heart of a person's fundamental sense of community. They remain, as they must, deeply subjective.

For the adventurer on a voyage of community knowledge building, this volume offers a network of roads to confidence in discovery; it provides a map of roads, double red lines for major arteries, single blue lines for narrower ones, all of which crisscross and intersect with one another long before they reach the Rome of truth and utility. As you peruse its contents, I recommend that even as you choose your road to community inquiry, you pause at each intersection to ponder all the other avenues toward confidence.

Nashville, Tennessee

ACKNOWLEDGMENTS

It is good to have the opportunity to acknowledge some of our friends and colleagues who have contributed to our ability to create this work.

The major single influence on Ed Susskind's development as a community psychologist was his training as a graduate student at the Yale Psycho-Educational Clinic (1964-1969). His teachers, Seymour Sarason, Murray Levine, and Ira Goldenberg, gave generously of themselves as they involved their students in the very creation of the newly emerging field of community psychology. The clinic was a very special, cohesive, and exciting place for the staff and students, who, during this period, also included: Ed Bennett, Dennis Cherlin, Elizabeth Fox, Gil Freitag, Frances Kaplan, Verne McArthur, Kate McGraw, Anita Miller, Jim Miller, Dick Reppucci, Esther Sarason, Andy Schwebel, and Rhona Weinstein.

During three years (1969-1972) as a faculty member in S.U.N.Y.-Buffalo's community psychology program, Ed continued to learn from Murray Levine, who was program director, as well as from other members of the warmly collegial graduate community (among them: Mike Domenico, Tony Graziano, Ed Katkin, Steve Lewis, Joe Masling, Irv Sigel, Ron Silverman, Karl Slaikieu, and Steve Tulkin). The department's request that he teach the graduate statistics sequence strongly affected the development of his professional interests in statistics and in paradigms for research. That interest continued to grow as he taught graduate statistics at the Psychology Department of The Hebrew University of Jerusalem during 1972-1975, where he worked with Kalman Binyamini, Charlie Greenbaum, and Zev Klein.

A similarly powerful influence on his growth as a clinical psychologist was fostered by psychotherapist Geraldine Slote Neugroschl, during his undergraduate years at Columbia (1960-1964). He gained a profound respect for the potency of psychotherapy and for the importance of naturalistic nonexperimental paradigms to capture the quality of central human experiences.

Don Klein's teachers whose influences are reflected in this volume include Egon Brunswik, Erik Erikson, Jean Walker Macfarlane, and Edward Tolman, who were faculty members during his graduate student years at the University of California at Berkeley (1947–1952). Others to whom he owes a considerable intellectual debt in regard to approaches to inquiry are Kenneth Benne, Robert Chin, Jack Glidewell, Erich Lindemann, and a host of NTL Institute colleagues who have kept alive the vital spirit of action research and laboratory learning which was inspired by Kurt Lewin. Finally, he takes this opportunity to express his affectionate appreciation to colleagues in community psychology who shared the excitement of the Swampscott Conference (where community psychology was born in the mid–1960s) and to the growing number of younger community psychologists with inquiring minds whose work is creating a solid substantive base for the field.

We are indebted to a number of members of the Psychology Department at the University of Maryland Baltimore County (UMBC). Aron Siegman, as Chairman of the Department, invited Don Klein to teach a graduate course on Research Methods in Community Psychology as a visiting professor. It was from that course, co-taught by us both, that the impetus for this book emerged, when we realized no textbook was available. We wish to thank our graduate students who joined us in the challenge of identifying and exploring a set of issues and approaches that were the beginning of this volume. Supportive colleagues Stanley Feldstein and Slobodan Petrovich encouraged our efforts through a long period of gestation. Madelon Kellough provided cheerful and skillful secretarial support, complemented by Mark Antell's precise proofreading. Our thanks to UMBC's administration for awarding Ed Susskind a sabbatical leave (1981–1982) to work on the book.

It has been a pleasure to work with George Zimmar, our editor from Praeger. Himself a psychologist, George appreciated the substance and spirit of the book, had many helpful suggestions to offer, and remained committed through several missed deadlines.

In addition, we celebrate one another and our collaboration. Individually, I, Ed Susskind, want to acknowledge Don for his combination of nonpunitive patience and empowering prodding. One of the most valuable learnings for me in our collaboration was experiencing his ability to adopt a Zen-like "don't push against the river," while still managing to irrigate the valley.

Individually, I, Don Klein, want to acknowledge Ed for three impressive qualities--enormously vital enthusiasm, imagination, and a high level of aspiration. These qualities led to the creation of a volume which far exceeds the more modest concept that was originally in my head. Ed's editorial skills also were a marvel to behold. Every chapter of this book was pruned, sharpened, and made far more readable because of his insistence on clarity and solid organization.

Finally, we thank the contributors to this volume for joining us and sharing in our belief that such a volume was important enough to merit their contribution, for responding thoughtfully to our editorial comments, and for persevering during the many and sometimes frustrating years it took to bring this project to fruition.

Columbia, Maryland
Fall, 1984

CONTENTS

COMMUNITY RESEARCH

1   A Multiparadigmatic Approach to Community Research: Paradigm Choice, Experiential Validity, and Commitment

Edwin C. Susskind

OUR RATIONALE AND GOALS

"The problem with having a hammer is that you may tend to treat everything as though it were a nail." Some popular but limited views of the nature of scientific inquiry constrain the tools available to community researchers to ones which may be inappropriate for or destructive to the medium with which these researchers work. This book is one attempt to present a broader view better suited to community research.

The thesis of this chapter, and the rationale for this book, is that:

1. Community researchers often accept inappropriate restrictions in the range of paradigms they may legitimately use as scientists.
2. As a result, they may adopt a paradigm that precludes their studying the phenomena of greatest concern to themselves, to their discipline, and to the broader society.
3. They may instead choose to study topics to which the paradigm is hospitable, even if these be less central to their discipline or trivial with respect to their discipline's objectives.
4. In the process, they may sacrifice external validity, experiential validity, and ecological validity, as well as passion and relevance.

1

5. As a consequence, their research (both its products and its process) loses a great deal of credibility and commitment from theoreticians, from clinical practitioners, from community leaders, and from the educated public at large.

6. Most importantly, by appropriately expanding the paradigms available to them, community researchers will be better equipped to engage in disciplined study of phenomena that are acknowledged as significant by all concerned.

The impetus for this book emerged from a seminar, cotaught by Donald Klein and Edwin Susskind, in which we and our graduate students sought to resolve some of the paradoxes or double binds of field research. One of these paradoxes is reflected in the following story:

> A man decided to treat himself for the first time to a custom-tailored suit. "Remarkable!" exclaimed the tailor, "I have just the thing for you--A very well-established customer of mine, who ordered a suit of the most exquisite and expensive fabric, has decided not to claim the garment, so you can have it at an incredible savings." However, the man noticed that the suit did not fit properly: it was tight across the shoulders, loose across the hips, and uneven on the left trouser leg. "Despair not," consoled the tailor, "all you need do is hunch up your left shoulder, stick out your right hip, and turn your left foot inward a bit, and you'll look like a million dollars."
>   As he hobbled down the street in his new garment, the man passed two women, one of whom frowned while the second beamed. "Oh my god," cried the first, "did you see that unfortunate cripple?" "Yes," replied the second, "but did you see what a magnificent tailor he has!

Often we find that in our attempts to fit the concerns of community research into well-established and powerful research paradigms, we must compromise either our concerns or the paradigms.

To help resolve that paradox, I will assume four tasks in this chapter. First, I will draw a distinction between naturalistic and designed data fields. Second, I will discuss three interwoven problems that result when one imposes designed-field paradigms on naturalistic phenomena; the three include the issues of experiential validity, ecological validity, and commitment. Third, I will discuss how three specific community psychologists (Ira Goldenberg, Murray Levine, and Seymour Sarason) have each contended with the paradox and have managed to conduct disciplined studies of naturalistic phenomena central to their discipline. Finally, I will indicate how the other nine chapters in this book relate to our thesis and to the resolution of the paradox.

You may have noticed that the tone in this chapter is more personal and informal than that typically found in the research literature and in many of the other chapters in this book. For example, in the preceding sentence I addressed you as "you," rather than as "the reader." My rationale for this personal tone will be made explicit ahead, toward the conclusion of the discussion of experiential validity.

NATURALISTIC VERSUS DESIGNED DATA FIELDS

There is a common methodological problem faced by researchers who study community phenomena, be they community psychologists, community social workers, empirical sociologists, epidemiologists, social anthropologists, or social psychiatrists. The research approaches most lauded during their graduate training typically draw only on a limited subset of methodologies used by some of the natural sciences. The data most suited to these methodologies can be labeled as ones generated in a designed data field. These approaches are typically not the methodology of choice for studying the events of primary interest to community researchers, which frequently occur in a naturalistic data field.

Eight Components of the Designed Data Field

The term designed is meant to convey that the investigator has considerable control over the research environment. There are at least eight components of that control. At this point, I will discuss each of the eight in some detail, so that we can later discuss their suitability and feasibility in community research.

Control over Group Membership

The experimenter has control over the membership of the various comparison groups in the study. Typically, he or she randomly assigns subjects to conditions (or employs matched pairs and/or repeated measures) to ensure the initial comparability of the groups.

Control over the Timing of Events

The experimenter determines the timing and magnitude of fluctuations in the manipulated independent variable. Further, the experimenter controls the frequency with which events occur, such that he or she can ensure a sufficient number of occurrences (or data points) to permit statistical analysis.

Perceptual Control during Measurement

Phenomena are measured "directly," that is, with a minimum of human inference, thereby minimizing the influence of those biases that otherwise distort human perception. There is a uniform (and often untested) discrediting of self-report or testimony by either subjects or observers.

Such direct measurement relies on a combination of three procedures. One is mechanical measurement by means of a physical device such as a thermometer or sphygmomanometer. A second is human recording of behavior, where the behaviors involved are simple, concrete, and external (or "public"), thereby requiring little or no inference on the observer's part; for example, the observer records the number of times a child was absent from school. That second approach has the value of focusing the research around actual behavior. In contrast, the third procedure, scale construction, requires a process of abstraction and inference that often radically departs from direct behavioral observation.

It appears that one has a choice to make when attempting to measure behaviors that are complex, abstract, or internal ("nonpublic"), such as "adjustment" or "rootedness." One alternative is to trust the sensitivity and relative accuracy of a human observer; in cases where the "stimulus" can be presented repeatedly to pairs of observers, one can even quantify one aspect of the observers' accuracy, that is, their reliability. However, the alternative commonly preferred in a designed data field is to create a scale, a method which raises at least two potential problems: (1) the complex, assumption-filled statistical techniques (for example, factor analysis) used to create the scale can leave one unsure as to what the scale is actually measuring; and (2) a frequent, though not necessary, concomitant is that the data components from which the scale is generated frequently involve subjects' responses to paper-and-pencil instruments, rather than the direct recording of actual behaviors.

Quantitative Control

It is assumed and required that the phenomenon under study has been adequately measured and quantified. Further, these measurements are assumed to satisfy a set of mathematical properties which make them amenable to specific inferential statistical analyses: the measurements constitute an interval scale; they are normally distributed; the operational measurements bear a linear relationship to the concept or "true score" they are intended to estimate; the various measures relate to each other in a primarily linear fashion; and in many instances, it is assumed that the comparison groups differ only in their means, while preserving homoscedasticity in their variances.

Emotional Control

The relationship between the researcher and the subject is explicitly and intentionally impersonal. The researcher is neither friend nor advocate for the subject. This impersonality may be further reflected in the stylistic conventions in the scientists' reporting of their findings.

Social Control

Creating many of the conditions of control described above may require the experimenter to maintain an authoritarian relationship with the subjects. Thus, the preferred subject may be a nonhuman organism or a college undergraduate. The subjects are not involved in the design of the study; further, they may be actively misled in an attempt to keep them "blind" concerning the project's goals.

Control over the Research Setting

Similarly, achieving the above levels of control may demand that the study be conducted in the investigator's own laboratory, rather than in the naturalistic setting of the subject's habitat.

Constraint on the Unit of Analysis

The requirement that the phenomena studied be ones that can be readily and repeatedly produced in the laboratory tends to restrict the concepts investigated to those drawn from the psychology of individual behavior, rather than from the behavior of groups, organizations, communities, or nations. For example, one is more likely to study conflict resolution and decision making using a pair of undergraduates in a "prisoner's dilemma" paradigm, than to examine how cultural norms may make it easier for one pair of nations (in contrast to another pair) to engage in de-escalation of international conflict or how their organizational structures may mitigate or exacerbate conflict between a company and its workers' union.

A Continuum

These eight components of control are present in varying degrees in different research studies. When all eight are fulfilled, we are faced with the extreme case of the designed data field. This situation constitutes one endpoint of a continuum. In contrast, as fewer and fewer of those conditions hold, we move toward the opposite endpoint of the continuum, namely the naturalistic data field, a point which is more characteristic of community phenomena.

Community Phenomena and the Naturalistic Data Field

Let us examine the extent to which the variables of community research conform to the eight components of control:

1. Frequently, the researcher studies "naturally occurring" groups, be they "emotionally disturbed versus normal populations," "high-crime versus low-crime neighbor-

hoods," "supportive versus nonsupportive social networks," or "open versus traditional schools."

2. While the timing of some interventions may be under the researcher's control (as in the program evaluation of a newly introduced "treatment"), many independent variables are beyond his or her ability to manipulate. Further, the amount of time required to create even one instance of the manipulation may be so great that the researcher is practically required to draw inferences from a single data point (see, for example, Goldenberg's analysis of the creation of The Residential Youth Center, discussed ahead).

3. The primary, or even exclusive, source of information about the phenomenon may be the observations and inferences of the researcher and his or her subjects. The phenomenon may inherently involve inferences about internal, nonpublic events (such as "the psychological sense of community").

4. Some of the primary data may be qualitative and descriptive, and thus not amenable to inferential statistical analysis. This may occur for at least two valid reasons: first, the human observer may be more accurate an instrument in describing or drawing inferences about the phenomenon than are any currently available quantitative scales; second, as noted in Point 2 above, the number of data points that can practically be amassed is limited when the unit of analysis is not the individual person but rather a larger social aggregate. Further, a statistically aware investigator (whether in community research or in another specialty) may not wish to be casual in assuming that his or her data meet the parametric requirements of inferential statistical tests.

5. In many cases, the investigator may have an intense personal relationship with the "subjects," as has been the norm in action research and anthropological participant observation; a similar norm of personalness is a vocally espoused tenet in current ecological research models, such as that presented by this text in the chapter by Trickett and his colleagues.

6. A second feature common to both action research and to Trickett's "spirit of ecological research" is a commitment to a collaborative, rather than authoritarian, relationship between researcher and subject. The researcher may choose to solicit the subjects' input when designing the study. For example, if one wants staff members of an

organization to feel a significant commitment to implement the conclusions drawn from a program evaluation, it is extremely important that the staff be involved in the original designing of the study. A collaborative stance may even be <u>required</u> when the researcher's access to the subjects depends on their active agreement (as, for example, in studies of intentional communities) or even on their financial sponsorship (as, for example, when funding is jointly applied for by a researcher and the agency to be studied).

7. It is typically the case that the phenomena of interest cannot be produced in the context of a laboratory but rather require the researcher to gather data in field settings.

8. As already noted, the unit of analysis is not the individual person but a larger social aggregate.

The distinction between naturalistic and designed data fields is not a dichotomous one. Rather, the two concepts define endpoints of a continuum. Many research designs contain a blend of components from both ends of the continuum. For example, a quasi-experimental study comparing differences between naturally occurring groups in field settings is one such hybrid.

Clearly, there are many instances in which the most appropriate and powerful research method is that of the direct experiment, whether in a laboratory or field station. One of this book's chapters (by Glenn Shippee) specifically champions community psychologists' adoption of "the true experiment"; a second chapter (by Stefan Hormuth, Nancy Fitzgerald, and Thomas Cook) lauds the advantages of quasi-experimental designs for field situations that do not fully meet the conditions of the true experiment. The experiment (whether "true" or "quasi") is a powerful hammer!

Similarly, it is crucial that community researchers be <u>statistically sophisticated</u>, given the complexity of the data field in which they operate. Our situation differs radically, for example, from that of the physiological psychologists who can typically demonstrate their effects by using a simple nonparametric Mann-Whitney U test with a sample of 12 subjects. It must be clear that in the specific instances when we espouse a nonstatistical observational study, as I will do in much of this chapter, we do so from an informed awareness that the descriptive approach is the most appropriate for that situation on both theoretical and practical grounds.

Nonetheless, Science is not served by the adulation and apotheosis of the laboratory experiment coupled with statistical inference as The Way to Truth; its evangelical devotees would have us equate Science (that is, the disciplined and systematic building of knowledge) with their single, preferred method. Further, they attempt to intimidate or excommunicate those who use other methods by saying, "Well, if that's the approach you take, you're not a scientist (or psychologist or sociologist or . . .) but just a philosopher or poet or muckraker." The experimental posture, like the missionary position, has its advantages, but it should not totally delimit our experience.

A discipline is not defined by or reducible to a specific set of research methods. Those methods may vary considerably as technology changes. One hundred years ago the inferential statisticians' call to prayer ("there is no god but the point-oh-five and Sir Ronald Fisher is her prophet") would have gone unheeded, because even the simplest inferential statistics (such as Student's t test) had not yet been created. A discipline is defined by the specific set of issues, variables, and relationships that it investigates in an ongoing, systematic, and disciplined manner.

A similar observation was offered by Emory Cowen in his 1976 presidential address to the American Psychological Association's Division of Community Psychology. Cowen acknowledged that in the spirit of the 1960s and the War on Poverty, community psychology had taken on a broad range of goals or dependent variables (for example, to enhance people's physical, economic, intellectual, emotional, and social well-being), goals which were addressed by other disciplines as well (for example, economics, epidemiology, and urban planning). He asserted that what distinguished community psychology from these other disciplines was its particular set of independent variables. Some current examples of such independent or intervening variables might include empowerment, natural support systems, and a psychological sense of community.

Because of the discrepancy between the typical hammers in many methodologists' toolboxes and the naturalistic medium of community researchers, investigators are often pressed to tailor community phenomena into research designs that are more appropriate to other levels of analysis and other content areas. The experience is much like carrying water in a straw basket; you lose a lot along the way.

Three of the major losses involve commitment, experiential validity, and ecological validity. Rather than beginning deductively with a formal definition of these terms, let us move inductively with some concrete examples, embodying the concepts, from which the definitions will emerge. As will be evident in the discussion to follow, the three are quite intertwined.

COMMITMENT, EXPERIENTIAL VALIDITY, AND ECOLOGICAL VALIDITY

While these three issues have an impact on all producers and consumers of research, they are particularly evident and cathected in the context of a graduate student contemplating selection of a community-oriented thesis or dissertation. Further, those students and their teachers are a primary group that this book aims to assist. Thus, I would like to begin our discussion in that general context. In passing, I will briefly relate the student's challenge to that described by Leo Buscaglia in his search for research on love and, more broadly, to Thomas Kuhn's analysis of the constraining effect of paradigms. This general discussion will be followed by a specific example involving one of my graduate students' master's thesis.

We will next broaden our focus to draw two additional examples from the clinical and social psychology literature. These are Irvin Yalom's analysis of psychotherapy research, in general, and of research on death, in particular, and Shlomo Breznitz's work on hope.

Selecting a Research Topic

Selecting a research topic can be an intensely personal and passionate choice, especially when one works in an applied area with concrete implications for people's lives. For many individuals this choice may involve an attempt to use the discipline of science to examine, modify, validate, or promulgate their values and to see whether this scientific process clarifies or enhances what they know "on a gut level," moving that knowledge from the status of a belief in the direction of becoming a fact. Similarly, for many the choice reflects an attempt to give meaningfully to others and an opportunity to see whether research will empower them to solve human problems.

Often the decision relates to a particular pain in the individual's past and constitutes a form of "belated mastery," as in the case of a former victim who goes on to study that process of victimization (for example, rape, substance abuse, or genocide). More cheerfully, the selection may draw on a peak experience (such as childbirth, nursing an infant, or meditation) or a successfully mastered hurdle (for example, overcoming a life-threatening illness) about which the individual wants more expertise and an opportunity to communicate.

All too often the passion is unfulfilled because the researcher is told that the topic he or she has chosen is not currently explorable in a "scientific" way. An analogous objection is described by Leo Buscaglia in his book Love:

> Only recently has it become at all defensible to even mention the word "love."
> Every time I go to speak somewhere, someone asks, "Will you talk about love?" I reply, "Sure," and they say, "What's your title?" I reply, "Let's just call it 'Love'. There's a brief hesitation, and then they say, "Well, you know, this is a professional meeting and it may not be understood. What will the press say?" So I suggest "Affect as a Behavior Modifier," and they agree that sounds more acceptable and scientific, and everyone is happy.
>   Love has been ignored by the scientists. It's amazing. My students and I did a study. We went through books in psychology. We went through books in sociology. We went through books in anthropology, and we were hardpressed to find even a reference to the word "love."
> (1972, pp. 16-17)

Clearly, the types of phenomena that researchers and their students are free to "study" depend heavily on the research paradigms that are both available and viewed as legitimate. In many cases we are constrained and frustrated by a paradigm shaft.

Scientists have become more conscious of the effects of paradigms in both guiding/focusing and narrowing/distorting their thoughts and very perceptions since the

1962 publication of Thomas Kuhn's influential book <u>The Structure of Scientific Revolutions</u>. The effect of this paradigm problem for community research has been discussed by Julian Rappaport in his textbook <u>Community Psychology: Values, Research and Action</u>:

> One of the things a paradigm provides for a scientific community is what Kuhn calls a criterion for choosing problems assumed to have solutions. The problems to which the paradigm leads are the only problems that the appropriate scientific community will consider to be scientific or worthy of its members' attention. In Kuhn's words ". . . other problems, including many that had previously been standard, are rejected as metaphysical, or the concern of another discipline, or sometimes as just too problematic to be worth the time. A paradigm can, for that matter, even insulate the community from those socially important problems that are not reducible to the puzzle form because they cannot be stated in terms of the conceptual and instrumental tools the paradigm supplies." (1977, pp. 18-19)

A graduate student is typically encouraged or required to demonstrate mastery of the technologies of the designed data field (for example, analysis of variance and multiple regression) within the dissertation. Finding a "lack of fit" between these technologies and the applied problems he or she had hoped to study, the student may abandon the original topic to seek a "safer" thesis. Many of us involved in training graduate students in community as well as clinical psychology have seen students choose a thesis topic totally outside their area of specialization because it appeared more "do-able." Such a choice might well be encouraged when it reflects intellectual breadth, but not when it signals a sense of the irrelevance of the research process to those issues to which the student is most personally committed.

The pressure to use a familiar or conventional paradigm is not necessarily imposed on the students by the faculty. Rather, the students themselves, facing the challenge of initiating their first original research project, may cling to the comfort of the conventional; they forsake an unfamiliar screwdriver which might open an exciting puzzle, for the safety of pounding with a recognized hammer.

More subtle and insidious than this direct abandonment of a specific research topic is a second potential loss, involving "fidelity to the phenomenon," a term we have borrowed from the Canadian community psychologist Benjamin Gottleib. Rather than rejecting the original research interest, the student may reformulate the problem in order to study one smaller, more focused, aspect. The student may create an analogue of the original concern, one or more steps removed from the original context of concern, to make the study more amenable to controlled laboratory experimentation and sophisticated quantitative analysis. In the process, the context may be so radically altered or the operationalized variables so changed that one is no longer studying the same phenomenon. The fact that one chooses to label the new variables as though they are identical or equivalent to the originals does not make them so; you may say that you have "fixed" a cat, but from the cat's point of view, it's been broken.

This pressure to study an analogue of the phenomenon rather than the phenomenon itself was grappled with recently by one of my graduate students, Debra Popeil. She has agreed to have that experience discussed in this chapter.

Popeil's Study of Rape Victims

Debra Popeil wanted to study whether the amount and types of support received by rape victims from their social network and from professionals influenced the victims' subsequent adjustment. A review of the literature revealed that little had been done to examine this specific issue. However, she faced a number of difficulties in translating this concern into a research design that she thought would be acceptable to her committee.

Among these difficulties were the facts (1) that subjects would be hard to recruit, which might reduce the sample size below the 30 subjects needed for univariate correlational analysis, not to mention the number needed for multiple regression; (2) that since it would be impossible to identify future subjects and to administer the adjustment measures <u>prior</u> to the rape, she would not be able to perform a pre-post comparison but would be limited to a post-only design; and (3) that since she would not be able to observe the supportive behaviors directly, she would have to rely on the subjects' recall and self-report, a potentially unreliable or confounded data source.

In light of these difficulties, she decided to modify her proposal. After passing through a number of incarnations, her proposal called for an interview with campus undergraduates, who would be asked how they felt about rape (for example, "to what extent or in what situations would you blame the woman?") and what types of support they would request, offer, or receive <u>if</u> they or someone close to them were raped. The proposal included an experimental manipulation: the subjects would participate in a two-hour workshop on understanding rape to be offered on campus by a local rape crisis center; the two groups of subjects (50 males and 50 females) would complete the attitude questionnaires ("what would you do <u>if</u> . . .") prior to and following the workshop.

The new proposal contained a number of attractions. It would be relatively easy to obtain subjects by relying on nominal payments or course credit or student goodwill and curiosity as incentives; there would be minimal problems of confidentiality, subjects' embarrassment or institutional approval (for example, by police departments or hospital emergency rooms). The design included an experimental manipulation and readily lent itself to a neat two-by-two, gender by pre-post, repeated measures analysis of variance, with one degree of freedom for each of the effects of interest. The combination of a repeated measures design (which reduces error variance) and the relatively large sample size insured that the design was well powered, making it likely that some of the dependent measures would yield statistically significant differences.

Nonetheless, she was dissatisfied, finding it hard to get excited about the research. "Is this something to which I want to devote a year of my life?" she wondered. Asking subjects to imagine (that is, to make believe) that they'd been assaulted and to hypothesize what they would do <u>if</u> . . . was very different from learning from the experiences of an actual victim. Such can be the problems when one studies an <u>analogue</u> of a phenomenon rather than the phenomenon itself: it is like reading an enticing

menu in a fine restaurant and deciding to chew the menu
instead of ordering the courses; often, the student is un-
interested in coming back for a second meal.

Ms. Popeil's predicament demonstrates two of the
losses of concern to us. First of all, what she sensed as
lacking in her new proposal was ecological validity. That
is, when the phenomenon, the conditions, and the subjects
being studied and measured in the research are sufficiently different from those to which we want to generalize "in
the real world," then one cannot validly draw any inferences from the sample that would necessarily hold true "in
the real world." To put it more simply, the research
findings are irrelevant to "real world" problems.

Secondly, as a consequence of this loss of ecological
validity, she encountered a potential second loss, the loss
of commitment to the research process. I am pleased to
report that, fortunately, we were able to help her to re-
structure the design in a manner that left her feeling that
she had a disciplined and meaningful, albeit imperfect,
vehicle to study the problem.

On the one hand, we agreed that she would use
actual victims as her subjects and clinical interviews as a
major data source. As a consequence, we understood that
a sample of 25 subjects was as large as would be feasible
for her to collect and that any statistical analyses would
be limited by the design's low statistical power. Further,
some of her key inferences about the support factors contributing to adjustment would be based on her subjective
integration of victims' personal "testimony."

On the other hand, she would also generate three
sets of more objective and quantitative data to be subjected to multiple regression and partial correlational
analyses. One set included eight measures of the apparent
severity or stressfulness of the assault (for example, the
extent of the physical injuries). A second set included
two established scales that have been used to measure
psychological adjustment. The third set involved a scale
that Ms. Popeil created to measure victims' perception of
the amount and kinds of support received from relatives,
friends, and professionals. A major hypothesis was that
the support ratings would meaningfully enhance the prediction of adjustment, beyond that predicted by the stressfulness measures. Ms. Popeil hoped that the effect magnitude of these relationships was sufficiently large to yield
results that were in the predicted direction (and possibly
significant as well), despite the small sample size.

Ms. Popeil completed her thesis in May of 1983, presented her findings to the Eastern Psychological Association in April of 1984, and currently has a journal article under review. However, the basic problem of potential disillusionment with and alienation from the research process goes well beyond her specific example.

Commitment to Research

We face a problem in the behavioral sciences in that many of the professionals we train avoid ever engaging again in research once they escape our clutches and depart graduate school. During the early 1970s, when I was a faculty member at the State University of New York, Buffalo, the director of our clinical training program, Murray Levine, discussed the statistics he had seen concerning this problem. He asked, "If you count the number of research publications completed by applied psychologists during the ten years after their doctorate that involve research beyond their doctoral dissertations, what is the average number per psychologist?" He shocked us all by reporting that the median figure was <u>zero</u>. That is, at least half of these Ph.D.s published <u>no research studies whatsoever</u> beyond their thesis data during those ten years.

A comparable criticism appears in Irvin Yalom's recent text <u>Existential Psychotherapy</u>. He states:

> It is common knowledge that psychotherapy research has had, in its thirty year history, little impact upon the practice of therapy. In fact, as Carl Rogers, the founding father of empirical psychotherapy research, sadly noted, not even psychotherapy researchers take their findings seriously enough to alter their approach to psychotherapy. It is also common knowledge that <u>the great majority of clinicians stop doing empirical research once they finish their dissertation or earn tenure</u> [italics mine]. . . . I believe that as the clinician gains maturity, he or she gradually begins to appreciate that there are staggering problems inherent in an empirical study of psychotherapy. (Yalom, 1980, p. 23)

Clearly there is a failure on the part of researchers to impress practitioners with the utility of both their findings as well as their very methods. There is a comparable failure on the part of clinicians to draw upon those findings and methods, or to propose more appropriate alternatives.

Perhaps some will explain that many of these professionals simply lack "the right stuff," and that there is only a small elite capable of either conducting meaningful research or of integrating its findings in clinical practice. However, I propose that these data reflect, at least in good part, our failure to demonstrate to graduate students that the research process is relevant to their finding powerful answers to important questions.

Yalom: Research on Psychotherapy and on Death

A similar point is presented more elegantly by Yalom: "Again and again one encounters a basic fact of life in psychotherapy research: the precision of the result is directly proportional to the triviality of the variables studied. A strange type of science!" (1980, p. 24)

Yalom's words are particularly impressive when one considers that he epitomizes, in many ways, the ideal of the "scientist-practitioner." A professor of psychiatry at Stanford University, he has published clinical research studies that have been well regarded for their content and methodology. Further, two of his integrative texts (The Theory and Practice of Group Psychotherapy and Existential Psychotherapy) are viewed by many as the definitive volumes in their area; both those texts demonstrate his broad scholarship, his articulateness and, most important to our discussion, his commitment to integrate findings from the research literature with those reported by theoreticians and practitioners.

There is an interesting parallel between Yalom's concerns and those voiced in Buscaglia's quotation earlier in this chapter. Buscaglia has criticized the behavioral sciences for failing to discuss as central a human concern as love. Yalom is similarly bothered by the failure of the research literature to address the four issues viewed by existentialists as the most fundamental sources of human anxiety (namely: death, freedom, isolation, and meaninglessness). For example, with respect to the topic of death, he notes:

> Over the past three decades there has been a continuous but feeble stream of empirical social science research on death . . . the contrast between the speculative or impressionistic writings on death and the methodical research into it is striking. . . . A bibliography on death up to 1972 listed over 2,600 books and articles; yet fewer than 2 percent report empirical research. (Yalom, 1980, pp. 49–50)

This theme, that the research literature avoids, ignores, or precludes an examination of major concepts central to human experience, recurs in many sources if one is alert to the issue. I had the pleasure of attending a recent colloquium address (February 16, 1984) entitled "The Psychology of Hope" given by Professor Shlomo Breznitz, an internationally recognized scholar and experimental social psychologist. His remarks about the research on hope complement those of Buscaglia on love and of Yalom on the existential concerns.

Breznitz's Research on Hope

Breznitz is interested in the process of hoping, and in how that process affects a person's ability to perform in the face of a challenge, for individuals ranging from marathon runners to cancer victims. He reports that when he searched the index of psychology and social science abstracts under "hope," he found no hope. The closest item he could find in the index was "Hopi Indians." Further, when he discusses his experiments in which it is clear to him that he has manipulated hope as an independent variable, he finds that some of his colleagues are upset with his use of the label hope. These critics would prefer that he use a term which describes the actual external manipulation (for example, variation in instructional set) without making inferences about what is going on inside the subject.

Breznitz's responses to that criticism reflect the fact that he is a mellow and nondogmatic person, his sharp wit notwithstanding. He accepts others' right to label the manipulation as other than hope. However, he does clearly point out that psychology has been reluctant to use concepts like hope, concepts whose validity we should accept in light of their power and persistence in the vocabulary of human experience. Further, he asserts that behavioral scientists' reluctance to deal with concepts like hope has contributed to the alienation that exists between the sciences and the humanities.

I would add that this reluctance has similarly contributed to the alienation between behavioral researchers, on the one hand, and practitioners, on the other, be they clinicians, community activists, business executives, or politicians. It is important that Breznitz continue to call his manipulated variable hope; to do otherwise would do violence to his research in a number of ways. For one, it is quite evident that Breznitz intends to manipulate hope and believes that he has manipulated hope. Further, many in his audience share his perception (or to play a bit with jargon, there is high inter-rater reliability in agreeing that he is actually manipulating hope); many in his audience find value in the research precisely because it illuminates the phenomenon that people call hope.

Experiential Validity

I would label this type of validity that Breznitz attributes to the term hope as experiential validity. While describing a phenomenon that is in many ways similar to face validity, the term experiential validity more powerfully asserts our willingness to take seriously our collective subjective experience. A study has experiential validity when a "reasonable" group of people (both lay as well as professional) concur that the phenomena, variables, and measures used in the study have been defined or operationalized in ways that are clearly and powerfully consistent with their individual experience.

Perhaps I can better convey the concept by comparing it to two analogous experiences: there are times when you are so powerfully moved by a novelist's description that you say to yourself, "I know that's true, my whole body and soul resonate to the description, and I know the novelist must be writing from personal experience because that's the only way she or he could describe the event

with such intimate knowledge"; similarly, there are times
when you have a sudden insight (whether during psychotherapy, or when awakening in the middle of the night
with a solution to a technical problem that had eluded you
during the day) where you say to yourself, "Aha! Eureka!
Oh my god, that's the answer!"

Clearly, the fact that an idividual experiences
"something" as experientially valid does not guarantee
that it is "true." Human perception and self-report,
whether by individuals or by groups, are sometimes invalid or biased. Perhaps the most salient examples of
strongly held perception which receive intragroup validation and are nonetheless erroneous include intergroup
prejudices and stereotypes. Similarly, an individual's
attempt to draw inferences about another person's internal
experience (for example, is the person experiencing hope?)
may be inaccurate.

However, these sources of information are not necessarily invalid; nor are they necessarily less valid or
more biased a source of information than are attempts to
understand the same phenomenon through "objective" measures of in-laboratory analogues of the phenomenon. One
can draw an analogy to the courtroom, where we accept a
witness's testimony as valid, provided that cross-examination does not show the witness to be incompetent or to have
a vested interest that would create a bias. Similarly, a
finding which elicits strong experiential validity should be
given credence or "the benefit of the doubt" in the absence
of specific evidence of bias. To borrow a metaphor cited
by Yalom (1980, p. 25), if you teach a dog to play the
violin, you don't need a string quartet to prove it.

There has been a bias in academic settings, assert-
ing that objective measurement of behavioral events in
controlled laboratory settings has greater external validity
and less distortion than does disciplined subjective human
observation and self-report of external behavior and internal events (for example, motivation) in field settings. In
contrast, I wish to assert that each of these two data
sources contains its own distortions and that the two approaches complement each other. It seems most reasonable
to trust that a "finding" is valid, and not a result of
either an experimental artifact or of human misperception,
when the criteria of both approaches have been satisfied.

The academic bias dismissing experiential evidence
is so intense that it is rarely perceived as a bias or even

as a postulate but rather as a self-evident truth. The bias exists within a closed system that is often not penetrated by conflicting evidence.

One example of what I mean by a closed system is the case of the psychologist lecturing to a group of alcoholics; he placed two glasses before him, one filled with water, the other with vodka, and dropped a worm in each; the worm in the water swam happily, while its inebriated colleague shriveled and died. When the psychologist asked the audience to draw the obvious conclusion, they replied, "If you drink, you won't get worms."

Perhaps one should not be at all surprised at the closedness of the system, given the following observation by Kuhn, in The Structure of Scientific Revolutions (1970):

> To the extent . . . that two scientific
> schools disagree about what is a problem
> and what a solution, they will inevitably
> talk through each other when debating the
> relative merits of their respective para-
> digms. In the partially circular arguments
> that regularly result, each paradigm will
> be shown to satisfy more or less the cri-
> teria that it dictates for itself and to fall
> short of a few of those dictated by its op-
> ponent. (Pp. 109-10)

The bias against experiential evidence is maintained despite the fact that it is inconsistent with most academic researchers' own behavior. Look at what researchers tend to do when faced with findings (their own or their colleagues') that run counter to their own experience and beliefs. Unless the study has very powerful external and experiential validity, the researchers will find some methodological flaw to explain away the findings. Discussion sections of journal articles are particularly acute in perceiving the studies' methodological flaws when a result diverges from the author's expectations. That is to say, in most cases, data are believed and accepted only when they also satisfy the criterion of experiential validity.

This point emerges even more forcefully when one observes that historically many of the major scientific revolutions and paradigm shifts owe their genesis not to a new quantitative or technical finding but rather to an experiential insight.

Experiential Validity and Scientific Revolution

What initiates the emergence of a new paradigm? To some extent it is "data based"; that is, it occurs when the "traditional" paradigm faces a "crisis" in its difficulty to account for some observation which can be more readily explained by the new paradigm. This model is quite famil- iar to many behavioral scientists, as it parallels Piaget's cycle of accommodation and assimilation. However, as Kuhn discusses in exquisite detail, this capacity to resolve the "crisis" is frequently absent when the new paradigm is first promulgated, and that capacity is rarely sufficient in itself to sustain the new paradigm.

As one example, Kuhn notes (1970, pp. 154-56) that Copernicus's heliocentric theory, when it was first proposed, was no more accurate than Ptolemy's geocentrism: it did not offer a superior calendar, nor significant improvement in the prediction of planetary orbits.

What then is it that attracts a small number of ini- tial "believers" to the new paradigm, who then begin to generate the "data" that will convert the general scien- tific community? Kuhn offers the following answer:

> These are the arguments, rarely made ex- plicit, that appeal to the individual's sense of the appropriate or the aesthetic [italics mine]--the new theory is said to be "neater," "more suitable," or "simpler" than the old. . . .
> The man who embraces a new para- digm at an early stage must often do so in defiance of the evidence provided by prob- lem-solving. . . . He must . . . have faith . . . ,though it need be neither rational nor ultimately correct . . . some- times it is only personal and inarticulate aesthetic considerations [italics mine] that can do that. Men have been converted by them when most of the articulable technical arguments pointed the other way. When first introduced, neither Copernican astro- nomical theory nor De Broglie's theory of matter had many other significant grounds of appeal. Even today Einstein's general theory attracts men principally on aesthetic grounds. (Pp. 155, 158)

Once initiated, the new paradigm may gain general acceptance if it generates convincing "data." Recall, however, that what constitutes valid data is often defined in a self-perpetuating way by the prevailing paradigm.

I have spent considerable time discussing experiential validity because I perceive it to be the most controversial point in this chapter. I regret the fact that some readers may reject this presentation as either heretical or, worse yet, as naively incompetent. The bias against the "experiential" runs so strong that I was tempted to back off and use a socially more acceptable term like face validity. I expect that some who skim this chapter will chuckle (or frown, in the case of those who are more punitive) the moment they see the term experiential validity and will succeed in immediately discrediting the concept by conjuring up an image of Fritz Perls bathing with a group in a California hot tub. However, if I can applaud Breznitz for openly calling his variable hope, I should show the same straightforwardness in my own use of labels. (Then, again, I should consider that Breznitz already has tenure.)

I would like to make two more observations about this bias before moving on.

One clear sign of the longstanding prejudice against the personal, subjective, and experiential sources of "truth" has been the cumbersome convention in traditional journal style to avoid writing in the first person. That is, the author engages in linguistic gymnastics to avoid using the words "I" or "we"; consequently, he or she tends to over-utilize the passive tense, adding to the tedium or dryness of the prose style. Similarly, we have been discouraged from addressing the reader directly as "you." Further, a personal tone, such as that explicitly chosen for this chapter, while welcomed at a colloquium address, might well be rejected by many scientific periodicals. Some of these stylistic conventions have only recently begun to change. Clearly, in this chapter I have allowed myself to deviate from them.

Part of my reason for doing so is that a major emphasis of this chapter is to assert the validity of disciplined subjective reporting and conceptualization of naturalistic observations. Thus, the personal medium is an integral part of the message. My choice is consistent with those of two of the role models to be presented later in this chapter: that is, Goldenberg and Sarason both advocate naturalistic description and frequently write in a similarly first-person style.

My second observation is to relate the bias against the "experiential" to a process which Ronald Laing has labeled mystification.

Mystification

In his book, The Politics of Experience, Laing describes how those in power (for example, a dominant parent or a colonial government) seek to maintain their dominance by altering the meaning of words in an Orwellian fashion to alienate subordinates from their own experience. For example, a child may learn to be submissive if most of his or her assertive acts are mislabeled as selfish or aggressive.

Similar mislabeling and mystification have occurred with regard to experiential validity. A major weakness exists in the traditional paradigm of laboratory experimentation. On the one hand that paradigm is excellently suited to the study of inanimate causal relationships. However, it is usually inapplicable as an exclusive technology when studying some of the major subjective concerns of human experience. Even where applicable, it may be sufficiently cumbersome not to be the most appropriate paradigm. Rather than acknowledge the limitations of the experimental paradigm, its adherents have redefined its weakness (that is, its discomfort with the "subjective") as its strength. In the process we are told that "truly experimental" approaches to the study of human experience are inherently superior to disciplined subjective observation in the knowledge they produce. Further, we are told that certain subjective concepts and methodologies are not appropriate for "scientific" inquiry.

In the very process of writing this chapter, I caught my own language being distorted by this process of mystification. I found myself using the words empirical and experiential as though they were opposites, as though you had to earn the right to call your work empirical by first doing an F test. After turning to the dictionary, I realized that the statistical investigators had simply arrogated the term and that the nonstatisticians had simply accepted their exclusive proprietorship. Webster's unabridged dictionary (1979) offers the following definitions for empirical: "1. relying or based solely on experiments or experience [italics mine]; as, the empirical method. 2. relying or based on practical experience, without reference to scientific principles; as, an empirical remedy."

Many community researchers have found that an exclusive reliance on non-naturalistic paradigms severely limits the experiential and ecological validity of their inquiry. In order to study the macroscopic molar phenomena central to their discipline, they have adopted other paradigms. I would like to present three such psychologists as potential role models.

THREE MODELS OF COMMUNITY INQUIRY: GOLDENBERG, SARASON, AND LEVINE

Ira Goldenberg, Seymour Sarason, and Murray Levine are three community psychologists who each demonstrate a different mode of coping with the paradox and conflicts that are the concern of this book. The three played a significant role in the very creation of community psychology in the mid-1960s as they worked together at the Yale Psycho-Educational Clinic. Each has found a way to employ disciplined subjective observation to study naturalistic community phenomena.

Ira Goldenberg

The most overtly passionate, rebellious, and stylistically flamboyant of the three, Goldenberg succeeded in his first book to capture the spirit and "schmaltz" of the 1960s War on Poverty:

> The birth of the Job Corps came as a signal that suddenly linked two generations of Americans. For those of us too young to remember the dust bowls and Hoovervilles and CCC Camps of the 1930's, the Job Corps became a tie with the past. It was a time when the long-dormant voices of Woodie Guthrie and Cisco Houston once again rose up. . . . it was a time when the voices of the Motown Sound, Murray the K, and James Brown joined with those of Hubert Humphrey and R. Sargent Shriver in a chorus of

"You're What's Happening, Baby."
(1971, p. 23)

In that excellent book, he powerfully describes an urban Job Corps Center that he created in New Haven, named The Residential Youth Center. That center was to become a prototype for national programs by the U.S. Department of Labor. His sensitivity to important detail, coupled with a charismatic prose that paralleled his charisma as the center's director, make him an excellent reporter. Further, he is very articulate in stating his sophisticated theory of organizational psychology that guided the creation of the center.

One of the book's 11 chapters presents a statistical analysis of the center's outcome data. However, the book's primary emphasis and contribution involves Goldenberg as a disciplined interventionist, observer, describer, and theoretician.

In his more recent writings, he has moved yet further away from traditional models of psychological writing and research. His 1978 book Oppression and Social Intervention is an intensely personal statement, involving both autobiographical material as well as his observations and conceptualizations about the nature of oppression. In his preface (p. x), he explicitly identifies himself as a community psychologist, stating that the book "is written from the perspective of what has been called 'community psychology.'" Nonetheless, there is hardly a single statistic in the volume. The book, which has been labeled a masterpiece by Professor Warren Bennis, a well-respected empirical social scientist, would not satisfy the methodological requirements for a master's thesis in most American psychology departments.

The strength of the book comes from its experiential validity, from Goldenberg's ability to observe, to conceptualize, and to describe the human condition. A brief example may help to convey the flavor of his writing. In a chapter titled "The Making of a Social Interventionist" he begins with an abstract definition of oppression, stating that

> a situation becomes oppressive when an individual is forced to tolerate behavior in himself and others for which there is no legitimate rationale other than survival. . . .
> The act is demeaning and there is a loss of integrity. (P. 37)

He then goes on to provide a series of autobiographical vignettes that clearly demonstrate his point. For example, he describes his childhood family's dependence on his mother's earnings in a garment district sweatshop and his annual Thanksgiving pilgrimage to be presented to her boss, Mr. Stern:

> I would extend my hand to the boss, smile as I had been instructed to do, and say: "How do you do, Mr. Stern." Mr. Stern would then bend over, grab me under the chin with his thumb and forefinger, shake my head and say: "Well sonny, are you being a good boy, or has your Momma been lying to me?" I would dutifully acknowledge that my mother wasn't a liar and begin to brace myself for the scene that invariably followed.
>
> Mr. Stern . . . would tell me what a "good girl" my mother was, how she came to work on time . . . I'd look at my mother. Her eyes no longer sparkled. They had a vacant look about them. . . . But Mr. Stern went on and on. . . . I tried to . . . sit on my growing anger as my mother had instructed me to do, or to sink into my favorite reverie, that of succeeding Phil Rizzuto as the next great shortstop of the New York Yankees. . . .
>
> Mr. Stern . . . would put a proprietory hand around my mother's shoulders, give her a squeeze, and reiterate what a "good girl" she was. . . . My insides would churn. . . . Again I looked at my mother. She seemed to have turned herself into a block of stone. (Pp. 40–41)

Goldenberg is highly critical of social scientists, arguing that the content of their research tends consistently to support the status quo and the hand that feeds them. He closes the book with Otto Rene Castillo's caustic poem "Apolitical Intellectuals." He does not explicitly note that the constraints on the content of research flow in part from the constraints, which we have described, on the methodologies that are viewed as legitimate science.

In many ways Goldenberg serves as an iconoclast and occasional gadfly for community psychologists. For example, during one of his infrequent addresses to the Division of Community Psychology, at the 1979 convention of the American Psychological Association (APA), he "congratulated" the Division for having come of age as evidenced by its ultimate achievement of having its own cocktail hour at the convention. His writing is similarly iconoclastic, in that he inherently rejects the requirement that psychological reporting need be based on statistical data analysis. Goldenberg makes no apologies for the fact that the data base for his book consists of his own observations and insights.

His iconoclasm has been coupled with his self-imposed relative isolation from the mainstream of organized community psychology (for example, its APA divisional activities and its scientific journals). An interesting contrast to him is provided by Seymour Sarason, who has calmly and non-confrontively adopted the role of "the psychologist as a disciplined observer-describer-conceptualizer of human behavior," while staying very much within the mainstream and intellectual leadership of American community psychology.

Seymour Sarason

Earlier in his academic career, Sarason established his scientific credentials using traditional experimental and correlational designs. To cite but one example, his work on test anxiety in children has spawned considerable quantitative research. However, contemporaneous with his growing interest in the phenomena of community psychology, he has become increasingly a naturalistic observer of the human condition. His voluminous writings are acclaimed, not because of the statistical power of his designs, but because of their scholarship, articulateness, and experiential validity.

In one of the earliest works on community psychology, Psychology in Community Settings (1966), he is primarily a describer and conceptualizer of nonquantitative case studies. Nonetheless, he continued to support the quantitative studies of his students and colleagues, as contained, for example, in Kaplan and Sarason's (1969) "The Psycho-Educational Clinic: Papers and Research Studies," Community Mental Health Monograph, 1969, 4.

His 1971 book <u>The Culture of the School and the Problem of Change</u> similarly reports a number of quantitative studies of recurrent patterns ("programmatic and behavioral regularities") in elementary schools. However, the book's primary offering is Sarason as the insightful observer and gatherer of <u>descriptive</u> data rather than of inferential statistics. Sarason is quite explicit in his call that researchers be encouraged to conduct descriptive studies involving the researcher as a participant observer.

> Descriptions of the change process in the school setting were very hard to come by . . . we are dealing with a problem of staggering complexity . . . to describe a natural, complicated, truly dynamic (non-static) social setting. It is no wonder that field research to the laboratory researcher, at least, is usually viewed as a messy business. Indeed it is, should be, and will be for a long time.
> . . . the complexity of the problem is . . . in the fact that we do not possess the security of feeling that we have experienced the problem to the extent that we are formulating the problem well. By "experiencing the problem" I mean initiating and engaging in the change efforts of others. . . . I am merely suggesting what we ought to be thinking about and experiencing in order to avoid the understandable but self-defeating tendency to flee from complexity at the expense of relevance.
> . . . let us not forget that the university culture does not make it easy for graduate students and ambitious young faculty members to work on messy problems in the field. (Pp. 31-32)

That same call is echoed in Sarason's 1976 <u>American Psychologist</u> article, "Community Psychology, Networks and 'Mr. Everyman,'" in which he publicly advocates a "divorce" between community and clinical psychology. Sarason asserts that the concepts of clinical psychology, based on the behavior of <u>individuals</u>, fail to grasp the complexity of <u>social</u> phenomena.

> The more clinical we are in our thinking
> and actions, the less we see the larger pic-
> ture as the social fabric. The individual
> tends to be figure and all else ground, and
> we are not even aware that there is a
> ground. And the kind of ground I am talk-
> ing about . . . has to be conceptualized
> . . . and the basis of that conceptualiza-
> tion is in fields other than psychology. At
> the very least they are conceptualizations
> that can never come out of clinical psy-
> chology. (Pp. 319–20)

To which "fields other than psychology" is Sarason
referring? The answer is more implicit than explicit in the
article's criticism of clinical psychology.

Anthropological participant–observation is clearly one
such field. Sarason describes the inability of well–inten-
tioned, sympathetic site visitors from the National Institute
of Mental Health (NIMH) to understand and fund the anthropological plans of his Psycho–Educational Clinic to study
the culture of the school. "Essentially, what we proposed
was to view the schools as a South Pacific island that we
wanted to observe, become participants in its activities,
and see where it took us" (p. 318).

A similar answer lies in Sarason's view of the ecological studies by Roger Barker and his colleagues. He
lauds Barker's goal of describing a total community; in
contrast, he criticizes mainstream clinical psychology for
ignoring Barker and failing to see the relevance of his
work. Sarason explains that one of the barriers that
makes Barker's work difficult for the psychological reader
is that his reports are primarily descriptive, lacking "what
we ordinarily call psychological data" (that is, summary
descriptive and inferential statistics).

A third answer is implicit in Sarason's response to
a student's criticism. The student challenged that the
ideal community psychologist, described by Sarason, held
no special professional skills but was simply using common
sense. In rebuttal, Sarason did not cite the psychologist's
methodological and statistical sophistication. Rather, he
turned to the discipline of history and to the response by
Carl Becker, a president of the American Historical Association, to a parallel criticism. Becker acknowledged that
the historical researcher uses many of the same principles

used by "Mr. Everyman." However, Becker asserted, in the case of the historian, the principles are "more conscientiously and expertly applied." Sarason concludes, "'More conscientiously and expertly applied'--that is the kernel of the answer I wish I had given my student critic" (p. 328).

So Sarason sees an affinity between his approach to those of anthropology, ecology, and history. He is willing to offer himself as a conscientious and expert naturalistic observer.

In explaining the grounds for his proposed divorce between clinical and community psychology, Sarason stresses the incompatibility caused by clinical psychology's conceptual focus on the individual. However, what one hears constantly lurking in the background is that this conceptual focus is closely tied to a paradigmatic question concerning methodology. For example, in his caustic evaluation of the relevance of social psychology to community psychology, Sarason states, "Social psychology--in its own ways an individualistic, experiment-worshipping fugitive from the social world in which we live our lives--provided no conceptual framework for either modern clinical psychology or the community mental health field" (p. 326).

I want to underline explicitly here that the conceptual problem described by Sarason is in fact a consequence of a methodological paradigmatic problem. So long as the methodologies of the designed data field are seen as the preferred (and even exclusive) paths to truth, those paths will not step beyond the door of the laboratory; the socially embedded phenomena, central to Sarason's thinking, will not be amenable to study.

This relationship between conceptualization and methodology is demonstrated in Sarason's more recent works. He has been dealing with increasingly broad concepts lying at the heart of community psychology which are difficult, impractical, and at points impossible to study in a non-naturalistic setting. Among these concepts are "the psychological sense of community" (for example, Sarason, 1974) and "the social and organizational networks" (for example, Sarason & Lorentz, 1979). As he moves from dealing with concepts at an individual level of analysis to those at an organizational or community level, he relies increasingly on nonstatistical historical analysis of the past and on naturalistic description of the present.

There is a similarity between Sarason and Goldenberg in that they both raise conceptual concerns that are implicitly related to the problem of paradigm choice. Further, both embody in their writings a departure from traditional paradigms of psychological research. A yet more explicit quest for alternative paradigms is found in the work of Murray Levine, to which we now turn.

Murray Levine

As did Sarason, Levine first established his scientific reputation as a prolific researcher while using traditional research designs. However, since his involvement at the Psycho-Educational Clinic in the 1960s, he has increasingly augmented his approaches by drawing on four other disciplines, outside psychology, which contend with the challenge of the naturalistic data field.

The first of these was anthropology. For example, in the 1960s, Levine encouraged his students and colleagues to read and emulate the works of the American anthropologist Jules Henry (such as Culture Against Man, 1963, and Jules Henry on Education, 1966). Henry applied anthropological methods to study contemporary American culture, in general, and the public schools, in particular. An example of Levine's anthropological influence on his students is found in two papers on participant observation by a Levine protege, Richard Balaban (1973, 1978). This anthropological orientation was similar to Sarason's, discussed above.

With regard to the second discipline, history, Levine is one of the few community psychologists to author a number of books whose primary focus was historical rather than psychological. For example, in 1970 he published A Social History of Helping Services, produced jointly with the sociologist Adeline Levine, with whom he shares an intense collaboration. Similarly coauthored by Levine and Levine was another 1970 publication, "The Gary Schools, a Socio-historical Study of the Process of Change." In 1975 he coedited the reprinting of an 1876 document, Mutual Criticism, which described some of the group dynamics in an "intentional community," the Oneida Community. More recently, he has completed The History and Politics of Community Mental Health (1981). There is a plethora of potential examples.

Levine has made a unique contribution in drawing on a third discipline, jurisprudence. In an impressive

tour de force in 1974, Levine pointed out the inherent similarity between the task of the naturalistic researcher and
that of the judicial system. His American Psychologist article "Scientific Method and the Adversary Model" begins
with a call for openness to alternative methodologies:

> Those who have worked with clinical and field
> problems have long chafed at the lack of fit
> of scientific method, as it is usually prac-
> ticed, to problems that we face daily. The
> soreness has been exacerbated by a social
> factor in which recognition, status, and
> power are granted to those who can fully
> apply the high-fashion designs. . . . Many
> have decried the artificiality and the ir-
> relevance of such research requirements to
> the field situation . . . in the search for
> methodological purity, we have frequently
> lost sight of the substance of the problems.
> (P. 661)

Levine notes that in the history of scientific method,
epistemologists used the word experimental to mean "referring to experience." An experiment was an action taken to
discover or demonstrate some truth:

> Experimental meant that which was reducible
> to observation, and observation meant
> human sensory observation. . . . The
> transformation of the requirement that we
> deal with observables to the requirement
> that we deal with quantified observables
> is responsible for a great deal of mischief.
> (P. 667)

Levine argues that scientific method does not require
that observations be quantitative, but rather that there be
controls to identify distortion and to determine if a particular observation is consistent with ones obtained from
other independent sources. He asks that we be given "a
social license to use our intelligence" (p. 668) as an observational research instrument in nonquantitative field
studies, which may be used not only for exploratory hypothesis generation but for confirmation of hypotheses as
well.

What might be a source of such "controls"? Levine points out that the legal system has had to make serious decisions (often involving life and death) while relying primarily on nonquantitative self-reports and observations of phenomena in a noncontrolled naturalistic setting.

> The courts are also in search of truth,
> and, over the centuries, methods for evalu-
> ating arguments and evidence have evolved.
> The courts have developed methods for deal-
> ing with whole human events in social and
> historical context, and as much as these
> methods have imperfections they also permit
> flexible dealing with a great variety of
> issues and of forms of evidence. No group
> has thought more carefully about the issue
> of evidence and the inferences that can be
> drawn from evidence than our legal profes-
> sion. (Pp. 669-70)

Levine advocates that social scientists adopt a "legal adversary" model to evaluate evidence, particularly evidence such as nonquantitative observational reports, which are akin to "testimony." In his article, he details how rules of evidence and cross-examination can be used to provide a set of alternative controls, rather than those demanded by the designed data field. A concrete application of this model is reported by Levine and others (1978) in an article entitled "Adapting the Jury Trial for Program Evaluation: A Report of an Experience."

Levine has been similarly creative in seeing the similarity between the problems of the observational psychologist and those of investigative reporters. In a 1980 article in the American Psychologist, titled "Investigative Reporting as a Research Method: An Analysis of Bernstein and Woodward's All the President's Men," he describes the disciplined methods used by reporters and editors to evaluate the validity of the testimony received from informants and reporters. He advocates that social scientists learn from those methods in order to develop their own disciplined approaches to field research and clinical case studies.

There are two consistent messages coming from Levine: (1) to meaningfully study community phenomena, we must give ourselves a "social license to use our intelligence" as naturalistic observers; however, (2) license does not mean licentiousness--there are a number of controls that can be exercised within a naturalistic data field to generate data that are no less valid than those of the designed data field.

THE ORGANIZATION OF THIS BOOK

This chapter has defined a continuum whose endpoints are the designed data field and the naturalistic data field. The chapter has clarified why community researchers need to draw their methodologies from multiple points along that continuum. I have noted the problems of commitment and experiential validity that result when one conforms to the pressures (imposed by oneself and by others) to rely exclusively on the methodologies of the designed data field.

This first chapter has focused to a considerable degree on anchoring and legitimizing one extreme endpoint of that continuum, namely, the case of nonquantitative naturalistic observation, which deviates from most of the eight controls demanded by the designed data field. Having anchored those endpoints, we can go on in the remainder of the text to consider in detail some of the alternatives that lie along the continuum.

Logically, this book is divided into two parts. The first section provides a broad conceptualization and overview of community research: in addition to this chapter, it includes a quantitative critique of published research in community psychology (Chapter 2) and an overview of the relationships and patterns of influence among community psychology's researchers (Chapter 3).

The second section provides detailed descriptions of a number of points on the continuum. We begin with two paradigms closest to the traditional methods of experimental psychology, namely, the "true" experiment (Chapter 4) and quasi-experimental designs (Chapter 5). The next three chapters move us closer to the naturalistic data field, in presenting ethological (Chapter 6), ecological (Chapter 7), and phenomenological (Chapter 8) research models. In Chapter 9, we return to Sarason's conceptual (rather than methodological) concern that community research be guided by an environmentally conscious (rather than an individual-focused) theory; we present a conceptual framework, the stress model, as one theoretical source to guide community research. Finally, in Chapter 10, we close with a potpourri, briefly reviewing seven alternative approaches.

We hope that the readers will allow themselves to draw freely, but selectively, from each of the orientations presented. Each of the approaches along the continuum has useful tools to offer. It is important that we avoid both Type I and Type II errors; that is, (1) let us not reject an orientation simply because historically it has belonged to another discipline or because some of its components are inappropriate for us, and (2) let us not exclusively embrace a single orientation and all of the components historically associated with it simply because it has been traditionally associated with our discipline or because some of its components are appropriate for us.

A story is told in the Talmud (tractate Kidushin, 39B) of a respected Rabbi Meir who shocked his students by spending much of a sabbath conversing with an apostate, Rabbi Elisha ben Abuya. Because of his heretical views, Rabbi Elisha had been shunned by the community. "How could you allow yourself to learn from such a man?" queried the students. Rabbi Meir replied, "When one has a pomegranate, it is possible to benefit from the fruit, while discarding the peel."

REFERENCES

Balaban, R. M. The contribution of participant observation to the study of process in program evaluation. International Journal of Mental Health, 1973, 2, 59-70.

Balaban, R. M. Participant observation--Rediscovering a research method. In L. Goldman (Ed.), Research methods for counselors. New York: John Wiley, 1978.

Breznitz, S. The psychology of hope. Colloquium address presented at the Department of Psychology, University of Maryland Baltimore County, Catonsville, Md., February 16, 1984.

Buscaglia, L. Love. New York: Fawcett Crest, 1972.

Cowen, E. Baby-steps toward primary prevention. American Journal of Community Psychology, 1977, 5, 1-22.

Goldenberg, I. I. Build me a mountain: Youth, poverty and the creation of new settings. Cambridge, Mass.: MIT Press, 1971.

Goldenberg, I. I. Oppression and social intervention. Chicago: Nelson Hall, 1978.

Henry, J. Culture against man. New York: Vintage Books, 1963.

Henry, J. Jules Henry on education. New York: Vintage Books, 1966.

Kaplan, F., & Sarason, S. The Psycho-Educational Clinic: Papers and research studies. Massachusetts Department of Mental Health, Community Mental Health Monograph, 1969, 4 (entire).

Kuhn, T. The structure of scientific revolutions. Chicago: University of Chicago Press, 1962, 1970.

Laing, R. D. The politics of experience. New York: Pantheon, 1967.

Levine, A., & Levine, M. The Gary Schools, a socio-historical study of the process of change. In R. S. Bourne (Ed.), The Gary Schools. Cambridge, Mass.: MIT Press, 1970.

Levine, M. Scientific method and the adversary model. American Psychologist, 1974, 29(9), 661-677.

Levine, M. Investigative reporting as a research method: An analysis of Bernstein and Woodward's All the President's Men. American Psychologist, 1980, 35(7), 626-638.

Levine, M. The history and politics of community mental health. New York: Oxford University Press, 1981.

Levine, M., Brown, E., Fitzgerald, C., Goplerud, E., Gordon, M., Jayne-Lazarus, C., Rosenberg, N., & Slater, J. Adapting the jury trial for program evaluation: A report of an experience. Evaluation and Program Planning, 1978, 1, 177-186.

Levine, M., & Bunker, B. B. (Eds.). Mutual criticism. Syracuse, N.Y.: Syracuse University Press, 1975.

Levine, M., & Levine, A. A social history of helping services. New York: Appleton-Century-Crofts, 1970.

Popiel, D. A. Impact of rape: Effect of family and friends' reactions. Master's thesis, University of Maryland Baltimore County, 1983.

Popiel, D. A., & Susskind, E. Impact of rape: Social support as a moderator of stress. Paper presented to the annual meeting of the Eastern Psychological Association, Baltimore, Md., April 13, 1984.

Rappaport, J. Community psychology: Values, research and action. New York: Holt, Rinehart & Winston, 1977.

Sarason, S. B. The culture of the school and the problem of change. Boston: Allyn & Bacon, 1971.

Sarason, S. B. Community psychology, networks and "Mr. Everyman." American Psychologist, May 1976, 31(5), 317-328.

Sarason, S. B. The psychological sense of community: Prospects for a community psychology. San Francisco: Jossey-Bass, 1974.

Sarason, S. B., Levine, M., Goldenberg, I. I., Cherlin, D. L., & Bennett, E. Psychology in community settings. New York: John Wiley, 1966.

Sarason, S. B., & Lorentz, E. The challenge of the resource exchange network: From concept to action. San Francisco: Jossey-Bass, 1979.

Yalom, I. D. The theory and practice of group psychotherapy. New York: Basic Books, 1975.

Yalom, I. D. Existential psychotherapy. New York: Basic Books, 1980.

2 A Content Analysis of Community Psychology Research

John W. Lounsbury, Michael P. Cook,

Dianne S. Leader, and Elizabeth P. Meares

INTRODUCTION

The study we report here began as an effort to answer a seemingly simple question: What kind of research
is being done in the name of community psychology? We
wondered if the body of community psychology research was
promoting a knowledge base which was representative of
the variegated concerns of this bustling new field and,
also, if the research was sound as measured by some of
the more traditional standards of quality employed in
other fields of psychology.

It is not necessary here to trace the emergence of
community psychology as a new field; others have done
so in an illuminating manner (for example, Iscoe, Bloom,
& Spielberger, 1977; Rappaport, 1977). That there is a
distinguishable field of community psychology can be witnessed by the facts that there is a division of community

---

The authors thank Margaret Morgan for her assistance in data tabulation and Morris Ehrenberg for his
help in coding and analyzing articles. We also thank Bob
Dipboye for sharing his ideas on content analysis with us.

This chapter represents a substantial revision and
update of an earlier article on this topic which appeared
in the American Journal of Community Psychology (Lounsbury,
Leader, Meares, & Cook, 1980).

psychology in the American Psychological Association, there have been two journals devoted to community psychology since 1973, there have appeared several textbooks on community psychology, and there are formally designated jobs in applied and academic settings for community psychologists.

What is not so clear are the boundaries of the field and what exactly is contained within those boundaries. Formal definitions of community psychology suggest a vast and potentially heterogeneous territory. Consider the definition offered by Murrell (1973):

> I would define community psychology as the area within the science of psychology that studies the transactions between social system networks, populations, and individuals; that develops and evaluates intervention methods which improve person-environment 'fits'; that designs and evaluates new social systems; and from such knowledge and change seeks to enhance the psychological opportunities of the individual. (P. 2)

Most definitions incorporate the perspective of an environmental, ecological, or systems viewpoint, as can be seen in the following conceptualizations:

"Community psychology is regarded as an approach to human behavior problems that emphasizes contributions made to their development by environmental forces, as well as the potential contributions to be made toward their alleviation by the use of these forces" (Zax & Specter, 1974, p. 2).

"Community psychology represents a new frontier in the study of human behavior which is broadly concerned with clarifying the complex interrelationships between individuals and their environment" (Spielberger & Iscoe, 1970, p. 244).

"The defining aspects of the perspective [of community psychology] are cultural relativity, diversity, and ecology: the fit between persons and environments." (Rappaport, 1977, p. 2).

The majority of community psychologists do appear to be united by a general concern for how individuals function within and between such systems or environments as schools, hospitals, criminal justice facilities, mental health centers, the workplace, and the family. There is substantially less consensus on such matters as the unit of analysis or where and how to intervene. For example, either restorative interventions or proactive prevention efforts might be directed toward the individual to improve his or her ability to function; on the other hand, intervention might be made into the larger system to create a better person–system fit. The relative importance attached to these activities and distinctions about their content vary considerably depending upon who writes about them (compare, for example, Zax & Specter, 1974; Dorr, 1977; Hodges, 1977; Goodstein & Sandler, 1978).

Along somewhat different lines, Reiff (1977) has identified three mainstream ideologies which characterize the field of community psychology: (1) a healing ideology, with an emphasis on "restoring the sick individual"; (2) a developmental ideology, with programs emphasizing "the realization of full potential of individuals"; and (3) a social problems or social change ideology, with emphasis on changing the social structure in which human problems are embedded. These ideologies are, of course, shared by many other fields such as clinical psychology, developmental psychology, and sociology, respectively, but they serve to highlight some of the more visible subdivisions within community psychology.

Our approach to this unsettled issue of field definition is concrete and operational. We elected to regard articles published in the two community psychology journals--the American Journal of Community Psychology (AJCP) and the Journal of Community Psychology (JCP)--as representative of the field of community psychology. Each of these journals has served as a forum for thinkpieces as well as a repository for empirical findings from research on a variety of topics. Moreover, we have chosen published research studies in these two journals as representative of current research in community psychology.

We note that some initial reporting along these lines has already occurred. In response to a conceptual analysis of community psychology by Goodstein and Sandler (1978), the present authors presented some preliminary findings (Lounsbury, Cook, Leader, Rubeiz, & Meares, 1979) from the investigation reported here. Those findings reported on the subject characteristics and types of variables analyzed in empirical research studies in a 50% sample of articles published between 1973 and 1978 in the

JCP and the AJCP. Novaco and Monahan (1980) also reported the results of a content analysis of community psychology research articles.[1] Their study primarily "examined the empirical reports with regard to their theoretical
basis and programmatic nature." They concluded that most
of the research had little to do with the stated objectives
of the discipline. Although Novaco and Monahan also
examined the explicitness of hypotheses, the setting in
which research was conducted, the type of design and
independent variables, and whether the article reported on
a prevention program, their content analysis was substantially narrower in scope and less detailed than the present
one. Also, their analysis was restricted to articles published only in the AJCP from 1973 to 1978. Despite their
claims that the AJCP is the definitive purveyor of quality
research in community psychology and it is representative
of research in the field, there are a number of differences
between the JCP and the AJCP in terms of research content
and quality, as shall be seen later in our Section V.

Our present report analyzes articles in both journals
from 1973 through 1982 in extensive detail, attempting to
portray accurately the content areas researched and the
methodologies employed. Description is the major purpose
of this study. Our aim is to provide a data base for
characterizing the field of community psychology, one comprehensive enough to generate further hypotheses and suggest directions for future inquiry in this area. Two general concerns guide our discussion of the results: (1) To
what extent does the empirical description generated overlap with the prescriptions for the field which abound?
(2) How adequate and appropriate are the research methodologies being used by community psychologists for addressing the issues involved?

A general strategy we employed in assessing the
existing research was to see if there was the rich diversity
of the field suggested by its definitions. Thus, as a
minimum, we expected the research investigations as a
whole to be varied and diversified with respect to a number of dimensions. Some of the dimensions we explored
were the topic area represented by a study, the purpose
served by the investigation (for example, describing a
social program or testing a theory); the type of subjects
involved (such as representation of adults and children,
males and females, and subjects with and without identified psychological problems), and the authors of published

reports (including their affiliation and region of residence). We further examined methodological dimensions, seeking variety in the type of research design employed (for example, whether a descriptive or experimental approach was adopted), the types of variables studied (for example, psychological variables such as attitudes, opinions, and behaviors; and sociological group process and other kinds and levels of variables), and the type of measurement methods used in a study (for example, paper-and-pencil tests, archival data, or observational techniques).

We were interested in finding out what defines this field as psychology at all, and what distinguishes it as community psychology in particular. With this aim in mind, we looked at the relative extent to which individual- and systems-level concerns were being emphasized and at what kinds of variables and subjects were being studied. More specifically, we looked for evidence that psychological variables were being attended to, such as individual adjustment, attitudes, and performance. We examined whether characteristics of communities were analyzed, such as degree of urbanization, stability, and demographic patterns. And we sought models and measures of intervening mechanisms which presumably link individuals to communities, such as social interaction, group cohesion, and role strain. We scrutinized the subjects employed in community psychology research, looking particularly at which segments of the community were represented (in terms of age, race, and sex) and noting the settings from which these were drawn (such as social institutions of various kinds and subgroups of the general population). In terms of the conceptualizations of the field presented previously, we wanted to assess the extent to which research was being conducted within the framework of a problem-centered, healing ideology versus the context of "normal" functioning. To this end, we were alert to the relative emphasis on topics, variables, subjects, and settings associated with psychopathology versus those representing more general human concerns and social interaction.

Although our primary concern was with the substantive question, "What is community psychology?" we also examined the empirical reports from a methodological perspective, attempting to characterize the type of research being conducted and the extent to which the empirical studies met several commonly accepted standards of research methodology. Looking at the body of research as a whole, we were interested to know which of the "two disciplines of scientific psychology" (correlational and experimental, as distinguished by Cronbach, 1957) predominated in the field, and whether a convergence of these traditions, as called for by Cronbach, could be discerned. We wondered to what extent the general research orientation was naturalistic versus controlled, so we examined whether investigations were conducted in the field or the laboratory and if researchers tended to observe or manipulate events. Underlying these analyses was a desire to determine the stage of development of community psychology research and its means of dealing with the issues confronting the field.

Individual studies were classified in terms of some specific features discussed or recommended by methodologists to enhance research validity. These included whether or not there was representative sampling of subjects; the use of comparison groups, and random assignment of subjects to conditions where appropriate; and the use of multiple occasions of measurement and multiple methods of measuring the key variables under consideration. In order to describe the studies fully, sample sizes were noted, as well as the significance level employed in analyzing data. We further looked at whether descriptive or inferential statistics were reported and what kind of statistical tests were used (for example, univariate or multivariate and parametric or nonparametric). We tried to ascertain if conceptual or empirical linkages among studies existed by looking at whether specific hypotheses were stated, if replications and extensions of previous work were undertaken, and whether implications were drawn from the research to theoretical and/or practical issues. The methodological critique focuses on the technical quality of the empirical work, and discussion of these results highlights the unique demands and problems of research in this field.

Our chapter, being primarily descriptive and spanning the variety of concerns discussed above, is detailed and wide ranging. It is organized into six sections:

I.   Method
II.   Results: Characteristics of Authors, Subjects, Topics, Purposes Served, and Implications Drawn
III.   Results: Research Design

A rather large amount of data is presented in Sections II–IV. In each of the sections in which findings are reported, we will briefly discuss the implications of the data and provide some evaluative comments. In Section V we examine some of the salient trends over time and differences between the two journals for variables on which the present content analysis was based. Moreover, in this section, we compare some of our findings with results obtained by analyses of research in other fields. Finally, in Section VI we summarize our findings in light of the general concerns which guided the investigation and consider some implications of the findings. Also in Section VI, suggestions are proposed for the further development of research in community psychology and our vision of trends for the future in this field is portrayed.

SECTION I: METHOD

A content analysis was performed on 935 of the articles published from 1973 through 1982 in the AJCP and JCP. These 935 articles represent a full census of articles in both journals from 1973 through 1980 and a 50% random sample of 1981–82 articles in both journals. The four authors and four graduate students served as analysts for this study.

After developing a standard coding form, the analysts were trained to a criterion of at least 80% agreement on every item in the form for ten consecutive articles. To control for possible coding biases between analysts, each analyst was randomly assigned to a series of issues for each journal, with the series counterbalanced to equate for issue number and year. For the 1981–82 issues, articles were randomly sampled from each issue.[2] Periodic spot checks of one analyst by another were conducted to help ensure that the established level of interanalyst agreement was in effect and to curb the tendency of an analyst to drift into an idiosyncratic interpretation of a particular category.

The results presented here are based only on those articles which reported the results of a research investigation. There were 728 of these articles, 322 from the AJCP and 406 from the JCP. Unless otherwise noted, the results are reported for both journals combined.

SECTION II: RESULTS: CHARACTERISTICS OF AUTHORS, TOPICS, SUBJECTS, PURPOSES SERVED, AND IMPLICATIONS DRAWN

Authors

The first characteristic of studies we examined was the authors of the article in which the study was reported. We examined the number of authors, wondering if there was much collaboration on studies as signified by multiple authors; the affiliation of authors, to see if nonuniversity affiliations were substantially in evidence or if there was primarily what one author (Renner, 1974) identified as "the academic sheltering of community psychology" research; and the geographic residence of authors, in an effort to see which regions, if any, were under- or overrepresented.

The number of authors per article indicates fairly extensive collaboration. Only 24% of the articles we examined had a single author, whereas 37% had two authors, 24% had three authors, 9% had four authors, and 5% had five or more authors.

Analysis of the primary affiliation of authors shows that in 67% of the articles the authors were affiliated only with a university or college, in 17% of the articles the authors were affiliated only with a nonuniversity setting, and in 16% of the cases both one or more authors were affiliated with a university and one or more were affiliated with a nonuniversity setting.[3] Thus, it appears that the bulk of published research in community psychology is emanating from academic settings. It may well be that there is much research of interest to community psychologists that is conducted for purposes other than publication in the professional literature (for example, for in-house reports, documents, and archives). Also, it may be that until recently there have not been that many practitioners with sufficient interest and/or training to carry out publishable research (although this will probably change as more and more Ph.D.-level community psychologists compete for and obtain positions in applied settings). For many reasons,[4] it seems to be desirable to have a strong, ongoing contribution from field settings into the community psychology research and efforts should be made by editors, conference planners, and others to help realize this contribution.

The region of residence of each author was also recorded. To simplify the presentation of the U.S. categories, the ten regional designations made in 1978 by the U.S. Department of Health, Education, and Welfare were used. The most frequent contributors by region are listed in Table 2.1.

As can be seen, four regions were represented in 10% or more of the studies: Region 4, or the southeastern United States, 21%; Region 5, or midwestern states, 15%; Region 9, including Arizona, California, and Nevada, 15%; and Region 2, including New York and New Jersey, 11%. It is interesting to note that the top contributing region also contains the present editorial office for the two journals (both in Tennessee, although the AJCP editorial office was located in Illinois during most of the period for which these articles were analyzed--which is in the second highest contributing region). This result may be related to the geographic distribution of community psychologists or the geographical propinquity of editors, reviewers, and contributors. In any case, community psychology research activity appears to be occurring in each region of the country and is not clustered mainly in heavily populated states and regions (whereas Richards & Gottfreedson, 1978, found that professional psychology activity as a whole tends to be rather concentrated in states with large populations).

Topic Area

As one might expect from reading the definitions and perspectives of the field, a vast array of specific topic areas have been claimed as legitimate concerns for community psychologists to pursue. For example, in 1965 at a national conference on "Education of Psychologists for Community Mental Health,"[5] six areas of needed community research were identified in the final report:

TABLE 2.1

Relative Frequency of Region of Residence of Authors

Rank	Region	Percentage of Articles Having Authors from This Region[a]	Relative Frequency of Authors by Region Corrected for Total Population[b]
1	U.S. #4 (Alabama, Florida, Georgia, Kentucky, Tennessee, North Carolina, South Carolina)	21	.66
2	U.S. #5 (Illinois, Indiana, Minnesota, Michigan, Ohio, Wisconsin)	15	.41
3	U.S. #9 (Arizona, California, Nevada, Guam)	15	.67
4	U.S. #2 (New York, New Jersey, Virgin Islands)	11	.47
5	U.S. #3 (Delaware, District of Columbia, Maryland, Pennsylvania, Virginia, West Virginia)	9	.47
6	U.S. #6 (Arkansas, Louisiana, New Mexico, Oklahoma, Texas)	6	.39
7	U.S. #1 (Connecticut, Maine, Massachusetts, New Hampshire, Rhode Island, Vermont)	6	.59
8	U.S. #8 (Colorado, Montana, North Dakota, South Dakota, Utah, Wyoming)	4	1.26
9	U.S. #7 (Iowa, Kansas, Missouri, Nebraska)	3	.36
10	U.S. #10 (Alaska, Idaho, Oregon, Washington)	2	.30
11	All other countries (except Canada)	2	(Not Estimated)
12	Canada (all provinces combined)	2	.13

[a]The percentages listed in this column are based on the full sample of 728 articles; the percentages sum to more than 100 because the region of each author was counted.

[b]To calculate this relative frequency, the percentage of articles having authors from each region was multiplied by a ratio of 100 million divided by the total population of the region (according to 1970 U.S. Census or 1976 Canadian National Government figures; source: World Almanac, 1978).

Note: The U.S. region numbers refer to the 1978 U.S. Department of Health, Education, and Welfare regions.

Source: Compiled by authors.

1. The study of man in the community, including the effects of varying physical and social environments upon his functioning both as an individual and as a member of social organization.

2. Assessment of the individual's reactions to planned change by varying methods of social intervention in a wide variety of human problems and concerns.

3. Basic research on the relationship between social-cultural conditions and personality functioning in order to add knowledge about the positive mastery of stress.

4. Examination of the effects of social organizations upon the individual, particularly those creating high-risk populations, and alternative social patterns which may serve to reduce their creation.

5. Facilitation of social-organizational change through modification of motivational and personality factors in the individual.

6. Evaluative research on consultation and other social change processes. (Bennett et al., 1966, p. 23)

In more recent years the concerns seem to have become more specialized. Thus, a relatively longer list of topic areas of concern to community psychologists can be compiled by perusing the proceedings of the 1975 Austin Conference on training in community psychology (compare Iscoe & Spielberger, 1977). The topics presented in this volume range from fairly specific concerns of mental health delivery systems (for example, needs assessment and aftercare programs), and other systems such as schools and courts, to more macro-level concerns such as community development and social change, and to many different problem or process issues (for example, attitudes toward mental health and mental illness, marriage and divorce, and the influence of the physical environment on behavior).

Although many of these topics have evoked consideration in the speculative body of community psychology literature, whether or not they have received empirical attention was an open question which we attempted to answer in our analysis of topic areas. Accordingly, we

formulated a list of topic areas which reflected the breadth
and variegation of topics as shown in the lists above and
which summarized the main subject matter to which the
individual articles were addressed. Our final list comprised 70 topic areas, and even at that we felt that we
had to shoehorn many ill-fitting topics into their categories. Although our classification scheme was intended to
be broad enough to bear witness to the diversity of this
field, it was sufficiently differentiated for key areas such
as mental health delivery systems to register the finer distinctions which have been popularized. There must necessarily be different levels of concepts in these topics and,
indeed, our list of topic areas is a mix of issues, systems,
problem areas, and processes. We have, however, organized these topic areas into larger categories for ease
of interpretation.

Each article was analyzed with respect to the main
topic under study and assigned to either one or two of the
70 topic codes. The results of this classification are summarized in Table 2.2.

The pattern of results for the topic analysis is not
simple; however, it does appear that there has been a
substantial amount of research--nearly one-half of the
studies--devoted to some aspect of mental health delivery
systems. Frequently studied areas within this broad grouping included some type of therapy (4%); clinical diagnosis,
assessment, or judgment (4%); crisis intervention (3%);
client reactions to a mental health center or program (4%);
intervention in an institutional setting (3%); some form of
consultation (3%); intervention in a natural noninstitutional
setting (3%); and admissions and intakes (3%). Other social systems were represented to a lesser degree among the
topics studied, notably research on topics relating to
criminal justice programs and penal or rehabilitation facilities (8%); and research dealing with public or private
school systems (8%).

Although much of the research could be viewed as
falling under the category of community mental health
concerns, there was also substantial representation of
topics which go beyond a traditional mental health framework. Thus, 50% of the studies dealt with a variety of
specific problem areas or issues: heading the list under
this category are individual adjustment or quality of life
in the community (10%); environmental psychology (15%);
attitudes and beliefs about mental health and mental

TABLE 2.2
Frequency of Topic Areas

Topic Area	Frequency	Percentage of Total Sample
Mental Health Delivery Concerns		
Therapy	33	4
Diagnosis, assessment, or clinical judgment	32	4
Crisis intervention	28	3
Client reactions (e.g., satisfaction) to a program or organization	27	3
Intervention in an institutional setting	25	3
Intervention in a natural, non-institutional setting	22	3
Consultation	22	3
Admissions and intake	18	3
Needs assessment	15	2
Dropouts and terminations	15	2
Organizational design, change, or assessment	12	2
Referrals	11	2
Consumer or citizen participation in delivery systems	10	1
Linkages between a mental health program or organization and the community		
Recidivism or rehospitalization	10	1
Administrative issues	9	1
Transitional facilities (e.g., half-way house, community lodge)	8	1
Partial hospitalization	6	1
Personnel concerns	6	1
Census reduction	6	1
Planning	4	1
Other	19	3
Total	342	47
Other Social Systems		
Schools (including alternative and preschools)	60	8
Criminal justice and rehabilitation	59	8
Total	119	16

(continued)

Table 2.2, continued

Topic Area	Frequency	Percentage of Total Sample
Specific Problem Areas and Issues		
Individual adjustment or quality of life in the community	70	10
Environmental psychology, environmental design and classification	37	5
Attitudes, opinions, and beliefs about mental health and mental illness	34	5
Prevention	32	4
Minority problems and concerns	30	4
Drugs and alcohol	27	4
Work, work adjustment; employment, unemployment	24	3
Community planning, development, or change	12	2
Parent training and parent effectiveness program	11	2
Social support systems	10	1
Suicide	9	1
Health or medical problems	8	1
Coordination, interaction, or gaps in services of general community organizations	8	1
Epidemiology	7	1
Ethical and legal issues	6	1
Rape	6	1
Disasters; disaster planning	4	1
Death and dying	4	1
Poverty	4	1
Vocational rehabilitation	4	1
Environmental quality; energy conservation	4	1
Other	14	2
Total	365	50
Provision of Human Resources		
Paraprofessionals	26	4
Training of mental health service providers	21	3

Topic Area	Frequency	Percentage of Total Sample
Provision of Human Resources (continued)		
Training of service providers (nonmental health)	19	3
Training programs for college students	17	2
Volunteers	15	2
Roles of other professionals (e.g., social workers, physicians, nurses) vis-à-vis mental health delivery	7	1
Roles of other professionals (e.g., social workers, physicians, nurses) vis-à-vis community psychology	5	1
Roles of other community members (e.g., bartenders, hairdressers) vis-à-vis mental health delivery	4	1
Other	5	1
Total	119	16
Measurement and Research Methodology		
Measurement methodology; test or scale development	62	9
Program evaluation methods	25	3
General research methodology; design issues	15	2
Research utilization	5	1
Total	107	14
Other Categories	18	2

Note: N = 728. The percentages add up to more than 100 because some articles were coded into two categories.

Source: Compiled by authors.

illness (5%); prevention in mental health related areas
(4%); problems of blacks, Chicanos, and other minority
members (4%); and drugs and alcohol (4%).

Sixteen percent of the studies were concerned with
the provision of human resources for social services, especially training people for community mental health services
or using the services of other professionals and nonpro-
fessionals in a mental health capacity. Finally, 14% of
the studies dealt with measurement, research, or evaluation
methodology, particularly test or scale development (9%).

If there is any apparent gap between the rhetoric
of topics advocated for the field and those actually researched, it is in the area of optimal environments/growth
enhancement and related categories for normal development
and healthy functioning of individuals. A liberal count
of such topics would tally 23%, or less than one-fourth of
the articles, including the topics of individual adjustment
or quality of life in the community (10%), person-environment
relations and environmental psychology (5%), prevention
(4%), community planning, development, or change (2%),
and parent-training programs (2%).

Purpose Served

Research in community psychology, like research in
other fields, is usually done for some broader purpose
than simply to inquire into a given topic area. Trickett
and Lustman (1977) identified two major purposes of research in community psychology: (1) to promote our understanding of that which is researched and (2) to serve as a
basis for social action. Analogous pairs of concepts are
theory-oriented versus decision-oriented research and basic
versus applied research. While such distinctions are useful, we did not find them sufficiently detailed to portray
the types of purposes which were stated by the authors of
community psychology research articles. After carefully
examining such purposes, we arrived at the following eight
categories.

1. Theory development. This refers to research
which articulates a formal theoretical model and emphasizes
development of the theory by expressly testing one or more
of its propositions. Articles classified as serving the
purpose of theory development were also usually charac-

terized by extensive discussion of construct relationships and implications for future research on the theory. Owing to the relative newness of the field and its emphasis on the application of knowledge, we did not expect to find much community psychology research which was oriented toward theory development as characterized here.

2. Program evaluation. This is research performed to evaluate or assess the worth of a program. Under the generic title of program, we included projects, sets of procedures, and other organized activities designed to carry out specified objectives. The emphasis in program evaluation research was typically on assessing program performance against a set of goals and objectives.

In view of the proliferation of new programs receiving the attention of community psychologists, as well as a prevailing concern among professionals, policymakers, and the public for the accountability of human service programs, we expected to find program evaluation a frequent purpose of community psychology research investigations.

3. Policy analysis and policy research. This is analysis and research which provides information that is used to formulate, revise, or verify policy (usually social or organizational policy). Following Coleman (1972), we viewed policy analysis and policy research as serving the purpose of guiding social action through the implications it draws for policy. In contrast to theory-oriented research, which can deal exclusively with unobservable and inferred variables, policy variables are those which can be made explicit and subject to direct policy manipulation (as in the number of children in a classroom or the caseload for a therapist in a mental health center).

We expected to find quite a few studies directed toward policy analysis and research, given the field's alleged involvement in social policy and programs and its interest in translating research findings into guidelines for action.

4. Description of Manipulation and 5. Description of Natural Process. Many studies serve to describe in a relatively detailed manner the process, structure, or functioning of some type of problem or program, or an aspect of individual or organizational functioning. Such descriptive research may have no direct bearing on theory, programming, or policies. In a new field like community psychology where innovations abound, descriptions are valuable for acquiring community information and facilitating

the diffusion of innovations. More fundamentally, careful and original descriptions of behavior at many different levels should furnish what Verplanck (1971) has labeled the "critical first stage" of a field, wherein "'observation' of the world that we experience is a starting point to which we go and to which we return again and again for further starts" (p. 482). This stage is critical, since without a sound descriptive base, one risks forming irrelevant or inadequate conceptualizations, both in terms of theory and application.

Descriptions were subdivided into two types: (1) those dealing with deliberate manipulations of the environment (for example, programs or services) and (2) those dealing with the impact of a natural event or process on the individual (for example, a tornado, a divorce, or moving to a new city). Frankly, we did not know how many studies would be classified as descriptions of either type, although we believed that the percentage should not be small.

6. Research or measurement methodology. Some studies are directed not toward a substantive theoretical, programmatic, or policy issue, nor toward describing phenomena, but are constructed to advance the state of the art of research or measurement methodology. Examples are studies which outline a new survey technique, propose an experimental design for community research, or assess the factor structure and psychometric qualities of a measurement instrument. Again, we had no clear expectations about the number of studies which would be categorized under this heading, but we believed it probably would not be small, since community psychology research will probably have to develop new measures and research methods—or at least apply techniques borrowed from other fields in a novel manner—in carrying out the other five types of research listed above.

7. Specific research. Although we had hoped that the first six topics would be exhaustive of the purposes served by articles, a sizable number of articles seemed to merit a separate category labeled specific research. Included under this category are articles which simply examined the relationship between two or more variables or investigated a specific hypothesis without reference to theory development, program evaluation, policy analysis and policy research, or measurement methodology. An example would

be a study which examined the relationship between self-esteem and attitudes toward mental illness.

    8. <u>General conceptualization</u>. A few articles served to outline or clarify a general conceptualization in the field of community psychology. Included among such conceptualizations are personal opinions, criticisms, recommendations, and other types of "think-pieces" concerning directions and progress in the field.[6]

    Up to two purposes were checked for each article. We found the following percentages accounted for by each of our categories:

Specific research topics	33%
Policy analysis and policy research	30%
Program evaluation	25%
Description of manipulation	14%
Research or measurement methodology	12%
Description of natural process	5%
Theory development	3%
General conceptualization	2%

    This distribution of purposes served by the articles exemplifies both the practicality and growth of the field of community psychology. The applied orientation is certainly strong, as can be seen in the 55% of articles concerned with policy analysis and policy research and program evaluation and another 14% describing programs and interventions. Up to this point, the research literature has been little concerned with theory development. This is probably a function of how young the field is and, really, how few theoretical models there are in community psychology, especially models that are unique to community psychology. Perhaps more attention should be devoted in community psychology literature to the formulation, development, and elaboration of theoretical models that reflect the goals, values, and perspectives of the field. These models may, in fact, tend toward "microtheories" applicable to generic situations or processes—such as models for understanding client responses to human services institutions—and they will almost certainly have to incorporate larger "contextual" factors—such as geographic locale, the economy, or prevailing cultural modes. But, regardless of the exact form of such models, we should expect more of the field than a long string of disparate and unconnected specific researches, evaluations, and analyses.

Hypothesis Stated

We also examined one separate purpose of the research articles: whether or not the study stated some form of testable hypothesis, including directional predictions and hypotheses of differences in either direction. Only 31% of the studies did so. In the other studies the purpose was either exploratory, descriptive, or hypothesis generating, which indicates that the field as a whole is at a relatively young stage of development with respect to the testing of models and hypotheses.

Subject Characteristics

To be truly a psychology of the whole community, the field should concern itself with the behavior of many different kinds of persons in many different milieus. Marginal as well as mainstream members of society, people at every point in the life span, participants in all manner of programs and organizations, and inhabitants of every conceivable setting should have an opportunity of claiming the attention of community psychologists. But do they? Such diversity should be reflected in the characteristics of persons who serve as subjects for community psychology research investigations. Accordingly, we examined some of the more salient subject characteristics, including presence of a psychological problem, gender, age level, ethnic status, and the type of setting from which subjects were drawn.

In 39% of the 681 articles in which humans (as opposed to some larger unit of analysis such as an organization or county) served as subjects and in which we could make such an identification, some or all of the subjects were identified as having some type of psychological problem, such as a problem in adjustment, psychopathology, or drug dependency. In only 16% of the studies were subjects nonvolunteers for the research; that is, participation was required (usually as a precondition for treatment or an obligation of incarceration). In 39% of the studies in which humans served as subjects, the sex of the subjects was not mentioned. Of those studies reporting the gender of subjects, 77% involved both male and female subjects; 14% males only; and 9% females only. For articles in which it was possible to calculate the relative frequencies

of males and females, the median percentage of male subjects was exactly 50%.

In 671 articles it was possible to identify broadly the
age status of subjects. In 4% of these articles preschool
children served as subjects; for 13%, primary school children served as subjects; for 13%, secondary school children
served as subjects, and in 68% of the articles, adults
served as subjects. It is interesting to note that in 15%
of the articles college students (also classified as adults)
served as subjects; and in 14%, mental health professionals
(also classified as adults) served as subjects.

In a full 71% of the articles in which humans served
as subjects, their ethnic status was not reported. Where it
was reported, 44% of the studies involved non-Caucasian
subjects.

There was considerable diversity in the settings from
which subjects were drawn, with affiliations as shown in
Table 2.3.

As can be seen from this table, the subjects of community psychology research studies came from a relatively
broad cross-section of settings. Leading the list were the
community at large (19% of the articles), mental health
centers (18%), colleges or universities (17%), public or
private schools (16%), mental hospitals or residential mental
institutions (11%), general social service organizations
other than mental health (9%), and prisons, penitentiaries,
or reformatories (6%).

On balance, it appears that there is a substantial
diversity of subjects and settings from which they were
drawn. Males and females were about equally represented,
and children at different age levels were fairly well represented among the subjects of studies. Although by one
classification over one-third of the studies identified some
or all subjects as having a psychological problem, and by
another classification over one-fourth of the studies' subjects were drawn from a mental health organization, in the
majority of studies subjects were not identified as having a
psychological problem and came from a number of different
settings. It is clear that the vast majority of studies
chose subjects who were affiliated with some type of institution, which probably reflects the field's commitment to
working in the context of specific programs, agencies, or
organizations. However, these may simply be the most
"accessible" places for community psychology researchers to

TABLE 2.3

Frequency of Settings with which Subjects Were Affiliated

Setting	Frequency	Percentage
The community (no program or organizational affiliation)	132	19
Mental health center or clinic	128	18
College or university	117	17
Private or public school	113	16
Mental hospital or residential institution	77	11
General social service organization (other than mental health)	63	9
Prison, penitentiary, or reformatory	45	6
General or medical hospital	25	4
Police department or law enforcement agency	13	2
Business or industrial organization	12	2
U.S. Navy, Army, or Air Force unit	11	2
Court or other agency of criminal justice system	9	1
People attending a specific conference or workshop	7	1
Drug or alcohol program or organization	5	1
American Psychological Association division	5	1
Other	42	6

Note: The total number of studies for which it was possible to determine an affiliation for subjects was 696. The percentages add up to more than 100 because in some studies subjects were selected on the basis of their affiliation with more than one setting. Settings which had less than 1% frequency are not reported here.

Source: Compiled by authors.

60

conduct their research and recruit their subjects. For example, it is probably much easier for many community psychology researchers to obtain subjects from a nearby mental health center, hospital, school system, general social service agency, or even their own university than it is for them to select from the community at large.

Finally, it is interesting to note that so few (8%) of the studies used a level of analysis greater than the individual. A hallmark of community psychology is its alleged mission of working with social systems, not individuals (compare Goodstein and Sandler, 1978). In this respect, it might seem disappointing for so few studies to use families, programs, or organizations as the smallest unit of analysis. On the other hand, the responses of individuals were often aggregated to the level of programs and organizations to make inferences about these larger units.

Implications Drawn in the Articles

In our overall assessment of an article we were interested in the general domain to which implications of the findings of the study were drawn. Besides the customary call for further research, were implications described for the community at large, for programs, or for a general problem area? We read several dozen articles to ascertain types of implications which were being drawn by the authors and were able to identify the seven broad categories listed below, which we used to record up to two types of implications drawn for each article.

A program or organization (specific or generic)	52%
The nature or extent of a problem or process	41%
Research methodology	14%
The community at large	7%
A field of psychology (including community psychology)	7%
Formal theory	5%
Society as a whole	5%

It was not possible in many studies to separate implications about programs from implications about organizations which administered these programs. Also, implications about the nature or extent of a problem (such as

drug dependence or recidivism) were mostly intertwined
with implications about the nature or extent of a process
to deal with that problem (such as planning a drug treatment program or training aftercare workers). The applied
orientation of the field is clearly reflected in the large
percentage of studies drawing implications to a program,
organization, or problem. Few implications were drawn to
the community or society, which we found surprising for a
field ostensibly concerned with phenomena at the level of
community and societal processes. The dearth of implications drawn to formal theory, or to the field of community psychology itself, seems to reflect the atheoretical
orientation of the investigations. If research in community
psychology is to better reflect the aspirations of the field,
researchers will need to pay more attention to the conceptual and cumulative implications of their work. We were
disappointed to find that a full 12% of the empirical studies
we reviewed drew no implications whatsoever from their
results.

SECTION III: RESULTS: RESEARCH DESIGN

Cronbach Category

In his presidential address at the 1957 convention
of the American Psychological Association, Lee J. Cronbach
characterized scientific psychology as not one but two independent disciplines, reflecting "two historic streams of
method, thought, and affiliation" (p. 671). Correlational
psychology is an approach that concerns itself with the
study of naturally existing variation; experimental psychology explores the consequences of creating variation by
interventions, or treatments. The scientific values of adherents to these approaches differ sharply, but both streams
have contributed valuable knowledge to the field of psychology, and Cronbach (1957) argued eloquently for a "true
federation" of the disciplines. "Kept independent," he
noted, "they can give only wrong answers, or no answers
at all regarding certain important problems" (p. 673).
We were interested in defining community psychology
research in terms of Cronbach's distinction between experimental and correlational psychology, and wondered whether
a "true federation" of the disciplines would be reflected in
this body of literature. In classifying a study as Cronbach

category experimental, we meant that the main approach was to estimate the effect of a treatment or process, typically an intervention or manipulation administered to subjects. The key to this code was that individual differences were treated as error variance, as in the case of a one-way analysis of variance. In addition, we classified the provision of a simple point-estimate in a survey (for example, 85% of the respondents reported having had a problem in the last year) as Cronbach category experimental when individual differences were not the subject of interest. In other words, studies classified as Cronbach category experimental were concerned with differences among groups rather than individuals, whether the grouping represented deliberate manipulations or naturally occurring classification of subjects in terms of some variable of interest.

In contrast, studies that focused on the variation among subjects were classified as Cronbach category correlational, and this term implied that individual differences were measured and considered to be important. A correlational design was often most easily identifiable by the type of statistical analysis used. For example, the use of correlation coefficients, multiple regression,[7] or canonical correlation usually indicated that individual variation among subjects was the primary focus of the investigator's attention, rather than average differences among groups. Some studies included both experimental and correlational analyses as defined above; we classified these as experimental and correlational, and regarded them as representing the joint application of approaches advocated by Cronbach. We found that 55% of the empirical articles reviewed were classified as experimental, indicating that research in community psychology largely reflects the experimental discipline. However, 23% of the studies were classified as correlational and 22% as both experimental and correlational, which implies that this field does draw somewhat on both traditions of psychology to frame questions and test answers. The combination of approaches within a single study, found in about one-fifth of the reports, further suggests that progress is being made within community psychology toward a federation of the two disciplines.

Research Strategy

Runkel and McGrath (1972) have described and compared some major research strategies (such as field studies, laboratory experiments, experimental simulations, and so forth) in terms of their relative capacities for giving differing amounts and kinds of information. Their analysis describes the strengths and weaknesses of each approach and stresses the complementary relationships among strategies, all of which are potentially useful as elements of programmatic investigation. We were interested in knowing which research strategies were being employed in community psychology studies and whether investigators were using a variety of strategies, or perhaps neglecting potentially useful types of empirical approaches.[8]

In our view, two general issues are involved in selecting a research strategy: (1) the extent to which the study captures or models the real-life situation of interest and (2) the amount of control exercised by the investigator. Researchers would like to optimize both the relevance and dependability of data obtained, but there are trade-offs involved in choosing any particular research strategy and these must be assessed in terms of the specific question under study. The aim is to capitalize on the relative advantages of the chosen method and to try to offset its disadvantages, which vary from situation to situation.

Accordingly, we classified the empirical studies into one of the following categories.

1. Field experiment--which we defined as a field investigation involving some deliberate modification of, or intervention into, some property of an environment or system. Studies of treatment, hospitalization, and therapy were regarded as studies of deliberate modifications and, thus, as field experiments.
2. Field study--which we defined as systematic observation of phenomena within "real-world" settings or "natural" behavior systems where no deliberate modification or intervention occurred, for example, studies of posthospital adjustment, community attitudes toward mental illness, smoking behavior, or bereavement.
3. Laboratory experiment--which we construed as systematic observation of phenomena under deliberately controlled conditions in an artificial setting.

Using these categories, the majority of investigations (61%) were classified as field studies. A further 36% were categorized as field experiments, and only 3% as laboratory experiments. These figures indicate a preponderance of field research in community psychology with minimal laboratory experimentation. The major advantage of field investigations is their realism; but, in general, the experimenter has relatively limited control in naturalistic settings. Laboratory experimentation involves converse strengths and weaknesses, and one might suggest that community psychology researchers consider including laboratory experimentation more often as a complementary strategy where appropriate, particularly in designing programmatic research. The predominance of field research in community psychology does, however, seem appropriate for an area dealing with complex issues of practical significance. Trickett and Lustman (1977) advocated such a naturalistic orientation in addressing the complicated questions faced by the field, and our data demonstrate that researchers have indeed adopted this approach. Training in community psychology research should therefore emphasize field research design and methodology, and deemphasize the classical laboratory techniques. Similarly, training in measurement principles, instrumentation, methods of data collection, and statistical analyses should be geared toward the requirements of field research.

In the field, both observation and experimentation are being employed. The majority of investigations were classified as field studies, indicating no deliberate intervention or modification of the environment, but a substantial proportion did include experimentation and were classified as field experiments. While observation and description provide a necessary foundation for research in this field, the most vital contributions of community psychology will not be served by observation or preservation of the status quo. They will come from innovative interventions into social systems, where the objective is improved functioning and enhanced quality of life for system participants. Empirical research is needed to verify the outcomes of these innovations. We follow Fairweather and Tornatzky (1977) in believing that the most productive strain of such research will be that which evaluates innovative models by means of naturalistic, scientific experiments; and so we were encouraged to find that so many studies were cast along the lines of what we have termed field experiments.

Validity Issues

So far we have discussed research design in general terms referring to the empirical literature as a whole.

However, it is the design of individual studies that determines their information yield, and the remainder of this section of the chapter will address some of the issues involved in designing a sound study to investigate problems in community psychology. The investigator is faced with decisions that influence validity at each point in the process of choosing a research strategy and designing a study. Even a seemingly simple field investigation requires the researcher to negotiate a morass of choice points. For example, one might be trying to estimate the number of drug abusers in a community. Some of the many questions which may arise include how to define a drug, a drug abuser, and a population at risk; how to select a representative sample of respondents; how to obtain consistent and accurate data; and how to obtain these data without sensitizing the respondents or violating their rights to confidentiality. On another level, the researchers in this situation must be concerned with larger issues like changes in legislation, seasonal variations in drug availability, law enforcement activities, and prevailing treatment and education efforts--all of which may influence the results of their study.

At the many decision points in designing a study, questions of internal and external validity dictate the choice of appropriate methods. Following Cook and Campbell (1979), by the term internal validity we refer to "the validity with which statements can be made about whether there is a causal relationship from one variable to another in the form in which the variables were manipulated or measured" (p. 38). External validity, then, refers to "the approximate validity with which conclusions are drawn about the generalizability of a causal relationship to and across populations of persons, settings, and times" (Cook & Campbell, 1979, p. 39). Questions of external validity are often crucial in this field, since the purpose of the research is usually to make inferences to populations and to generalize to diverse groupings of persons, programs, and environments. But questions of internal validity are equally important to community psychology researchers because of the lack of control which often exists in the settings with which they deal. (For a more thorough cataloguing of validity threats in field studies, see Cook and Campbell, 1979.)

Unfortunately, the requirements of internal validity often may conflict with the requirements of external validity.

For example, using homogenous subjects in tightly controlled settings or employing highly standardized measurement devices which are insensitive to individual differences among subjects may enhance internal validity by improving the power to detect a treatment effect, but these same restrictions may diminish the generalizability or external validity of the findings. We believe that in the final analysis, the optimum research methods needed to balance the different requirements of internal and external validity must be determined by the purpose and scope of each separate inquiry. We were interested in assessing the extent to which the research designs reported in the community psychology journals took account of some of the major issues concerning internal and external validity.

Comparison Groups and Random Assignment

Two important design features which enhance the internal validity of a study are the use of control or comparison groups and the random assignment of subjects to conditions. While they do not ensure internal validity, these features are the most effective means of ruling out many of the alternative hypotheses which might explain obtained results. We believe their effectiveness justifies the expenditure of considerable effort to include comparison groups and random assignment in community psychology research designs, and we wondered to what extent this was being accomplished. In 59% of the studies, one or more control or comparison groups were used, usually to augment the analysis of whether or not a manipulation was effective, but sometimes merely to compare levels or rates on selected process variables (for example, recidivism rates by demographic subgroups). We considered a control or comparison group to be one which was formed on the basis of an indenedent variable, such as absence of a treatment, or on the basis of some classification variable, such as sex, age, socioeconomic status, or IQ score. Of these 423 studies, full random assignment of subjects to groups was accomplished in only 40 cases. Matching was a technique used specifically to equate groups in 14% of the studies not employing full random assignment.

These figures indicate deficiencies in research design with respect to internal validity, which is described by Campbell and Stanley (1966) as "the basic minimum without which any experiment is uninterpretable" (p. 5).

We are of course aware of the difficulty in field research
of obtaining appropriate comparison groups, maintaining
their independence, and particularly of assigning subjects
randomly to conditions in the face of administrative opposition or alternative priorities. Nevertheless, in advocating
naturalistic experimentation as a productive approach to
community psychology research, we stress the importance of
including comparison groups and random assignment in designing studies.

Factorial Designs

For studies with comparison groups we looked at
whether a factorial design was used, that is, whether two
or more levels or categories of one independent variable
were crossed with two or more levels or categories of at
least one other independent variable. Factorial designs
permit an assessment of the statistical interaction between
the crossed independent variables, and hence allow one to
draw inferences about the interaction of treatments and individuals, or about the simultaneous effects of other variables of interest. The definitions of community psychology
suggest that complex interactions among variables are of
central importance, and particularly those among individual-
level and systems-level variables. Factorial designs are
therefore necessary to capture this complexity, but we found
only 21% of the studies with comparison groups were designed in this way. More adequate designs are indicated
for community psychology research to deal with the intrica-
cies of this field.

Occasion of Measurement

We were interested to know when measures were
taken on the dependent variable(s) and whether multiple
occasions of measurement characterized the research designs,
which would allow comparisons over time. We found that
most often (66% of the studies) a single occasion of measurement was used, which we designated post only. In 2% of
the studies a postmeasure plus one extra follow-up measure
was taken (post-post), in 17% of the studies pre-post measures were taken, and in 15% of the studies more than two
measures were taken, which we labeled time-series occasion
of measurement.

The predominance of designs employing a single
occasion of measurement indicates a potential weakness of

the research we reviewed. More general use of multiple occasions of measurement is needed to investigate changes in behavior over time and to draw inferences about the stability of effects over time.

Using the categories as described, we tabulated the frequency of designs schematically as shown in Table 2.4.

Thus, for example, it can be seen that four studies, or nearly 1% of the total, employed research designs using multiple comparison groups, formed on the basis of manipulated independent variables, with random assignment of subjects to conditions, in a factorial design and with more than two occasions of measurement.

Statistical Power and Sample Size

Another design issue we looked at was sample size, which has a profound impact on the statistical power of the research. Across all studies the median total number of subjects serving in the primary statistical analysis of an investigation was 92. The median cell size was 34. More specifically, the median sample size for studies analyzing the responses of a single group of subjects was 84. For studies comparing groups of subjects, the median cell size was 28.

The small sample sizes reported in most of the community psychology studies we examined call into question their statistical power. By statistical power we mean the probability of rejecting the null hypothesis when it is false (that is, the probability of obtaining statistically significant results). Statistical power is crucial for adequately testing any hypothesized relationship, whether the concern is with theoretical models, construct relations, or the ability of a program or service to achieve specified outcomes. At low levels of power even negative findings or null results are rendered ambiguous.

Although we are interested here in relating statistical power to sample size, we must first outline several related factors which must also be considered when analyzing statistical power. As noted by Cohen (1977), statistical power depends on the effect size or "degree" to which the phenomenon is present in the population, that is, the "degree to which the null hypothesis is false" (p. 9). The larger the effect size, the greater the power of a statistical test. Statistical power also depends on the significance criterion set by an investigator (for example, α = .05). Other things being equal, the more stringent the

TABLE 2.4
Frequency of Research Design by Type of Design and Occasion of Measurement

			Number and Occasion of Measurement			
			1 Post Only	2 Pre/Post	2 Post/Post	3+ Time Series
			472 (66)	124 (17)	11 (02)	106 (15)
Single Group 290 (41)			205 (29)	36 (05)	1 (<01)	48 (07)
Classification 277 (39)	Nonfactorial 226 (32)		176 (25)	31 (04)	4 (01)	15 (02)
	Factorial 51 (07)		41 (06)	5 (01)	0 (00)	5 (01)
Multiple (Two or More) Groups 423 (59)	Nonfactorial 109 (15)	Without Randomization 62 (09)	26 (04)	17 (02)	5 (01)	14 (02)
		Partial Randomization 20 (03)	6 (01)	8 (01)	0 (00)	6 (01)
		Full Randomization 27 (04)	4 (01)	14 (02)	0 (00)	9 (01)
Manipulation 146 (20)	Factorial 37 (05)	Without Randomization 14 (02)	4 (01)	7 (01)	1 (<01)	2 (<01)
		Partial Randomization 10 (01)	3 (<01)	4 (01)	0 (00)	3 (<01)
		Full Randomization 13 (02)	7 (01)	2 (<01)	0 (00)	4 (01)

Note: The first number in each cell or section represents the number of studies which used that type of design. The number in the parentheses is the percentage (out of 713) of studies that used that type of design. An explanation for the row and column headings is given in the text.

Source: Compiled by authors.

significance criterion (that is, the lower the α level), the lower the statistical power. Statistical power is also a function of the reliability or precision of a sample value, which refers to the degree to which a sample value approximates the relevant population value. The reliability of a statistic can be expressed in terms of its standard error, which in turn is a function of sample size. In general, the larger the sample size, the greater the power of a statistical test. Finally, in talking about the power of a statistical test and factors which influence power, one should specify the type of statistical test, as the relationships between power and the other factors will depend on the test statistic considered.

Cohen has provided a series of tables for estimating the power of statistical tests for varying combinations of sample size, alpha level, and effect size and for determining the sample size required to achieve specified levels of significance at varying effect sizes and power levels. Based on the latter series of tables, we have summarized some selected sample size values in Table 2.5 for "small" and "medium" effect sizes at the α = .05 level for .80 and .90 levels of statistical power.[9]   The terms small and medium are obviously arbitrary--for example, Cohen labels a medium effect as one which is "large enough to be visible to the naked eye" (p. 26)--but they serve as useful frames of reference in new areas of research like community psychology where most of the phenomena have not been well studied and effect sizes may be rather small at first.

As can be seen in Table 2.5, the cell sizes necessary to detect "small" effects are substantially larger than those found in the typical community psychology research investigation. In fact, in no cases of testing for a medium-size effect does the typical cell size of 28 lend sufficient power to have an 80% chance of rejecting the null hypothesis. The reader should note that the values summarized here are cell sizes, not total sample sizes.[10]   Thus, one would have to multiply the cell sizes shown in Table 2.5 by two to estimate the total number of subjects necessary in the case of a t test of differences between means in a two-group experiment. Similarly, the cell size values for the F statistic are based on three degrees of freedom, which would require multiplication by four to estimate the total number of subjects required in a design comparing four groups of subjects. We wonder how many community psychology researchers would go to the effort to recruit, say, 1,552 subjects to test differences between four different treatment groups. It is likely that the published studies in community psychology journals had larger sample sizes than the unpublished ones, and it may be that many interesting findings were undetected (and unreported) owing to inadequate statistical power. As a minimum, we recommend that community psychology researchers investigate whether they have sufficient power to reject the null hypothesis before they conduct a study. Power analysis may also be helpful to those investigators who have completed a study and would like to know whether they really had sufficient power to detect effects which did not prove to be significant.

TABLE 2.5
Examples of Estimated Cell Sizes

| Effect Size[a] | Power | Statistical Test[b] | | |
		$\underline{t}$	$\underline{r}$	$\underline{F}$ (3, $\underline{N}$-4)
"Small"	.80	393	783	383
	.90	526	1,046	483
"Medium"	.80	64	84	63
	.90	85	112	78

[a]The source for these estimates is Cohen (1977), especially pages 55, 102, and 381. The "small" and "medium" effect sizes he suggests for each statistical test were employed here: viz., $\underline{d}$ = .2 and .50, respectively, for $\underline{t}$; $\underline{r}$ = .10 and .30, respectively, for the Pearson product-moment correlation, $\underline{r}$; and $\underline{f}$ = .10 and .25, respectively, for the one-way, fixed factors $\underline{F}$ ratio where each cell has an equal number of subjects.

[b]For the $\underline{t}$ and $\underline{r}$ tests the significance criterion was set at the two-tailed α = .025 (or total α for both tails of the distribution = .05). For $\underline{F}$ the one-tailed α = .05 level was used.

Note: The cell size ($\underline{N}$) refers to the number of subjects required in each cell. It is assumed that there is one cell, or group, used to compute $\underline{r}$ and two equal-sized cells or groups used to compute $\underline{t}$. Four groups with equal cell sizes were assumed for the $\underline{F}$ ratio. Thus, for example, a total of 1,932 subjects would be needed to conduct an experiment to have a .90 chance of detecting a "small" difference in means among four comparison groups at the α = .05 level using the $\underline{F}$ test.

Before leaving the issue of statistical power, we note that power problems stemming from small sample sizes are most likely compounded in most studies by two other factors which we did not analyze--range restriction and unreliability.   By range restriction we refer to any selection of subjects in a design or any choice of a measurement device which reduces the variability of scores (that is, reduces the standard deviation of scores).   Examples of range restrictions would be measuring feelings of tension among residents of a community threatened by a hurricane or measuring life satisfaction among pregnant teenagers (where in each there would be a smaller range of responses by more concentration around an extreme value).   By unreliability we refer to any reduction in the accuracy of measurement caused by random errors of measurement.   Both these factors can reduce the power of any statistical test. For example, Schmidt, Hunter, and Urry (1976) present tables for the statistical power of validity coefficients which show that a sample size of 959 would be necessary to detect a true correlation of .35 with .90 confidence if the reliability for one measure were .50 and if the top 10% of the scores in the population distribution for the other measure had been selected for estimating the correlation.

Sampling

In considering external validity, the sampling of subjects was assessed, with the focus on whether or not the obtained sample was representative of the population which was claimed to be under study.   In 7% of the studies a full census of some population (usually all patients in a particular hospital or all new clients in a mental health center or crisis center) was taken.   In another 12% of the studies a representative sample of subjects was obtained through the use of such techniques as simple, systematic, or stratified random sampling.   In the other 79% of the studies, the obtained sample was either nonrepresentative by design, by outcome (we used an arbitrary cutoff of 10% or greater attrition of subjects from a design which was intended to be representative to constitute grounds for classification as nonrepresentative),[11] or the type of sampling procedure could not be determined.   The prevalence of nonrepresentative sampling of subjects is particularly problematic in an applied field such as community psychology where the aim of most studies is to draw inferences to a larger population. Attempting to obtain representative samples is a clear imperative of research design in the field.

In general, our analysis indicates that research designs employed have not met the technical standards of sound experiments. Only 19% of the studies we reviewed provided evidence that a representative sample or full census of subjects had been obtained; only 5% used two or more comparison groups and randomly assigned subjects to conditions; and only one study, or less than one-sixth of 1%, reported using both random sampling and random assignment of subjects to conditions. There were far too many studies which evaluated a treatment simply by comparing effects pre- and post-treatment for a single group or that made their analysis by comparing post-only measures among nonequivalent comparison groups. (One study, for example, looked at the effects of recent relocation upon housewives by comparing their effective states with three other groups: successful university students, recently hospitalized psychiatric patients, and women who had recently had a child.)

We are aware of the extraordinary problems faced by community psychology researchers in designing studies; they must deal with a complex reality, include both individual- and systems-level variables, and try to exert some control in a dynamic environment. However, we are convinced of the benefits of investing time, effort, and ingenuity in improving the design of research studies, particularly in obtaining representative samples large enough to ensure powerful research designs, using appropriate comparison groups, and employing random assignment of subjects to conditions whenever possible. The task of designing and conducting sound field research is indeed demanding, but the search for vigorous generalizations and innovative solutions to social problems calls for nothing less.

SECTION IV: RESULTS: MEASUREMENT AND STATISTICAL ANALYSIS

Measurement Characteristics

Without adequate measurement even the most brilliantly conceived research design and analysis can be rendered meaningless. In thinking about the question of measurement adequacy we came to ask the question of what really is the purpose of measurement in community psychology (or any other field) research. A fundamental purpose of measurement is to accurately model some aspect of the observable world. But on nearly every front, community psychology researchers are faced with enormous complexities, all of which contribute to a generic measurement problem of how to accurately model a complex reality. Whether that reality is a "natural" process such as social change or recidivism, or a planned intervention, such as an aftercare program or a drug treatment facility, there are invariably many knotty problems of how to depict a system of independent variables, document its process, and measure the myriad effects which it may register on an individual, group, or larger configuration. And all this is to be accomplished in a milieu in which social systems and their participants are constantly changing and interacting! One test of measurement accuracy, then, is to ask whether the set of measures used in a study is "rich" enough or sufficiently complex to capture the full range of effects which might be expected to occur in the setting. Moreover, from the standpoint of community psychology research, a related question is whether there is diversity in the variables examined and methods used to measure these variables. Reliance upon, say, paper-and-pencil measures of adjustment would afford a rather narrow view of reality and would hardly do justice to the lofty goals of the field.

With these considerations in mind, we elected to analyze some relatively simple features, such as the types of dependent variables studied, the methods used to collect data, and whether multiple methods were used. Obviously, other measurement aspects could be analyzed, but as will be seen below, even these few features provide an interesting insight into the current state of measurement in community psychology research.

We note first that in 717 of the studies some type of dependent variable was explicitly analyzed and associated measurement procedures were described. Of these studies, 90% analyzed more than one type of dependent variable. We categorized studies as using one or more of the following methods to collect data, with results as listed below:

Paper-and-pencil tests, questionnaires, or
inventories used   66%

Interviews conducted	24%
Archival data sources, records, or registers used	22%
Behavior measured by direct observation	16%

In 89% of the studies where a self-report measure in either a paper-and-pencil or interview format was used, there was no form of direct observation of behavior employed for any variable. Further, only 7% of the studies used some form of multiple operationism, wherein two or more different methods were used to assess the same construct or the same kind of specific variable (see, for example, Webb et al., 1966, for discussion of this concept). This shortage of method cross-checking limits the generalizability of conclusions and is an area needing improvement in future studies.

The types of dependent variables analyzed in studies were also recorded, with the relative frequencies of the major different types summarized in Table 2.6. As can be seen from this table, there was substantial emphasis on general constructs as well as specific variables. For example, over two-fifths of the studies analyzed personality or adjustment constructs, and 38% analyzed psychological sentiments (including attitudes, interests, satisfaction, and values), but 54% analyzed a specific action, behavior, or activity (such as returning to a mental hospital or leaving a program, number of cigarettes smoked, and so on). One wonders if there might not be an even greater number of studies measuring some type of general construct if there were more attention given to theory development.

That the majority of the studies examined a specific action, behavior, activity, or event is consistent with the field's extensive involvement in policy research and program evaluation where such variables often represent important outcomes. Also, the high proportion of studies measuring personality and adjustment variables is consistent with the mental health orientation of the field, noted earlier. It is interesting to note the heavy concentration of constructs and variables measured at the level of the individual.

Only 16% of the studies tapped social interactional variables; only 5% examined organizational constructs; and only 4% sociological constructs. These latter percentages seem to us to be rather small. Even if we view the mission of community psychology as the study of individual behavior in relation to social systems (compare Murrell,

TABLE 2.6

Frequency of Studies Analyzing Different Types of
Dependent Variables

Type of Dependent Variable	Frequency	Percentage
General Constructs		
Personality and adjustments	311	43
Sentiment (attitudes, interests, opinions, satisfactions, values)	275	38
Cognitions, beliefs, and expectancies	177	25
Social interaction	117	16
Achievement (e.g., math, reading)	72	10
Mental abilities (e.g., IQ, spatial relations)	44	6
Mental health skills	41	6
Physical, motor, or sensory functions	38	5
Organizational constructs (e.g., formalization of rules and roles; organizational climate)	36	5
Sociological constructs (e.g., stratification, decentralization)	25	4
Work-related constructs (e.g., job involvement, work-role strain)	21	3
Specific Variables		
Specific actions, behaviors, activities, or events	387	54
Demographic data, biodata	286	40
Specific content analysis of verbal material	119	17
Judged attribute of a physical object (e.g., readability of a brochure)	4	1

Note: N = 721. These percentages add up to more than
100 because in most studies more than one type of variable was
measured.

Source: Compiled by authors.

77

1973), there will still be a need to systematically measure some attributes of systems like family, organization, and community.

We also examined the extent to which the variables listed in Table 2.6 were examined in isolation or in combination in each study. In 20% of the studies only one of these types of variables (especially sentiments and specific actions, behaviors, or events) was measured, and in another 6% of the studies only two types of variables were measured. The most frequent combinations of two types of variables assessed were demographic data with personality or adjustment constructs, constructs measuring sentiments, and social interactional variables. It seems to us that there has not been sufficient differentiation of behavior in naturalistic settings or employment of multifaceted measurements of behavior. We believe that this deficiency in the representation of behavior results generally in a failure to assess relationships among different classes of behavior (for example, attitudes versus actions) and thus leads to a diminished, if not distorted, view of reality.

Finally, many of the measures reported appear to have been constructed just for the purpose of this study. We ascertained that in 37% of the studies none of the measures had been used previously (as indicated by the absence of citations to previous use); in 18% of the studies one or more of the measures had not been used previously; and in 45% of the studies reference was made to prior usage of all the measures.

Measurement Recommendations

We conclude that a basic shortcoming of research in community psychology to date can be expressed as a lack of complexity of the measurement process, including both the selection of the types of variables to be analyzed and the method of measurement used to collect data. By complexity we do not mean simply unsystematic addition to measurement. Rather, we mean (1) systematically selecting varied measures which, as a whole, possess enough content validity to represent the domain of interest and (2) systematically varying the methods used, to permit assessment of convergent validity (compare Campbell & Fiske, 1959).

A simplified illustration of this issue can be portrayed if we think of two dimensions considered jointly in

graph form. One axis we can label the complexity of measurement (including, as mentioned above, complexity through
planned variation in constructs/variables and method); the
other axis, the complexity of the stimulus situation (including the milieu of persons, social and physical environments, time frame, and so on, in which the behavior under
study occurs). These two dimensions can be diagramed as
shown in Figure 2.1.

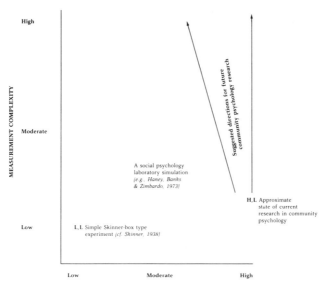

FIGURE 2.1
Complexity of Measurement and of Stimulus Situation in
Relation to Types of Psychological Research

    Although this is admittedly a gross generalization,
we think that the current body of research in community
psychology can be roughly located in the lower right corner of this diagram (high stimulus complexity, low measurement complexity). Other points of reference might be a
simple animal conditioning experiment using a Skinner box
(Skinner, 1938) in the lower left corner (low stimulus complexity, low measurement complexity), and a social psychology simulation study conducted in the laboratory such
as Haney, Banks, and Zimbardo's (1973) "prison study,"
which might be identified somewhere just below the middle
of the diagram.
    In our opinion, community psychology research
should systematically increase the level of measurement

complexity, perhaps (but not necessarily) arriving at a point in the upper right corner of Figure 2.1. A more crucial general strategy might be to investigate the theoretical and practical yield of systematically covarying the complexity of the stimulus situation and the measurement process. We might find that the state of the art would be advanced most by studies employing moderate control over the environment, as in a naturalistic field experiment, and using a very complex measurement technology.

As a final set of measurement concerns, we note (but did not count) that very few studies reported information about the psychometric quality of the instruments used. For example, the reliability of a measure was rarely reported. [12] Information about the psychometric properties of the measurement devices were particularly needed in the 37% of the studies where only "homemade" or unreferenced measures were used.

Statistical Analysis

We examined four features of the statistical analysis procedures used in the studies. Thus, we determined (1) whether descriptive or inferential statistics were reported, (2) whether univariate or multivariate statistics were used, and (3) whether parametric or nonparametric statistics were used; and (4) for each study reporting an inferential statistical test, we recorded the most lenient alpha level used to claim statistical significance.

Our only a priori expectation concerning these features involved the relative use of descriptive and inferential statistics. In view of the newness of the field and its attendant research, we anticipated frequent use of descriptive statistics and moderate use of inferential statistics, mainly to test hypotheses about new programs, policies, and procedures.

In 697 of the 728 studies, some type of statistic was reported. (The other 31 studies simply described the results without using numbers). In 89% of these 697 studies, descriptive statistics (for example, percentages, means, and standard deviations) were reported; and in 86%, some type of inferential statistic (for example, F, t, or chi-square tests) was reported.

The type (or types) of statistical analysis used in each of the 598 studies reporting a statistical test was classified into one or more of the following categories, with the following results: 85% used either a univariate statistical procedure (that is, having one dependent variable, such as the Student's t test) or bivariate statistical tests (that is, tests involving two variables such as the Pearson product-moment correlation coefficient); 15% used a multivariate statistical procedure (such as factor analysis or canonical correlation); 74% used a parametric statistical test; and 29% used a nonparametric statistical test.

Although the emphasis on parametric, univariate statistics is not surprising, it is interesting to note that so few studies employed multivariate statistical procedures. Multivariate tests can be very appropriate for community psychology research insofar as they permit the investigator to ascertain the effects of programs, policies, procedures, and other "treatments" on multiple dependent variables in a single test or single statistical procedure.

We also recorded the most lenient level of statistical significance (at the two-tailed probability level) presented in each study reporting a test of significance. Of these 569 studies, 106 or 19% interpreted a result as statistically significant when the probability value was greater than .05 (typically .10), while 354 or 62% used the conventional alpha = .05 level of significance, and 109 or 19% determined significance at a $p < .01$ level. We were surprised to find so many studies using a $p > .05$ significance level, particularly since there was so little reliance on theory or previous related research, thereby making it difficult for the investigator in these cases to justify, say, a two-tailed alpha = .10 significance level by making a test at the one-tailed .05 level.

SECTION V: COMPARISONS OVER TIME, ACROSS
JOURNALS, AND ACROSS FIELDS

Trends over Time

We were interested in whether the variables reported above displayed any change in relative frequency over time. Accordingly, we divided the ten years' worth of studies into two groups: (1) the first five years contained all the studies analyzed which appeared in the 1973–77 journals; (2) the second five years contained all the studies analyzed which came from the 1978–82 journals. These two time periods were compared on each of the variables listed above to depict trends over time. In many cases it was necessary to condense the variable values so that there would neither be too many empty cells nor cells with low frequencies. Chi-square tests were used in the case of nominal data (for example, types of topics), and t tests were used in the case of discrete data (for example, number of authors). The results reported here summarize just the significant findings; in the other cases no significant differences between the two five-year periods were observed.

There was a significant difference between the first and second five-year period on university/nonuniversity affiliations of authors [chi-square (2 df) = 26.34 p < .01], with the relative frequency of only university-based authors increasing from 60% of the studies analyzed to 76%; and nonuniversity-based authors decreasing from 22% to 9% from the first to the second five-year period.

There was also a general shift in the topics addressed by the studies over time [chi-square (4 df) = 24.91, p < .01], with the second five-year period characterized by fewer studies concerned with some aspect of mental health delivery (40% compared to 55% for the first five years), less emphasis on research or measurement methodology (11% versus 18%), but more emphasis on specific problem areas and issues (77% versus 63%).

A significant difference [chi-square (7 df) = 24.91, p < .01] between the two periods was found in the purpose served by the studies, with the later group being distinguished by less emphasis on theory development (1% in the second five years versus 4% in the first five years), less emphasis on studies concerned with describing some type of manipulation (8% versus 18%), less emphasis on studies concerned with program evaluation (17% versus 30%), and more emphasis on what we labeled specific-research investigations (50% versus 24%).

Three basic differences in subject characteristics were observed between the two periods. First, in terms of the settings from which subjects for studies were drawn, there was a significant difference [chi-square (5 df) = 34.56 p < .01], indicating that in the second five years relatively fewer subjects were drawn from a mental hospital or residential institution (8% versus 18% for the first five years) and more subjects drawn from the community at large (30% versus 17%). Second, in the 1978-82 studies there were relatively fewer studies in which some or all of the subjects had identified psychological problems than in the 1973-77 studies [32% versus 45%, respectively, with chi-square (1 df) = 11.23, p < .01]. Third, there was a shift in the gender of subjects over time, with later studies characterized by more studies employing both male and female subjects (59% versus 37% for the first five-year period), fewer studies employing only male subjects (4% versus 12%), and more studies reporting the gender of subjects (68% versus 55%). [The latter differences were observed in a single test, with chi-square (3 df) = 35.74, p < .01:]

A significant difference was also observed in the Cronbach category [chi-square (2 df) = 12.00, p < .01], with the 1978-82 studies more frequently classified as correlational (28% versus 19%) and "both correlational and experimental" (25% versus 19%). The 1973-77 studies were more often classified as experimental (60% versus 49%).

Several differences were observed in the types of dependent variables studied with the 1978-82 studies more frequently (38% versus 14%) assessing cognitions/beliefs/expectancies [chi-square (1 df) = 52.06, p < .01]; less frequently (3% versus 9%) assessing mental abilities [chi-square (1 df) = 8.20, p < .01]; less frequently (3% versus 7%) measuring physical, motor, or sensory functions [chi-square (1 df) = 6.27]; and less frequently (45% versus 60%) analyzing specific actions or events [chi-square (1 df) = 15.65, p < .01].

Two significant differences were observed in the types of statistics employed. In the second five years, studies more frequently (79% versus 70%) utilized some type of parametric statistic [chi-square (1 df) = 7.43, p < .01] and they more frequently (19% versus 11%) used some type of multivariate statistic [chi-square (1 df) = 7.24, p < .01].

A final difference between the earlier and later periods concerned the implications drawn from the studies [chi-square (6 df) = 47.69], with the 1978-82 studies more frequently drawing implications to a problem or process (52% versus 32%) and more frequently to a field of psychology, including community psychology (10% versus 5%); at the same time, the 1978-82 studies less frequently derived implications concerning a program or organization (42% versus 60%) and to the community as a whole (4% versus 10%).

In summary, one of the major trends over time in the first decade of community psychology research seems to be a growing academic emphasis at the expense of a more applied orientation, particularly a more traditional mental health orientation. This can be seen in the increased percentage of authors from a college or university setting. Moreover, there were fewer studies devoted to mental health delivery topics and more emphasis on specific problems and issues. Similarly, the purpose served by articles appears to be decreasing with respect to an emphasis on program evaluation and descriptions of new programs and interventions, but increasing in terms of emphasis on specific research questions. Consistent with this trend is the decreased frequency of subjects drawn from mental health facilities and fewer studies conducted with subjects who had identified psychological problems. As might be expected from such a trend, there were also fewer implications drawn to programs or organizations and the community as a whole, but more frequent inferences drawn to specific problems and processes.

There was some evidence to suggest that the subject base is broadening over time in that more of the later studies sampled subjects from the community at large and more of the later studies utilized both male and female subjects. There were few indications of improved research of statistical methodology from the first five years to the second five years, with one exception being that slightly more frequent use was made of multivariate statistical methods in the later studies.

Journal Comparisons

We examined the differences between the research articles published in the AJCP and the JCP, wondering to what extent the same picture of community psychology research was represented in both journals. The variables examined and types of statistical tests made to compare the two journals were the same as in the previous section summarizing differences between the two time periods.

One difference in the affiliation of authors was noted. Regarding the university/nonuniversity affiliation [chi-square (2 df) = 47.82, p < .01], the AJCP authors of an article had only an academic affiliation more frequently than did JCP authors (78% compared to 49%), whereas the authors of JCP studies were found to have only a nonacademic affiliation more frequently than the authors of AJCP studies (24% versus 9%, respectively).

An examination of whether a hypothesis was explicitly stated in an article revealed that AJCP articles more frequently contained explicit statements than did JCP articles [36% versus 28%, with chi-square (1 df) = 4.93, $p < .05$].

Four differences between the two journals were observed in subject characteristics. First, some or all subjects in JCP articles more frequently were identified as having an identified psychological problem than subjects in AJCP articles [45% versus 33%, with chi-square (1 df) = 9.50, $p < .01$]. Second, there was a difference between the two journals in settings from which subjects were drawn [chi-square (5 df) = 33.27, $p < .01$]. Specifically, subjects in JCP articles were more frequently drawn from mental health centers or clinics (26% versus 19%) and more frequently from mental hospitals or residential institutions (20% versus 7%) but less frequently from school systems (14% versus 27%) than subjects in AJCP articles. Third, there was a difference between journals in the age groupings of subjects [chi-square (5 df) = 14.58, $p < .01$], with AJCP subjects being more frequently identified as being of primary school age (16% versus 12%) but less frequently identified as either secondary school children (8% versus 18%) or adults (68% versus 75%) than JCP subjects. Fourth, in studies where the gender of subjects could be identified, the average percentage of subjects who were male was found to be higher in the JCP articles than the AJCP articles [61% versus 55%, with t (332 df) = 1.95, $p < .01$].

Representative subject samples were found to be obtained more frequently in AJCP articles than in JCP articles [16% versus 9%, with chi-square (2 df) = 6.71, $p < .05$]. Also, there was a significant difference between the journals on the Cronbach category for the research strategy [chi-square (2 df) = 12.00, $p < .01$]. Specifically, the JCP articles were found to more frequently employ an experimental strategy (61% versus 27%), whereas the AJCP studies more frequently employed research strategies that were correlational (27% versus 20%) and "both correlational and experimental" (25% versus 19%).

Three significant differences emerged for the types of dependent variables studied, with AJCP studies more frequently analyzing cognitions/beliefs/expectancies [31% versus 20%, with chi-square (1 df) = 11.18, $p < .05$], work-related variables [5% versus 2%, with chi-square (1 df) = 5.39, $p \lessdot .05$], and sociological variables [6% versus 2%, with chi-square (1 df) = 9.29, $p < .05$] than JCP studies.

One significant difference between the two journals was found on the type of statistical test used: AJCP studies more frequently employed some type of multivariate statistic than did JCP studies [19% versus 12%, with chi-square = 6.46, $p < .05$].

Finally, AJCP studies more frequently noted the reliability of one or more of the measurement devices used than did the JCP articles [44% versus 30%, with chi-square (1 df) = 4.01 $p < .05$].

In summary, it appears that there are several important similarities between the two journals with no essential differences found on such key variables as the topics addressed by the studies, the purpose served, the implications drawn, and the types of design. However, AJCP authors were more often affiliated with university settings than their JCP counterparts. The JCP authors appeared to be more interested in studying subjects with problems and subjects affiliated with mental health facilities. There was also some evidence that AJCP studies incorporated a somewhat more rigorous approach to conducting or reporting research (or both) as can be seen in their more frequent statement of explicit hypotheses, more frequent reporting of reliability of one or more the measures used, and more frequent use of multivariate statistics. One conclusion to be drawn from this analysis is that while both journals are similar in the topics and purposes of their research investigations, there are several other differences which suggest that a slightly different picture of research in community psychology research would emerge if an investigation such as this one were to focus on only one of the two journals.

Comparisons with Other Fields

In looking at the results of any study of this nature which confines itself to a single field, it is difficult to maintain perspective and know how the field compares

with other fields on the dimensions analyzed. In this section we make a limited number of such comparisons to
other fields of inquiry.

There have been few systematic analyses of research
methods and content in other applied fields of social sciences; however, four studies permit limited comparison on
common dimensions to the present content analysis. The
first is a doctoral dissertation by Jones (1981) that compared the fields of community psychology and social work on
selected variables. In this study, Jones analyzed the 51
empirical articles appearing in the 1973 and 1978 volumes
of two journals, Social Work and Social Work Research and
Abstracts. In another comparative content analysis,
Ehrenberg (1983) analyzed 306 empirical articles from the
1964-82 issues of the Community Mental Health Journal and
compared them on a number of variables to articles published in the AJCP and the JCP. Another extensive investigation is a content analysis reported by Dipboye and
Flanagan (1979) on research in industrial-organizational
psychology (also see Dipboye & Flanagan, 1977; Flanagan &
Dipboye, 1977). They analyzed all 490 empirical articles
from the 1966, 1970, and 1974 volumes of the Journal of
Applied Psychology, Organizatonal Behavior and Human
Performance, and Personnel Psychology. A fourth data
base is provided by White and Mitchell (1976), who examined methods of research employed in 44 studies of organization development (OD) wherein the research pertained to a
long-range organization improvement program and appeared
in a published book, journal, or periodical (examples
being the Journal of Applied Behavoral Science and the
Training and Development Journal). For several items
direct comparisons between the results for our categories
and the ones used in those studies can be made, but we
did have to aggregate some of the original categories in
these studies to make them comparable.

To make the comparisons easier to see, in Table 2.7
we have presented the percentages found in our study
along with the percentages found in the other four studies.
Unless otherwise noted, the meanings of the categories presented in this table are essentially the same as described
earlier in the chapter.

Three of these applied fields appear to be most frequently represented by university-affiliated authors. Thus,
one can see from Table 2.7 that the percentage of studies
which had only university-affiliated authors was 67% for

TABLE 2.7

Summary of Findings of Content Analyses in Community Psychology, Community Mental Health, Social Work, Industrial-Organizational Psychology, and Organization Development

Variable Analyzed	Percentage of Articles in Each Field				
	Community Psychology[a] (N=728)	Community Mental Health[b] (N=306)	Social Work[c] (N=51)	Industrial-Organizational Psychology[d] (N=490)	Organization Development[e] (N=51)
Affiliation of Authors:					
University based	67	39	57	72	--
Nonuniversity based	17	34	26	18	--
Both university and nonuniversity based	16	27	17	10	--
Subjects:					
College students served as subjects	15	8	13	37	--
Subjects were identified as nonvolunteers	16	12	10	--	--
Where gender could be determined:					
Males only served as subjects	14	10	--	50	--
Females only served as subjects	9	14	--	14	--
Both males and females served as subjects	77	76	--	36	--
Gender of subjects could not be determined	39	58	42	42	--
Some or all subjects had identified psychological problems	39	49	16	--	--
Hypothesis Was Stated	31	22	36	45	--
Type of Research Design:					
Field experiment	36	20	17	5	41
Field study (includes sample surveys and case studies)	61	79	83	54	54
Laboratory experiment	3	1	00	37	5
Two or more comparison groups were used	59	62	52	--	25

Occasion of Measurement:					
Post-only measures	66	74	82	88	55
Pre-post measure	17	14	12	10	18
Multiple (more than two) post measures	17	12	6	--	27
Other	--	--	--	2	--
Type of Measures Used:					
Self-report measures[f]	89	55	78	--	74
Direct observation	16	14	6	--	--
Archival data	22	32	22	--	5
Statistical Analysis Procedures:					
Parametric statistics used	74	52	66	79	--
Nonparametric statistics used	29	31	55	19	--
Univariate or bivariate statistics used	85	56	93	72	--
Multivariate statistics used	15	11	11	24	--

[a]The data for community psychology are the ones which have been presented earlier in this chapter and, unless otherwise noted, the meaning of each variable is as described earlier.

[b]Source: Ehrenberg, M. An empirical analysis of the boundaries between community psychology and community mental health. Doctoral dissertation, in progress, University of Tennessee, 1983.

[c]Source: Jones, T. W. A conceptual and empirical comparison of the fields of community psychology and social work. Unpublished doctoral dissertation. University of Tennessee, June 1981.

[d]Source: Dipboye, R. L., & Flanagan, M. F. Research settings in industrial and organizational psychology. American Psychologist, 1979, 34, 141-150.

[e]Source: White, S. E., & Mitchell, T. R. Organization development: A review of research content and research design. Academy of Management Review, 1976, 1, 57-73.

[f]Included in this category are self-report paper-and-pencil measures as well as self-report interviews.

Note: The use of -- indicates that the variable was not analyzed or is not available for that field.

Source: Compiled by authors.

community psychology (CP), 72% in industrial-organizational psychology (IOP) studies, 57% in social work (SW) studies, and 39% in the community mental health (CMH) studies.

Although not shown in Table 2.7, we note that the 76% rate of multiple authorship of studies appearing in CP journals may be slightly higher than the rate for other fields. By way of example, Lindsey (1978) analyzed journals listed in the Social Science Citation Index and the Science Citation Index from 1970 to 1975 and found that the number of single-author articles in all fields of psychology combined was 45% of the total of the psychology articles. Corresponding figures for other fields were biochemistry, 19%; economics, 83%; psychiatry, 53%; social work, 75%; and sociology, 75%. It could be that community psychology research requires more active collaboration with other people to carry all the tasks associated with a community field experiment or field study; or, it may just be that researchers in community psychology like to work in groups more often than researchers in other areas of social science.

Concerning characteristics of subjects, 15% of the CP studies used college students as subjects versus 8% for CMH, 13% for SW, and 37% for IOP studies. Part of the greater emphasis on college students by IOP may be based on their more frequent usage of laboratory studies than CP (37% versus 3%, respectively). Community psychology studies appear to be more broadly based in terms of using both male and female subjects than IOP studies. Community psychology, social work, and industrial-organizational psychology studies all were about equally deficient in terms of not reporting the gender of subjects. It is interesting to note that even studies in social work, a field which is purportedly much concerned with disadvantaged and disenfranchised persons, focused on subjects with identified psychological problems less frequently than CP studies (16% versus 39%, respectively). On the other hand, the rhetorical assertion of many community psychology thinkers that CP is less concerned with individual dysfunctioning than CMH is supported by the respective figures for studies using some or all subjects with identified psychological problems (49% for CMH versus 39% for CP).

We were somewhat surprised that in none of these fields was an explicit research hypothesis stated in a majority of the studies. The IOP studies appeared to do best in this regard, with 45% of its studies stating a hypothesis, versus 31% for CP studies, 36% for SW studies, and 22% for CMH studies.

Studies in all five fields were found to use a field study strategy about equally frequently and at least in a majority of the studies (61% for CP, 79% for CMH, 83% for SW, 54% for IOP, and 54% for OD). Field experiments appear to have been used more frequently in OD studies (41%) and CP studies (36%) than in SW studies (17%) or IOP studies (5%). The latter results may be partially a function of a strong interest in IOP in correlational designs assessing individual difference variables (as in studies dealing with personnel selection, test validation, and characteristics of managers and supervisors), whereas the OD investigations often attempt to evaluate the effectiveness of a new intervention strategy and CP investigations often study a new program or method of delivering services which require an experimental research strategy. In all five fields post-only designs predominated (66% for CP, 74% for CMH, 82% for SW, 88% for IOP, and 55% for OD). Community psychology studies used comparison or control groups about as often as CMH and SW studies (59%, 62%, and 52%, respectively), and much more often than OD studies (25%).

Community psychology, community mental health, social work, and organization development studies frequently employed self-report measures (89%, 55%, 78%, and 74%, respectively). Community psychology and CMH studies made more frequent use of direct observation of behavior (16% and 14%, respectively, versus 6% for SW). The CP, CMH, and SW studies made more frequent use of archival data sources than did OD studies (22%, 32%, 22%, and 5%, respectively).

Finally, parametric statistics were used most frequently in IOP studies (76%), followed by CP (74%), SW (66%), and CMH (52%) studies. Only SW studies employed nonparametric statistics in a majority (55%) of the studies. Univariate statistics were used more often in SW studies (93%) than CP (85%), IOP (72%), or CMH (56%) studies. The IOP studies most frequently used some form of multivariate statistic--24% versus 15% for CP studies and 11% each for CMH and SW studies.

What, then, can be concluded from these comparisons of community psychology studies with studies in the fields of community mental health, social work, industrial-organizational psychology, and organization development? First, taking the broad view, the CP studies do not appear to be unique in many ways from the other fields. Thus, for example, there appears to be a disproportionate representation of university-based authors in CP, SW, and IOP. Further, studies in at least four or more of these fields, including CP, tended to rely heavily on post-only designs, self-report measures, and univariate, parametric statistical tests as research and analysis strategies. One might take comfort in CP's relative equality on these dimensions, or one might fault all the fields for not being more rigorous in their designs.

On the other hand, CP research can be viewed as being perhaps overinvolved in the use of subjects with psychological problems. Also, by making comparison to at least one other of the fields presented here, one could say that CP research could improve on such other factors as stating explicit hypotheses and using multivariate statistics. Finally, CP studies appear to be doing relatively well compared to the other fields in the frequency of use of field experiments and use of direct observation of behavior. Our overall assessment is that in terms of the research parameters across the five fields, CP is doing a comparable job but requires much room for improvement if it is to become an exemplary discipline for applied behavioral research.

SECTION VI: CONCLUSIONS

We set out to chart the content and state of the art of community psychology research with no clear expectation of what lay ahead. We were aware of numerous definitions which outlined desirable missions of the field or catalogued a variety of topics representing the domains of interest, but we had no idea how or whether the diversity of ideas we encountered could be integrated into a coherent body of scientific endeavor. And, indeed, we found that community psychology researchers had traversed a wide terrain and established a loosely federated and varied discipline. We were pleased to find many kinds of diversity in the research literature as a whole: participation by university and nonuniversity researchers; substantial representation among the subjects of studies by females as well as males, children, and persons without identified psychological problems; and, despite a conspicuous commitment to studying various aspects of mental health delivery, investigations of a broad variety of topics.   The topic areas covered many aspects of individual functioning, social programs, educational concerns, and community activities. However, certain areas of investigation which had loomed large in the field's definitions were infrequently researched or totally neglected in the literature we reviewed. Among these were prevention, optimal environments, the psychological sense of community, and the role of social institutions in shaping behavior.

One way to capture the flavor of any new field is to examine the type of questions guiding the research. To do so, we classified the purpose served by each article and found most studies (55%) to be classifiable as policy analysis and policy research or program evaluation, while only 3% could be regarded as theory development (articulating a model or testing specific theoretical propositions). Community psychology research has not been directed toward theoretical issues in general; rather, it has developed largely in response to practical questions about the best kinds of programs and policies for a diversity of people in a variety of circumstances. A number of field definitions have stressed the important role of interventions and action research in guiding policies and programs and of the need for community psychology research to be responsive to the practical problems facing people in communities; we were pleased to find such an applied orientation reflected in the literature.

However, the underemphasis on theoretical research indicates this field is still at an early stage of development; conceptual base building is essential for the growth of a cumulative body of scientific knowledge. Indeed, we found community psychology research to be action oriented and diverse, a promising beginning, but somewhat unfocused in that few studies were related to conceptual frameworks or to one another. We suggest not necessarily that formal theory development be an important priority at this stage in integrating a field so heterogeneous and applied, but that concept- and model-building are urgently required before community psychology can develop coherent perspectives on the issues being addressed. Productive thinking and research in this area could probably best be served by the construction, elaboration, and programmatic testing of applied models under varying conditions. Research should also be designed with an emphasis on generalizing across persons, behaviors, times, and settings to encourage cumulative research and the development of conceptual models.

We examined the empirical studies with an eye to assessing how adequately the research strategies and methods used served the purposes of the field and dealt with the complexities of the subject matter. Field research dominated the literature; we found this naturalistic orientation entirely appropriate to the applied questions being addressed, and in line with previous exhortations to "move the research out of the laboratory."

However, the reported studies were less adept at dealing with the complexities involved in community psychology research. Conceptions of the field stress that it includes both individual- and systems-level processes as well as their interrelationships. Few studies measured variables at the level of social systems (group, organization, or community), and hardly any integrated a psychological and community perspective simultaneously (measuring variables at both levels and examining their interaction). The researcher in this field deals with a complex reality in studying persons and systems interacting in real life settings and is faced with the difficult task of modeling these complex processes operationally. We found a narrowness in the use of measurements, in terms of both the range of variables examined and the virtual absence of the use of different methods to measure specific variables. There is a clear need for community psychology researchers to devote more attention to the measures they employ, use measures that are diverse enough to model the complexities being studied, guard against method-induced bias in drawing conclusions by using a greater variety of data-gathering methods, and determine and document more fully the reliability and discriminating power of their measuring devices. That there was evidence of concern with measurement and research methodology is indicated by the fact that 12% of the articles were designed to address such issues; nevertheless, many individual studies were deficient in both measurement and research design.

We were disappointed by several factors which reduced the statistical power of most research designs and lowered the confidence with which we could draw meaningful conclusions from them. Among these factors were unrepresentative sampling of subjects, small sample size, use of nonequivalent comparison groups or no comparison group at all, and designs involving a single occasion of measurement. Although cognizant of design difficulties in field research, we believe that until community psychologists channel their energies into creating more powerful research designs, the potential of the field will remain largely unfulfilled. Meaningful questions about complicated processes can only be addressed by research that can handle the level of complexity involved in terms of conceptual analysis, measurement, research design, and statistical procedures. Community psychology will progress rapidly once investigators are committed and trained to upgrade these aspects of their research.

In general we were encouraged by the diversity, applied orientation, and naturalistic approach reflected in community psychology research. However, the field suffers from inadequacies in the conception, design, and analysis of empirical studies. These, one hopes, can be rectified by further efforts to develop a cumulative body of knowledge, thorough training in research methodology for future community psychologists, and the adaptation and integration of relevant techniques from other areas. In this regard, fields such as operations research, decision theory, quantitative sociology, policy analysis, psychometrics, and mathematical psychology have much to offer. In the not-too-distant future we expect to see community psychology researchers employ such techniques as path analysis, structural equations, ridge regression, time-series analysis, Markov chain modeling, optimum-level and mix analysis, and a variety of new nonlinear and multivariate statistical techniques.

We feel uneasy about the lack of a community perspective in most of the research articles we examined. Rappaport (1977) noted the inherent difficulty in even bringing together the terms community—which suggests individuals related to each other through shared social behavior or individuals sharing a geographic locale—and psychology—which refers to the individual. Most studies certainly emphasized the viewpoint of the individual, as is evidenced by the nearly exclusive focus on the individual as the unit of analysis and the emphasis on measuring psychological variables, such as those dealing with personality, attitudes, or individual achievement. Far less clear is how the researchers conceptualized the community. For most of them, the term community appears to signify the locus of their research: namely, that their research was conducted outside of an academic setting (especially outside of a psychological laboratory) and it was conducted in a public setting or in a public-sponsored agency or

program (as opposed to a private or profit-making organization). Not much else in the way of a community perspective can be identified in their work. If the research locus
so delineated is the only prerequisite for psychological research to qualify for the label community, then there is
undoubtedly much research in many other recognized fields
(for example, developmental, applied social, clinical,
school, and industrial psychology) which should be grouped
under the community psychology banner.

Perhaps a better test of a community perspective is
that of the domain to which the implications of a study are
drawn. As noted earlier, most studies drew conclusions
for only a small segment of the community, usually a particular program or process, and in only 7% of the articles
was there a concerted attempt to relate findings to the
community as a whole. A healthy exercise for all researchers in the field might be to have them explain why their
research should be considered community psychology (versus
some other kind of research) and how their findings can be
interpreted from a community perspective. Such an exercise should be in order, for example, when a contributor
decides whether to submit an article to a community psychology, community mental health, clinical psychology, or
some other journal. Some community psychology journal
editors have encouraged this exercise, but stronger encouragement is needed in view of the prevalence of articles
which simply study individual functioning without considering relationships with the larger social context, or which
study single social programs without reference to other
sources of behavior variance.

Another of our concerns about the state of the art
of research in community psychology stems from the generalization problem. As we noted earlier, it is difficult to
generalize from any of the research findings established in
most individual studies. As most studies were independent
of one another in terms of topic, if not also method of investigation, there is not even the reassurance of similar
types of studies pointing toward the same general conclusions. We think there is and will continue to be little
impetus for researchers to begin to attack systematically
the problem of generalization, but we believe it represents
a fundamental obstacle to valid application of any research
findings in community psychology. Given the internal-
validity threats inherent in many studies, coupled with the
lack of evidence for generalization across time, places,

persons, or methods in nearly all of the studies, we must
conclude that there is little reason for clients to choose
services, for practitioners to plan programs, or for policymakers to allocate funds on the basis of knowledge based
on community psychology research.

One important strategy for promoting the generalization of community psychology research findings is to attempt to replicate findings. Cook and Campbell (1979)
note that one can attempt a simultaneous or consecutive
replication with virtually identical conditions in effect; or,
replications can be attempted by the same or independent
investigators. Also, a replication can be undertaken when
one or more of the important dimensions of a study have
varied from the original study. Thus, explicit recognition
might be taken of differences in subjects, situations, times,
organizations, or communities in an effort to achieve generalization across the different conditions. As a first step,
one might identify a limited set of dimensions which are
likely candidates for influencing the results of a study and
develop a series of replications around systematically varied parameters of these dimensions. Although there will
probably never be a set of uniform guidelines for selecting
which dimensions to study in such a procedure, in many
cases the potential universe of generalization can be delimited by practical considerations. Thus, if a well-
documented treatment program was shown to be successful in
ameliorating the problems of white teenage male clients,
service providers might want to see the results of a replic-
cation study based on clients who differ on ethnic status,
age, and gender.

The question of generalization across settings begs
another fundamental question confronting the field of community psychology (as well as other fields): How shall
settings be measured? Moos (1974) has described seven
distinct approaches to classifying settings, environments,
or situations, including taxonomies based on geographical
and meteorological variables; architectural and physical
design variables; organizational structure; personal characteristics of the inhabitants of a milieu; psychological
characteristics and organizational climate; and the behavior-
setting scheme of Roger Barker and his associates. However, none of these approaches has gained much general
acceptance or application in community psychology research
endeavors. Furthermore, it is open to question whether
any of these approaches provides a satisfactory basis for

describing such complex systems as a mental health center, self-help group, prevention program, crisis center, and so on. We were unable to apply Moos's sevenfold classification in any meaningful or reliable way to published research studies in community psychology; neither were we able to come up with any usable system of our own for classifying settings.

And what of the course of future research in community psychology? If the grand definitions and aspirations of community psychology are to be realized, we should witness the blossoming of many new topics in the field. Some logical areas into which the field may branch out include research on planned communities and residential environments; efforts to improve environmental quality and to increase energy conservation; alienation and its converse--a psychological sense of community; the classification and explication of human environments and behavior settings; community support systems as they are used by individuals to offset stress and illness and to optimize functioning; the role of experiences in one life domain, such as work, in influencing experiences in another domain, such as the family or community participation; and, similarly, the maintenance of behavior change from one setting to another.

On the other hand, there is at present a large, if not critical, mass of research devoted to mental health concerns. If there is a cumulative body of knowledge in the field which develops over time, it is equally logical to expect to see the field continue to concentrate on matters pertaining to mental health delivery systems and what is recognized by others (for example, Bloom, 1977) as community mental health. We might witness a vast amount of research which will be characterized by an increasing differentiation and expansion of topics dealing with therapy, diagnosis, intervention, and consultation.

We also anticipate more specified purposes to be served by the next generation of community psychology research. There will undoubtedly be more refined model testing in every arena as we formulate more complex models of individual behavior and more elaborate models of programs, organizations, delivery systems, and so on. There should also be a growing concern for linking research to action. This concern may take many forms, such as using a decision-theoretic framework to specify costs and alternative policies (see, for example, Nagel & Neef, 1979) or studying processes by which validated research findings can be translated into social programs and diffused into society at large.

We predict that community psychology researchers will become more and more involved in program planning, development, and implementation. Indeed, such involvement may be necessary if their research is to be externally valid and have any utility outside an academic context. This approach is perhaps best illustrated at present in the experimental social innovation model advanced by Fairweather (1967, 1972, 1977), described in Chapter 4 of this volume.

As the field of community psychology becomes more involved in the overlapping spheres of social systems and individual behaviors, it will require more and more sophisticated, generalizable, and timely research for feedback and guidance. Then, too, the pursuit of ways to enhance the quality of life for persons and communities will undoubtedly require imaginative new methods of designing studies and measuring effects. The danger is that the research base of community psychology will not keep pace with the field's growing involvement in an increasingly complex world. We hope that future analyses of research in community psychology will show that it is meeting these challenges.

NOTES

Requests for reprints and other information concerning this study should be directed to John W. Lounsbury, Department of Psychology, University of Tennessee, Knoxville, TN 37916.

1. It is interesting to note that both our initial analysis and that of Novaco and Monahan were carried out independently and at about the same time.

2. Thus, for example, Analyst One was responsible for coding the following issues of the JCP: 1973--#1, 1974--#2, 1975--#3, 1976--#4, 1977--#1, 1978--#2; and similarly, for the AJCP to 1973--#4, 1974--#3, 1975--#2, 1976--#1, 1977--#4, and 1978--#3 and one-half of the issue of #6 (because for the first time in 1978 the AJCP began publishing six issues per year instead of the previous four per year.

3. Some of the predominant university affiliations were a psychology department (32% of all cases); a medical school or department of psychiatry (13%); a university-based research institute (2%); and a department of education (1%). The most frequent nonuniversity affiliations were a mental health center or clinic (11%); a mental or psychiatric hospital (4%); some type of special purpose institute (4%); a correctional or criminal justice agency (3%); a state, county, or city mental health division or department (2%); and the U.S. Navy (2%).

4. Some of these reasons are that researchers operating in an applied setting are often in a much better position than their university counterparts to test conceptual models in the crucible of practice; draw out more fine-grained distinctions and implications concerning policies, procedures, and programs; and be able to act in and to implement changes in practice suggested by research results. Moreover, they may pose different questions, look at different topics, study different subjects, and use different measures in ways that can only enhance the vigor of the field.

5. Although the conference title employed the term community mental health, conference participants chose to embrace instead the term community psychology. The Boston conference is regarded as a seminal contributor to the evolution of community psychology (Iscoe & Spielberger, 1977).

6. Of course one would expect such articles to be few in number in this analysis of the 478 research articles in the two journals. Most of the 137 nonresearch articles would be checked once for the purpose of general conceptualization.

7. We do recognize that multiple-regression techniques can be used to analyze the effects of independent variables or factors in what we have termed here experimental designs (for example, through contrast coding or effects coding). (For further elaboration of such approaches, see Cohen, 1968; Cohen & Cohen, 1975.) However, in nearly all of the present cases, multiple regression analysis was used to analyze variables in a nonexperimental, correlational framework.

8. We investigated differences in all the variables listed in this section by means of chi-square analyses. Although we used a criterion of $p < .05$ to indicate significant differences on a single variable, the true p value for

these comparisons cannot be determined, since so many runs were made and we did not select variables for comparison a priori. Our aim was exploratory, and our interest, therefore, was to pinpoint variables that showed differences and try to make sense of the patterns found. The results of our tests should be regarded as hypotheses generated by the data.

9. Our readings of the literature on applied psychological research suggest that one frequently mentioned minimum value for power is .80. However, some authors (for example, Schmidt, Hunter, & Urry, 1976) consider .90 to be a reasonable minimum statistical power value which a researcher should be assured of before carrying out his or her study.

10. The reader should also note that the different statistical tests in these examples ask different questions and that it would be inappropriate to use these estimates to compare the relative efficiency of the different statistics. Thus, for example, at power equal to .80 (and alpha equal to .05) only approximately 84 subjects would be required to detect a "medium" effect using the Pearson r as the statistical test for a significant relationship between two variables. On the other hand, at the same power level, 252 subjects would be needed for the F test to detect a significant "medium" effect difference among the mean values of a dependent variable among the four comparison groups.

11. Our rationale for this arbitrary cutoff was that a loss of 10% or more of the subjects would cast doubt on the representativeness of the remaining sample, unless the author is provided specific evidence that the attrition was not systematic and did not affect the representativeness of the remaining sample.

12. Moreover, we did not find a single study which reported the reliability of measurement in the context of more than one facet of a measuring operation (as in unreliability owing to both the lack of agreement between raters and between occasions of rating). In this regard, the powerful technique of generalizability analysis formulated by Cronbach, Gleser, Nanda, and Rajaratnam (1972) should be noted, wherein facets of a measuring operation are explicitly considered for their unique and interactive contribution to the overall dependability of a measured variable.

REFERENCES

Bennett, C. C., Anderson, L. S., Cooper, S., Hassol, L.,
    Klein, D. C., & Rosenblum, G. Community psychology:
    A report of the Boston conference on the education of
    psychologists for community mental health. Boston:
    Boston University Press, 1966.
Bloom, B. L. Community mental health (A general intro-
    duction). Monterey, Calif.: Brooks/Cole, 1977.
Campbell, D. T., & Fiske, D. W. Convergent and dis-
    criminant validation by the multitrait–multimethod
    matrix. Psychological Bulletin, 1959, 56, 81–105.
Campbell, D. T., & Stanley, J. C. Experimental and quasi-
    experimental designs for research. Chicago: Rand
    McNally, 1966.
Cohen, J. Multiple regression as a general data-analytic
    system. Psychological Bulletin, 1968, 70, 426–443.
Cohen, J. Statistical power analysis for the behavioral
    sciences. New York: Academic Press, 1977.
Cohen, J., & Cohen, P. Applied multiple regression/
    correlation analysis for the behavioral sciences.
    Hillsdale, N.J.: Erlbaum, 1975.
Coleman, J. S. Policy research in the social sciences.
    Morristown, N.J.: General Learning Press, 1972.
Cook, T. D., & Campbell, D. T. Quasi-experimentation
    design and analysis issues for field settings. New
    York: Rand McNally, 1979.
Cronbach, L. J. The two disciplines of scientific psychol-
    ogy. American Psychologist, 1957, 12, 671–684.
Cronbach, L. J., Gleser, G. C., Nanda, H., & Rajaratnam, N.
    The dependability of behavioral measurements: Theory
    of generalizability for scores and profiles. New York:
    John Wiley, 1972.
Dipboye, R. L., & Flanagan, M. F. Research settings in
    industrial and organizational psychology: II. Are
    findings in the field more generalizable than in the
    laboratory? West Lafayette, Ind.: Purdue University,
    Krannert Graduate School of Management, Paper No. 646,
    December 1977.
Dipboye, R. L., & Flanagan, M. F. Research settings in
    industrial and organizational psychology. American
    Psychologist, 1979, 34, 141–150.
Dorr, D. Intervention and prevention: I. Preventive
    intervention. In I. Iscoe, B. L. Cloom, & C. D.
    Spielberger (Eds.), Community psychology in transition.
    New York: Hemisphere Press, 1977.

Ehrenberg, M. An empirical analysis of the boundaries between community psychology and community mental health. Doctoral dissertation in progress, University of Tennessee, 1983.

Fairweather, G. W. Methods for experimental social innovation. New York: John Wiley, 1967.

Fairweather, G. W. Social change: The challenge to survival. Morristown, N.J.: General Learning Press, 1972.

Fairweather, G. W. A process of innovation and dissemination experimentation. In L. Rutman (Ed.), Evaluation research methods: A basic guide. Beverly Hills, Calif.: Sage, 1977.

Fairweather, G. W. (Ed.) Social psychology in treating mental illness: An experimental approach. New York: John Wiley, 1964.

Fairweather, G. W., Sanders, D. H., Cressler, D. L., & Maynard, H. Community life for the mentally ill. Chicago: Aldine, 1969.

Fairweather, G. W., Sanders, D. H., & Tornatzky, L. G. Creating change in mental health organizations. New York: Pergamon Press, 1974.

Fairweather, G. W., & Tornatzky, L. G. Experimental methods for social policy research. Oxford: Pergamon Press, 1977.

Flanagan, M. F., & Dipboye, R. L. Research settings in industrial and organizational psychology: I. Characteristics of research in laboratory and field settings. West Lafayette, Ind.: Purdue University, Krannert Graduate School of Management, Paper No. 645, December 1977.

Goodstein, L. D., & Sandler, I. Using psychology to promote human welfare: A conceptual analysis of the role of community psychology. American Psychologist, 1978, 33, 882–892.

Haney, L., Banks, L., & Zimbardo, P. Interpersonal dynamics in a simulated prison. International Journal of Criminology and Penology, 1973, 1, 69–97.

Hodges, W. F. Intervention and prevention: III. The enhancement of competency. In I. Iscoe, B. L. Bloom, & C. D. Spielberger (Eds.), Community psychology in transition. New York: Hemisphere Press, 1977.

Iscoe, I., Bloom, B. L., & Spielberger, C. D. Community psychology in transition. New York: John Wiley, 1977.

Iscoe, I., & Spielberger, C. D. Community psychology: The historical context. In I. Iscoe, B. L. Bloom, & C. D. Spielberger (Eds.), Community psychology in transition. New York: Hemisphere Press, 1977.

Jones, T. W. A conceptual and empirical comparison of the fields of community psychology and social work. Unpublished doctoral dissertation, University of Tennessee, June 1981.

Lindsey, D. The scientific publication system in social science. San Francisco: Jossey-Bass, 1978.

Lounsbury, J. W., Cook, M. P., Leader, D. S., Rubeiz, G., & Mears, E. P. Community psychology: Boundary problems, psychological perspectives, and an empirical overview of the field. American Psychologist, 1978, 34, 554-557.

Lounsbury, J. W., Leader, D. S., Meares, E. P., & Cook, M. P. An analytic review of research in community psychology. American Journal of Community Psychology, 1980, 8, 415-441.

Moos, R. H. Systems for the assessment and classification of human environments: An overview. In R. H. Moos & P. M. Insel (Eds.), Issues in social ecology. Palo Alto, Calif.: National Press, 1974.

Murrell, S. A. Community psychology and social systems. New York: Behavioral Publications, 1973.

Nagel, S. S., & Neef, M. Policy analysis in social science research. Beverly Hills, Calif.: Sage Library of Social Research, Volume 72, 1979.

Rappaport, J. C. Community psychology (Values, research and action). New York: Holt, Rinehart & Winston, 1977.

Reiff, R. Social intervention and the problem of psychological analysis. American Psychologist, 1968, 23, 524-531.

Reiff, R. Ya gotta believe. In I. Iscoe, B. L. Bloom, & C. D. Spielberger (Eds.), Community psychology in transition. New York: John Wiley, 1977.

Renner, K. E. Some issues surrounding the academic sheltering of community psychology. American Journal of Community Psychology, 1974, 2, 95-105.

Richards, J. M., Jr., & Gottfreedson, G. D. Geographic distribution of U.S. psychologists (A human ecological analysis). American Psychologist, 1978, 33, 1-9.

Runkel, P. J., & McGrath, J. E. Research on human behavior: A systematic guide to method. New York: Holt, Rinehart & Winston, 1972.

Schmidt, F. L., Hunter, J. E., & Urry, V. W. Statistical power in criterion-related validation studies. Journal of Applied Psychology, 1976, 64, 473–485.

Skinner, B. F. The behavior of organisms: An experimental analysis. New York: Appleton-Century-Crofts, 1938.

Spielberger, C. D., & Iscoe, I. The current status of training in community psychology. In I. Iscoe & C. D. Spielberger (Eds.), Community psychology: Perspectives in training and research. New York: Appleton-Century-Crofts, 1970.

Tornatzky, L. G., Fergus, E. O., Avellar, J. W., & Fairweather, G. W. Innovation and social process. New York: Pergamon Press, 1980.

Trickett, E. J., & Lustman, N. M. Research, knowledge, and professional growth. In I. Iscoe, B. L. Bloom, & C. D. Spielberger (Eds.), Community psychology in transition. New York: Hemisphere Press, 1977.

Verplanck, W. S. Further overstatements of a phenomenological behaviorist. The Psychological Record, 1971, 21, 481–486.

Webb, E. J., Campbell, D. T., Schwartz, R. D., & Sechrest, L. Unobtrusive measures: Nonreactive research in the social sciences. Chicago: Rand McNally, 1966.

White, S. E., & Mitchell, T. R. Organization development: A review of research content and research design. Academy of Management Review, 1976, 1, 57–73.

World Almanac & Book of Facts 1978. New York: Newspaper Enterprise Association, 1977.

Zax, M., & Specter, G. An introduction to community psychology. New York: John Wiley, 1974.

3 Studying the Emerging Community of Community Psychology

James H. Dalton, Maurice J. Elias,
and George W. Howe

As community psychology nears the end of its second decade, the nature of its research and scholarly activity comes under increasing scrutiny. Most analyses have concentrated on the <u>content</u> of research--its concepts, methods, and underlying values and assumptions, or its findings (Heller & Monahan, 1977; Lounsbury et al., 1980; McClure et al., 1980; Rappaport, 1977; see also Chapter 2 of this volume). The alternative perspective which we will use in

The authors would like to gratefully acknowledge the assistance of Carolyn Dalton, Ellen Elias, Robert Franco, Ann Bonnano, Elizabeth Colapietro, and Sharon Riebe with data collection and preparation. Candy Won of the American Psychological Association graciously provided us with convention programs. We thank Reuben Baron of the University of Connecticut for suggesting that we read Thomas Kuhn's work and for nurturing our interests during the early stages of our work. Irving Kirsch also provided us with resources to begin our work. Emory Cowen provided pithy comments and insightful suggestions about aspects of study three and suggested the term <u>imprinting</u> for graduate school experiences. Ed Susskind and Don Klein, our editors, provided thorough and helpful suggestions which enabled us to articulate our findings and concepts more clearly. Manuscript preparation was carefully performed by Libby Brusca and Harriet Cohen of Rutgers University, Sandra Long and Susan Petty of Bloomsburg University, and Hazel Donnell of Peabody College.

this chapter is concerned with the social structure of community psychology as an emerging discipline. Our units
of analysis are the clusters or networks of scientist-
professionals who communicate and collaborate intensively
in the production of knowledge in community psychology.
A discipline cannot develop sets of methods, values, and
findings without these clusters. In this chapter, we present several empirical methods for identifying and describing such clusters. In addition, we will propose a developmental model which depicts how clusters grow through time
and the role they play in the emergence of an applied
discipline. By fitting our empirical findings into this developmental framework, we will generate a heuristic portrayal of the present status of community psychology as an
emerging discipline as well as of some challenges it faces
in the immediate future. We caution the reader that our
primary purpose is to propose an alternative perspective
for assessing community psychology and explore briefly
its methodology and implications. We intend our methods
and findings as heuristic and suggestive, not definitive--
we seek to illustrate rather than evaluate.

To accomplish these goals, this chapter is divided
into five sections. In the first, we define the concept of
a cluster of a discipline's members and outline the basis
of this concept in Thomas Kuhn's concepts of paradigm and
disciplinary matrix (Kuhn, 1970). The first section also
includes our Kuhnian-based developmental model delineating
how clusters of scientist-professionals coalesce and grow in
an applied discipline such as community psychology.

We devote the second section to identifying methods
for the measurement of clusters. The cluster of individuals
is considered as a hypothetical construct, analogous to the
hypothetical personality constructs defined by Cronbach and
Meehl (1955). In the manner suggested by Cronbach and
Meehl, we propose methods for building a nomological "net"
of empirical indicators of the cluster construct.

In the third section, we present three exploratory
empirical studies of clusters among scholars in community
psychology. These studies illustrate alternative methods
for identifying and describing such clusters, based on
archival data sources. The findings of these studies are
summarized in the following section. In the last section,
we discuss the heuristic implications of the findings
from these studies by fitting them into the developmental
framework proposed earlier in the chapter. We also identify

four metaphors for community psychology and outline how they are related to our findings and to the future of the discipline.

CLUSTERS OF SCHOLARS AND THE GROWTH OF AN APPLIED DISCIPLINE: AN OVERVIEW

The analysis of science provided in Thomas Kuhn's The Structure of Scientific Revolutions (1970) provides a rich heuristic for understanding the development of scientific disciplines. This treatise has popularized a view of science as a distinctively human, dynamic enterprise, rather than the rational, linear accretion of irrefutable facts and theories. Perhaps Kuhn's major contribution is the concept of paradigm, which includes three major components: (1) a body of beliefs and assumptions concerning appropriate problems and theories for investigation; (2) a cohesive group of practitioners--the "disciplinary matrix"-- who perform research, communicate with each other, and indoctrinate graduate students into the consensually validated set of beliefs and assumptions; and (3) a set of exemplary studies which contain the model problems and methods for research--the practical, tacit knowledge of the discipline.

Kuhn vividly describes the process of scientific revolution and change. An emerging discipline passes through three stages: preparadigmatic, transitional, and paradigmatic. While his description is compelling, the model must be supplemented in order to apply it to community psychology. Perhaps because his focus is on the relatively autonomous basic natural sciences, Kuhn does not devote much attention to sociopolitical forces outside the discipline. These forces certainly affect applied disciplines greatly, and their impact on community psychology is emphasized in almost any history of the field (compare Rappaport, 1977, or Bloom, 1975). In addition, Kuhn does not address the issue of interdisciplinary collaboration as a source of novel concepts and enrichment of scientific work. Community psychology has emphasized such interdisciplinary ties (Chinsky, 1977); a model of the discipline's development must address the issue. Finally, we found useful and relevant the scientific literatures on group formation and cohesiveness (for example, Hollander, 1971; Myers & Lamb, 1976), social networks (for example,

Mitchell, 1969; Tichy, Tushman, & Fombrun, 1980; Wellman, 1981), and the sociology of science (Price & Beaver, 1966; Gieryn, 1978). With these concerns in mind, we extended Kuhn's concept of disciplinary matrix to construct a heuristic, global model of the development of an applied discipline such as community psychology. This model focuses on stages in the growth and functioning of clusters or networks of scientific practitioners. This model has proven useful in performing several empirical studies of community psychology (Elias, Dalton, & Howe, 1981; Elias, Dalton, Franco, & Howe, in press). In what follows, we present our most elaborate and specific statement of this model to date. This furnishes the background for the remainder of the chapter and also provides a heuristic basis for further research.

A Developmental Model of Applied Disciplines

Stage One: Reactive

Ullman (1969) has noted that the primary impetus for a discipline's development usually comes as a reaction to an established discipline. The reactors generally serve as a shadow cabinet, an opposition party that is quicker to criticize than to provide constructive alternatives. They share a sense of solidarity in that there is a common "foe"; differences can be put aside or ignored as long as there is a focus on the opposition (Myers & Lamb, 1976). In a very real sense, members of the new approach need the presence of the "old guard" to give them a focus for their efforts.

Stage Two: Transition

In stage two, the opposition party begins to articulate a position of its own. Through theoretical refinements and/or empirical evidence, these scholars begin to develop a coherent viewpoint at a global level, although this does not yet lead to conceptual or methodological consensus. As this process occurs, clusters of scientists may form. These are the "building blocks" of a new discipline, the "invisible colleges" studied by Price and Beaver (1966). They are composed of scholars who communicate models, methods, and findings; exchange ideas and resources (including apprentices); and may eventually undertake collaborative work. These clusters may begin in a single setting, but eventually they must expand their communication and exchange to other settings if they are to have an impact on disciplinary development. A cluster develops a content focus, that is, a set of concepts and phenomena studied with a consensually preferred set of methods. These are often represented in exemplary studies. The cluster may be based originally on geographic proximity of researchers with similar interests or on an intellectual "lineage" of mentors and students who begin collaboration during the graduate students' training years. The socialization of the budding scholar in the mentoring relationship is strong; students' basic assumptions and methods are often conditioned by their initial experiences in research and practice. It is important to note that in an applied discipline, clusters perform other functions in addition to research, for example, professional service delivery, training of students or interns, or administration. Their intercommunication does not concern solely research topics.

Clusters may compete with each other for intellectual or ideological hegemony as well as control of resources, for example, faculty or professional positions, grant money, students, and "freshly minted" graduates. At the same time, they are almost certainly competing for those resources with the established discipline against which they rebelled in stage one. During the transition phase, however, the spirit becomes that of "building our own community." If clusters do not emerge, the stage one reaction begins to dissipate. Researchers begin to merge with other groups or function as "mavericks" outside any established network or discipline. Further disciplinary development is stymied. A discipline cannot develop its own structure and viewpoint unless communication and collaboration among its members reach some critical level of interrelationship.

Stage Three: Convergence

If networks form in the transition phase, and if these networks provide durable, productive working relationships among researchers, then movement occurs into a convergence phase. Intercommunication increases as collaboration within clusters expands to include multiple settings. Contact between clusters increases in frequency. A key role in this process is played by individuals who "bridge" separate networks and by "liaisons" between scholars in differing clusters (Sarason & Lorentz, 1979;

Tichy, Tushman, & Fombrun, 1980). Single-setting clusters and individual "maverick" researchers become less common and less influential. In an applied discipline, a key step in the cluster-building of the convergence phase is the forging of durable linkages with applied practitioners in nonacademic settings. This is related to the ongoing process of adaptation (see stage five). As cluster connections grow, so does consensus among researchers on preferred concepts, methods, and findings. The content focus of the discipline becomes clearer, although it is more general than the content focus of specific clusters.

Stage Four: Identity

When a discipline establishes an identity, it has a relatively clear set of concepts and methods, a defined body of knowledge, a coherent set of procedures with which to train future members of the discipline, and a set of defined roles that members of the discipline can fill once they have completed training. The training element provides the potential for the ongoing maintenance of the discipline and for the continuation of its particular paradigm.

Stage Five: Adaptation

The long-term prospects for a profession depend on the extent to which it has a niche within a given ecological context. For individuals in the discipline, this niche provides a basis of shared expectations and a variety of interpersonal incentives to diligent work (such as access to valued social roles or material rewards). The niche generally establishes one's occupational role as important in the ecosystem (Glidewell, 1972). For instance, it is the basis of one's professional identity among local colleagues. For a discipline, it provides guidelines for boundary relationships with other academic disciplines, with nonacademic practitioners of the disciplines, and with economic, political, and consumer forces influencing the discipline.

Boundary relationships of a mature discipline with other disciplines vary along a continuum. At one pole a discipline can rigidify by increasing intracommunication and resisting alternative viewpoints, seeing these as threats rather than resources. At the opposite pole is a discipline that actively seeks to build relationships with its own practitioners as well as other disciplines. Such a discipline is open to alternative theories and methods, and likely to be more adaptive. The relationhip between discipline and environment is a dialectical process of adaptation, analogous to that used by Piaget to explain the operation of cognitive structures (Flavell, 1963) or by Mills and Kelly (1972) to describe the evolution of communities.

A key factor in the passage of a discipline through these stages is the development of clusters among members of the new discipline. These networks form the "critical mass" necessary for forming a new discipline, and they are the most basic social unit for the development of scientific knowledge. They provide avenues of mutual influence, ultimately fostering the development of consensus and sense of identity described in stages four and five. Clusters can be understood as a set of communication linkages, or relationships, among individual scholars. These linkages can be conduits for the exchange of social support (Gottlieb, 1981), information and technical assistance (Sarason & Lorentz, 1979), and intellectual or ideological influence (Mitchell, 1969). By focusing on the development of these clusters and their role in the growth of an applied discipline, we do not assert that clusters "cause" the other phenomena of a scientific discipline, or that these social groupings are merely effects of other forces. Rather, the interpersonal dynamics we describe here form social structures in transaction with intellectual and sociopolitical trends; a scientific discipline is the result.

METHODS FOR IDENTIFYING AND
MEASURING CLUSTERS

Clusters of scholars can be considered a hypothetical construct, analogous to the hypothetical personality constructs described by Cronbach and Meehl (1955). To use the cluster construct in research examining the growth of community psychology, we must specify observable means of measuring clusters. The cluster construct is useful if empirical studies using alternative operational definitions of clusters can best be integrated using the cluster construct. To do so, studies should identify groupings of members of a discipline which exhibit the characteristics of ongoing communication and collaboration and identify key clusters of community psychologists who appear together across studies using different measurement methods.

If clusters form a useful explanatory construct for these empirical findings, then they can be used within the developmental model proposed earlier to portray in a global way the level of development of community psychology as an applied discipline. In this section, we discuss methods for operationalizing the cluster concept and empirically identifying clusters of scholars in an applied discipline. This discussion forms the background for description of our research in the next section. It also provides a heuristic guide for further research.

Our use of the concept of a cluster is based on several assumptions, which are summarized in Table 3.1. These assumptions are of three types: (1) criteria for identifying networks, (2) hypotheses regarding the characteristics of networks, and (3) hypotheses regarding the relationship between networks and our model of disciplinary development. Let us discuss these assumptions in turn.

Criteria for Identifying Clusters

Clusters are identified on the basis of relationships or linkages among individuals (see Criterion 1 in Table 3.1). A cluster can be "mapped" by identifying instances of intercommunication among individuals, for instance, coauthorship of papers or citation of another's work. Thus, a cluster can be empirically identified as a set of researchers with observable communication linkages between them.

Communication can occur through formal channels, such as published papers, or through informal contact. In addition, linkages between two or more researchers may be direct or indirect. Indirect linkages occur where researchers communicate and influence each other only through mediating members of a network; direct linkages involve straightforward communication (written or oral) without such mediation. Support, information, and influence pass readily through both types of linkages (Mitchell, 1969; Sarason & Lorentz, 1979; Tichy, Tushman, & Fombrun, 1980).

In our studies, we have operationally defined these linkages among researchers in terms of four types of communication through which influence can occur:

1. Close cooperation in research, resulting in coauthorship of a paper.

TABLE 3.1
Summary of Assumptions Regarding Networks

Criteria for Identifying Networks

1. Communication. Research in a scientific discipline is
   produced by researchers embedded in a cluster or network
   of individuals who communicate with each other regarding
   their work. This communication occurs in formal channels
   (that is, coauthorship or citation of published papers) or
   informal contacts, and it may be direct (between two individuals) or indirect (through separate communications with
   mediating researchers).

   A scholar within a given cluster will communicate more
   often with members of that network than with members of
   other networks.

2. Durability. Continued communication over time among members of a cluster is an indicator of the sustained utility
   of the cluster to its members.

3. Productivity. The production of research reports or
   scholarly papers by members of a cluster is a necessary,
   but not sufficient, activity in order for that cluster to
   influence the development of their discipline.

4. Impact. The works of cluster members must have observable
   impact on members of the discipline outside the cluster in
   order to influence the development of the discipline. This
   can be measured, for instance, by the citation by scholars
   outside the cluster of work reported by cluster members.

Hypotheses Regarding Clusters

5. Content focus. As communication and mutual influence
   occur within a cluster, a stable, relatively narrow content or topical focus will emerge. This focus can be
   observed in the content of articles, abstracts, or titles
   of published work.

6. Proximity. Geographic proximity facilitates collaboration.
   Most clusters will have a focal group of members in one or
   two settings or geographic areas.

114

7. Imprinting. The educational experiences of scholars, particularly graduate school relationships, strongly affect the development of clusters. Members of a discipline tend to continue work within the frameworks they have learned. Therefore, we can expect collaborative "lineages" within clusters, based on mentor-student or colleague relationships which originated in shared educational experiences.

Clusters as Indicators of Disciplinary Development

8. Critical mass. Clusters are the primary social unit within which knowledge and research develop. Their appearance is necessary for disciplinary development and first occurs in the transition phase of our model.

9. Communication between settings. In order to build greater communication and influence, clusters must move beyond the constraints of geography and build ties between settings. This process occurs during the transition phase.

10. Exhaustiveness. As a discipline develops, more of its members will generate or join clusters. Thus, the clusters will become more exhaustive, accounting for more of the discipline's membership and a larger proportion of its research. This process becomes important later in the transition phase.

11. Cluster interrelationships. Developing interrelationships of communication (including citation) between clusters is an indicator of progress toward and into the convergence phase.

12. External communication. Adaptation by the discipline to changes in sociopolitical forces is enhanced by communicative and collaborative ties with other disciplines and with nonacademic institutions or groups. This assumption is associated with all states of our model.

Source: Compiled by the authors.

115

2. Exchange and <u>critique</u> of <u>unpublished manuscripts</u>, indicated by acknowledgment of this contribution in a published paper.
3. <u>Coparticipation</u> in convention symposia.
4. Reading and <u>citation</u> of published work.

These linkages are indicators of a variety of events in the production and dissemination of research. When community psychologists collaborate in performing a research study or writing a theoretical paper, they must come to an agreement on such issues as general topic area, appropriate methods and units of analysis, and the meaning and generality of their findings or theories. Coauthorship of a paper is a direct indication that such collaboration and mutual influence have occurred.

A less obvious form of communication takes place when investigators exchange unpublished papers and findings. Often this process occurs when a researcher sends a draft of an as-yet-unpublished paper to a colleague, whose critique is utilized in preparing a final draft. The critique can have a good deal of influence over the presentation of the research findings, as well as on the choice of problems and methods in the writer's future research. If the paper is eventually published, the involvement and influence of such colleagues are generally acknowledged in a footnote.

Community psychologists who participate together in a convention symposium may influence each other in a variety of ways. At the very least, hearing other researchers discuss their findings can serve as a means of influence. Symposium participants may also have influenced each other in more active ways, as seen in the subtle "networking" involved in the organization of topics and participants for symposia.

Finally, influence takes place when researchers read the work of other investigators and then build their future work on this background. Acknowledgment of such influence, in the form of notes or bibliographic citations, is one indicator of this process.

Using these operational definitions, we can map clusters of members of a discipline. Identifying these clusters is analogous to defining a personality construct from divergent observable measures. We look for <u>conver-gence</u>--the presence of observable linkages between researchers. This is analogous to the convergent validity of a construct (Campbell & Fiske, 1959). At the same time, we assess the independence of a cluster from other clusters. This is analogous to the assessment of discriminant forms of validity of personality constructs (Campbell & Fiske, 1959). Some linkage between clusters is expected and, indeed, is a major element in the progression to the convergence and identity phases of our developmental model. However, to be the basic unit of analysis for quantitative study, a cluster must be a relatively independent, identifiable structure.

Our conception of clusters is somewhat similar to the concept of a social network (Wellman, 1981). Both constructs are inferred from evidence of communication linkages among individuals. However, there are two differences between the ways in which we use the cluster construct and the uses of the social network construct as it is commonly used in community psychology. First, we are concerned with not only social support (for example, Leavy, 1983) but the entire range of communication exchanged between members of a cluster. Second, most studies of social support networks cited in Leavy's 1983 review and in the Gottlieb (1981) volume analyze networks with an individual person as the focal point of support received. In the studies reported in this chapter, we use archival data to construct clusters which do not necessarily have a focal person but do have a set of identifiable linkages. Third, the exploratory findings we report in this chapter do not include the more advanced techniques of network analysis, such as a reachability analysis (Tichy, Tushman, & Fombrun, 1980). Our use of density data in study two is the sole present step in that direction.

Three other criteria are important in describing clusters in terms of communication linkages; these are defined in Criteria 2, 3, and 4 in Table 3.1. Groupings which exchange ongoing communication and influence are likely to be more important in the developmental progress of a discipline. Consequently, in our studies we looked for evidence of durable communication and influence (Criterion 2). In addition, we have assumed that clusters which produce and disseminate a relatively large amount of research are more influential, and have more of an impact on the discipline, than those which produce less (Criterion 3). Finally, productivity alone does not create influence, and the impact of a cluster must be assessed more directly. Those with high impact on other researchers—

measured by citation of their work--are more likely to influence their discipline (Criterion 4). Using these criteria of durability, productivity, and impact to simplify the complexities of communication among researchers, we can identify ongoing networks of researchers which are likely to influence the course of the discipline's development.

Hypotheses Regarding Cluster Functioning

In Table 3.1, we also present three hypotheses about the characteristics of clusters. These hypotheses concern the formation of a content focus for the cluster and the influence of geographic proximity and of imprinting on cluster development. In our exploratory studies, we did not test these hypotheses in a rigorous, quantitative manner. However, we carefully examined the clusters which we identified for these characteristics.

A cluster is likely to develop a relatively specific focus, in terms of the phenomena studied, methods considered appropriate, and theoretical constructs used to explain the findings (Hypothesis 1 in Table 3.1). A developed cluster or network will be marked by a high degree of consensus on these issues, which can be assessed through content analysis of their published reports and often even through content analysis of report titles. We hypothesize a direct relationship (for example, correlation) here: durable, productive clusters, marked by frequent intercommunication, will have a consistent content focus. We are not hypothesizing that either the formation of a group or the collective choice of a content focus "causes" the other.

Our two other hypotheses concern antecedents of network formation. These can be understood as enabling conditions rather than as precipitating factors for the establishment of linkages of communication and influence. Geographic proximity (Hypothesis 2) enables influence and collaboration in research work, and it can easily be assessed by recording institutional affiliation. Beyond such physical propinquity, the influence of educational (especially graduate school) experiences is so strong that we chose to call it imprinting (Hypothesis 3). Within mentor, student, and colleague relationships, views and assumptions are exchanged which have influence well beyond the educational years. We operationalized this in our studies by tracing "lineages" of graduate or post graduate mentor-student and

student-colleague relationships in the networks we had
identified. Thus, we hypothesize that clusters will be
more likely to contain researchers in geographically proximal settings than in settings widely distant from each
other, at least in the early stages of disciplinary growth.
In addition, clusters will include linkages which were initiated during the educational years of at least some of the
individual scholars linked by ongoing communication.

Hypotheses Regarding Clusters and
Disciplinary Development

Where do these clusters fit in our developmental
model? Several assumptions concerning this issue are
also summarized in Table 3.1. Clusters begin to appear
in stage two, especially in a few influential settings (Hypothesis 4). As communication, collaboration, and mutual
influence develop, multiple-setting clusters appear (Hypothesis 5). More individuals and settings are drawn into the
discipline's set of interrelationships. The clusters become
more exhaustive in the sense that their networks include
more of the researchers and settings involved in the discipline (Hypothesis 6). A small number of clusters may compete for hegemony as the discipline moves into stage three,
but the most important indicator of the convergence phase
is the growth of communication and interrelationships between clusters (Hypothesis 7). Finally, an applied discipline, in our view, can adapt more successfully within its
environment—at almost any developmental level—if it col-
laborates with other disciplines and with nonacademic community groups (Hypothesis 8).

If communication and collaboration do not develop,
however, clusters remain small and isolated, closely tied
to single settings and early patterns of imprinting. They
are not exhaustive; a number of mavericks work alone or
with members of groups outside the discipline. This interdisciplinary activity results not in an adaptive exchange
of views within the discipline but in the discipline's dissolution.

The developmental model and assumptions which we
have elaborated directly influenced the empirical work we
report here. In three studies utilizing independent data
sources and alternative methods, we identified clusters of
scholars in community psychology, using the observable

criteria defined in Criteria 1 through 4. We assessed these clusters informally for evidence of the relationships proposed in Hypotheses 1 through 3. Finally, we utilized Hypotheses 4 through 8 to assess these clusters for indicators of the developmental level of research in the discipline, within the Kuhnian framework we have proposed.

THREE EMPIRICAL STUDIES OF CLUSTERS IN COMMUNITY PSYCHOLOGY

The empirical studies which we report in this section utilize alternative operational definitions of the cluster concept. We want to emphasize that our purpose is to illustrate methods of identifying and describing clusters in community psychology, and (in the next section) to fit our findings regarding these clusters into a heuristic model of disciplinary development.

In Table 3.2, we summarize the methodological differences among our studies. Archival data sources were used for all three studies, but each utilized a different source which complemented the others. Study one focused on all articles published by community psychologists, study two on convention symposia, study three on a single influential journal. Time periods studied were varied, as were the specific observable definitions of communication used to define linkages. The criteria used to refine and simplify lists of clusters differ slightly among the studies, but all are based on the criteria presented in Table 3.1. Finally, studies one and two investigated clusters of individual scholars, while study three focused on linkages among settings rather than individuals.

STUDY ONE

In study one we identified clusters of scholars linked to each other by coauthorship. We focused on clusters productive over a three-year period. We also examined the impact of these networks on community psychology by investigating the extent to which researchers outside the cluster cited works produced within the cluster.

TABLE 3.2
Summary of Designs of the Three Studies

	Study One	Study Two	Study Three
Data base	Articles by Division 27 members catalogued in So- cial Sciences Citation Index	APA convention symposia, Divi- sion 27 primary sponsor	Articles in American Journal of Community Psychology
Time period surveyed	1976–78	1973–79	1975–79
Observable definition of communi- cation	Coauthorship of articles	Coparticipation in symposia	Coauthorship of articles; ac- knowledgment of prepublication critique of manu- script; change of affiliation
Other cri- teria used in identi- fying net- works	Durability, productivity	Durability	Productivity
Network components	Individuals	Individuals	Settings

Source: Compiled by the authors.

Method

Data Source

The original data base for study one was a list of 478 scientific articles, published in 1976, which had at least one author who was a member of American Psychologi- cal Association (APA) Division 27. Characteristics of these articles were reported in Elias, Dalton, and Howe (1981). These articles were written by 676 authors. The articles were identified by using a 1976 Division 27 membership list (students excluded) and the 1977 source index of the Social Sciences Citation Index (SSCI).

Procedure

A direct linkage between any two authors was recorded for any instance of coauthorship during 1976. After initial examination of the data, we applied two simplification criteria. First, to isolate clusters which were productive as a group, we eliminated all authors not involved in a network which published six or more reports during that year.[1] Second, we eliminated a small number of clusters in which the average number of authors per article was greater than three. These steps removed clusters which were large yet produced few papers and appeared to lack meaningful intercommunication. We thus identified 12 productive, cohesive clusters involving a total of 81 researchers, a group based almost exclusively in academia. Characteristics of these clusters were reported in Elias, Dalton, and Howe (1981). In order to study the durability of these clusters, we returned to the SSCI source index to record 1977-78 publications by all 81 authors, thus expanding our data base to a three-year period. As a measure of cluster impact, we also recorded the citations recorded in 1977-78 articles of 1976-77 articles coauthored by any of our 81 original individuals. The contents of the articles were judged from titles, and institutional affiliations of authors were identified from the Division 27 membership list.

Results

Two of the original 12 clusters demonstrated much greater productivity and impact than the others. These two clusters were the only ones to produce ten or more articles during the three-year period. On the average, they produced several times the number of articles written by other clusters and were cited much more often by authors outside their networks.

The focal setting for the first cluster was the University of Rochester. Emory Cowen and Ray Lorion were the focal individuals who continued collaborative work through the period surveyed; they were joined by Ellis Gesten in 1977-78. This cluster produced 28 articles during the period surveyed and cited previous cluster articles 12 times in 1977-78. The content focus of their work concerned preventive programs in school mental health. Research produced by this network was cited 12 times in two years in papers produced outside the cluster, usually in general reviews of research.

The second major cluster was centered at Pennsylvania State University. Its focal researchers were Anthony D'Augelli and Steven Danish. The cluster members produced 19 articles in 1976-78 and also cited their own previous work 12 times in 1977-78. Their content focus concerned development and evaluation of paraprofessional training programs. The 24 citations of this network's work by authors outside the cluster were contained more often in specific, empirical research reports rather than general reviews.

Both these clusters show evidence of communication and influence within themselves, indicated by the productive coauthorship and citation among the researchers within the network. They also demonstrate considerable impact on other scholars in terms of the citations of their work by individuals outside the cluster. However, these two clusters appear to have had little impact on each other—there were only two instances of cross-citation in the two-year period we studied. Each of these networks is centered almost exclusively in a single geographic setting. Both include mentor-student linkages (for example, Cowen with Lorion and Gesten) in which imprinting is likely to have occurred.

STUDY TWO

Study one was concerned with linkages reflected in the written work of scholars produced through a wide number of published outlets. Study two, by contrast, is focused on a relatively narrow outlet for research findings—the annual convention of the APA. In addition, it involved clusters which seem more flexible and reflect more immediately the focus and flavor of research. Our data base was convention symposia—which are arranged over less than a year's time and often report data which have not surfaced through journals' publication lag. Symposia are influenced by "networking" efforts and usually bring together individuals from different settings and research programs. Clusters based on symposium participation might be expected to be somewhat larger and more dispersed than those in study one, in terms of geography and content focus. We also expected convention participants to include more non-academic practitioners of community psychology.

Method

Data Source

Using convention program guides for the APA conventions from 1973 through 1979, we identified 145 symposia which were sponsored either solely or primarily by Division 27. Paper-and-poster sessions and invited addresses were excluded. In all, 855 individuals (including symposia chairs and discussants) gave 1,054 presentations in these symposia.

Procedure

Communication linkages were operationally defined in study two as "coparticipation" in symposia. Coparticipants were not necessarily coauthors of a paper, but they participated in the same symposium. We identified durable networks as consisting of linkages representing coparticipation recurring in at least two symposia during separate conventions in the seven-year period of the study. This procedure isolated clusters which were relatively stable over time. Only 55 researchers (6% of the sample) were involved in such networks. The contents of symposia involving these 55 researchers were judged from symposium titles. Setting affiliations were recorded from the convention guides.

Results

We identified 17 durable clusters. One of these was large and dispersed, the others smaller and denser with greater likelihood of direct links between members. The large network had 13 members in 12 settings and a density of .19 (this is the proportion of possible linkages among network members which was actually observed). No other cluster had more than six members, five settings, or a density of less than .40. Eight clusters were composed only of pairs of researchers; only four networks had four or more members.

The two largest clusters were connected by a single link but were different in size, density, and content focus. The individuals linking these two clusters were J. R. Newbrough and S. Murrell. The largest network, which we labeled the central cluster, had a core of five members who participated together in a series of two symposia regarding the Austin Conference (Iscoe, Bloom, & Speilberger, 1977) on Training in Community Psychology. Eight satellite members were linked to the core group but less often to each other. The central cluster continues to be a highly influential group--perhaps an elite--in community psychology today. Its members included the editors of the two major journals (J. Glidewell and J. Newbrough) as well as six past or recently elected presidents of Division 27 (I. Iscoe, J. Newbrough, J. Rappaport, D. Stenmark, J. Kelly, and E. Trickett). Ira Iscoe appears to be the primary organizer of this cluster. He chaired the two symposia on training which included the core group and several satellite members. In addition, he is included in a three-generation mentor-student linkage within this network, composed of Iscoe, Kelly, and Trickett. The network's 13 members represented 12 different settings for most of the seven-year period of the study. While the core-group symposia had a consistent content focus, links with satellites were based on symposia with a diversity of themes. Two other characteristics of this group are worth noting: all members were men and all were based in universities.

The remaining clusters were smaller, and more limited in terms of cross-setting collaboration and content focus. The second-largest network had six members, four of whom worked in a single city, Louisville. Five members of this network participated in a series of three symposia over a three-year period (1973-75). The content focus of this group was evaluation research in community mental health. It is also noteworthy because of the presence of both a sociologist--the only incidence of interdisciplinary linkage in this study--and the administrator of a community mental health center.

A third cluster was very similar to the Penn State network in study one. Its content focus was paraprofessional training. Three of its six members were based at Penn State, and all six were in university settings.

A fourth cluster of four members is remarkable because it was the only group consisting solely of practitioners outside academia. No other cluster had more than two applied practitioners. The content focus of this network was community treatment in mental health. Its members represented the Mendota Mental Health Institute (Wisconsin) and the Southwest Denver Community Mental Health Center.

STUDY THREE

In this study, we returned to investigation of published literature. Unlike study one, however, we concentrated on clusters of researchers publishing through a single journal—the American Journal of Community Psychology (AJCP).

Two methodological procedures are noteworthy. First, we operationally defined communication linkage in terms of not only coauthorship but also prepublication assistance or critique as acknowledged in article footnotes. Second, we identified clusters in terms of linkage among settings rather than individuals.

The latter distinction compels further discussion. This analysis is performed at a different conceptual level than analysis of networks among individuals. A setting is a physical location in which researchers are provided resources for their work. Defining clusters in terms of these settings highlights the influence of geographic proximity and the importance of cross-setting communication, as well as the necessity of material support from an institution beyond the social support of colleagues. In practice, it is often difficult at first to distinguish a setting from a focal individual or group, for instance, to distinguish the University of Rochester, a setting in community psychology research, from the person of Emory Cowen. However, scattered individuals without the sources of a few focal, influential settings will not develop a continuing research paradigm or a new discipline. Identifying these focal settings is just as important as identifying influential scholars.

In addition to defining these clusters based on linkages of coauthorship and prepublication assistance, we also assessed their impact as indicated by patterns of citation of published work.

Method

Data Source

The data base consisted of all AJCP articles from January 1975 through June 1979. During this four and one-half year period, 208 articles were produced in 160 settings by 436 authors.

Procedure

We recorded all communication linkages between settings; such a linkage consisted of two or more instances of
coauthorship or prepublication assistance between researchers in different settings. Settings were identified from published institutional affiliations of authors. If a researcher
changed settings during the period studied, we also counted
this as a linkage between the two settings. This created a
preliminary list of 17 settings involving 144 researchers.
We then removed the names of 102 researchers involved in
the production of less than two articles during the study
period. This removed cross-setting linkages involving four
settings, thus reducing to 13 the number of productive settings involved in multiple-setting networks. Contents of
articles produced in these settings were then judged from
the titles.[2]

To assess the impact of research supported by these
settings, we also recorded bibliographic citations in all
208 AJCP articles published during the study period. In
these articles we counted citations of the articles produced
in the 13 productive settings during the period studied.

Results

Three multiple-setting networks appeared. These
three clusters produced about one-fifth of the articles
printed in AJCP during the study period. Of the 13 settings involved in these networks, 12 were universities; the
other was affiliated with a university medical school.

Two of the multiple-setting clusters were similar to
major clusters in studies one and two. The Rochester network in this study also appeared in study one. In the
AJCP data, this cluster included five settings and appeared
primarily concerned with prevention and enhancement interventions in schools. This cluster produced 18 articles in
the AJCP during the period of our study. Cluster members
cited their own work 36 times, but the work of the other
clusters only twice. The effect of mentor-student imprinting
was strong, with Emory Cowen as mentor.

A second network of three settings lacked a clear
focal setting; we named it the North Carolina/Texas/Louis-
ville (NCTL) cluster. This network intersected in some
ways with the Louisville cluster in study two, and similar

content themes of planning and evaluation research in community mental health settings appeared in both studies. This cluster produced nine articles in AJCP during the period, citing its own work 14 times and that of the other two clusters twice.

A third cluster included five settings apparently focused on the Universities of Oregon and Nebraska. The content focus of this cluster was less clear, but it largely concerned alternative models for community service delivery. This cluster produced 14 AJCP articles during the study period, citing its own work six times and that of other clusters three times.

SUMMARY OF FINDINGS

In this section we summarize the findings from our three studies, discussing the ways in which they converge on a common portrayal of community psychology. We then apply our heuristic model to these findings to describe the developmental level of community psychology's social structure.

Convergent Descriptions of Clusters

Communication Clusters (Criterion 1)

Several clusters appeared in two or more of our studies. A Rochester cluster appears in studies one and three. Emory Cowen is clearly the focal person of this network. In both studies in which it appears, this cluster is highly productive. Its content is consistently concerned with preventive programs in schools. Finally, this cluster appears in study three as a multiple-setting network, apparently based on the imprinting of Rochester work on Cowen students who have moved to other settings. The failure of this cluster to appear in study two could reflect several factors. One explanation could be a cluster preference for presentation through published channels; an alternative could be that APA presentations by this cluster are not organized as symposia or not submitted to Division 27 for primary sponsorship.

A Penn State network emerged in studies one and two. Its primary members are Steven Danish and Anthony

D'Augelli. The content focus consistently appears as the development and evaluation of paraprofessional training programs. Across studies, the cluster is productive and durable, although its size and the extent of cross-setting collaboration differ.

A third cluster also appears which is less consistent in structure across studies. In study two, a cohesive, focused Louisville cluster appears. Its counterpart in study three (NCTL) lacks a clear focal setting, has a fairly wide range of research content, yet demonstrates productivity and collaboration as a network.

Although we have concentrated on clusters as the basic unit of analysis in this chapter, some noteworthy individuals appear to play major roles in the functioning of these clusters. Emory Cowen consistently appears at the core of the Rochester network, and Anthony D'Augelli and Steven Danish do likewise for the Penn State cluster. Ira Iscoe chaired the two major training-oriented symposia which formed the large network initially identified in study two. James Kelly was a central figure in the Oregon-Nebraska network in study three, as well as in a smaller group in study two. Sarason and Lorentz (1979) have described how a central "networker" is often the most important factor in establishing and maintaining a network; the repeated appearance of these individuals suggests that they may be playing such a role in community psychology.

Durability and Productivity (Criteria 2 and 3)

In all three of our studies, we encountered a similar phenomenon. The initial data set often showed a large number of individuals and settings, sometimes with a number of linkages among these. However, when we applied even minimal standards of durability or productivity, the number of individuals and settings eliminated was very large--usually most of the original sample. In study one, we started with 676 authors involved in 478 articles. After applying what we considered moderately stringent productivity criteria, we were left with only 81 authors. Only two clusters produced more than ten articles during a three-year period. In study two, most symposium clusters also lacked durability. Only 6% of the individuals in the sample coparticipated with another individual at more than one convention. Our durability criterion here is set at the lowest level possible. Furthermore, the figure of 6% seems too low to be attributed solely to the desires of program planners for variety in convention presentations. Study three continued this trend. When we operationally defined a linkage between settings as two instances, in four and one-half years, of any of the three types of communication we had recorded (hardly an exclusive criterion, we believe), 12% of the researchers and 10% of the settings of our original sample were involved in such linkages.

We did not design our criteria in these studies to eliminate large numbers of scholars. Indeed, we were surprised at what seemed to be the rather ephemeral nature of much of the collaboration in community psychology. An alternative explanation of these findings would be that analysis of face-to-face or other contacts not recorded in the formal literature would reveal more interconnectedness among community psychologists. If this is true, however, study two—an analysis of unpublished papers and symposia—should reveal more durable clustering than studies one and three. In fact, it reveals somewhat less.

Impact (Criterion 4)

In Criterion 4, we stated that the clusters which influence the course of their discipline will be those which are read and cited by others. Both study one and study three addressed this issue. The most impressive figure was that the Penn State cluster in study one was cited 24 times in two years by other researchers. In neither study, however, did the major clusters have much impact on each other. The two clusters in study one cited each other only twice in two years; the three multiple-setting clusters in study three cited each other only seven times in almost five years.

Hypotheses Regarding Network Functioning

Content Focus (Hypothesis 1)

A review of the three sets of findings shows covariability of social structure and content of research. Two clusters identified across studies (Rochester and Penn State) are engaged in clearly definable research programs. The third network (Louisville/NCTL) shows some similarity of content across studies in the area of community mental health program planning and evaluation. In study two, most of the smaller clusters also demonstrate content interests of varying scope. On the basis of informal inspection of research work, intercommunication does seem associated with a consistent content focus.

Proximity and Imprinting (Hypotheses 2 and 3)

Across the three studies, almost all major clusters identified appear to be based in one or two geographic settings, or at least to have been originally established there. This is evidence of the importance of proximity as an enabling condition for cluster formation. The effects of educational imprinting were more difficult to trace than those of proximity. Three examples of mentor-student links in clusters emerged. The centrality of Emory Cowen and his students in the Rochester group was clear. Similarly, the relationships between Anthony D'Augelli, Steve Danish, and their Penn State students were traceable. Ira Iscoe, James Kelly, and Ed Trickett formed a "three-generation lineage" with durable links in study two. Other imprinting relationships were difficult to identify. These findings could reflect differences in how different networks function or in how their functioning is reflected in the data sources we used.

Hypotheses Regarding Disciplinary Development

The findings from these three studies converge to portray community psychology as a discipline at the crossroads of the transition phase. In each study relatively small networks appear which are cohesive and productive. These groups have clearly moved beyond the reactive phase and begun the task of generating consensual knowledge for a new discipline (critical mass, Hypothesis 4). They are beginning to extend beyond single-setting research programs to develop the broader communication and consensus on which Kuhnian paradigms are built (communication between settings, Hypothesis 5). However, the evidence indicates that these trends are limited and that dissolution rather than convergence is still a very conceivable outcome. In all three studies, only a small number of community psychologists and settings were involved in clusters. Many mavericks still appear to work outside the networks, de-spite our efforts to design linkage criteria which were minimally exclusive yet indicative of productive, durable relationships (exhaustiveness, Hypothesis 6). Only in study two did an overarching network link a large number of individuals and settings. In addition, in studies one and three, we found limited impact of any network's research on the work of other clusters (cluster interrelationships, Hypothesis 7). There was little evidence of the forging of durable adaptive links with other disciplines or with com-munity settings outside academia (external communication, Hypothesis 8).

IMPLICATIONS OF METHODS AND FINDINGS

The implications of our work can be summarized in two statements. First, we seek to communicate a conceptual perspective on the development of applied disciplines, espe-cially community psychology. We do not wish to reify a set of exploratory findings, but to use them to illustrate the value of studying social structure as one indicator of disci-plinary development. Our primary purpose is the heuristic facilitation of further research. Second, the desirable social structure for an applied discipline--the nature of the clusters it seeks to encourage--depends a great deal on the goals of the discipline and its emerging identity. That identity is rooted in the metaphors used by its members--often tacitly--to represent their collective goals and values. We will elaborate on these issues in turn.

Further Research

In undertaking the work we have described in this chapter, our primary purpose has been to generate an al-ternative perspective from which to describe community psy-chology and, ultimately, other applied disciplines. Most applications of Thomas Kuhn's conception of scientific revo-lutions to community psychology have emphasized the intel-lectual content of paradigms (for example, Rappaport, 1977). We seek to complement those analyses with a conceptual framework which brings into focus the creative, fallible, human builders of paradigms and the nature of their inter-personal ties. Toward that end, we have presented in this

chapter a conception of clusters of individual members of a
discipline, a developmental model which summarizes the role
of such clusters in the development of that discipline, and
three studies which illustrate alternative methods for operationalizing and measuring these constructs. The specific
empirical findings we have generated are illustrative, not
definitive. The data are from the 1970s; if our model is
valid, discernible movement toward the convergence phase
could have occurred by the time this volume appears in
print. In addition, many alternative measures of communication links can be used in further work. The value of
our findings lies primarily in their use as examples of the
relationships among the cluster construct, the developmental
model, and the empirical indicators of communication as it
occurs among members of a discipline.

Four Metaphors to Describe
an Applied Discipline

      For community psychology and other applied disci-
plines, the practical implications of our study depend on
the goals and values chosen for the discipline. These can
be expressed in terms of four metaphors: community psychology as a viewpoint rather than social institution, as a
participatory democracy, as an emerging species, and as
an experimenting society.
      If the value of community psychology is primarily
contributing a new viewpoint to traditional areas of inquiry
and service, rather than building the institutions of a new
discipline with its own identity, our findings are neither
surprising nor disquieting. In this view, the role of community psychologists is disseminating knowledge, sharing
values, and developing a new approach to services in mental health, education, criminal justice, and other fields.
The key problem here is that without the development of a
disciplinary identity, reflected in social units such as
clusters, the strength of the community viewpoint dissipates.
It will be absorbed into the work of other fields not necessarily systematically or completely.
      A second metaphor for community psychology is that
of a participatory democracy, a political entity. Its members define issues and goals, form constituencies, and engage in mutual influence--while maintaining an overarching
solidarity as members of a community. These processes are

beginning to occur in community psychology. The establishment of task forces (for minorities, women, applied practitioners, and other groups) in Division 27 represents such activity. The appearance of regional student conferences and meetings at regional conventions is also a positive sign of cluster building and intercommunication. If our data accurately describe community psychology, however, much more network building needs to be done.

Two difficulties arise here. First, such "networking" takes time and energy to go beyond the single-setting collaboration often associated with research. This is especially true for the focal individuals of a network, who shoulder much of the organizational effort in the early days of a network's functioning. Second, the defining of constituencies, in our view, needs to be pursued with efforts to link these groups with each other and to define common grounds of interest. Otherwise, disputes can erupt over who represents "true" community psychology and the discipline reverts to the reactive phase.

Community psychology can also be portrayed as an emerging species seeking an adaptive niche. A major issue here is the Darwinian dictum that more than one species cannot occupy a given niche. For community psychology, the question is most simply posed: What can we do that others--clinical or organizational psychologists, social workers, or community activists, perhaps--do not do? In the study of ecology, paradoxes in this area have been resolved by increasing the complexity of the concept of niche and the number of niches available in a given habitat (Worster, 1977). In this way, species which seemed to be competing for the same niche have been shown to be occupying subtly different niches. In addition, it seems likely that creation and occupation of a niche is a process in which species and environment influence each other. For community psychologists the task becomes creating and defining activities and competencies which are useful in their environs, which complement the competencies of other disciplines, and which provide an identity for the discipline (Glidewell, 1977). The major clusters in our studies appear to have found local niches of their own. It is unclear from their diverse content and sparse intercommunication whether these can be integrated into a disciplinary identity.

The ecological metaphor highlights a second issue: adaptive flexibility. The ability of an applied science discipline to adapt to changes in its sociopolitical environs can be enhanced by initiating two activities: (1) adapting itself to a variety of habitats and (2) building mutually supportive and influential relationships with other disciplines and community groups. The findings we have presented concern the community psychologists who are most active in defining the future of the discipline through scholarly activity. These community psychologists are heavily concentrated in one habitat--the university psychology department. Interdependent, mutually influential relationships with other disciplines and in the community appear limited in our data. These factors leave the discipline in a position that is extremely vulnerable to shifts in priority by funding groups, decreases in college enrollment and legislative support, and other changes in availability of resources. Overdependence on a threatened habitat makes for an endangered species, no matter how great its numbers.

A fourth metaphor for community psychology is the "experimenting society" (Campbell, 1969). From this perspective, psychology is in an enviable position. As a discipline, it can use familiar methods and concepts to plan proactively for the future and to monitor empirically its own development. For example, alternative interventions, designed to foster communication and interdependence among community psychologists and with other groups, could be implemented on a regional basis. The outcomes of such efforts could be evaluated and compared empirically, with study of the methods of both successes and failures. Information can be collected regarding disciplinary development among similar applied social sciences and compared with data for community psychology. Finally, the data we have reported could form a baseline for monitoring of changes in the research community of the discipline.

These metaphors are neither unfamiliar nor mutually exclusive. They have been central themes in community psychology. In a time of transition from a passionate party of opposition to a convergent, identifiable discipline, the application of the concepts, values, and methods of community psychology to the building of its own scholarly community is an important task for the discipline.

NOTES

1. The reader should note that in the empirical studies to be discussed we have attempted to use produc-

tivity criteria which are at most only moderately stringent. We recognize that valuable scientific work often does not facilitate frequent publication, but this must be balanced with a concern for identifying networks engaged in sustained research. In study one, we counted articles by anyone in the network published in 1976. Book reviews, editorials, letters, and abstracts of conferences were omitted.

2. A 46-item checklist of key words was used to analyze titles. This checklist was sufficiently varied and sensitive to show clear divergence of content between AJCP and the Journal of Consulting and Clinical Psychology. The checklist and further information on it may be obtained from Maurice Elias, Department of Psychology, Livingston Campus, Rutgers University, New Brunswick, New Jersey 08903.

REFERENCES

Bloom, B. L. Community mental health: A general introduction. Monterey, Calif.: Brooks/Cole-Wadsworth, 1975.

Campbell, D. T. Reforms as experiments. American Psychologist, 1969, 24, 409-429.

Campbell, D. T., & Fiske, D. W. Convergent and discriminant validation by multitrait-multimethod matrix. Psychological Bulletin, 1959, 56, 81-105.

Chinsky, J. M. Nine coalescing themes at the Austin Conference. In I. Iscoe, B. Bloom, & C. Spielberger (Eds.), Community psychology in transition. New York: Wiley, 1977.

Cronbach, L. J., & Meehl, P. E. Construct validity in psychological tests. Psychological Bulletin, 1955, 52, 281-302.

Elias, M. J., Dalton, J. H., & Howe, G. W. Studying community psychology as a community of professionals: An empirical approach. Professional Psychology, 1981, 12, 363-376.

Elias, M. J., Dalton, J. H., Franco, R., & Howe, G. W. Academic and nonacademic community psychologists: An analysis of divergence in settings, roles, and values. American Journal of Community Psychology, in press.

Flavell, J. H. The developmental psychology of Jean Piaget. New York: Van Nostrand, 1963.

Gieryn, T. F. Problem retention and problem change in science. In J. Gaston (Ed.), Sociology of science: Problems, approaches, and research. San Francisco: Jossey-Bass, 1978.

Glidewell, J. A social psychology of mental health. In S. Golann & C. Eisdorfer (Eds.), Handbook of community mental health. New York: Appleton-Century-Crofts, 1972.

Glidewell, J. Competence and conflict in community psychology. In I. Iscoe, B. Bloom, & C. Spielberger (Eds.), Community psychology in transition. Washington, D.C.: Hemisphere Press, 1977.

Gottlieb, B. H. (Ed.). Social networks and social support. Beverly Hills, Calif.: Sage, 1981.

Heller, K., & Monahan, J. Psychology and community change. Homewood, Ill.: Dorsey, 1977.

Hollander, E. P. Principles and methods of social psychology (2nd ed.). New York: Oxford University Press, 1971.

Iscoe, I., Bloom, B., & Spielberger, C. (Eds.). Community psychology in transition: Proceedings of the national conference on training in community psychology. Washington, D.C.: Hemisphere Press, 1977.

Kuhn, T. S. The structure of scientific revolutions (2nd ed.). Chicago: University of Chicago Press, 1970.

Leavy, R. L. Social support and psychological disorder: A review. Journal of Community Psychology, 1983, 11, 3-21.

Lounsbury, J. W., Leader, D. S., Meares, E. P., & Cook, M. P. An analytic review of research in community psychology. American Journal of Community Psychology, 1980, 8, 415-442.

McClure, L. F., Cannon, D., Belton, E., D'Ascoli, C., Sullivan, B., Allen, S., Connor, P., Stone, P., and McClure, G. Community psychology concepts and research base: Promise and product. American Psychologist, 1980, 35, 1000-1011.

Mills, R. C., & Kelly, J. G. Cultural adaptation and ecological analogies: Analysis of three Mexican villages. In S. Golann & C. Eisdorfer (Eds.), Handbook of community mental health. New York: Appleton-Century-Crofts, 1972.

Mitchell, J. C. The concept and use of social networks. In J. C. Mitchell (Ed.), Social networks in urban situations: Analyses of personal relationships in central African towns. Manchester, England: Manchester University Press, 1969.

Myers, D. G., & Lamb, H. The group polarization phenomenon. Psychological Bulletin, 1976, 83, 602–627.

Price, D. J., & Beaver, D. Collaboration in an invisible college. American Psychologist, 1966, 21, 1011–1018.

Rappaport, J. Community psychology: Values, research and action. New York: Holt, Rinehart & Winston, 1977.

Sarason, S. B., & Lorentz, E. The challenge of the resource exchange network. San Francisco: Jossey-Bass, 1979.

Social Sciences Citation Index. Philadelphia: Institute for Scientific Information, 1976–1978.

Tichy, N. M., Tushman, M. L., & Fombrun, C. Network analysis in organizations. In E. Lawler III, D. Nadler, & C. Cammann (Eds.), Organizational assessment: Perspective on the measurement of organizational behavior and the quality of work life. New York: John Wiley, 1980.

Ullman, L. Behavior therapy as a social movement. In C. M. Franks (Ed.), Behavior therapy: Appraisal and status. New York: McGraw-Hill, 1969.

Wellman, B. Applying network analysis to the study of support. In B. H. Gottlieb (Ed.), Social networks and social support. Beverly Hills, Calif.: Sage, 1981.

Worster, D. Nature's economy: The roots of ecology. San Francisco: Sierra Club Books, 1977.

4   Community Psychology, Experimental Social Innovation, and the Role of the "True Experiment"

Glenn Shippee

In recent years a paradox has come to characterize the youthful but quickly maturing discipline of community psychology. The recent, sagelike recommendations for more rigorous research paradigms reflect considerable disenchantment with the lack of methodological sophistication characterizing community psychological research (Cowen, 1973; Cowen, Gardner, & Zax, 1967; Kelly, Snowden, & Munoz, 1977). At the same time, however, the research literature includes many contributions which champion less rigorous, "quasi-experimental techniques." Some researchers even go so far as to denigrate directly or by implication the "true experiment" as a method for investigating the effects of innovative community interventions (for example, Edwards & Guttentag, 1975; Edwards, Guttentag, & Snapper, 1975; Goldberger, 1973; Guttentag, 1973; Hollister, 1974; Levine, 1974; Schulberg & Perloff, 1979; Weiss, 1972).

The paradox can be simplified if community psychology is conceived of as a youth with an unusually severe case of acne. While the discipline continues to ingest, undiscerningly, a "poor diet" of new, ill-defined, and statistically unjustifiable research methods, periodic self-scrutiny reveals a worsening dermatological condition. It will be the primary purpose of the present chapter to argue that

---

The author would like to thank George W. Fairweather who insightfully commented on an earlier draft of this chapter.

the cure for this affliction lies in tempering the discipline's craving for nonexperimental methodologies, while at the same time optimizing the validity of research results through the increased utilization of the true experiment.

In pursuing this goal, the first section of the chapter addresses some of the criticisms which have been leveled at the true experiment as a paradigm for community research. In addition, the various quasi-experimental techniques which have been advocated as replacement paradigms for the true experiment are critically assessed. By way of a brief preview, this section attempts to demonstrate that because of severe internal validity problems, quasi-experiments should supplement or augment the true experiment and not replace it as the primary methodological paradigm in community or social policy research. The section suggests that (1) the appropriate application of quasi-experimental designs occurs in the context of preintervention, knowledge-building research in community psychology; (2) the true experiment is most suitable for intervention or program development research in community psychology.

The second major section describes a research and training model which provides a conceptual, philosophical, and methodological backdrop for the integration of quasi-experimental methods with the use of the true experiment. The experimental social innovation research model developed by George W. Fairweather and his associates (Fairweather, 1967; Fairweather & Tornatzky, 1977; Shippee, 1979; Tornatzky, 1976) provides community researchers with a set of humanitarian values which stress the social accountability of the scientist and with a comprehensive problem-solving research model which is applicable to the social, environmental, and community mental health maladies of our communities.

The final section provides a working example of the experimental social innovation research paradigm. The example is based on the demonstration and dissemination researches with the community lodge conducted by Fairweather and his colleagues (Fairweather, Sanders, Maynard, & Cressler, 1969; Fairweather, Sanders, & Tornatzky, 1974; Tornatzky et al., in press). The community lodge research exemplifies the experimental social innovation process, underscores the humanitarian value orientation of the experimental social innovator, and demonstrates how quasi-experimental methods can productively supplement the true experiment in community research.

THE QUASI-EXPERIMENT AS THE SINE
QUA NON OF COMMUNITY PSYCHOLOGY?

Before progressing to a discussion of true or quasi-experimental designs, it is necessary to differentiate these designs conceptually and operationally. The distinguishing feature of the true experiment lies in the researcher's ability to control the scheduling of experimental stimuli (the when and to whom of treatment interventions). More precisely, the random assignment of a randomly selected sample of treatment recipients to experimental conditions distinguishes the true experimental design from the various quasi-experimental designs (Campbell & Stanley, 1966; Cook & Campbell, 1976). When the rule of complete randomization is violated, then the experimental design, by definition, becomes a quasi-experimental design.

The second important parameter characterizing the true experiment, and closely related to the concept of randomization, is a controlled exposure to a treatment. What this means operationally is that the researcher must control the provision and time of onset of experimental treatments. That is, once a sample has been randomly assigned to a set of experimental conditions, the researcher must initiate the treatments at a similar point in time across the experimental groups. (Of course, treatments can also be assigned to recipients randomly over time.) Further, the quality or intensity of the treatment originally scheduled for a particular experimental group must be maintained following the assignment of research participants to treatments.

As a means of clarifying the above distinctions, consider the following hypothetical examples. Suppose a state desires to develop a network of community mental health centers (CMHC) whose services would be expanded to include natural disaster crisis-intervention programs. One method for evaluating the effects of this service would be to randomly assign the entire statewide network of CMHCs to either one of two treatment conditions. One condition would include the establishment of the service, while the remaining conditions would reflect the maintenance of current CMHC services. Prior to the introduction of treatments, communities serviced by the CMHCs would be surveyed to obtain a measure of "community adjustment," the primary dependent variable in this hypothetical example. Following the implementation of the program, suppose a series of earthquakes, floods, or tornadoes struck various areas of the state. In the case of each of these disasters, to evaluate the effects of the crisis-intervention service on the community adjustment index, the pre-experimental and the postexperimental data for the experimental group would be contrasted with adjustment data from a similarly affected control group of CMHCs in a two-by-two (time x treatment) analysis of variance. While extremely crude in many respects, this example captures the essence of true experimentation where the researcher maintains control over the provision of treatments.

A quasi-experimental approach to the evaluation of the postdisaster crisis-intervention services might be represented as follows. Rather than randomly assigning CMHCs to the services (through a random provision of funding, for example), the program would be offered to any CMHC desiring to establish it. A second group of CMHCs not adopting the program would serve as a no-service control. With the inclusion of both pre- and postdisaster measures, as in the above true experiment, such a design would be referred to as a pre-post nonequivalent control-group design.

In addition to the nonequivalent control-group design, there exist several other varieties of quasi-designs. Since several comprehensive descriptions of these designs are readily available in the literature (for example, Campbell & Stanley, 1966; Cook & Campbell, 1976; Hersen & Barlow, 1976; Kazdin, 1973, 1978; Mahoney, 1978; Sidman, 1960), they will not be reviewed here. However, what is important to note is that the conditions of randomization and control over the provision of treatments are the distinctive characteristics of the true experiment.

Criticisms of the True Experiment

It is ironic that those characteristics of the true experiment which make it the most scientifically valid method of establishing causality between variables (randomization and control of treatment) are the same factors which greatly impede the widespread utilization of the true experiment in community research. The rationale underlying this statement is inextricably tied to the political and organizational realities faced by those mounting community researches. Stated succinctly, to obtain the degree of control necessary for the conduct of true field experiments, the community psychologist must become actively involved in the organizational, administrative, and highly political contexts in which program development and design decision making occur.

Among academic psychologists, the possibility of becoming "entangled" in such decision-making processes has traditionally been viewed as distasteful at best and "unscientific" at worst (Kelly, 1971; Sarason, 1974). This attitude undoubtedly prevails because of the apparent incongruity that exists between the behaviors of cajoling, persuading, politicizing, bargaining, negotiating, and compromising and the logical and rational research decision-making atmosphere which most academics are accustomed to. Some analysts have even gone so far as to suggest that the detachment and autonomy recently being advocated for program evaluators (often cloaked behind an objectivity argument) (for example, Campbell, 1969; Hargreaves, Attkisson, Horowitz, & Sorenson, 1978; Weiss, 1977; Wortman, 1975) may stem from a desire to maintain academic decision-making styles for the program evaluation research-design process (for example, Fergus, 1979; Tornatzky, 1979).

In addition to strictly political and organizational considerations, there exist several additional arguments which critics of the true experiment have relied on to justify the utilization of quasi-experimental techniques. Essentially, these criticisms can be classified under four general categories. These are (1) logistical problems posed by experimentation, (2) the ethicality of experimentation, (3) problems of scope, and (4) the information value of experiments for policymakers. In the sections which follow, these criticisms are presented and critically assessed.

Logistical Problems Posed by Experimentation

The most frequently cited set of logistical problems believed to impede the fielding of true experiments in the community are those of administrative support, time, and excessive expense. Of these, obtaining the support of administrative personnel within service-rendering agencies is often seen as the most formidable obstruction to true experimentation. In particular, it is believed by some critics that the objectivity of the community researcher should not be sacrificed through undue participation in administrative decisions concerning program design and implementation.

Administrative Support. While the sheer number of instances in which administrative pressures have prevented or subverted a piece of experimental research is unknown, it is probably the case that a few glaring failures to implant or complete a true experiment in the community are more familiar to community psychologists than are the numerous successes (nearly 300) documented in recent years (for example, Boruch, McSweeney, & Soderstrom, 1977). Complementing these successes are the 21 true experiments which have been completed or are in progress for dissertational research in the ecological psychology program headed by George W. Fairweather at Michigan State University. A great deal of informal observational evidence suggests that the successful implementation and completion of a true experiment in the community is contingent on the consummation of a formal administrative agreement between the researcher and the relevant community organizations (Fairweather, 1967; Fairweather & Tornatzky, 1977). The establishment of this agreement, or contract, in turn, is generally dependent on the relationship which the community researcher establishes with the personnel of the host agencies in which the research is to be conducted.

In the case of most community research projects, it is essential that the researcher be perceived as "a part" of the organization. Through an extended association with the agency or organization (sometimes on a voluntary basis) the researcher must establish legitimacy and credibility within the organization. Specifically, the researcher must be seen as an individual who is interested and committed to assisting the organization in the search for solutions to problems confronting the organization. Prior to even proposing a piece of research, it is usually necessary for the researcher to assist the organization on other ongoing projects as a means of demonstrating sincerity and commitment to the organization. It is not uncommon for researchers to invest three to four months of time within an organization prior to the research-proposal stage.

The researcher's long-term association with a community agency or organization dealing with a particular problem area has a number of favorable by-products. Among them are a set of firsthand experiences with a problem population, their needs, and their judgments concerning potential solutions to the problem. Through extended contacts with administrators, service personnel, paraprofessionals, and other persons within the organization, the researcher is also likely to gain knowledge of these professionals' views of a social or environmental problem.

Very often administrative support for true experimentation materializes because the researcher seeks out members of agency staffs and the problem population for the purpose of consulting with them about a potential research project. Rather than "being allowed to participate" in the research-design endeavor, the researcher actively solicits the views, perceptions, and opinions of members of the problem population and those of organizational personnel. It is in a collaborative and participative atmosphere where organizational and grass-roots support for the research enterprise emerges. In the same context, it is also possible for the researcher to paint a rough scenario of the conditions which will be necessary for the implementation of random assignment procedures. Here also the researcher can introduce the necessity of maintaining the integrity of the experimental interventions. Following these deliberations with agency personnel, service providers, members of the problem population, and other relevant persons, a formal, written administrative agreement should be consummated. This agreement should be arrived at in a spirit of cooperation, mutual support, commitment, and trust. Further, it is often useful if the agreement is perceived as a memorandum which traces the historical progression of the research collaboration process between the researcher and the organization. As Fairweather and Tornatzky (1977) suggest, the agreement should contain provisions for the following contingencies, events, and activities:

1. Authority for researchers to select and randomly assign persons to conditions according to an experimental plan.
2. Research money allocations.
3. Management of space, funding, or personnel issues.
4. A commitment to support and defend the integrity of the experiment.
5. An agreement to release data to researchers.
6. An understanding concerning sample size and the dimensions of the experimental design.
7. A commitment to follow organizational norms and bureaucratic procedures.
8. Provision of feedback and a final report to research participants and to the host agency or agencies.
9. Deviation from the experimental procedure only with the consent of the agency or agency personnel.

Expense. Critics of the use of the true experiment often argue that the expense incurred through the conduct of experimentation does not justify the benefits which result. This general argument usually relates to two aspects of the true experiment. First, some critics hold that the provision of a potentially beneficial social or mental health intervention should be maximally supported by as large an allocation of funds as is available to the organization. That is, in order that as many individuals as possible receive the program or treatment, all monies should be allocated for the purpose of delivering service. Second, a less extreme but related argument holds that while some evaluation of program effects is necessary, it is inappropriate to "waste" valuable resources for control groups.

Rather than the expense involved in conducting true experiments (or any evaluation research for that matter), it is the expense which is incurred by not conducting optimally valid research which emerges as a primary consideration. Very often, ameliorative human service programs are disseminated and implemented on a national basis without empirical evidence demonstrating their likely effectiveness. Equally as often, there is no a priori design or plan for evaluating federal programs following their dissemination. Yet, the cost-benefit outcomes of massive federal efforts launched in all types of social and environmental problem areas would be enhanced through the conduct of small-scale, experimental research which would establish the effectiveness of programs prior to their national dissemination. At a fraction of the cost of implementing programs of unknown merit nationally, it would be possible to engage in small-scale experimentation (with a national program of small replicates) to determine the effectiveness of ameliorative programming prior to implementation.

Time. Very closely related to the criticisms of true experiment which emphasize their excessive expense are those arguments which hold that experimentation is overly time-consuming. In particular, this rationale maintains that the current policy-making apparatus characterizing federal, state, and local decision making prevents the utilization of longitudinal experimentation as an information resource for policy making. For example, often federal decisionmakers are confronted with immediate policy decisions brought about by crisis situations requiring prompt action. Critics suggest that the experimentation process is simply unresponsive to these types of situations.

To address this criticism, it is necessary to view it through a broader value perspective. First, acceptance of this argument implies support for the misinformed policies often resulting from a policy-making structure which frequently does not value issue-relevant information as a decision-making aid. Support of such a policy-making structure is unthinkable to scientists who value logic and rationality as components of decision making. Second, the pressures thrust upon the extant decision-making system by crises might very well be reduced if the process of research and social experimentation became sanctioned and valued elements of governmental policy-making activities.

Consider that many of the social and environmental dilemmas this nation faces presently--and in the immediate future--had their antecedents two decades ago. In the realm of environmental problems, a prime example is afforded by the recent tragedy of Three Mile Island. Nuclear power plants began full-scale operation in this country as early as the late 1950s. A longitudinal, national experiment could have been designed and conducted to compare nuclear energy generation technologies to conventional generation technologies in a randomized experimental design. The social, economic, political, and environmental impact of such technologies could then have been evaluatively assessed across matched geographic areas and then randomly assigned to a nuclear or traditional type of energy-production technology. Such an experiment would have been able to assess the specific impact of nuclear technologies on employment, industrial growth, environment, health, and public response to the technology; and more importantly, on the possible consequences of plant malfunctions. While at first glance such a plan seems absurd in view of the political and logistical difficulties involved, additional reflection on the wealth of comparative data which could have resulted from such an experiment sobers much skepticism. Note that both sides of the currently embroiled nuclear power debate have advanced competing claims of benefits or hazards of the technologies. The time-series data currently available is completely malleable to any interpretation any interest wishes to impose. Utility companies claim increased production, increased employment, and cheaper utility costs, while opponents point to greater costs, decreased employment, and lessened production. A longi-

tudinal experiment initiated in 1959 and continuously monitored to the present would have resolved these issues and,
further, would have provided the most valid information resource possible for governmental policymakers in this area.

The point of the above example is that many problems likely to confront this nation can be anticipated to
some degree prior to the time at which decisions at the
policy-making level are necessary. Prominent examples
which quickly come to mind are national health insurance,
transportation alternatives, housing policy, alternatives to
social security, breakdowns in affirmative action programs,
and the problems confronted by the growing number of elderly persons. Experimentation which comparatively assessed alternative technologies, services, and programs in
differing geographic areas of the nation could serve as the
primary knowledge base for future policy decisions and
planning when these problems reach "crisis proportion."
By anticipating future problems such as these with a continuing program of experimental research, then the "short-
term," and "stop-gap" decision-making characteristic of governmental policy formation might be reduced considerably.

The Scope of True Experiments

Many critics of the true experiment stereotypically
equate its use with the neglect of nonexperimental, impressionistic sources of data derived from informal participant-
observation or with the exclusion of sociodemographic data,
social indicators, and research-participant characteristics.
More specifically, censurers of the true experiment hold
that the use of the experimental paradigm leads the researcher to ignore anecdotal and archival sources of evidence which can be acquired throughout the life span of a
community intervention.

Nonexperimental Sources of Data. The experimental paradigm
neither explicitly nor implicitly precludes the collection of
experiential and impressionistic data. In fact, there exist
several formal and informal mechanisms which are designed
to facilitate the collection and analysis of "soft data" in
experiments. One of the less formal techniques for collecting these types of descriptive accounts is the research-
team diary. This diary can be periodically completed by
members of the research team and extraordinary, noteworthy,
or special events which occur during an intervention period

can be recorded and later compiled. As an excellent example of the research diary, consider an experiment by Whitney (1974). Whitney designed an experiment which assessed the effects of a cooperative auto mechanics training program for juvenile delinquents in a two-condition, completely randomized experimental design. The control group of his study reflected the then-current method of rehabilitating juvenile delinquents (a private employment training and placement program). Note the lucid detail of the following account, which describes some of the difficulties Whitney confronted when initially establishing the cooperative.

> Many people did not have a business attitude in working. Therefore, a lot of time had to be spent on developing appropriate job behavior; developing the fact that this was a business and not an agency; that as a business certain types of behavior must be controlled when working in the program. . . .
>
> It had to be stressed time and time again that it was a business and individuals had to display appropriate behavior. For example, a customer would walk in and individuals would be horse-playing, cursing, or talking in a very loud manner. These types of behaviors detracted from the business and caused great concern among many customers. Therefore, many weekly meetings were spent merely in telling the individuals about appropriate behavior. . . .
>
> Another major problem associated with the new model was concerned with keeping equipment to do the work. During the first two months of operating the business, the equipment disappeared at a very rapid rate. Individuals who were employed here did not feel or understand that the equipment was necessary in order for the employees to have a job and to satisfy the customers—the equipment was theirs and they were stealing from themselves. To correct the situation, every time a part was missing the money to pay for it would

be taken out of everyone's check. The result of doing this . . . was that the equipment started being returned, primarily because individuals who did not take equipment were not willing to pay for the missing equipment. . . .

Another major problem associated with
the behavior of participants in the model
that detracted from the business was getting to work on time. Many of the young
people did not think of getting up at
eight o'clock in the morning at the beginning of the operation of the co-op. Many
times when I went down to open the garage
I was the first one there. I had to call
individuals up; go pick up those that
lived near in order for them to come to
work. Soon a policy was set in a group
meeting that all persons attended. They
decided that if an individual was late or
absent three times then he would be suspended or not paid for the total days
missed. (Pp. 15-16)

The same richness of description can be found in an
experimental report authored by Beck (1975). This experiment contrasted an innovative consumer-participation model
with a traditional administrative decision-making structure
in health care planning contexts. Beck's account highlights the difficulty originally plaguing the establishment
of her innovative intervention.

The problems that emerged in the beginning
of the experiment were with some incompatibilities between the plan of the research
and what the consumers would actually let
happen. In this research there was a general plan of action which the volunteers
agreed to, such as carrying out periodic
meetings and how they would be conducted.
But the main theme of the new model was
that the consumers would be encouraged to
conduct the program as they wished so that
as the consumer group training program began these incompatibilities became obvious.

The first problem to emerge was in group
development. The researchers were trying
to let the natural leadership of the group
develop. One member decided that he was
going to turn the autonomous group meeting
into his own political platform and try to
rearrange the way in which the program
was run. A great deal of hostility developed over this but eventually, after some
of the group left and after disrupting several meetings, the group voted against his
plan [and plans] and about the fourth meeting he left. (P. 46)

What the above examples should demonstrate is that the
use of the true experiment does not preclude the researcher
from collecting and using anecdotal accounts of the effects
of innovative community interventions.

There exist several more formalized methods to
collect and analyze the "human response" to innovative
community programs. For instance, various correlative
methods such as cluster analytic techniques (Tryon &
Bailey, 1970) can be utilized to assess the relationships
between treatment outcomes and social process measures
obtained with structured instruments. Cluster analysis
was utilized by Tucker (1974) in an experiment which contrasted two models for teaching reading to disadvantaged
black youth. Tucker utilized this analysis to assess the
relationships between improvement in reading achievement
scores (the primary dependent variable) and process measures such as students' attitudes toward the school, students' parents, and students' self-concepts. Interestingly,
and contrary to a number of theoretical perspectives prevalent in the education literature, reading improvement
showed no relationship to these other attitudinal and social dimensions.

Social Indicators and Sociodemographic Data. Examples
abound of the use of sociodemographic data, social indicators, and archival data sources in true field experiments.
Consider the juvenile delinquency diversion research conducted by Davidson and his associates (1977). In this research, juvenile delinquents are randomly diverted from
formal processing in the juvenile justice system and are
assigned to various intervention programs staffed by uni-

versity undergraduate paraprofessionals. Davidson's research has heavily utilized various archival data sources
as dependent variables. Court records (recidivism) are
utilized as the primary outcome measure and participant
characteristics (for both paraprofessionals and delinquent
youth) are utilized to discover successful predictors of positive program outcomes. Other variables in the prediction
work of the Davidson group have included prior delinquency,
family characteristics, race, sex, age, school achievement,
and so forth.

It should be clear from the above examples that the
use of true experiments in no way militates against the
use of subjective, descriptive accounts of program effects,
social indicators, or sociodemographic data from program
participants. Further, it can be argued cogently that
true experiments enhance the utilization of such data,
since the actual manipulation of social and environmental
conditions may have differing effects on these types of indexes and on the social processes which mediate particular
interventions. Careful observation and formal correlative
analyses can be employed fruitfully to elucidate these effects within and between experimental conditions.

Ethical Dilemmas Posed by the Experiment

It is often the case that some program administrators and service providers question the ethicality of true
experimentation, arguing that it is ethically unjustifiable
and inhumane to deprive a supposedly beneficial treatment
program from any individual.

The most common response to this contention by
methodologists and community researchers has been the use
of the "waiting control group" design (Campbell, 1969;
Wortman, 1975). Specifically, in the case of most community
intervention programs, there exists insufficient manpower
and/or financial resources to serve all members of a problem population at any given point in time. As a result,
persons are selected randomly to receive the experimental
treatment while other persons wait in an untreated control
group until such time as treatment becomes available. Of
course, there exist numerous instances where sufficient resources do exist for the provision of a particular treatment
to all who require it. It is in these cases in which the
ethicality of experimentation becomes an especially salient
consideration.

At a minimum, it is the moral responsibility of re-searchers to provide some type of treatment to suffering others. That is, the position of the responsible scientist on this issue should be that treatment should never be withheld from an individual or group requiring assistance. However, it is not incumbent on the researcher to provide a treatment that exceeds in quality that which is normally and traditionally provided to persons with similar prob-lems. What this view suggests is that the "control group" in any true experiment devoted to the solution of human problems should never be represented by a standard of treatment below that which currently characterizes a prob-lem area. In sum, control groups in community experimen-tation should reflect that treatment, program, or interven-tion which is currently functioning and in place in the community.

Implicit in the above rationale is the belief that variations in treatment are not always going to produce more advantageous outcomes than those characterizing a traditional and extant treatment modality (in fact, one might argue tenuously that the very existence of a par-ticular treatment practice bears testimony to its effective-ness relative to other methods). Ostensibly beneficial treatments have often led to extremely negative and dele-terious states in their recipients. One only has to consider the effects of the various fertility drugs administered dur-ing the 1950s to be reminded of the fact that not all sup-posedly superior treatments result in positive outcomes. Unfortunately, the same may hold true for various social interventions. Clearly, it is the uncertainty of the effects of alternative community interventions which provides the raison d'être for true experimentation.

A final point which deserves introduction in discus-sions of the ethicality of true experimentation has been raised by Fairweather (1972). Fairweather has argued that simply by virtue of being members of our society per-sons have been part and parcel of the experimental process throughout history. The development of a new government in the 1700s, manipulations of the environment, nuclear weaponry, the New Deal, television, or the introduction of any social and technological innovation means that an en-tire society potentially will serve as subjects in social experiments of colossal proportions. In these instances, the experimental design is defined more formally as a pre-test/post-test one-group design, yet as a society we are all required to experience man-made interventions of one sort or another. If we are all to be participants in such experiments, then perhaps, as Fairweather (1972) suggests, society should demand that such experimentation be conducted in such a fashion as to guarantee an enhanced quality of life for all. At the very least, society should be assured that prior to the widespread dissemination of a social or technological innovation, a scientifically valid program of research was conducted which established the positive and negative effects of an innovation, social or otherwise. Viewed in this broader context, the perceived value of social experimentation as a means of improving humankind's existence would be recognized and the acceptance of experimental technology in social policy making would be enhanced.

Information Value to Policymakers

Many governmental policymakers or legislative decisionmakers scoff at the value of social scientific research as an information resource for social policy making. These individuals often maintain that it is naive to subjugate intuitive decision making to a "handful" of experiments which more often than not are fraught with methodological problems and may be of limited generalizability. Of course, it could be asserted that such a rationale conveniently cloaks a nonobvious preference on the part of policymakers for decision-making processes reflective of political efficacy rather than rational consideration of available evidence. Rational, scientific evidence about the effectiveness or ineffectiveness of a program occasionally flies in the face of legislative appropriations for various special interest groups.

It is understandable why these particular attitudes are so prevalent among governmental decisionmakers. One primary reason for their existence is that there is a definite paucity of well-done, policy-relevant research in the social sciences. For example, following the completion of the New Jersey and Pennsylvania Negative Income Tax experiments, some social scientists expected federal decisionmakers to respond to the evidence collected in the experiment by legislatively mandating a Negative Income Tax structure (Rossi & Wright, in press). This is far from what occurred, however. Instead, federal policymakers questioned the generalizability of the research, since the effects of the various tax payback structures were assessed only in New Jersey (Trenton, Paterson-Passaiç, and Jersey City) and in one city in Pennsylvania (Scranton). Other criticisms leveled at the experiment concerned confounded variables. As the Negative Income Tax experiment proceeded, it became unclear as to what exactly was being manipulated (Rossi & Wright, in press). Originally, it had been expected that the treatments (payback formula calculated on the basis of percentage of guaranteed income and tax rate of earned income) comprised the sole independent variables being varied in the experiment. Operationally, however, implementing these variables required different administrative procedures, thereby confounding the tax structure with these extraneous administrative variables. The exact nature of these latter variables was such that the differing payback structures required differing levels and types of administrative contact with program participants. It was these variations in the operationalization of the primary independent variables that could have produced the results obtained in the experiment. These difficulties, in addition to a number of other more microscopic methodological problems, led governmental decisionmakers to defer a legislative decision on the Negative Income Tax until additional experimental data with a larger sample could be collected. Subsequent studies (ongoing in Seattle, Denver, Gary, and Windsor, Canada) should provide a more confident data set on which to base Negative Income Tax legislation.

The Negative Income Tax experience shows that social scientists and governmental decisionmakers have incongruent perceptions of the role of policy-relevant community research in legislative decision making. Fortunately, this dissimilarity in perspectives may well reflect the current status of social-policy research as an unsystematic, nonlongitudinal, and nonprogrammatic activity, rather than representing active discrimination against true experimentation per se. At this point, however, it is not difficult for policymakers to be skeptical of social experimentation, since there exists little precedence for directly tailoring national policy decisions to experimental work. A second misconception of experimentation held by policymakers is considerably more damaging to the future of social experimentation. Some professionals believe that field experimentation (and program evaluation more generally) inhibits the creation of new programs and, further, does little to improve upon extant programs established to ameliorate a particular problem. In particular, these professionals hold that ongoing experimentation does not permit new programs to be easily and quickly implemented in a community setting because an experimental comparison of some form is required prior to implementation. A secondary issue which often accompanies this line of reasoning is the notion that the "rigidity" imposed by true experimental designs often interferes with the ideal operationalization of the conceptual underpinnings of an innovative program. More precisely, some professionals in the community believe that the organizational and logistical demands of true experimentation will cause alterations in the design of new programming to ensure the integrity of an experimental analysis.

There is some merit to both these beliefs. There are undoubtedly many situations where a new program was not initiated because of a desire to complete an experimental research already in progress. Research in progress usually renders unavailable the necessary comparison groups to which the new program could be contrasted. In addition, new programs have often been altered substantially (with respect to their underlying theoretical conceptualization) to conform to logistical constraints which inevitably affect the design of true experiments. Yet, with respect to the former contention, it makes little sense to create and implement new programs injudiciously or faddishly if they cannot be contrasted in the same experimental design with traditional programs already in place. To be of value in a policy-making sense, community experimentation should be programmatic in the sense of new programs being built upon, or integrated with, older programs. In addition, this process should proceed according to a logical and rational decision process whereby new programs are designed and comparatively contrasted with the most effective traditional ones even as future programs are being formulated for later experimentation. This research strategy also permits the utilization of invaluable data gleaned from the measurement of mediating processes characterizing previously assessed interventions in the formulation of new and more effective problem-solving models. In the absence of a sequential programmatic research effort, the process data gained from prior research cannot easily be translated into new intervention strategies. As was suggested in the preceding section, the insight gained through correlative analyses of mediating variables and processes which covary strongly with outcome measures can serve as the spawning ground for new and more focused community interventions. What this section suggests is that not only can a long-term program of experimentation be utilized to evaluate innovative new programs, but in addition, the conceptual developments resulting from this work can be utilized as the formative material for future programs.

Just as ongoing true experimentation may function to inhibit the immediate implementation of new programs, occasionally the design constraints imposed by true experiments require changes in how a community intervention is operationalized. For example, often an innovative program cannot be implemented as originally designed because of a lack of resources or staff shortages. As a hypothetical example, suppose an intervention designed to reduce post-prison recidivism requires that the ex-offender receive 24-hour per day supervision in the community. Further, suppose that only nine staff persons are available for the program. With only nine staff persons available it would be possible for only three ex-offenders to be serviced by such a program (assuming an eight-hour day for each staff person). Such a small number of program recipients would hardly allow for a meaningful statistical comparison between this innovative program and a traditional unsupervised parole intervention. In response to these contingencies, the program developer is compelled by experimental design and statistical considerations to change the nature of the intervention in order to increase sample size. The process by which such changes are arrived at is much like a proverbial balancing act wherein the researcher attempts to satisfy statistical and experimental design constraints and logistical constraints by changing the program elements comprising the intervention. In this example, the researcher might reduce staff-offender supervision periods to eight hours. Such a change would permit a larger sample of ex-offenders to be included in the program, and yet the "in vivo" essence of the original program would still be maintained.

As is evident from the above example, decisions concerning design and program changes pose a value dilemma to the researcher. This dilemma ultimately comes down to a decision either to proceed with a methodology of questionable scientific validity (through the design of an observational-demonstration research) or to redesign an intervention in order that it may be made amenable to evaluation through true experimentation. Fortunately, such forced choices are usually circumventable through careful planning by the experimentalist.

In summary, this section has presented the criticisms of true experimentation most often expressed by professionals in the community and in academia who disfavor its use and staunchly advocate quasi-experimentation. These criticisms were grouped into four categories (logistical problems, ethical dilemmas, problems of scope, and policy relevance). In each case exemplary community researches and counterarguments were cited which challenged the validity of the majority of censuring contentions. In the next section, the alternatives to true experimentation are considered.

QUASI-EXPERIMENTATION AS AN ALTERNATIVE TO THE TRUE EXPERIMENT: TYPES OF VALIDITY

In order to review quasi-experimental methodology, it is necessary to introduce a set of evaluative criteria by which the quasi-designs can be assessed. Ironically, the two authors who have worked extensively on the development of quasi-experimental methodology (Thomas D. Cook and Donald T. Campbell) have provided the most well-articulated set of dimensions or standards for judging the quality of experimental designs. Cook and Campbell (1976) have described four types of validity which should be considered in the interpretation of data resulting from both quasi-experimental and true experimental designs (Mahoney, 1978, and Nunnally & Durham, 1975, have provided similar typologies of validity).

The first type of validity is internal validity, which refers to the degree of confidence one possesses concerning the existence of a true causal relationship between two variables (most typically an independent and a dependent variable). The major threat to the internal validity of an experimental design is posed by the existence of alternative explanations which could account for a pattern of results obtained in an experiment. Major sources of internal invalidity include:

1. extraneous events which occur between pre-test and post-test;
2. differences in maturation which occur between pre-test and post-test;

3. changes in outcomes due to the effects of repeated measurement;
4. changes in measuring instruments themselves;
5. the tendency of scores to regress to the mean following selection;
6. systematic differences in selection of groups of respondents;
7. attrition of subjects due to intervention conditions;
8. possibility of bidirectional causality;
9. diffusion of effects among controls who become aware of treatments;
10. competition among groups which contaminates treatment;
11. uncooperative attitudes among control group members;
12. differing impacts of treatment because of varied local conditions (Cook and Campbell, 1976)[1]

While these alternative explanations are not threats to every field research, varying numbers of the sources of invalidity usually require conceptual resolution in most field researches. For example, the now-classic (and often maligned) "Hawthorne Experiments" were characterized by several internal validity problems. This research was designed in the late 1920s and early 1930s to discover the most effective means of increasing the productivity of assembly-line factory workers at Western Electric's Hawthorne assembly plant (Roethlisberger & Dickson, 1964). The experimental group for the research consisted of six female factory workers who were separated from their coworkers in a special testing area for a period of nearly four years. Utilizing an A-B-A repeated-measures design with the females serving as their own controls, the research attempted to identify the effects of several differing contingency plans and working conditions designs (varying lengths of rest periods, shift length, and the provision of company-sponsored lunches and beverages, for example) on productivity. The major result of the research was that regardless of the nature of the experimental treatments introduced over the course of the experiment, productivity continued to increase (for example, from a 40% to 62% increase over the four years of the research).
Among the numerous threats to the internal validity of this research was a maturation confound. That is, the group of segregated women developed an esprit de corps and sense of cohesiveness between the pretest baseline period and the introduction of the varying experimental

treatments. Consequently, the increase in productivity demonstrated by the workers over time cannot be causally explained unambiguously. The introduction of more favorable working conditions, a developing sense of social cohesiveness and morale, or some form of interaction between these states may have produced the treatment effects. This example reflects the primary difficulty posed by internal validity problems. Their existence does not permit clear causal statements concerning observed treatment effects.

A second form of validity identified by Cook and Campbell (1976) is statistical conclusion validity, which is concerned with the correct and appropriate application of statistical testing procedures to the results of quasi-experiments and true experiments. The inappropriate use of a particular statistical technique or arriving at an erroneous decision to reject or not reject the null hypothesis constitute the major sources of statistical conclusion invalidity. The Hawthorne Experiments again represent an extreme example of a research in which the statistical validity criterion was not considered. Statistical tests were not utilized as an aid to data interpretation in the Hawthorne studies. Without the application of inferential statistics, it is not known if the results obtained in this experiment deviated significantly from those that would have been expected to result by chance.

The third type of validity is that of construct validity. Threats to construct validity stem from two sources. The first of these concerns the degree to which a particular operationalization of an independent variable reflects the theoretical and conceptual rationale which underlies an intervention. The second source of a threat to the construct validity of a field research lies in the extent to which an outcome measure actually and reliably reflects the outcomes theoretically predicted to result from a treatment or intervention program.

Similar to the threats to internal validity, a threat to the construct validity of an independent or dependent variable implies the existence of an alternative account for the effects obtained in a quasi- or true experimental design. Unlike the former threats, however, threats to construct validity stem from a conceptual confound present in the treatment intervention procedure or in the selection or construction of outcome measures. More specifically, the various threats to internal validity are usually tied to some form of participant-selection bias which permitted differences in participant characteristics (history, maturation, attrition, and so forth) to covary with assignment to a particular treatment group. In contrast, threats to construct validity involve the presence of differing conceptual interpretations concerning exactly what was varied or measured in a research.

The Hawthorne studies again may be used to illustrate at least one form of deficient construct validity. While a maturation explanation can account for the results of this experiment, an equally plausible explanation surrounds the manner in which the various experimental treatments were introduced. Recall that the six female members of the experimental group were physically separated from their peers (over 100 other workers) in a special testing facility. Further, these females were under continuous surveillance from the research team and this surveillance also included a group physical examination at a local hospital every three months. As a result of these elements of the intervention program, it could be hypothesized that the increase in productivity exhibited by the females was due to an emergent sense of "specialness" or "uniqueness" on the part of the females which translated into enhanced productivity.[2] Perhaps the female workers came to feel that their behaviors were a significant part of the research process; hence they optimized their productivity levels to confirm the expectations of the researchers. Regardless of the specific perceptual response of the females, a legitimate alternative explanation for the increased productivity of the workers in the Hawthorne studies centers around their self-perceived "specialness." This state engendered through the introduction of the treatments now serves as a confounding variable vis-à-vis the intended experimental treatments.

A similar state of affairs can occur when researchers attempt to operationalize a dependent variable. Returning to the Hawthorne studies, suppose the researchers had not employed an actual productivity index but instead had relied on supervisor estimates of productivity. If only this measure had been employed, perhaps actual productivity increases would not have resulted. On the other hand, if increased productivity had resulted, it might be argued that supervisors were purposely responding so as to maximize the effects of the research project, perhaps as a means of enhancing their status within the factory. As with threats to the construct validity of an independent variable, threats to the construct validity of dependent variables reflect a poor fit between conceptualized outcomes and the outcomes that are actually measured.

Finally, the last type of validity described by Cook and Campbell (1976) is that of external validity, which refers to the degree to which an experimental effect is generalizable or applicable to differing persons and differing social and organizational contexts. An analysis of the Hawthorne studies more than adequately illustrates this type of validity. The increase in productivity observed in this longitudinal experiment would probably be replicated only under conditions where a small, segregated group of workers in a factory context were carefully observed and provided with a sequence of experimental treatments designed to enhance their productivity. To extend the generalizability of this work would require empirical replication in differing industrial settings.

Quasi-experiments: Validity Problems

Many of the quasi-experimental designs which have been extensively used in the community psychology literature are of the type which are unacceptable to even the staunchest defenders of quasi-experimental designs (see the Novaco and Vaux chapter in this volume). Such "uninterpretable designs" include the "one-shot case study," the one-group pretest-post-test design, and the nonequivalent control group post-test-only design. All these designs are so susceptible to threats to internal validity that many design experts (for example, Cook & Campbell, 1976; Mahoney, 1978) consider them useless for assessing the effects of community interventions. It is not so much that researches which employ these designs are of no value in the development of community psychology theory, but rather that program interventions evaluated through such designs cannot be considered as candidates for widespread utilization and dissemination until such time as they are subjected to more rigorous evaluation.

In addition to the above simpler quasi-experimental designs, recent years have witnessed the continued development and refinement of more sophisticated nonrandomized designs. These designs are extensively discussed in Cook and Campbell (1976); Campbell (1969); Campbell and Stanley (1966); Kazdin (1973, 1978); Hersen and Barlow (1976);

Mahoney (1978); and Greenwald (1976). The general classes of these designs include the nonequivalent control group designs, cohort designs, single-subject and multiple-subject repeated-treatment designs and reversal designs, the regression-discontinuity design, time-series designs, and the various causal-modeling techniques (path analysis, cross-lagged panel analysis).[3]

The nonequivalent control group and cohort designs involve the formation of nonrandom comparison groups which are later provided with differing experimental treatments. These groups are then compared to determine if the treatments differentially affected some outcome measure common to both groups. The cohort designs are special cases of the nonequivalent control group designs in that nonrandom comparison groups are formed with persons who share a common setting (for example, siblings in the same family; persons who experience the same treatment program over time are considered cohorts).

The multiple-treatment designs and reversal designs are those in which repeated experimental treatments are provided to a group of research participants over time. Certain "hybrid" versions of these designs involve the use of two independent groups such as the multiple-treatment reversal design where after receiving a common, often superior treatment, one group continues to receive the superior treatment while the second group receives a treatment expected to reproduce the prior, pre-experimental forms of behavior.

The regression-discontinuity design is a special-purpose design for situations where a stratified sample will or will not receive an experimental treatment, contingent on their standing on the stratification index. Persons falling near a median cutting point are randomly selected to receive or not receive treatment, and their outcomes are later utilized to determine the continuity or discontinuity of a regression line defining the relationship between an individual's standing on the stratification variable and a treatment outcome measure.

The time-series designs are a family of designs whereby the relationship between two variables (time and another variable) is monitored over time both prior and subsequent to the introduction of an experimental intervention (usually to an entire population). The effects of treatment are assessed by analyzing the slope of and intercept of regression lines resulting before and after the introduction of an intervention.

The various causal- or structural-modeling procedures typically involve the formation of causal models defining the relationship between a set of independent and
dependent variables. The relationships are defined through
the prior specification of the values and patterns of correlations (actually partial regression coefficients) between
variables obtained cross-sectionally. In simple terms, the
researcher attempts to formulate hypothetical causal rela-
tions (for example, $A \rightarrow B \rightarrow C$), shaped by estimates of temporal occurrence; and later, to assess their validity by an
analysis of the strength of the intercorrelations between
the variables in the model.

In the case of each of these designs, at this stage
of their development there exist serious validity problems
with regard to at least one of the four types of validity
criteria introduced by Cook and Campbell (1976). The
most serious deficiency of most of these quasi-designs is
their failure to directly control for many of the threats to
internal validity listed above. When treatment recipients
are randomly assigned to conditions, as in the case of the
true experiment, most threats to internal validity are ne-
gated through randomization. As sample size across treatment interventions increases, it becomes more unlikely
that persons receiving a particular treatment will differ in
development, experience, and the like from those in another treatment condition. Random assignment to interventions, in effect, "rules out" a number of threats to internal
validity which rely on the possibility that differences in
the characteristics of treatment recipients led to a particular pattern of results. These sources of invalidity (for
example, history, maturation, and selection) are particularly potent sources of alternative explanations for the
effects of an intervention. Problems of interpretation become especially acute when preintervention differences on
dependent variables characterize the treatment conditions
of the design. Contrary to the beliefs of many, there exists no acceptable statistical procedure for "equating" pre-
experimental differences between treatment groups, including
analysis of covariance (for example, Cronbach & Furby,
1970; Lord, 1960, 1969; Porter, 1967).

As an example of the susceptibility of quasi-experiments to these sources of invalidity, consider the following
hypothetical investigation. Suppose a research was to introduce a preventative mental health program into eight
nonrandomly selected schools that had volunteered to receive

the intervention. Further, suppose that eight highly similar schools not as amenable to the program served as a no-prevention program control (these schools continued to respond with traditional psychological services to those children in need). Assume that the researcher has both pre- and postintervention measures of adjustment for all students in each school for two years prior and one year after the introduction of the preventative program. Of the several potential outcomes for this quasi-experiment, suppose a statistical comparison of the schools' preintervention adjustment scores revealed no significant differences between the schools, but following the intervention program a positive difference emerged which favored the prevention program. (Note that this is the ideal outcome for most quasi-experimental designs of this type, since no pre-experimental differences in adjustment are apparently present on the pretest, but a significant difference emerged on the post-test adjustment index.) In such a case, some researchers would assume the existence of no pre-experimental differences of any kind between the schools and would ignore the possibility of other threats to internal validity. Most informed adherents of quasi-experimental designs, however, urge caution and suggest that the researcher initiate a deductive/conceptual process whereby plausible explanations which correspond to each of the threats to the validity of the outcomes are assessed. For the purposes of the present example, the threat of history will be utilized as an instance of this process.

Suppose the schools have experienced a different set of historical antecedents prior to the introduction of the experimental treatment. Assume that in the eight schools which served in the prevention program group, the principals were democratically selected, which in turn led to extremely high faculty support and morale. Such considerations would be overlooked if researchers assessed the effects of "history" by utilizing only readily available data such as school achievement data and students' attendance records. If no differences between schools emerged on these various measures, the researcher might erroneously conclude that historical differences between the schools provide an unlikely alternative explanation for the effects obtained in the quasi-experimental design. However, while extreme differences in faculty morale between the schools might not be reflected on measures of student achievement, attendance, or adjustment, it is highly probable that receptivity to a preventative program sponsored by a respected and admired principal would lead to greater faculty support of the program (that is, to greater willingness on the part of the faculty to implement various in-class aspects of the program). The point here is that there are likely to be any number of differences characterizing schools or treatment recipients, only one of which might produce an experimental artifact which disguises itself as a treatment effect. The measurement of some portion of these differences for the purpose of demonstrating equivalence between nonrandomly assigned groups or treatment recipients is simply not an acceptable substitute for true random assignment to conditions. <u>Causality, then, can never be inferred with any degree of confidence from such designs, since there will always exist m-k possible alternative explanations for postintervention effects obtained in nonrandom designs (where k equals measures utilized and m equals number of measures which could have been utilized).</u>

Quasi-experimental designs become even more uninterpretable when pre-experimental differences on a primary dependent variable do emerge. It has been standard practice among community researchers to resolve this problem through the use of analysis of covariance. However, two problems characterize this strategy: (1) researchers frequently violate the assumptions of the analysis of covariance in performing these analyses (namely the assumption of homogeneity of within-group regression coefficients between groups); (2) these analyses require a reliability of .90 or above for the covariate. This requirement is rarely met in psychological research (Nunnally, 1978; Lord, 1960, 1967, 1969; Cronbach & Furby, 1970). Quite simply, as measurement error characterizing the covariate increases, treatment means will reflect to an increasing extent treatment effects along with the pre-experimental differences which are unsuccessfully partialed out by the analysis of covariance.

For each of the remaining classes of less frequently used quasi-experimental designs which are not of the nonequivalent control group variety, there exist similar deficiencies with regard to the threats to internal validity listed above. Despite arguments to the contrary, the one-group interrupted time-series design is difficult to discriminate from the one-group pretest-post-test design. Although time-series designs typically possess multiple baseline and postintervention measures, most of the sources of invalidity attributed to the earlier "uninterpretable" one-group designs characterize the one-group interrupted time-series design. Some of these internal validity concerns, as well as external validity considerations, are reduced if an entire population is represented in the design (Kazdin, 1978). However, this frequently is not the case in most smaller-scale researches conducted by community psychologists. The use of an entire population of research participants (for example, an entire population of a state) eliminates many selection-related biases (selection, mortality, and interaction of other threats with selection); yet psychologists rarely have access to populations of this magnitude for intervention research. The major problem of the time-series designs, however, is that posed by the internal validity threats of history, maturation, and statistical regression.

Another problem with the time-series designs is that frequently the introduction of an intervention is accompanied by the simultaneous introduction of several extraneous variables. When several variables are introduced simultaneously, the construct validity of the time-series design is challenged. For example, in Campbell's (1969) commonly cited "Connecticut speeding crackdown" time-series study it is not possible, as with most time-series designs, to determine what elements of the intervention were ineffective. While the Connecticut crackdown study seemed to indicate that the entire intervention package was ineffective, if the opposite result had occurred, it would have been impossible to determine the important or necessary elements of the intervention program.

A third deficiency of the time-series designs is related to the statistical models which are available for the analysis of the results of these designs. Thus far, the statistical models available for these designs are mostly of a univariate nature and do not permit the utilization of multivariate statistical methods. This state of affairs makes it extremely difficult to obtain convergence with several dependent variables--especially those that might be only mildly intercorrelated. Of greater concern is the possibility that the correlations between the dependent variables will not remain static over the duration of the time series. If the correlations between outcome measures were to vary significantly over time, convergent results with multiple dependent variables would be almost impossible to obtain or to consider in the interpretation of analyses.

As the above section indicates, there are several problems with the statistical conclusion validity of many quasi-experimental designs. To this point in time there exists no definite set of accepted statistical procedures for many of the quasi-experimental designs. Cook and Campbell (1976) aptly summarize this state of affairs:

> But it is a sad fact that research on the statistical evaluation of quasi-experiments has not reached the stage of definitiveness that currently characterizes the state of the statistical art for randomized experiments. In particular, no adequate statistical tests yet exist for the most frequently used quasi-experimental design in which nonequated groups, whose pretest performance levels vary, receive different treatments. Even with time-series analysis (in which observations are made at multiple times before and after treatments), there is no definitiveness yet despite much vigorous and enlightened research that we shall mention later which promises well for the not-so-distant future. (P. 232)

It can be cogently argued that the statistical conclusion validity of most quasi-experiments is much more tenuous than the above comment would indicate. All inferential statistical tests which involve the estimation of population parameters assume a random selection of samples to be utilized for such tests. As Winer (1971) states:

> Statistics obtained from samples drawn by means of sampling plans which are not random have sampling distributions which are either unknown or which can only be approximated with unknown precision. Good approximation to sampling distributions are required if one is to evaluate the precision of inferences made from sample data. (Pp. 6-7)

In general, researchers have hardly heeded such warnings and have continued to utilize parametric statistical tests (for example, the F test) for the analysis of data from designs which were constructed nonrandomly. Without delving extensively into sampling theory, it can be demonstrated that the mathematical logic underlying the use of most of the sampling distributions of variability (for example, the t or F distributions) requires the assumption of randomly selected samples.

To this point, the major validity problems inherent in quasi-experiments have been briefly overviewed and a limited number of examples have been introduced to clarify these deficiencies. Unlike the other forms of validity, it is not readily apparent that quasi-experiments differ from the true experiment on an external validity criterion. Whichever one of these major types of designs is employed by the researcher, extreme caution is required when assessing the generalizability of an intervention's effectiveness.

There are some isolated forms of quasi-experimental designs, however, which possess design features that are not reflective of many social problem contexts. One such set of designs is the various repeated-measures designs and the treatment-withdrawal-treatment, or A-B-A, designs. In the repeated-measures designs, a group of subjects will serve as their own controls and will receive exposure to a series of interventions over time. Two differing schedules of treatments are generally utilized with these designs. Sometimes treatment order is counterbalanced, although more frequently treatments are presented via randomly determined sequences. While practice effects or "carry-over" effects often plague the internal validity of the complete within-subject designs, external validity concerns also accompany the use of these designs.

First, in most ameliorative community settings persons rarely receive many different and conceptually orthogonal treatments over time. That is, rarely do ex-criminal offenders receive sequentially an employment training program, a college-credit study program, a paraprofessional advocacy program, a half way house experience, and the like. More typically, such interventions are grouped to form a composite or "blanket" form of program which contains, simultaneously, many separate program elements. Second, and related to the first point, even if sequential assignment to programs does occur, rarely does participation in such programs occur on the basis of random sequencing. Instead, there usually exist logical program sequences based on the objective of the overall treatment program. This invariable program order reduces the possibility of randomly determining or counterbalancing program sequences. Without the inclusion of these essential features of within-subject designs, order effects overwhelm the possibility of clearly interpreting the results of these designs. In such cases, it is preferable to conceptually lump differing program elements to form "total programs" of differing intensities. This is accomplished by systematically adding and deleting differing program elements and treatment conditions. Multiclassification factorial design can be used to directly manipulate the presence or absence of various treatment elements. In most cases, such a procedure is likely to more accurately reflect the logistics of most service-providing agencies and to result in greater confidence in the external validity of the experiment.

The Proper Use of Quasi-experimentation in Community Psychology

The primary aim of the preceding section was to comment on the various quasi-experimental designs with regard to their merit as scientifically valid research methodologies. In this section, a set of broader concerns related to the role of quasi-experimentation in community psychology is addressed. In general, it is proposed that quasi-experimental designs should be utilized solely in the province of knowledge-generation and theory-building activities in community psychology. In contrast, the true experiment has superior status as a research methodology for contexts where specific problem-solving interventions are being assessed evaluatively.

To comprehend the above distinction, it is necessary to conceive of the research enterprise in community psychology as comprised of two related activities. Basic community research and product-development research are convenient labels for these activities. Basic community research is concerned with the discovery of orderly relationships between social or environmental variables and community processes, structures, or problems. Product development in community psychology is concerned with harnessing or catalyzing a known relationship between variables through the development, evaluation, and dissemination of a social technology.

As an example of how these scientific activities dovetail, consider the recently demonstrated relationship between the quality of social support networks and positive mental health (Craven & Wellman, 1973; Gottlieb & Todd, 1979). Having established this relationship through basic research, the objective of community psychologists concerned with product development is to use experimentation to design and evaluate a set of alternative social technologies to enhance the formation of these networks. This process would ideally culminate in the wide-scale dissemination of the most effective technologies available for facilitating social support networking in the community.

What the above reasoning implies is that "the choice" between quasi-experimental and true experimental methodologies should be guided by the futuristic consideration of the ultimate objective or purpose of any piece of community research. To arrive at such a prognosis the researcher must consider carefully the relationship of the proposed research to both knowledge generation and product development. When a piece of research contains a product or innovation designed to capitalize on a known relationship between variables for the purpose of creating social change, then it is incumbent upon the researcher to guarantee that the product or social innovation does produce the outcomes anticipated.

It is the contention of this chapter that only the true experiment provides an unambiguous answer to such a question. The primary reason for this position is that the outcomes of product-development research, unlike those of research concerned with establishing theoretical relationships, assume center stage in the policy-formation domain of human welfare. Administrative decisionmakers in schools, governmental organizations, public service agencies, and the like adopt and implement programs or products designed to solve particular social problems. In these contexts, knowledge about a problem, while important, assumes a secondary role in the day-to-day decision making of these organizations and social institutions.

Since ameliorative social technology and innovative social programs will directly affect society, it is essential that the scientist responsible for the evaluation and dissemination of such products understand the likely effectiveness of such programs. As Fairweather (1972) has suggested, the scientist, through the development and evaluation of social technology, is actually privy to and a part of a mammoth program of social change. As the next section of this chapter suggests, participation in this process requires a humanitarian value orientation which prescribes that the scientist place the ultimate welfare of the community before all other aspects of the scientific process.

An important assumption implicit in the above view concerning the role of social-technological developments in community psychology is the assumption that the creation of knowledge about communities and the problems they confront does not have the same direct impact on society that product-development research outcomes have. For example, throughout recent history, philosophers, scientists, educators, and others have debated polemically the nature/nurture bases of human intelligence. The opposing camps on this issue have conducted and marshaled literally thousands of pieces of basic research and the numerous theoretical developments in this area to support their chosen perspective. However, in a policy-formation sense, it is difficult to see the actual social outcomes of these purely scientific activities.

In contrast, what impact will the product-development research which is now ongoing in this area have on social policy? From various news-media accounts, product-development research has now been initiated whose objective is the production of offspring of superior intelligence through the utilization of the sperm of famous Nobel-laureate scientists. It is the view of this chapter that in the majority of cases product-development research (which actualizes hypothesized relationships between variables into products or programs) heavily affects public and social policy.

This belief should not be taken to mean that knowledge creation is unimportant in problem-solving contexts. To the contrary, knowledge generation is an essential first step in any problem-solving endeavor. However, an erroneous or poorly formulated knowledge base, in itself, is not as likely to have as extreme an effect on society as an erroneous decision to implement an ineffective social or technological innovation. That is, the knowledge-generation process tends to be a self-correcting process, whereas the development and widespread dissemination of inappropriate or deleterious social programming tend to be non-self-correcting. The reasons for this undoubtedly have to do with variables and processes which are peculiar to the interpersonal and situational contexts in which each of these scientific activities occurs. Extended to community psychology, basic community researchers, who maximally utilize rational and logical reasoning in the consideration of relevant evidence, tend to accept change more readily in the theoretical marketplace. However, in the province of product development, more varied population groups, who often hold vested and conflicting interests in the continuation of a service-delivery program, are not as amenable to change.

For example, consider the process of psychotherapy. While over time the personality theories which served as the foundation of the therapeutic process have changed markedly, the basic parameters characterizing the ecology of the psychotherapeutic process have not changed appreciably. This maintenance of the status quo has occurred in spite of the growing evidence which questions the value of psychotherapy in many differing problem-solving contexts (Cowen, 1973; Sarason, 1974). Yet, because of variables (for example, status, professional roles, and monetary power) exogenous to the actual knowledge that psychotherapy as a product or innovation may be ineffective for many applications, its widespread use persists.

There is a second reason why knowledge acquisition will rarely have the same impact on society as do products or social technologies developed to ameliorate community problems. When a set of conceptual relationships is eventually developed into a product and evaluated, this process serves as a society's "second line of defense" against the widespread dissemination of erroneous knowledge or theory. Throughout this chapter it has been advocated that product development in community psychology should proceed initially on a small scale. Cursory but well-designed experiments such as these would provide the opportunity for technologies to be evaluated before their widespread dissemination. However, it is through such experimental tests that basic research knowledge can be reassessed for its validity. If an optimum combination of programming components which, according to theory, should produce an effect on some outcome does not do so, then such data can alert researchers to the possibility that a finding emanating from basic research is not reliable or generalizable. The lack of success of innovative programs, then, can provoke a reexamination of the alleged relationship between variables established through basic research.

In sum, the distinction between basic community research and the development of innovative social products has implications for the choice of methodology when planning a community research program.   Research oriented toward the establishment of basic relationships between social problems, community structures, community processes, and the like should be less constrained with respect to a choice in methodology than research concerned with innovative program development.   Since the latter type of research could ultimately serve as the foundation for social change, there is much less flexibility in product-development activities.   As a result, true experimentation (given the present level of development of quasi-experimental techniques) is the optimum choice for the latter type of research.   This view is strengthened in the next section of the chapter, which outlines a value system and research paradigm which more explicitly justifies the above prescription.

EXPERIMENTAL SOCIAL INNOVATION: A MODEL
FOR COMMUNITY PSYCHOLOGY RESEARCH

The 1967 volume Methods for Experimental Social Innovation, authored by George W. Fairweather, represents the landmark work in the formation and development of the experimental social innovation research and training model. Followed by a revised edition of the book by Fairweather and Louis G. Tornatzky in 1977, and by several shorter journal articles (for example, Shippee, 1979; Tornatzky, Fairweather, & O'Kelly, 1970; Tornatzky, 1976), the experimental social innovation model has continued to provide a philosophical foundation and methodological paradigm for the conduct of community psychological and social policy research.   The model provides a concise and cogent research paradigm.   The value of the model lies in its breadth as a guide for the formation of ethical values. In this section, the value orientation characteristic of the experimental social innovator is presented.   A description of the experimental social innovation research model follows.

The Values of the Experimental Social Innovator

The most critical value orientation held by the experimental social innovator is a deep-rooted humanitarian concern for the social and biological welfare of human beings. More specifically, the experimental social innovator is committed to improving the quality of human existence through the design of innovative solutions to contemporary and future human problems. Included in this orientation are the creation, assessment, and dissemination of preventative and problem-oriented social and ecological models. It is these day-to-day activities (design and implementation of alternative models, for example), in turn, which serve as the sequential phases of the experimental social innovation research model.

A humanitarian concern for people also carries with it several other value orientations which guide and flavor community research activities. First among these is the notion that alternative social and ecological models have to be innovative and not constrained by traditional academic boundaries. The severity of most social and environmental problems renders them particularly resistant to traditional or paradigmatic forms of solution imposed by the traditional disciplinary approaches and status quo systems of problem amelioration. Innovation flourishes in a multidisciplinary atmosphere where the contributions of all disciplines can be adapted, synthesized, combined, or integrated to assist in the formulation of alternative social and ecological models. The experimental social innovator approaches all problem areas with this multidisciplinary perspective to maximize the potential for the creation of truly innovative models. Theory, research methods, and service perspectives from psychology, sociology, urban planning, economics, anthropology, human ecology, health, education, social work, and communication are only a few of the resources relevant to contemporary human problems.

Four additional and interrelated value positions also stem from the humanitarian value orientation characteristic of the experimental social innovator. Innovative models should be problem relevant, usable, action oriented, and based on democratic participation. Each of these perspectives is considered in turn.

Problem Relevant

Too often the research and theories generated by psychologists (including even some of the work of community psychologists) have not been directly relevant to human and environmental problems. To many scientists this type of basic research and theorizing is essential, since it reflects the popular credo, Knowledge for knowledge's sake. Yet given the severity of the ecological, social, and economic maladies which currently characterize the human condition, it is doubtful that psychologists have the luxury any more of generating, ruminating over, or empirically testing irrelevant theoretical perspectives which are not directly applicable to human-problem contexts or to efforts to improve the quality of human existence.

This nation confronts serious social and ecological dilemmas which will severely challenge our problem-solving abilities. Urban blight, energy availability, child abuse and neglect, the humiliation experienced by welfare recipients and the elderly, unemployment, less than successful (and in some cases backsliding) affirmative action programs, crime and delinquency, the possible environmental consequences of a nuclear-powered society, all are problem areas which require the full and immediate, and not the distant and peripheral, attention of social scientists, particularly community psychologists. Further, as these problems indicate, the training of community psychologists cannot continue to remain exclusively mental health oriented. Community psychologists have a unique set of conceptual and methodological skills which are applicable to a broader range of social problems than those currently in vogue, including environmental problems. In short, without regard to specific problem areas, the experimental social innovator's activities are totally oriented to problem-relevant researches.

Usable

It often occurs that knowledge and programs generated by community psychologists which are problem relevant are, nevertheless, neither feasible nor implementable in the community. It is the responsibility of the experimental social innovator to ensure that social innovations provide usable solutions in contemporary and future problem areas. This is not to say that innovative programs have to be easily implementable with respect to organizational or political considerations. In fact, many creative social innovations which are extremely effective in solving a particular problem are not favorably received by service personnel or administrators of potentially adopting agencies and organizations. The community lodge developed by Fairweather and his associates (1969) clearly demonstrates that effective innovations may be highly usable (at the ease-of-implementation level), but receive little support in terms of organizational support or enthusiasm. In cases like the community lodge, where extremely favorable outcomes characterize the innovation, this circumstance compels the researcher to advocate its use for the benefit of the problem population for which it was intended, despite political sources of resistance which may emerge in agencies.

In short, the usability criterion of an innovation refers to its logistical ease and practicality with regard to local organizational staff and facilities and not the political receptivity of an organization to its use.

Action Oriented

A cornerstone of experimental social innovation is the notion that the scientist should function as an activist in the community on behalf of positive social change. In particular, this action orientation should be translated into the experimental manipulation of social processes and ecological settings, rather than the passive measurement or modeling of the status quo. Much of what occurs under the guise of community psychology is simply the passive assessment of societal conditions through the use of survey techniques or other highly sophisticated statistical procedures (for example, path analysis, regression designs, and causal modeling) and observational methods. While these types of researches serve a purpose for the experimental social innovator as the precursors of innovation, the primary research activity of the experimental social innovator is the active creation of alternative social models, ecological settings, or organizational contexts. In blunt terms, the experimental social innovator actively and experimentally manipulates social variables and processes for the purpose of discovering more effective solutions to social and environmental problems. These types of researches are pursued at the expense of engaging solely in passive, observational investigations of community phenomena and community processes.

Democratic Participation

From the above section it could be assumed that the experimental social innovator manipulates variables in the community at will. This assumption is erroneous. The experimental social innovator must actively encourage and solicit, through the democratic participation of professionals, lay persons, and problem population representatives, the involvement and input of all concerned persons in the community prior to the conduct of a research. A high level of democratic participation in the design and implementation of innovative social and ecological models is absolutely essential from the standpoint of determining informed opinions concerning the models likely to be most effective in problem solution and the context-specific barriers which might impede the implementation of experimental models. As was noted in a previous section, these arrangements are established through the pursuit of a trusting and collaborative relationship with community agencies and through the formation of administrative agreements with these groups.

The high level of humanitarian concern embraced by the experimental social innovator is also dependent upon two additional value orientations, scientific accountability and scientific rigor in evaluation.

Scientific Accountability

In many ways scientific accountability can be viewed as an umbrella term which encompasses the values of problem relevance, usability, action-oriented research, and democratic participation. However, in addition to these connotations, the term scientific accountability also implies the notion of the scientist being accountable or responsible for the appropriate utilization of the knowledge or products which result from the scientist's research. The experimental social innovator believes that scientists are responsible for the dissemination of their innovations to the using populations of society. Many scientists believe that product or program utilization automatically occurs following the publication of results. In point of fact, much of the evidence available suggests that written publication is an extremely ineffective means of disseminating problem-solving innovations (Havelock, 1969; Fairweather, 1972; Fairweather, Sanders, & Tornatzky, 1974; Fairweather & Tornatzky, 1977). To ensure the dissemination of innovations, it is necessary for the scientist to adopt the role of advocate for an innovation. In this role, the scientist actively pursues opportunities where the innovation might be adopted. An advocacy posture, however, does not mean that the scientist must abort scientific methodology. To the contrary, an experimental approach to innovation dissemination is called for. That is, in order to determine effective dissemination strategies, as well as to firmly establish the organizational parameters which facilitate or impede the adoption of innovations, it is necessary to experimentally validate dissemination principles. Furthermore, this validation process must be continuous in nature, since differing approaches are likely to be necessary for differing social innovations in differing community organizations. A concrete example of how empirical dissemination research can be integrated with an advocacy posture is presented later in this chapter.

Scientific Rigor in Evaluation

Another critical value held by the experimental social innovator logically follows from the philosophical position of scientific accountability. Given a belief in the necessity for an active approach to dissemination, it follows that when juxtaposed with an overriding humanitarian concern, experimental social innovators have to be extremely confident of the effectiveness of the programs or models which they are attempting to disseminate. With respect to the highly sophisticated (and enticing) methodological technologies available in the social scenes presently, the true experiment, as was argued earlier, still remains the only sure methodological technique available for determining the validity of a program or intervention. While even true experiments can lead the researcher to an erroneous conclusion concerning the effectiveness of an intervention (for example, Lakatos, 1970; Mahoney, 1978), they can, given suitable replication, minimize the errors associated with the causal-inference process.

It is essential to minimize errors of causal inference in the evaluation of social models because the dissemination of models discovered to enhance societal quality usually proceeds on as broad a scale (even nationally) as is possible to mount. In the case of the community lodge, the dissemination effort has spanned a ten-year period and has been of national scope (Fairweather, Sanders, & Tornatzky, 1974; Tornatzky, Fairweather, Fergus, & Avellar, in press). To have initiated such a dissemination effort with an innovation which affected marginal outcomes, or to disseminate an innovation whose benefits were demonstrated solely through the use of quasi-experimental techniques, involves the adoption of an unacceptably high degree of possible error (in terms of program outcomes). In terms of economic considerations, the expenditure of huge sums of money for the dissemination of an ineffective program, in the long term, means that these monies are not available for further efforts at innovative program development. It is for these reasons, then, that the true experiment is the primary methodological paradigm for the experimental social innovator. Through its use, the community psychologist does not have to compromise on methodological quality or on causal-inference prowess.

The marriage between humanitarian concern and methodological rigor which the experimental social innovation model has attempted to consummate also has implications for other methodological and statistical practices. First, the experimental social innovator chooses those statistical procedures which are most conservative with respect to identifying statistically significant differences. That is, statistical procedures which artificially inflate alpha (the probability that a statistically significant effect is present) are avoided, since a rejection of the null hypothesis, in statistical terms, implies a successful model for dissemination. Failures to reject the null hypothesis, however, are equally informative, since they imply that additional research and development with the innovative program will be necessary before it can be disseminated.

In sum, this section has portrayed the array of value orientations which characterizes the philosophy of experimental social innovation. These values can be viewed as a "philosophical guidance system" which governs the research and professional activities of the experimental social innovator. The actual experimental social innovation research paradigm is presented in the next section.

The Experimental Social Innovation
Research Paradigm

The experimental social innovation research model is a six-step model which guides the research activities of the experimental social innovator. The list below identifies each phase of the model, described here in detail.

1. Define Problem.
2. Design Innovative Model.
3. Create Experimental Design.

4. Implement Models.
5. Evaluate Models.
6. Disseminate Models.

Problem Definition

The beginning step in the experimental social innovation process is the definition of a significant social or environmental problem. Occasionally, it is the life experience of the experimental social innovator which leads to the initial contact with a particular social or environmental problem. Other researchers are attracted to a problem area through vicarious exposure to the problem via the literature or the mass media. Following an initial exposure, the experimental social innovator embarks on a multidisciplinary problem-definition process which results in the identification of the important variables, processes, and parameters characteristic of the problem.

One source of information concerning a particular social or environmental problem is the literature which has been devoted to it. An interdisciplinary review of the literature often results in the collection of knowledge and/or observations which lead to the development of the conceptual framework underlying a potential intervention. For example, the author's work in the energy conservation area was firmly grounded on principles established through prior research in the energy-behavior area (Shippee, 1980; in press). This research examined the effectiveness of an innovative community awareness campaign for reducing energy consumption among commercial energy users.

A second resource necessary for the design of innovative community interventions is acquired through the use of participant-observation methods to determine the day-to-day manifestations of problems in the actual community contexts in which they occur. In particular, the researcher should be concerned with assessing the nature of the problem from the perspective of those persons experiencing the problem. A participant-observation methodology can also be productively employed with respect to obtaining the perspective of those professionals who have direct contact with problem areas and who are in a position to contribute insightfully into long-range planning processes in a particular area.

Finally, the comprehensiveness of problem-definition activities can be enhanced through the use of more formal survey instruments or program follow-up activities. For example, in the areas in which human services are directly provided to ameliorate human problems, a post hoc follow-up of treatment participants may reveal several areas in which a particular program is deficient. With the acquisition of such data, supplementary innovative programming can be directed toward solving certain deficiencies. A needs-assessment strategy (Siegel, Atkisson, & Cohn, 1974); Warheit, Bell, & Schwab, 1977) can also be used as a more general method for problem identification in the community. Particular needs-assessment methods such as interviews with professionals and other key informants in the community, community forums, and the analysis of demographic data can often lead to the discovery of problem parameters and to innovative ideas for interventions.

More formal quasi-experimental methodologies can also be employed in the problem-definition phase. For example, the participant data available within community agencies dealing with a problem may help to identify relevant and promising problem solutions. Statistical techniques such as discriminant analyses and multiple regression can be extremely helpful at this stage. In short, quasi-experimental technology can be of considerable benefit in gaining an understanding of the important parameters and/or causal antecedents of social and ecological problems during problem-definition activities.

Designing Innovative Social and Ecological Models

The problem-definition phase should yield the identification of a meaningful target population which is experiencing a problem, an in-depth understanding of the problem from the standpoint of both the population affected and professionals who deal with it, an understanding of the present efforts which exist in the community for ameliorating the problem, and a set of ideas concerning its core causes.

Armed with this knowledge, the experimental social innovator attempts to devise an effective ameliorative intervention or set of interventions. Typically, the creation of these interventions occurs in a collaborative atmosphere where the researcher and field personnel cooperatively design the program elements to be included in a set of alternative interventions. The community lodge example to be described below exemplifies this collaborative process and the synthesis of observations and information required for the creation of effective community interventions.

It is common at this stage of the process for the researcher to pilot test differing innovations. At this preliminary point, the experimental social innovator could select a suitable quasi-experimental design to obtain a global picture of the likely success of various innovations. For example, the researcher might implement an experimental program in the context of a time-series design with a small group of participants. The nonequivalent group designs might also be productively utilized at this point to pilot test an innovative program and thereby determine its feasibility. Beck (1975), for example, utilized such a design to assess the effects and feasibility of a health consumer participation training program prior to its assessment in a true experiment. Utilizing nonrandomly selected samples of intact volunteer groups, she was able to demonstrate increases in perceived competence and a sense of decision-making power in the training groups when contrasted to an intact control group. The program-design phase of the experimental social innovation model, much like the problem-definition phase of the model, provides a suitable context for the application of quasi-experimental methodology.

Creating an Experimental Design

The design and/or pilot testing of a set of innovative programs is followed by translating them into a true experimental design. However, the design of true experiments has to be tempered with the logistical constraints imposed by community settings and organizational contexts. Constantly shifting particulars of an experimental design, such as the unit of analysis, number of treatment recipients, number and type of cooperating agencies, and so forth, quite frequently demands constant revisions in the experimental design itself or in the nature of the interventions being experimentally assessed. Funding constraints can also alter the nature of the experimental design.

Despite these logistical and organizational forces which often force modifications in the experimental design, there do exist some stable principles of design which the experimental social innovator will rarely compromise. First, experiments should be longitudinal in nature, sometimes running for periods as long as one to two years, depending upon the particular intervention being assessed. The primary reason for advocating longitudinal experiments is that intervention strategies can sometimes produce outcomes very late in the experiment, or interventions can have immediate effects which dissipate over time. A longitudinal experiment provides the researcher with data concerning time trends and can also provide detailed information regarding the possibility of time-x-treatment interactions. Time-x-treatment interactions can have important implications for the design of innovative community programs. For example, one intervention or social model may be more effective than another in the short term, whereas the intervention not especially effective over the short term will be more effective in the long term. Such a pattern of results can be extremely useful for the innovator, since it suggests the possibility of combining the interventions in the future for optimal impact.

The second major principle governing the experimental design process concerns the construction and use of outcome and process instruments. In the case of outcome measures, it is essential that a variety of outcome measures be included in the overall experimental plan. Behavioral, cognitive, attitudinal, affective, and unobtrusive indexes of outcomes should accompany the design of field experiments. In addition to outcome measures, the potential processes which might mediate the effectiveness of an intervention should also be assessed. Behavior, perceptions, and social processes which covary with effective interventions can often clarify the whys of an intervention's effectiveness and help in the development of new innovative models.

Finally, much recent theorizing has suggested that effective social interventions are likely to have effects at multiple levels of social and community functioning (for example, Rappaport, 1977; Seidman, 1976). This concept suggests that in addition to measuring change which is likely to occur among the primary targets of an intervention, it is also important to measure concurrently potential changes at other levels of community functioning. That is, while an intervention may be focused on behavior at one level of analysis (for example, the individual level), interventions can also influence other levels of the community (small groups, organizations, or political processes). Measures of the multiple effects of interventions should be included in all experimental comparisons of social models in order that these effects might be identified. Much like social-process measures, these measures can often provide the conceptual framework for new and creative social innovations.

Implementation of Innovative Models

Implementing innovative social and environmental interventions in community settings for evaluation purposes entails the performance of several related activities which have been addressed to a considerable extent in the previous sections of this chapter. As indicated earlier, the foundation of true community experimentation lies in administrative agreements established by the researcher with cooperating community organizations and their personnel.

Innovative Models, Experimental Design,
and Implementation

All the phases outlined above are extremely interactive and dynamic in a systems sense. Often, a change in an implementation activity will necessitate a change in the experimental design or in the nature of the models being evaluated. It is this systems-like dependence between the phases of the experimental social innovation model which demands long-term planning and extensive pre-experimental preparation. Even with a maximally effective planning effort, however, contingencies may force experimentalists to modify their social models, the experimental design, or both. For example, a set of innovations can be devised, an experimental design formulated, and administrative agreements established, only to have the entire project not receive the funding necessary for completion.

Alternatively, funding for a project will materialize, but a set of institutional agreements will break down, thereby changing the nature and/or the number of innovative models that can be assessed in the experimental design. For example, in a study with three innovative models, with six agencies assigned to the models, a loss of two or three agencies might compel the experimentalist to combine two of the innovative models. In this case, a two-model experimental design would result.

What the above examples should convey is that the creation, design, and implementation of social and ecological models is a process which is continuously "in flux," and in the initial stages of planning and implementation, any number of contingencies can arise, thereby changing the products generated in the other phases.[4]

Evaluation and Dissemination
of Innovative Models

The scope of this chapter prohibits any detailed
analysis of the evaluation and dissemination procedures
which the experimental social innovator utilizes to comparatively evaluate innovative models (such discussions are
well described in Fairweather and Tornatzky, 1977). In
general, the experimental social innovator contrasts the
outcomes of the alternative models in the experimental design utilizing inferential statistical methods and multivariate correlative procedures to discover relationships between
outcomes and social processes. If an effective social or
ecological model results from the experiment, it is necessary
for the socially responsible researcher to actively prolif-
erate the effective innovation through the use of various
dissemination strategies.

At the level of organizations, very little is known
about the innovation adoption process or the organizational
parameters which facilitate or impede social innovation.
Most of the social scientific knowledge of innovation dissemination has been generated via case history methodologies. Consequently, very few empirically validated principles of dissemination are available in the literature (Berman & McLaughlin, 1978; Havelock, 1969; Rogers & Shoemaker, 1971; Yin, Quick, Bateman, & Marks, 1978; Zaltman
& Duncan, 1977).

The paucity of knowledge concerning the dissemination of innovations compels the experimental social innovator to experimentally assess alternative dissemination
strategies. Additionally, the experimental analysis of alternative dissemination techniques provides the experimental
social innovator with immediate feedback concerning the
effectiveness of his or her activities. Finally, the necessity for a continuous experimental program of dissemination
research is highlighted when the variability that characterizes social innovations and the organizations which are
potential adopters of various innovations is acknowledged.
Social service organizations are likely to differ on several
criteria including personnel's training and background,
size, structure, formality, openness, communication patterns, decision-making processes, and the like.

Given this diversity, it is important to determine if
these organizational parameters are related in any systematic fashion, across social innovations, to the innovation

adoption process. It is also important to determine if the introduction of differing innovations interacts with organizational or personnel characteristics to maximize or obstruct innovation adoption.

When questions such as these are addressed experimentally, dissemination principles result which can then be utilized to provide a rough format for other dissemination efforts. Further, as noted earlier, the experimental method provides the experimental social innovator with an important source of feedback concerning nonpersuasible organizations. Those organizations that do not adopt a particular innovation can be reused or "recycled" in the next dissemination effort. Such an effort might assess a new set of approach and persuasion strategies. Dissemination is a never-ending research process, until such time as a majority of organizations have adopted a demonstrably effective treatment program.

To summarize, the experimental social innovation research model, with its accompanying value orientation, provides a set of guiding philosophical principles and a systematic but flexible paradigm. In the section that follows, a working example of the experimental social innovation process is presented along with integrative commentary which demonstrates the value orientations of the experimental social innovator, as well as the methodological phases of the experimental social innovation research paradigm.

THE COMMUNITY LODGE: A WORKING EXAMPLE OF
EXPERIMENTAL SOCIAL INNOVATION

Over the last three decades, the empirical research with the community lodge conducted by George W. Fairweather and his colleagues exemplifies the experimental social innovator's approach to community psychology research. In the late 1950s Fairweather became interested in the problems posed by the long-term and destructive hospitalization periods endured by the mentally ill. Because of his direct exposure to the chronically mentally ill, Fairweather became acutely concerned about the excessive length of hospitalization for those admitted to mental hospitals. Related to this problem was the "revolving door syndrome" which accompanied institutionalization. Survey evidence from multiple follow-up survey investigations suggested that nearly 75% of those persons released from the hospital would ultimately return to the hospital within 18 months of their time of discharge. With respect to the length of hospitalization, only a minimal proportion of those persons hospitalized for periods of greater than one year were ever released into the community (Fairweather, Sanders, Maynard, & Cressler, 1969).

With this skeletal evidence serving as a set of defining parameters, Fairweather went on to further elucidate the problem of chronic hospitalization through the conduct of quasi-experiments and a subsequent true experiment (Lindemann, Fairweather, Stone, & Smith, 1959; Fairweather & Simon, 1963; Fairweather et al., 1960; Forsyth & Fairweather, 1961). The quasi-experiments attempted to elucidate the important characteristics of those persons whose periods of hospitalization were excessive. The true experiment conducted by Fairweather and his associates (1960) attempted to determine the efficacy of traditional approaches utilized to prepare chronic persons for a positive adjustment to the community. The specific questions addressed by this work were these:

1. Are any of the traditional approaches to treatment more effective than others in bringing about discharge and positive adjustment in the community?
2. Did persons with differing diagnoses respond differentially to the various approaches to treatment?
3. What relationship existed between various outcome criteria traditionally utilized to assess patient's community adjustment?

As can be seen, the primary objective of this early work of Fairweather and his colleagues was to further clarify and refine the nature of recidivism and excessive periods of hospitalization as mental health problems. Further, this early research was evaluative in nature, since various traditional methods employed to ameliorate these problems were subjected to a comparative evaluation in the context of a true experiment.

The true experiment contrasted individual psychotherapy, group psychotherapy, group living, and a work-only treatment as alternative therapeutic approaches. This experiment demonstrated that these, then popular, approaches did not differ in effectiveness, and further, that the provision of therapy of any type did little to improve

upon the levels of adjustment exhibited by work-only patients. With respect to patients possessing differing diagnostic labels, 72.4% of those persons considered chronic
returned to the hospital from the community within 18
months. Neurotics failed at a 55.6% rate and acute psy-
chotics exhibited a 29% return rate by 18 months. Finally,
in terms of the relationships between outcome measures,
several results emerged which were of considerable methodological significance. First, the outcome measures traditionally utilized to assess adjustment were uncorrelated with
each other (for example, the Minnesota Multiphasic Personality Inventory, ward-behavior ratings, self-concept measures, and various projective techniques). More important,
these measures were uncorrelated with indexes of community
adjustment such as employment, desirable family relationships, and the like.

These results suggested to Fairweather that since
traditional treatment methods were not differentially effective in enhancing the community adjustment of the mentally
ill, it was necessary to innovate new programs, or social
models, designed to improve the probability that chronic
patients would make a positive and lasting adjustment in
the community. The research also served to further de-
lineate the critical target population for future interventions. The results of the work clearly indicated that the
chronic patient groups were those persons most in need of
an innovative approach to treatment. Methodologically, the
work also suggested that any innovative treatment program
had to be assessed multivariately, since most in-hospital
outcome measures were uncorrelated, and further, such measures were not correlated with indexes of community adjustment.

With these data providing a backdrop for problem-
solving activities, an innovative treatment began to take
shape. Informal observations by Fairweather and his colleagues suggested that the most critical period for the
successful adjustment of the chronic patient occurred during the first few days of autonomous community living.
The notion that a support group comprised of patients
could provide mutual support for their changed lifestyles
began to dominate the thinking of Fairweather and his colleagues. To further elucidate the potential effectiveness
of such an approach, a series of investigations was conducted to determine the feasibility of forming such groups
with chronic patients and the extent to which such groups

would actually improve the adjustment of the mentally ill person upon the person's release into the community. Along with addressing these questions, these investigations also represented an attempt to formatively isolate the group structure and group processes necessary for the success of the small-group model (Scriven, 1967; Suchman, 1967).

Lerner and Fairweather (1963) began this process by assessing the level of autonomy which should optimally characterize the small groups of patients. In a completely randomized two-group design, Lerner and Fairweather varied the presence or absence of hospital staff as leaders of the small-patient groups' activities. This initial study demonstrated that the small-group concept was feasible, and, in addition, the study also revealed that the level of support or cohesiveness generated in such groups (a characteristic essential for community adjustment) developed more freely and fully in groups provided with minimal staff supervision.

Fairweather (1964) extended this work by conducting a second randomized experiment whereby the work-only treatment condition examined earlier (Fairweather et al., 1960) was comparatively contrasted to the small-group treatment model. This small-group treatment research can be viewed as a second piece of formative evaluation (Scriven, 1967), since the necessary ingredients for the success of patient groups (for example, their structure and reward system), to that point, had been based entirely on the researchers' collective intuition. The innovative small-group ward model devised by Fairweather attempted to maximize autonomous patient decision making at the expense of staff-dominated decision making. This form of autonomous decision making was encouraged by training the ward staff to serve solely as information resources for patient decision making. Ward staff, in turn, attempted to facilitate actual patient decision making concerning various phases of patients' lives on the ward. The reward structure of the group was such that the staff provided encouragement and social reinforcement for rational responses, group contributions, and practical group decisions, but the staff negatively reinforced impractical and irrational group decisions and individual contributions.

The results of this longitudinal study, when combined with the earlier work, suggested that the formation and maintenance of small groups of chronic patients were feasible and logistically operational. Further, the small-group ward program, relative to controls, produced superior within-hospital adjustment levels, social interactions of enhanced quality, and more positive staff and patient expectancies and satisfaction levels. However, when indexes of community adjustment (for example, recidivism, employment, quality of social relationships, and so forth) were examined, differences between the treatments disappeared. This result led Fairweather and his associates to perceive the need for transferring the small-group innovation into the community, since it appeared that positive community adjustment was totally dependent on the maintenance of the small-group structure (and the support it provided) immediately following release.

This awareness, along with some additional sociological notions concerning social labeling, social roles, and social status, led Fairweather and his colleagues to design the community lodge society. That is, informal observation and more formal follow-up data led Fairweather to the conclusion that simple social support might not be sufficient by itself as a mechanism for reducing recidivism and optimizing patients' posthospitalization adjustment. In Fairweather's view, a stronger intervention was necessary which would function to improve not only patients' cognitive appraisal of themselves or their progress in the community but, in addition, more tangible aspects of the patient's life such as bolstering patients' social status or social position in the community. The community lodge society, then, was built on a broad conceptual framework which included these notions of the patient's role and status in the community.

The community lodge treatment program emerged as the culmination of a longitudinal, systematic, and formative research process whereby empirical evidence gleaned from quasi-experiments and true experiments, professional opinion, problem-population participation, and an interdisciplinary view of community life were synthesized into the formation of the community lodge intervention. Once designed, the lodge was subjected to a true experimental test where it was comparatively evaluated with the within-hospital small-group treatment program originally designed by Fairweather (1964; Fairweather et al., 1969). The actual implementation of the community lodge was characterized by a myriad of administrative agreements between organizations with which Fairweather was affiliated (Stanford University, the Veterans Administration hospital in Palo

Alto, the National Institute of Mental Health, and a small nonprofit corporation formed to coordinate the employment of lodge members).[5]

The lodge was designed to be a small, autonomous, self-governing society of chronic ex-patients living in the community. An old motel was leased for the group to reside in and a small gardening-janitorial business was established as an employment opportunity for patients. Staff involvement in the operational functioning of the lodge was minimized, with only one staff member being on 24-hour per day call to the lodge.

Multiple outcome and process measures were included in the experimental design for the research. Anticipating Rappaport's notion of multiple intervention levels (1977), Fairweather and his associates determined that neighborhood attitudes toward the lodge improved over the four-year period of the lodge's existence. Lodge participants' levels of satisfaction with the lodge also improved over time. In terms of other outcome measures, the lodge society produced superior outcomes to those obtained in the "traditional" small-group ward condition. Lodge members showed a significantly reduced recidivism rate and an increased employment rate compared to their traditional ward counterparts. In terms of a cost-benefit analysis, the lodge program was one-third as expensive as traditional hospitalization.

With respect to social processes (which are covered comprehensively and entertainingly in Fairweather et al., 1969), several differences characterized the lodge and hospital treatment groups. Patients in each experimental group were administered social-process measures each 90 days over the duration of the experiment. These measures included indexes of group cohesiveness, morale, attraction, satisfaction with group leadership, perceived group acceptance, and group performance measures. In both the lodge and in-hospital groups, cluster analyses revealed that performance was related to group cohesiveness and attraction to the group. However, in the lodge, the development of strong indigenous leadership came to play an increasingly important role over time, whereas with in-hospital groups, emergent patient leadership bore little relationship to group performance. What this finding suggests is that the role of the professional staff in the case of the chronically ill is an assumable role for emergent patient leaders when in small groups.

The above research conducted by Fairweather exemplifies several important characteristics of the experimental social innovation research model and value system. First, the devotion of nearly 20 years to the discovery and ultimate utilization of the small-group principles by Fairweather demonstrated an unwavering humanitarian commitment to the problems associated with the hospitalization and treatment of the chronically mentally ill. The community lodge represented the asymptote of participative planning, organizational coordination and collaboration, and formative evaluation of differing innovative models through the utilization of quasi-experimental and true experimental research methods. This policy-relevant research was also conducted with an interdisciplinary flavor, since the sociological concepts of role, status, and community organization were ultimately made operational and integrated with the community lodge innovation. The lodge innovation, however, was above all a problem-oriented application of scientific methods for the purpose of first identifying and then deriving valid solutions to the problems posed by chronic hospitalization. The resultant product of this research was a usable program, demonstrated to be effective as a mental health innovation through an experimental, action-oriented research program.

The research with the community lodge represents only the initial portion of the experimental social innovation research model and value system formulated by Fairweather (1967). What is absent is that portion of the model which prescribes a change agent-advocate role for the experimental social innovator. The experimental social innovator's role as an advocate of social change stems from the innovator's attempts to actively disseminate an innovation discovered to be an effective solution to a social problem. As was noted in a previous section, the experimental social innovator cannot be truly socially responsible and concerned about the alleviation of human problems if an innovation is not utilized to the benefit of humankind. The experimental assessment and rigorous evaluation of social and environmental innovations, then, is only an essential first step in the experimental social innovation process.

The dissemination effort conducted with the community lodge was initiated by Fairweather and his colleagues in 1969. An analysis of the traditional community-wide organizational structure of professional mental health services suggested that a national sample of mental institutions should serve as the primary targets for the dissemination of the community lodge. Following a rudimentary conceptualization of the innovation dissemination process outlined by Rogers (1962), Fairweather, Sanders, and Tornatzky (1974) conceived of the innovation dissemination process as a four-stage, sequential process. The first stage of the process was the approach phase, whereby an organization is initially contacted by the dissemination agent. This phase typically involves the presentation of information about the innovation or social technology. The second phase of the process is the persuasion phase. In this phase the dissemination agent attempts to "unfreeze" the organization for the purpose of convincing the organization to attempt to adopt the innovative program (for example, Lewin, 1947). The activation phase involves an attempt on the part of an outside change agent to try to induce movement within the organization from a verbal commitment to adopt the innovation to the actual emission of innovation implementation behaviors. Finally, the fourth phase of the innovation dissemination process is the diffusion phase whereby organizations that have adopted an innovation are encouraged by the outside change agent to disseminate it to other organizations that might be potential adopters.

The first national dissemination experiment initially assessed the effects of three approach-persuasion techniques on the adoption of the community lodge by mental institutions (Fairweather, Sanders, & Tornatzky, 1974). Two hundred and fifty-five mental hospitals were randomly assigned to one of three approach-persuasion strategies. These methods included a brochure condition, a face-to-face workshop condition, and an innovation demonstration condition. Completely crossed with this variable in a factorial design was a factor which varied the status of the professional staff person initially approached about the lodge innovation within the organization. Various administrative and service personnel within the mental hospitals were ranked into a status hierarchy which included the hospital superintendent, psychiatrists, psychologists, social workers, and nurses, respectively. A person of a status corresponding to these positions was initially contacted at hospitals which were randomly assigned to one of these status of initial contact conditions. Two other blocking variables assessed in the approach-persuasion phase design were type of hospitals (state or federal) and the hospital's geographic location (rural or urban). The primary dependent variable was a verbal commitment to proceed with lodge adoption or a verbal report that the organization was not interested in pursuing the lodge innovation. Measures of hospital decision processes, communication processes, and organizational members' assessments of the lodge innovation were also collected and analyzed correlatively.

The results of this first dissemination experiment indicated that while a passive strategy (sending a written brochure) yielded the highest level of initial interest, later adoption of the lodge most frequently occurred in those organizations that agreed to house a pilot lodge demonstration ward in their hospitals. More interestingly, the status of the initial contact person within organizations bore little relationship to the rates of ultimate lodge adoption. Geographic location and type of hospital also did not affect decisions to attempt to adopt the lodge. The former finding is extremely important, for it suggests that organizational change and the introduction of social innovations can be initiated at any level of an organizational hierarchy.

The second experiment conducted by Fairweather, Sanders, and Tornatzky (1974) corresponded to the activation phase of the innovation dissemination process. Those hospitals (N = 25) that were successfully persuaded to make a verbal commitment to attempt to adopt the lodge were randomly assigned to an active consultation or to a passive consultation condition. In the latter condition, only a written set of implementation manuals was sent to the hospitals. In the active consultation condition, an outside change agent actively assisted and consulted with the hospitals in various stages of the lodge adoption process. The results of this experiment demonstrated that continuous, active consultation with an outside consultant-advocate was essential for the ultimate adoption of the community lodge.

The second major lodge dissemination project was initiated by Fairweather and his colleagues in 1974 and attempted to experimentally assess several of the correlative findings discovered in the first set of dissemination experiments (Tornatzky, Fairweather, Fergus, and Avellar, in press). One set of correlative outcomes obtained in the initial studies suggested that the adoption of the lodge was positively related to high levels of democratic, participative decision making by persons holding many different roles and statuses within the hospital organizations. To assess this relationship experimentally, a two–by–two–by–three factorial experiment was designed to correspond to the persuasion phase of the approach–diffusion dissemination model.

Utilizing the insight gained from the first lodge dissemination research, all institutions ($\underline{N}$ = 108 nonadopting hospitals from the first lodge dissemination research) were first approached utilizing a combined passive–active (brochure–workshop) approach sequence. Following the approach phase of the experiment, hospitals were requested to involve either many or few persons in the decision to attempt lodge adoption. Hospitals were also requested either to enhance the typical amount of staff discussion and interaction in organizational decision making or to leave unaltered the extant decision-making processes in hospitals. Finally, the composition of the decision-making groups in each hospital responsible for organizational change decisions (such as lodge adoption) was varied. For two–thirds of the hospitals homogeneous groups composed of treatment staff or hospital administrators were requested to participate in adoption decision making. In the remaining one-third of the hospitals, a heterogeneous group composed of both administrators and staff participated in the lodge adoption decision.

Among the various effects to emerge from this study, the most important was the experimental validation of the earlier correlative finding concerning the composition of groups charged with lodge adoption decision making (Tornatzky, Fairweather, Fergus, & Avellar, in press). This study indicated that to ensure movement toward lodge adoption it was necessary to involve in decision making those persons whose roles were such that they were closest to the day-to-day provision of services to patients. Specifically, hospitals were more likely to be amenable to lodge adoption if treatment staff or both treatment staff and administrators were involved in the lodge decision-making process. An affirmative lodge decision was most unlikely when only hospital administrators were allowed to participate in the adoption decision.

The second experiment of the second major lodge dissemination project extended the activation–phase experiment of the first lodge dissemination project. In this study (conducted with hospitals that were successfully persuaded to begin actual lodge implementation activities), hospitals were randomly assigned to a task consultation condition or to a task consultation condition which was accompanied with an intervention based on organizational development principles (Blake & Mouton, 1969; Lubin, Goodstein, & Lubin, 1979). In the former condition, as in the active consultation condition of the first activation phase study, consultant change agents made periodic visits to hospitals for the purpose of troubleshooting problems with lodge implementation activities encountered by hospitals and their staffs. In the task consultation–organizational development condition, the outside change agent not only provided problem–relevant consultation but also attempted to increase the cohesiveness of within–hospital groups formed to implement the lodge. This was accomplished by the application of various organizational development training exercises. These activities included group exercises such as role clarification and interpersonal affective feedback provision.

The major result of the activation–phase experiment was that the hospitals receiving task consultation–organizational development were more likely to move behaviorally toward lodge adoption than were hospitals receiving the task consultation only. In addition to being one of the first experimental demonstrations of the effectiveness of organizational development strategies, the above study experimentally demonstrated the importance of group cohesiveness as a necessary condition for facilitating the adoption of social innovations such as the community lodge.

In summary, the community lodge dissemination research demonstrates that scientific methodology can be applied to the social change process. The experimental social innovator can utilize the true experiment to advocate the adoption of an innovation, as well as to discover the principles governing the dissemination of social technology. In two senses, the Fairweather dissemination researches should be viewed as "model investigations." First, contrasted to the several hundred correlative investigations which have examined the dissemination of innovations, the results obtained by the projects of Fairweather and his associates (Fairweather, Sanders, & Tornatzky, 1974; Tornatzky et al., in press) can be embraced more confidently, since much of the knowledge of dissemination processes gained from this work is experimentally validated. Perhaps even more valuable, however, are the changes in the treatment of the chronically mentally ill that resulted from the dissemination work. Presently, there exist nearly 25 independent community lodges nationally. Given the initial low levels of support for the lodge concept among professionals, this is quite remarkable, yet heartening from the perspective of those who are concerned about the plight of the mentally ill.

CONCLUSIONS

This chapter has addressed a biased imbalance which has come to characterize the choice in methodologies for community psychological research. To an increasing degree, quasi-experimentation has come to dominate the discipline of community psychology, while at the same time periodic reviews of the discipline call for greater methodological sophistication in the conduct of community research. The present chapter has attempted to provide a set of logical arguments which favor increased utilization of the true experiment: first, by dispelling some of the more "popular myths" about true experimentation as a methodological paradigm; second, by assessing the current status of quasi-experimental designs for the purpose of pointing out both their usefulness and shortcomings as valid scientific methodologies.

Conceptually, philosophically, and methodologically it is possible to integrate the quasi-experimental and the true experimental methods to the benefit of community psychology as a discipline. The experimental social innovation research model, with its emphasis on human-service program development and its accompanying value orientation, provides a framework for accomplishing this integration. The community lodge work conducted by George Fairweather and his associates highlights the successful integration of these methods.

The national lodge dissemination experiments and the social science literature devoted to innovation dissemination have repeatedly discovered that the printed word-- brochures, books, information sheets, newspapers, and the like--is extremely deficient as a dissemination technology (Fairweather, Sanders, & Tornatzky, 1974; Tornatzky et al., in press; Havelock, 1969). Yet, perhaps the message offered here to community psychologists and others will contradict this generalization. The intent of this chapter has been to foster on the part of community psychologists

an increased recognition of the influence their research
has on social change processes. In the mundane, day-to-
day world of conducting community research, it is easy to
lose sight of the potentiality for social change inherent in
all scientific research. Indeed, beneficial social change
in our society is best accomplished through the application
of rational and valid scientific methodology to the solution
of human problems. The experimental social innovation research model, with its emphasis on the true experiment, is
a means of ensuring this desirable end for community psychology and for our society.

NOTES

1. The scope of this chapter prevents an in-depth
discussion of each of these threats to internal validity.
The interested reader is directed to Cook and Campbell
(1976, pp. 227-230).

2. This, of course, is now labeled the Hawthorne
effect and refers to the notion that the provision of any
treatment under conditions where the experimental group is
aware of the existence of an untreated control group may
lead the former participants to respond more positively to
treatment.

3. It is far beyond the scope of this chapter to
present each class of designs in detail. For path analytic
procedures, the interested reader is directed to Blalock
(1971). The remaining designs are given excellent treatment in Cook and Campbell (1976).

4. The uncertainty produced through the conduct
of experimentation in community settings highlights the importance of developing a set of professional values similar
to those outlined by James Kelly (1971). The experimental
social innovator develops a high tolerance for ambiguity,
is perseverent, maintains diverse community networks, and
as Kelly advocates, develops a balance between long-term
and short-term objectives for professional and community
development.

5. The exact nature of these agreements as well as
other aspects of the lodge research are well beyond the
scope of this chapter. They are comprehensively described
in Fairweather, Sanders, Maynard, and Cressler (1969).

REFERENCES

Beck, A. A. The application of small group techniques to training in community participation: A field experiment. Unpublished dissertation, Michigan State University, 1975.

Berman, P., & McLaughlin, M. Programs supporting educational change (Vol. 7). Santa Monica, Calif.: The Rand Corporation, 1978 (R-1589/8-HEW).

Berman, P., & McLaughlin, M. Federal programs supporting educational change (Vol. 8). Santa Monica, Calif.: The Rand Corporation, 1978 (R-1589/8-HEW).

Blake, R. R., & Mouton, J. S. Building a dynamic corporation through grid organization development. Reading, Mass.: Addison-Wesley, 1969.

Boruch, R., McSweeney, A. J., & Soderstrom, E. J. Randomized field experiments for program development and evaluation: An illustrative bibliography. Unpublished paper, Northwestern University, 1977.

Campbell, D. T. Reforms as experiments. American Psychologist, 1969, 24, 409-429.

Campbell, D. T., & Stanley, J. C. Experimental and quasi-experimental designs for research. Chicago: Rand McNally, 1966.

Cook, T. D., & Campbell, D. T. The design and conduct of quasi-experiments and true experiments in field settings. In M. D. Dunnette & J. P. Campbell (Eds.), Handbook of industrial and organizational research. Chicago: Rand McNally, 1976.

Cowen, E. L. Social and community interventions. Annual Review of Psychology, 1973, 24, 423-472.

Cowen, E. L., Gardner, E. A., & Zax, M. (Eds.). Emergent approaches to mental health problems. New York: Appleton-Century-Crofts, 1967.

Craven, P., & Wellman, B. The network city. Sociological Inquiry, 1973, 43, 57-88.

Cronbach, L. J., & Furby, L. How should we measure "change"--or should we? Psychological Bulletin, 1970, 74, 68-80.

Davidson, W. S., Seidman, E., Rappaport, J., Rapp, N., Rhodes, W., & Herring, J. The diversion of juvenile offenders: Some empirical light on the subject. Social Work Research and Abstracts, 1977, 13, 40-49.

Edwards, W., & Guttentag, M. Experiments and evaluations: A re-examination. In C. Bennett & A. Lumsdaine (Eds.), Experiments and evaluations. New York: Academic Press, 1975.

Edwards, W., Guttentag, M., & Snapper, K. A decision-theoretic approach to evaluation research. In E. Struening & M. Guttentag (Eds.), Handbook of evaluation research. Beverly Hills, Calif.: Sage, 1975.

Fairweather, G. W. (Ed.). Social psychology in treating mental illness: An experimental approach. New York: John Wiley, 1964.

Fairweather, G. W. Methods for experimental social innovation. New York: John Wiley, 1967.

Fairweather, G. W. Social change: The challenge to survival. Morristown, N.J.: General Learning Press, 1972.

Fairweather, G. W., Sanders, D. H., Maynard, H., & Cressler, D. L. Community life for the mentally ill. Chicago: Aldine, 1969.

Fairweather, G. W., Sanders, D. H., & Tornatzky, L. G. Creating change in mental health organizations. New York: Pergamon Press, 1974.

Fairweather, G. W., & Simon, R. A further follow-up comparison of psychotherapeutic programs. Journal of Consulting Psychology, 1963, 27, 186.

Fairweather, G. W., Simon, R., Gebhard, M. E., Weingarten, E., Holland, J. L., Sanders, R., Stone, G. B., & Reahl, G. E. Relative effectiveness of psychotherapeutic programs. A multicriteria comparison for four programs for three different groups. Psychological Monographs, 1960, 74 (Whole No. 492).

Fairweather, G. W., & Tornatzky, L. G. Experimental methods for social policy research. New York: Pergamon Press, 1977.

Fergus, E. O. The role of telephonic consultation in creating innovation adoption in health organizations. Unpublished dissertation, Michigan State University, 1973.

Fergus, E. O. The future evaluator: A renaissance person with a humanitarian approach to social change. Evaluation and Program Planning, 1979, 2, 149-150.

Forsyth, R. P., & Fairweather, G. W. Psychotherapeutic and other hospital treatment criteria. The dilemma. Journal of Abnormal and Social Psychology, 1961, 62, 598-604.

Goldberger, A. S. Structural equation models: An overview. In A. S. Goldberger & O. D. Duncan (Eds.), Structural equation models in the social sciences. New York: Academic Press, 1973.

Gottlieb, B. H., & Todd, D. M. Characterizing and promoting social support in natural settings. In R. F. Munoz, L. R. Snowden, & J. G. Kelly (Eds.), Social and psychological research in community settings. San Francisco: Jossey-Bass, 1979.

Greenwald, A. G. Within-subjects designs: To use or not to use? Psychological Bulletin, 1976, 83, 314-320.

Guttentag, M. Subjectivity and its use in evaluation research. Evaluation, 1973, 1, 60-65.

Hargreaves, W., Attkisson, C., Horowitz, M., & Sorenson, J. The education of evaluators. In C. Attkisson, W. Hargreaves, M. Horowitz, & J. Sorenson (Eds.), Evaluation of human service programs. New York: Academic Press, 1978.

Havelock, R. G. Planning for innovation for dissemination and utilization of knowledge. Ann Arbor, Mich.: Institute for Social Research, 1969.

Hersen, M., & Barlow, D. H. Single case experimental designs. New York: Pergamon Press, 1976.

Hollister, R. The role of experimentation in policy decision-making. In R. F. Boruch & H. W. Riecken (Eds.), Experimental testing of public policy. Boulder, Colo.: Westview, 1974.

Kazdin, A. E. Methodological and assessment considerations in evaluating reinforcement programs in applied settings. Journal of Applied Behavior Analysis, 1973, 6, 511-531.

Kazdin, A. E. Methodological and interpretive problems of single-case experimental designs. Journal of Consulting and Clinical Psychology, 1978, 46, 629-642.

Kelly, J. G. Qualities for the community psychologist. American Psychologist, 1971, 26, 897-903.

Kelly, J. G., Snowden, L. R., & Munoz, R. F. Social and community interventions. Annual Review of Psychology, 1977, 28, 323-361.

Lakatos, I. Falsification and the methodology of scientific research programs. In I. Lakatos & A. Musgrave (Eds.), Criticism and the growth of knowledge. Cambridge, England: Cambridge University Press, 1970.

Lerner, M. J., & Fairweather, G. W. The social behavior of chronic schizophrenics in supervised and unsupervised work groups. Journal of Abnormal and Social Psychology, 1963, 67, 219-225.

Levine, M. Scientific method and the adversary model: Some preliminary thoughts. American Psychologist, 1974, 29, 661-677.

Lewin, K. Frontiers in group dynamics. Human Relations, 1947, 1, 5-41.

Lindemann, J. E., Fairweather, G. W., Stone, G. B., & Smith, R. S. The use of demographic characteristics in predicting length of neuropsychiatric hospital stay. Journal of Consulting Psychology, 1959, 23, 85-89.

Lord, F. M. Large-scale covariance analysis when the control variable is fallible. Journal of the American Statistical Association, 1960, 55, 307-321.

Lord, F. M. A paradox in the interpretation of group comparisons. Psychological Bulletin, 1967, 68, 304-305.

Lord, F. M. Statistical adjustments when comparing pre-existing groups. Psychological Bulletin, 1969, 72, 336-337.

Lubin, B., Goodstein, L. D., & Lubin, A. W. (Eds.). Organizational change source-book: Cases in organizational development. La Jolla, Calif.: University Associates, 1979.

Mahoney, M. J. Experimental methods and outcome evaluation. Journal of Consulting and Clinical Psychology, 1978, 46, 660-672.

Nunnally, J. C., & Durham, R. L. Validity, reliability, and special problems of measurement in evaluation research. In E. L. Struening & M. Guttentag (Eds.), Handbook of evaluation research. Beverly Hills, Calif.: Sage, 1975.

Nunnally, J. C. Psychometric theory. New York: McGraw-Hill, 1978.

Porter, A. C. The effects of using fallible variables in the analysis of covariance. Unpublished dissertation, University of Wisconsin, Madison, 1967.

Rappaport, J. Community psychology: Values, research, and action. New York: Holt, Rinehart & Winston, 1977.

Rappaport, J., Seidman, E., & Davidson, W. S. Demonstration research and manifest versus true adoption. In R. F. Munoz, L. R. Snowden, & J. G. Kelly (Eds.), Social and psychological research in community settings. San Francisco: Jossey-Bass, 1979.

Roethlisberger, F. J., & Dickson, W. J. Management and the worker. Cambridge, Mass.: Harvard University Press, 1964.

Rogers, E. M. Diffusion of innovations. New York: Free Press, 1962.

Rogers, E. M., & Shoemaker, F. F. Communication of innovations: A cross-cultural approach. New York: Free Press, 1971.

Rossi, P. H., & Wright, S. R. A faltering giant step forward: A critique of the New Jersey–Pennsylvania negative income tax experiment. In D. Bybee & L. G. Tornatzky (Eds.), Nonrandom error: Issues in social experimentation and program evaluation. Philadelphia: University of Pennsylvania Press, in press.

Sarason, S. B. The psychological sense of community: Prospect for a community psychology. San Francisco: Jossey-Bass, 1974.

Schulberg, H. C., & Perloff, R. Academia and the training of human service delivery program evaluators. American Psychologist, 1979, 34, 247–254.

Scriven, M. The methodology of evaluation. In R. W. Tyler, R. M. Gagné, & M. Scriven (Eds.), Perspectives on curriculum evaluation. Chicago: Rand McNally, 1967.

Seidman, E. Steps towards the development of useful social and public policies. Unpublished manuscript. University of Illinois, Urbana–Champaign, 1976.

Shippee, G. E. Experimental social innovation as an alternative to a "pseudo-relevant" social psychology. Personality and Social Psychology Bulletin, 1979, 5, 491–498.

Shippee, G. E. The psychology of energy consumption and conservation: A review and conceptual analysis. Environmental Management, 1980, 4, 297–314.

Shippee, G. E. Conservation as a renewable resource and the role of social science. Energy Policy, in press.

Sidman, M. Tactics of scientific research: Evaluating experimental data in psychology. New York: Basic Books, 1960.

Siegel, L. M., Attkisson, C. C., & Cohn, A. H. Mental health needs assessments: Strategies and techniques. Report for NIMH, 1974.

Suchman, E. A. Evaluative research: Principles and practice in public service and social action programs. New York: Russell Sage Foundation, 1967.

Tornatzky, L. G. How a Ph.D. program aimed at survival survived. American Psychologist, 1976, 31, 189–191.

Tornatzky, L. G. The triple-threat evaluator. Evaluation and program planning, 1979, 2, 111–115.

Tornatzky, L. G., Fairweather, G. W., Fergus, E. O., & Avellar, J. Social processes and social innovation: A national experiment in the dissemination and implementation of social technology. New York: Pergamon Press, in press.

Tornatzky, L. G., Fairweather, G. W., & O'Kelly, L. I. A Ph.D. program aimed at survival. American Psychologist, 1970, 25, 884–888.

Tryon, R. C., & Bailey, D. E. Cluster analysis. New York: McGraw-Hill, 1970.

Tucker, C. The role of reading, speaking dialects, and associative bridging in behavior achievement. Unpublished doctoral dissertation, Michigan State University, 1974.

Warheit, G. J., Bell, R. A., & Schwab, J. J. Needs assessment approaches: Concepts and methods (DHEW Publication No. AD AMA-77 472). Washington, D.C.: U.S. Government Printing Office, 1977.

Weiss, C. Evaluating action programs: Reading in social action and education. Boston: Allyn & Bacon, 1972.

Weiss, C. Using social research in public policy making. Lexington, Mass.: Heath, 1977.

Whitney, W. M. An evaluation of a community based delinquency prevention program on the basis of group and individual employment. Unpublished doctoral dissertation, Michigan State University, 1974.

Winer, B. J. Statistical principles in experimental design. New York: McGraw-Hill, 1971.

Wortman, P. M. Evaluation research: A psychological perspective. American Psychologist, 1975, 30, 562–575.

Yin, R. K., Quick, S. K., Bateman, P. M., & Marks, E. L. Changing urban bureaucracies: How new practices become routinized. Santa Monica, Calif.: The Rand Corporation, 1978.

Zaltman, G., & Duncan, R. Strategies for planning change. New York: John Wiley, 1977.

5   Quasi-experimental Methods for Community-based Research

Stefan E. Hormuth, Nancy M. Fitzgerald, and Thomas D. Cook

STRATEGIES FOR RESEARCH IN COMMUNITY PSYCHOLOGY--AN OVERVIEW

The design problems encountered by community psychology researchers depend to some degree on the goals and purposes of their study. Different research goals require different levels of explanation. A very low level of description can be the simple statement of the co-occurrence of two events, frequently described in terms of correlations. On the other end of the range is the micro level of causal explanation as it is usually sought in experimental research of a basic nature. The decision about the level of explanation considered desirable and possible in a given research context should be made with the goals of the research in mind.

Which level of explanation is prevalent in community psychology journals? Novaco and Monahan (1980) reviewed the articles from the first six years of the <u>American Journal of Community Psychology</u> (AJCP). Although the majority (71.5%) of the 235 articles published during those years were broadly classified as empirical, only one study in ten employed a randomized control group design. More than half of the empirical studies involved correlational

The authors thank Anthony D'Augelli, Meg Gerrard, Mark Ginsberg, Eva Lantos Rezmovic, William Shadish, and the editors for comments on earlier drafts.

analyses or one-time measurements with no comparisons of control groups. McClure and associates (1980) similarly critiqued a sample of articles from community psychology and community mental health journals. They classified articles in AJCP and the Journal of Community Psychology (JCP) according to design: 20% employed either quasi-experimental (9%) or experimental design (11%); 80% were classified as either generally theoretical (24%), generally uninterpretable (15%), or correlational (41%).

This appears to be an inordinately high proportion of studies that do not permit reasonable causal inference. Without a comparison group of similarly critiqued journals, we cannot say with assurance that articles in AJCP and JCP exhibit less methodological sophistication than articles appearing elsewhere. Our guess is that when comparisons are made with mainstream psychology journals (for instance, in personality, social, or cognitive-experimental journals) the incidence of nonexperimental studies would be higher in community psychology journals. If comparisons are made with journals representing disciplines with applied emphases similar to community psychology, such as social work, criminal justice, and ecological psychology, AJCP and JCP may not be unique. The point here is neither to condemn nor justify the current state of research design but to understand some of the unique problems that community psychologists face in doing research.

The demand for a more stringent causal explanation of the relationship between variables of interest to community psychologists can easily be countered by pointing to the problems inherent in field research that forbid the precision of experimentation. And, of course, the abstraction, reduction, and isolation of variables undertaken by experimental researchers in the laboratory are not necessarily goals of interest to community psychologists. The model of explanation for basic experimentation is not necessarily appropriate for community psychology. To explain this last point we shall discuss briefly the relationship between causal relationships and explanations.

Cook and Campbell (1979) state, in the first of eight statements on causality, that "causal assertions are meaningful at the molar level even when the ultimate micromediation is not known" (p. 32). The practical implication of this statement is that it is useful to have information about a causal relationship (what is the result of X happening?) even if an explanation (why does X lead to Y?) cannot be achieved based on the conditions under which the research is conducted. For instance, the finding that one type of prerelease counseling in an institution is more successful than another can, under certain instances, be all that is needed to institute a general prerelease counseling program. Whether the effect of the counseling can be better explained by providing motivation or information interests neither the counselors nor those they counsel.

The level of causal explanation that community researchers should seek is dictated, in part, by the intended audience and the use to which the findings will be put. Policymakers, including community psychologists in policy-making roles, are typically less concerned with why a program works and more interested in whether a program has a given desired outcome. Outcome evaluation involves establishing whether a causal relationship exists between a programmatic treatment and a specified effect.

A fuller specification of the causal links between a program and its effect is important to the community psychologist-as-experimenter. This exploration of causal links can take place at various levels. At the molar extreme, one might test whether community support for a program "caused" it to be more or less effective by comparing the effectiveness, that is, by comparing the different degrees of community support each enjoys. Other approaches might compare program effectiveness by varying the type of staff employed (professional versus peers) or the type of counseling offered (social-skills versus job-skills training). At a more micro-level of analysis, one could study a program's ability to raise individuals' self-esteem that was, in turn, expected to mediate clients' motivation to do well. Regardless of the level of explanation at which a researcher is working, specifying causal linkages provides more opportunities for intervention. Understanding causal processes makes it possible, for instance, to streamline a program into its most essential components or to heighten its effectiveness with various types of clients.

While we have formulated these examples of levels of explanation, we have assumed that community psychologists are primarily interested in seeking explanations at the level of manipulable causes that are potentially open to intervention. Hence, if we were interested in studying the effects of nursing home relocation on elderly persons, we might do a descriptive study correlating indexes of health, satisfaction, and well-being for residents before and after the move. This would tell us some things about the effects of relocation, perhaps that health and feelings of well-being decline temporarily subsequent to the move. Assuming, however, that relocations are unavoidable and sometimes necessitated by nursing home closings, overcrowding, and the like, we might prefer to study potentially manipulable aspects of the relocation, such as distance moved, degree of choice, and preparation time allowed, and the process of introducing residents to a new home. Varying these factors may suggest which cause or combination of causes is largely responsible for the temporary decline and potentially worth trying to modify. The burden is now on us to illustrate how such studies can be done.

Inferring Causal Relationships

The process of inferring causal relationships is mainly one of obtaining a pattern of data commensurate with cause, developing a list of plausible rival hypotheses, and exploring these in order to reject some and be left with as few plausible alternatives as possible. Experimentation systematizes this process by manipulating potential causes to test whether predicted patterns are obtained and by eliminating rival explanations by generating comparable experimental groups and by manipulating or measuring in ways that unconfound competing constructs. The randomized experiment is one of the best means for inferring causality. To be clear about the advantages provided by randomized design helps in recognizing what is involved in drawing causal inferences other designs.

Advantages of Randomized Experiments

The defining attribute of randomized experiments is the creation of different groups whose members one has assigned at random. This creates an initial comparability between the treatment and nontreatment units in each group. The classic randomized pretest-post test control group design is generally considered one of the best experimental means for testing causal hypotheses. Its merit is the relative ease with which important questions about causality can be addressed. The most basic question--Is the treatment associated with the intended effect?--can be answered by noting any changes in the treatment group from the time of the pretest to the post-test. The more difficult question,--Could the change in the treatment have been caused by factors other than the treatment?--can be answered partially by comparing pretest-post test changes in the treatment group with those in the control group. When the changes differ, a number of rival explanations to treatment as the cause can be eliminated, for example, selection, testing effects, statistical regression, maturation, and so on (for a more detailed discussion see Campbell & Stanley, 1963; Cook & Campbell, 1979). Such explanations are rendered implausible because had the artifact in question operated, it should have affected the treatment and control groups equally.

Other potential factors that could differentially affect the treatment or control groups--such as, higher motivation in the case of the treatment group, or demoralization in the case of the controls--remain as rival explanations for observed changes in the treatment group or lack of change in the control group. Discounting the plausibility of such factors depends on the researcher's ability to bring evidence to bear concerning them.

Advantages of Quasi-experimental Designs

Quasi-experimentation is a term referring to experimental designs that are not based on the random assignment of treatment and control groups. Rather, quasi-experimental designs rely on many methods, principally the use of nonequivalent control groups and multiple times of observation, in order to determine whether change occurred and to address the relative contribution of the treatment versus alternative explanations for the observed change.

Quasi-experimental techniques are useful when a randomized design was planned and implemented but cannot be maintained for the course of the study. Not unlike researchers in other applied settings, community psychologists find it difficult to maintain randomized designs as they were implemented (Cowen, 1978). Specific precautions can be taken at various stages of the experimental process, from initial decisions in selecting participants to vigilance in the randomization procedures through compensatory attention to control participants. Still, attrition can result in noncomparable groups at the time of post-testing.

Treatment conditions may become diffused or participants may select one treatment condition rather than another. The conditions of the randomized control-group design may also be violated for various other reasons. By anticipating such violations, community psychologists often can utilize quasi-experimental designs to analyze the data and help rule out rival explanations for any observed changes in the treatment group.

Researchers also may turn to quasi-experimental designs at the very start when it is clear that random assignment of units to treatment conditions is impossible. As an alternative, a researcher may obtain a group similar to the treatment participants who act as a "noncomparable" control. Many quasi-experimental designs are aimed at the problems of unconfounding causality when intact groups, rather than individuals, different in unknown ways, are selected into treatment or nontreatment conditions.

Finally, quasi-experimental methods may be useful when community psychologists encounter particular design problems that arise from the very nature of the phenomena being studied. In studying environmental settings, institutions, or communities, there are sometimes few, if any, comparable units available for comparison. Furthermore, many socially relevant phenomena do not afford the researcher the control over the assignment of treatment, the timing of treatment, the duration of treatment, and so forth. We are referring here to a wide range of community problems: the effects on inmates of crowding in prisons, mental health adjustment after legislated deinstitutionalization of patients, and community responses to natural disasters. Studies of problems such as these do not lend themselves to an experimental framework. There are, however, some principles of quasi-experimentation that could be helpful in maximizing the possibilities for causal inferences.

In the remainder of the chapter, we will specify and illustrate the above three uses. In the first section we encourage community psychologists to attempt randomized experiments in field research. We show the benefits and fall-back options of doing so even if the randomization ultimately breaks down. We have tried to anticipate common sources of failure and to show how research projects, which might otherwise have been uninterpretable, have been salvaged.

In the second section, we recognize that community psychologists are often in a position where randomized experiments are not feasible or not desirable because of cost or increased artificiality. Accordingly, we discuss the boon to interpretation of causality provided by non-comparable control-group designs or designs involving such strategies as multiple times of measurement or the direct measurement of potential threats to interpretation.

In the third section, we explore the match between some quasi-experimental strategies and particular problems faced by community psychologists, for example, studying whole communities or nonexperimentally induced independent variables, such as the installation of public housing in an established community or the closing of neighborhood schools.

WHEN RANDOMIZED EXPERIMENTS FAIL

The advantages of randomized control-group designs in making causal inferences have been well argued (Campbell & Stanley, 1963; Cook & Campbell, 1979; Cook, in press). In addition, the feasibility of doing randomized experiments in applied settings has been well documented (Boruch, 1975, 1977; Boruch, McSweeny & Soderstrom, 1978; Cook & Campbell, 1979). Conner (1977) and Cook and Campbell (1979) have cited precautions that can be taken to minimize the breakdown of random designs. Even if comparability becomes compromised, the ability to draw causal inferences is still likely to be better if one starts with randomized groupings than if one does not. Among the numerous threats to maintaining randomization once it has been implemented are attrition of participation, failure of participants to receive the treatment to which they were assigned, and demoralization of participants because they are receiving one form of treatment and not another. When these threats do in fact operate, randomized experiments fail to produce the comparable treatment and non-treatment groups on which strong causal inference depends. However, in many situations the degree of noncomparability when a randomized experiment breaks down may still be less than if the researcher had started with groups that were self-selected or selected by administrators.

We turn our attention now to specific threats to randomized designs—how they affect interpretability, how to judge their seriousness, and how to avoid them.

When Attrition Occurs

Perhaps attrition of participants is the biggest problem faced by researchers in applied settings. Some loss of subjects from treatment and control groups is almost inevitable. Knowing the potential for attrition, researchers can often take steps to minimize and measure its occurrence.

Random and Systematic Attrition

Attrition patterns can be random. Participants' reasons for not continuing in a study may be unrelated to the purposes of the study or the treatment condition to which they are assigned. Sickness, weather, or work-related problems may truly be randomly related to the experimental conditions, in which case the original design can be preserved with unequal numbers of participants.

Attrition is more problematic when it is systematically related either to the kinds of participants who drop out or to the nature of the treatment from which they withdrew. For instance, participants may elect to drop out because of disinterest or suspicion about the researchers' motives. To the extent that such participants drop out at similar rates from all the treatment groups, the problem becomes one of external generalizability. The results cannot be generalized to the population of potentially disinterested or suspicious participants. Internal validity and causal interpretation are not affected, however, since eliminating rival explanations is associated with treatment groups being comparable in all ways except the presence of the treatment itself. To the degree that attrition is uniform among groups, such comparability is preserved.

Unfortunately, attrition tends to be treatment related, with the least desirable conditions and the no-attention controls evidencing the greatest frequency of withdrawal. Frequency and descriptions of participant attrition can provide the researcher with some basis for making reasonable judgments about the resulting comparability among treatment and control groups. Given the nature of the study, the researcher has to decide whether it is plausible that the loss of participants in one or another group would interact with the treatment to provide spurious results.

Consider, for example, a randomized experiment that takes advantage of a counseling agency's waiting list.

The researcher hypothesizes that all clients will show some improvement ("spontaneous recovery") but that those receiving a packet of self-help materials will show greater improvement. After an initial screening, clients are randomly assigned to receive in the mail either the self-help materials (treatment group) or a general information packet about the agency (placebo group). Two months later, they are screened and evaluated again, just prior to being offered actual counseling.

Anticipating attrition, the researcher might easily collect information at the initial screening on relevant characteristics. Such information might include the nature and seriousness of the clients' problems, a logical variable to use in checking whether random assignment had in fact resulted in initially comparable groups. Other data might include previous involvements with mental health or counseling services, other kinds of professional or nonprofessional help already sought, self-perceived ability to deal with the problem, and self-perceived need for immediate help.

If attrition occurs after the initial pretest screening interview, the researcher can use information on clients' characteristics to compare the participants remaining in the study with those who drop out. Suppose the researcher finds that the clients for whom he is not able to obtain post-treatment data are, in fact, those with chronic histories of mental health problems and repeated counseling or institutionalization. The attrition has implications for external validity; namely, the results of the study can no longer be generalized to all wait-listed agency clients.

In addition, suppose these chronic clients drop out of the treatment and placebo groups in different proportions. Assume further that the treatment group showed greater improvement from the initial screening to the second screening than did the placebo group; the confidence that can be placed in the finding depends on the attrition differences. If the treatment group had the greatest number of wait list dropouts, there is the possibility the treatment appeared successful only because the clients with the most chronic problems were underrepresented in the treatment group. Similarly, we might suspect that the treatment group was overrepresented by clients who were more motivated, or more optimistic about overcoming problems than was the placebo group. Consequently, the rate of recovery for the two groups would have been different regardless of the treatment intervention.

On the other hand, attrition of clients with chronic problems could be primarily from the placebo group, probably because they were dissatisfied with the materials provided. In that case, we would expect less motivated, more chronic clients to be over-represented in the treatment group. Thus a finding of greater improvement in the treatment group than in the placebo group would suggest that the effectiveness of the treatment might be underestimated! When attrition is systematic and differs among treatment groups, any finding of significance must be interpreted in terms of the potential biasing (for or against the treatment as cause) that it introduces.

Minimizing Attrition

Often it is helpful for researchers to develop a theory of attrition, that is, a set of expectations that addresses the types of participants most likely to drop out, the treatment conditions most likely to produce dropouts, and the potential interaction between these two. There are a number of advantages to developing such a set of expectations early in the planning stages of a field experiment.

A theory about why attrition occurs should suggest what steps might be taken to minimize its occurrence. Problems such as seasonal or weather conditions or access to transportation may be anticipated or even alleviated for participants. Sometimes incentives can be incorporated into a research plan to decrease the likelihood that participants will drop out. By having theories (and even better, some relevant evidence) about who is at risk of attrition and what might motivate them to remain, researchers can target more effective incentives for maintaining participation.

When attrition is differentially affected by the desirability of the treatment offered to a group, one strategy is to provide compensations only for those treatment conditions that might otherwise be considered less desirable. A group designated as a control for one experiment could be offered attention or services in ways that are not related to the intended treatment. Clearly, such special attention has to be worked out carefully so that effects of the "compensation" treatment do not overlap with the effects expected from the experimental treatment, thus destroying any value the compensated group might have as a control.

A theory of attrition also provides a framework for measuring and interpreting dropout patterns. When researchers expect certain participants or conditions to be more prone to attrition, direct measures may be incorporated into a research design to ensure that necessary information is available to make this determination. As outlined above, even when direct measurement is not possible, theories about attrition can aid in the interpretation of results. Different patterns of attrition can have different implications for the confidence placed both on generalizability and causal inference.

When Treatment Contamination Occurs

By treatment contamination we refer to a number of phenomena that may mar or blur the comparable groupings created by random assignment. One kind of contamination occurs when groups receiving different forms of treatments are not sufficiently isolated from each other. One group may learn about the conditions to which another group is being exposed with the resulting consequence that either one or more groups are exposed to aspects of the same treatment or group members become demoralized, angry, or otherwise reactive to being treated differently.

Treatment contamination can also take the form of variability of exposure to the treatment among participants within the same treatment conditions. In many situations, participants exert some control over their own exposure to the treatment manipulation. For instance, in education, training, or other treatments extended over a series of sessions, variations in exposure to treatment can be detected in obvious ways, such as attendance or absence at sessions. More subtle are within-treatment variations due to participants' abilities to read and comprehend materials given them, or their levels of interest, boredom, and openness in regard to the conditions to which they are exposed. Differential exposure to the treatment means, simply, that in the end participants in the same group have experienced different treatments.

When treatment contamination occurs, it becomes difficult to detect change due to treatment. Mullen, Chazin, and Feldstein (1972) compared an innovative counseling project for welfare recipients with traditional counseling techniques. They found astounding variability of treatment

delivery within the innovation project. Personal interviews with counselors varied from a low of 1 interview in
over one year for some recipients to a high of 129 interviews for the same time period, with the median being 15
interviews. Similarly, the range of telephone and letter
contact was from 0 to 81, with a median of about 10 contacts. What constituted treatment differed for recipients
greatly within the same treatment group. In fact, the
experience of recipients receiving few or no contacts was
more akin to control conditions. Given such a wide fluc-
tuation in treatment, it becomes difficult to detect treatment-
related change.

Avoiding Treatment Contamination

A number of precautions are possible for preventing
treatment contamination. Treatment procedures should be
standardized as much as possible and monitored to determine the nature and extent of participants' differential
exposure to the procedures. Steps should be taken to increase the desirability of less attractive treatments; often
incentives can be built into treatment options unrelated to
the purpose of the treatment. Similar considerations should
be given to the control group's experience: How can its
membership be preserved and its naiveté about other conditions assured? Cook and Campbell (1979) have suggested
that, with innovative forethought, experiences can be
planned for the control group which are unrelated to the
treatment but which can sustain control members' involvement by addressing other interests, problems, or needed
services. Social agencies whose ethical considerations may
preclude withholding treatment from clients for control
purposes may find offering alternative services more acceptable.

Of equal importance is the monitoring of the experiences of both the experimental and control groups.
Not only is it essential to catch instances of contamination
early, but detailed information is necessary if and when
contamination occurs.

Data Analysis Options When Attrition or
Contamination Occurs

One essential axiom should be understood when trying to analyze data from designs in which treatment con-

tamination or treatment-related attrition has taken place. No single analysis is likely to be sufficient; rather, a series of analyses, each with various strengths and weakness, is almost always indicated. Here the researcher becomes a detective who pieces together evidence of causality and weighs the relative contribution of each piece.

An essential step in the investigatory process is to determine the extent and nature of attrition or contamination. In a reanalysis of the evaluation of "Sesame Street," T. D. Cook and his associates (1975) found that although some control children had watched the program on a number of occasions (contamination), there were still clear differences between the experimental and control groups in the frequency with which children had viewed the program. As part of their reanalysis, Cook and his associates (1975) preserved the original randomized design by comparing children in the groups to which they had been assigned. They recognized, however, that this test of the effectiveness of "Sesame Street" was particularly stringent. If watching "Sesame Street" increased children's learning performance (and some of these effects were evidenced by control children who watched the program a little), then the analysis was essentially looking for significant differences between frequent viewers and infrequent viewers--a more exacting measure of the program's effects. In this case the contamination did not pose a major problem for the data analysis, since the contamination biased the results against the treatment program and the program, nonetheless, was shown to have a significant effect.

In order to take full advantage of available data, we suggest doing two types of analysis: (1) the analysis of data for only those cases which received the treatment as planned, in accordance with the original randomized design, and (2) the analysis of all cases, grouped according to amount or kind of treatment received (sometimes called partitioning), using a quasi-experimental approach for noncomparable groups. The first analysis would provide the most internally valid test of causality for the treatment but would limit the generalizability to the unrepresentative subgroup of participants under model treatment conditions. The second quasi-experimental design tests the effects of the treatment as it is probably experienced in actuality, thereby allowing additional conclusions about generalizability. This quasi-experimental design is, however, often difficult to interpret by itself.

Matched with the conservatively biased first analysis of randomly formed groups, the quasi-experimental analysis gains credibility.

Wan, Weissert, and Livieratos (1980) provide a good example of the logic behind this repeated-analysis strategy. They encountered serious attrition in a congressionally mandated experimental study to test how two innovative programs, geriatric day care and homemaker services, influenced the physical, mental, and social well-being of elderly persons. Elderly persons referred for services were randomly assigned to one of four conditions: (1) to be involved in a health-oriented day-care program only, (2) to receive homemaker assistance only, (3) to receive a combined program of the two services, or (4) to act as controls receiving no special services.

A number of factors contributed to attrition. Some of those assigned to the innovative programs did not use the services offered. Others received demonstration services to which they were not assigned. Assessment data were incomplete for still others who were not available, due partially to mortality. Of the 1,871 elderly persons initially included in the study, 718 had to be excluded.

Wan and his colleagues examined the data to determine how their analyses might be biased by such attrition. They found that across the three experimental conditions nonusers of the innovative programs tended to be older, sicker, and more likely to die than users of the services. This difference held when comparisons were made between dropouts from the experimental and control conditions. In addition, a higher proportion of experimental (rather than control) dropouts were seriously disabled. They concluded that the dropout pattern favored finding effects for the innovative program as compared to the control group, since the innovative conditions would in the final analysis contain a smaller proportion of seriously disabled participants. Of course, differential effects found between the experimental groups would not be similarly biased, since their patient samples were equivalent.

Wan and his colleagues proceeded to test the consequences of this bias favoring the program groups. They reanalyzed the data in two ways. In one set of analyses, they compared participants assigned to the experimental conditions with those assigned to controls, regardless of whether the participants made use of the services offered. In parallel analyses, users of the services were compared with nonusers, regardless of whether they had originally been assigned to an experimental or control condition. The results of these two analyses were considered to be analogous to a kind of confidence interval around the "true" experimental effects. In the first analyses, the test of the programs' effects was highly stringent, since included in the experimental group were persons who had never received the assigned services. In the second analyses, the test was biased toward detecting experimental effects, since users and nonusers of services were compared without any attempt to control for the differences between the groups in numbers of seriously disabled members. In the end the results of the two sets of analyses were comparable, lessenening considerably concerns about attrition being a threat to the internal validity of the experiment.

When Measurement Biases Occur

Comparability among treatment groups is threatened when measurement of the effects is unintentionally applied differently in one treatment group than in another. Such systematic biases can occur both when observers or testers are involved in measuring the effects of treatment and when self-report data are collected.

Two obvious precautions are to develop measures that require minimal personal discretion and to train testers or observers to perform in a standard manner. An additional precaution is to randomly assign participants to observers as well as to treatment conditions. Then any effects due to systematic differences between observers can be tested in an analysis of variance.

However, the reality of applied settings seldom lends itself to such control. In actuality, testers and observers are probably assigned to participants or groups of participants most often on the basis of scheduling or abilities. When such is the case, a minimal precaution against systematic biasing is to vary observers and testers over conditions as much as possible. Doing so prevents interpreting as treatment effects differences that in reality are due to the observers or testers associated with various treatment conditions. The disadvantage presented by tester-observer heterogeneity is that it introduces random error into the analysis of experimental effects, thereby increasing error variance. This makes real treatment effects more difficult to observe.

Cowen (1978) cites problems in self-report measurement which pose threats to determining true treatment effects in community program evaluation research. These problems are perhaps best exemplified by the tendency of participants to respond in a socially desirable fashion or in ways that second-guess experimenters' intentions. When such tendencies are reflected equally in treatment and control groups, comparability is not at issue. Instead, as Cowen (1978) aptly argues, one may need to call into question the meaningfulness of an effect demonstrated by participants, all of whom were presumably affected in "unnatural" ways by the research.

Self-report can also be biased when the experimental group has developed some relationship with the researcher that the control group has not. This relationshp would affect data from experimental and control groups in noncomparable ways. A randomized control-group design cannot guarantee against self-report biasing that may grow out of some aspect of the experimental treatment. However, it may be possible to test for the occurrence of self-report bias by looking at two dependent measures of the same treatment effect, which can be expected to be differentially influenced by self-report bias. An effect due to self-report bias would show only on that dependent variable more susceptible to it. If, on the other hand, two different dependent variables show a similar treatment effect, even the one susceptible to bias is more to be trusted.

Summary

We recommend that researchers implement randomized experiments in field settings whenever it is feasible to do so. A few circumstances are particularly suitable to randomized experiments—such as when demand for services is greater than availability of services (see Cook & Campbell, 1979, pp. 371-383, for suggestions of other situations conducive to randomized experiments). Researchers must have a good deal of control over resources in a setting to execute randomized designs. In reality, they will often have to argue persistently and persuasively for the controls that are needed for well-designed experimental studies. Even when problems in measurement, attrition, or treatment contamination threaten to bias the findings, initial comparability of experimental groups can be invaluable in determining whether the bias favors finding an effect in

the treatment group. Sometimes, parts of the initial randomized design can be analyzed as planned and, in conjunction with quasi-experimental back-up designs, can
create a confidence interval within which to judge the
reliability of any findings. To do this, data should be
collected so that the extent and nature of attrition, contamination, or measurement problems can be detected.

If researchers do repeated analyses reflecting both
the original design plan and the treatment as it was actually implemented, the analyses may not always converge
as they did for Cook and his associates (1975) and Wan
and his associates (1980). When the various analyses
yield conflicting results, the best approach, in our opinion, is to report each analysis and the biases and limitations associated with each to the extent they are known.
No individual study should ever be expected to be definitive. Rather, knowledge is cumulative and a study that
is clearly labeled for what it is contributes to this ac-
cumulation.

WHEN RANDOMIZED EXPERIMENTS ARE NOT POSSIBLE

Some circumstances make randomized experiments impossible or even undesirable. Some potential causal variables, such as gender or race, cannot be assigned.

Similarly, studying differences among naturally
formed groups (employed versus nonemployed mothers or
elderly reporting memory impairment versus those reporting
no impairment) or among communities or neighborhoods
precludes the possibility of assigning individuals to these
memberships. In other settings, the researcher may simply
not be in a position to assign participants to conditions
at random. Communities are included or excluded in a
research project on the basis of their willingness to participate. Agency clients participate in one research component rather than another because they are willing to
commit themselves to different days and times of the week.
These are the actualities of research in applied settings
that create experimental groupings which are noncomparable
in unknown ways.

Mounting a randomized experiment typically requires
more planning time than do studies that take advantage of
naturally formed groups and natural variation to define
the independent variables. Differences in costliness of the

research may arise more from the increased time and preparation required for randomized experiments and less as the direct result of the method of assignment per se.

The consequence of not being able to form treatment and control groups at random is that the groups may be different in ways other than the treatment they receive. Any potential differences, then, remain as rival explanations to treatment that may account for effects observed in the treatment group. Quasi-experimental designs provide systematic ways for establishing which rival explanations may explain the observed effects. At best, some (but seldom all) of the rival explanations can be dismissed as unlikely. In this section, we will describe quasi-experimental designs that most often increase the interpretability of research findings. (By interpretability we mean the ability to narrow the number of potential causes.)

In some cases, the researcher may have information that renders a commonplace explanation implausible. For instance, when a treatment is expected to produce a response that is so unique it would hardly ever occur spontaneously, explanations such as natural maturation are unlikely threats. To eliminate threats a priori, one must rely heavily on established theories or research findings. But theories and previous knowledge, though not required in quasi-experimental research, can also assist in designing the strongest design that given settings and resources will allow.

Noncomparable Control-Group Design

When randomized experiments are not realizable, an alternative involves locating a group to act as a plausible noncomparable control. Often individuals are assembled or an intact control group is identified that resembles the experimental group on demographic, social, or intellectual characteristics pertinent to the study. We persist in using the term noncomparable, however, since the likelihood of the two groups differing in unidentified ways is still considerably greater than if they had been formed through randomization. The decided advantage of the noncomparable control-group design is that treatment effects often become interpretable, while a single pretest-post-test design with no control group never permits ruling out rival explanations for change.

The noncomparable control-group design (in its simplest form) involves administering pre- and post-test measurements to two groups at the same point in time and under the same conditions. The design parallels the classic pretest-post test random control-group design, except that the groups have not been randomly formed.

Interpreting an Example

To illustrate the advantages and disadvantages associated with interpreting the noncomparable control-group design, we preferred to use some (not necessarily ideal) examples from the literature. In Figure 5.1, data are presented from a drug abuse prevention study conducted in a number of New York school districts (Stoessel, 1974). The purpose of the New York study was to evaluate the effects of different school-based drug prevention programs on sixth and seventh grade students' attitudes toward drug use.

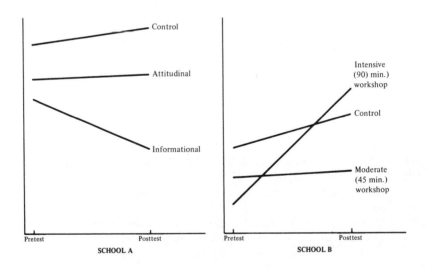

FIGURE 5.1
Effects of School Programs on Drug Attitudes of Students. (Source: Data presented here are modified from tables appearing in Stoessel, R. E. A cross-modality evaluation of drug abuse prevention program effectiveness. Unpublished report, 1974.)

Each school used a different programmatic attack. School A represented in Figure 5.1 offered two different forms of instruction: one program was concerned with providing <u>information</u> about drugs and drug use; the other program emphasized <u>personal attitudes</u> and <u>decision making</u> about drug use. At School B, two communications skills workshops were initiated that emphasized group dynamics and decision making in groups. The formats of the workshops at School B were intended to vary primarily in their intensity: one group met for 45 minutes weekly while the other met for 90 minutes. At each school, students not involved in the drug education programs were randomly chosen to act as controls. In both cases, the dependent measure of the programs' effectiveness was a drug attitude index, developed and validated to reflect the drug-taking propensity of individual students. Individuals' scores might range on a continuum from −190 to +190, with more positive scores indicating less propensity to drug use.

The task now is to determine what confidence we can place in attributing change in drug attitudes to the various school programs. The constraints include the lack of random assignment, either of students to groups or groups to conditions; the resulting large discrepancies among groups at the time of pretesting; and in both cases the initial superiority of control groups over the experimental groups. Based on the appearance of the data, we can speculate about how the treatment groups were chosen. We note that students in the treatment groups were initially worse than the controls. Therefore, the treatment groups, particularly at School B, may have been chosen or formed because these students were seen as more prone to drug abuse and identified as needing special attention.

A number of other studies considered for description here had similar relationships between the experimental and the control groups: the experimental participants were earmarked for ameliorative treatment and those with less serious problems acted as control groups. We suspect that this pattern of pretest performance may frequently occur in community-based experiments.

We now deal in turn with each of some common threats that potentially rival the experimental treatment as a cause for change from pretest to post-test. As far as applicable, we will examine the school results to determine the plausibility that a given threat is a reasonable cause of observed change.

Local History

The threat of local history refers to any number of kinds of events occurring between pre- and post-test observations that although irrelevant to the purpose of the experimental treatment could nevertheless cause changes in the experimental group. To avoid potential contamination through history, researchers should ideally attempt to provide identical experiences for control and experimental groups, except for the treatment itself. Any extraneous events or influences should then be experienced similarly by both groups.

Considering our example of drug abuse programs in schools, one would be concerned, for instance, if a drug crackdown occurred in the local community during the time the program was being conducted or if the policies of the school administration toward student supervision changed during the interim weeks. Under randomized conditions, one would expect such incidents to affect all groups equally. When research groups are not comparable, however, incidents may interact more with one group than with another. For example, if the more drug-prone students comprised the experimental groups, these groups may be more sensitive and reactive to incidents such as crackdowns and stricter policies than the less drug-prone controls.

If an incident such as a drug crackdown actually had taken place during the time of the programs, we would want to determine in what ways the direction of the results might have been influenced. Looking at the graphs for School A, we would find little support for the concern that the incident affected the pattern of results. First, while it seems reasonable to assume that a drug crackdown might "cause" drug-prone students to improve their self-reports of possible drug use, it is harder to find reasons why such an event would cause a sizable negative trend as shown by the attitudinal program group. Second, if such a negative reaction was, in fact, operating, we might expect to see some evidence of it in the attitudinal program group, which presumably was also suggested for experimental treatment because of its members' propensity to use drugs. Instead, the informational group shows a slight positive shift in attitudes. It is unlikely that such a threat operated to produce the pattern of results seen in School A.

At School B, however, the possibility would have to be seriously entertained that such an incident might have produced the pattern of results. The large positive change in attitude exhibited by the intensive-training group might be due to the treatment, but could also be an artifact of students monitoring more carefully their responses to "drug questions." Additional information—such as estimates of communication skills improvement in the intensive-training group—might be brought to bear. A finding that students in the intensive-skills group improved as predicted on various communication and decision-making measures would strengthen the case that treatment (and not history effects) made the difference in their attitude change.

Events external to the treatment sessions are only one kind of local history threat. Threats can also arise when groups experience differences that are related, but not relevant, to the treatment. For instance, one might propose that the informational group at School A showed a move toward a more negative drug-use behavior as a reaction to having been singled out to be part of the program.

Testing

The effects of repeated measurement or testing are threats to interpretability to the extent that participants score better or worse from pretest to post-test, not because of changes induced by treatment, but because they are reacting differently to the measurement. Participants may remember items from earlier testing, may have caught on to the purpose of the questions, or may have become disillusioned and refused to keep trying.

Generally, even a noncomparable control group provides a degree of protection against misinterpreting testing effects as being due to treatment. For instance, assume there is a problem because the time between testings is so short that participants remember many items and therefore answer differently: such behavior should be reflected equally in experimental and control participants. But in noncomparable control-group designs, the threat can interact selectively with one group and not the other. Given our example, the control group may not only be less drug prone but also brighter, which could mean that they remember the pretest items better.

Instrumentation

Instrumentation refers to changes in the measuring instruments themselves from one time to the next. The performance of observers or coders may improve from pre-test to post-test measurement; raters or evaluators may change their criteria. In addition, instrumentation effects may enter in when scaling limitations in a test or measuring instrument artificially restrain the range of change (so-called floor or ceiling effects) or otherwise shift the relative value of change (for example, when a two-point gain midscale is easier to achieve than a two-point gain at the extremities of the scale). Instrumentation becomes a threat to interpretability when, for instance, pretest scores are free to vary because they are positioned at the middle of the scale, but post-test scores are less variable (that is, can reflect less gain or loss) because they are clustered at the extreme top of the scale. Such scaling artifacts can lead to either underestimates or overestimates of treatment change.

The lack of change in the control group for School A could be suspected to be due to a ceiling effect. To be sure, one would want to inspect the distribution of pretest and post-test scores for the groups to determine if the control scores were skewed, a usual sign of scaling problems. However, for School B data, ceiling effects are an implausible explanation for limited change in that control group, since the post-test mean of one of the experimental groups exceeds the control-group mean.

Maturation

Maturation refers to naturally occurring change over time that is seen in individuals, groups, communities, and most other vital systems. When individuals or groups are randomly assigned to experimental conditions, any change due simply to maturation should be reflected equally in all groups. When noncomparable control-group designs are employed, however, groups may be maturing at different rates with presumably different potentials for affecting treatment effects.

When we consider the term maturation, we think of individuals' intellectual, physical, and social development. One group of study participants may be brighter, more socially adept, or otherwise more experienced than another group, implying that the groups are changing at different rates regardless of treatments. Estimating exactly how these rates of maturation should differ between pretest and post-test is clearly difficult, even when there are relevant theories available.

Inspecting the results from School A, one might argue, for instance, that the decline evidenced in the informational group was not the result of the treatment but simply reflected a natural progression in drug-prone children as they grow older. Unfortunately, the pattern of results for the control group provides little evidence to confirm or discount this argument. The control group's level of propensity to use drugs at the onset of the study was not comparable to that of the informational group. However, the additional experimental group (attitudinal program) shows none of the informational group's decline, although both are more drug prone initially than the control group. This comparison seems to discount the influence of maturation, although one still might argue that the attitudinal program was simply more effective at arresting but not reversing decline.

Statistical Regression

Due to error in measurement, individuals' scores tend to fluctuate from one time to the next. When experimental groups have been formed on the basis of pretest scores that are extremely high or low--as often happens when groups are identified for ameliorative programs--the likelihood is for their scores to shift from the extremes at the time of retesting. This shift occurs independently of any experimental treatment effect, but the apparent "change" might falsely be attributed to the treatment.

The pattern of results for School A would indicate that statistical regression is an unlikely threat. Statistical regression would suggest that the low pretest scores for the informational group would become more moderate, and not more extreme, at the time of the post-test. For School B, statistical regression would have been a serious threat if there had not been a crossover in the pattern of results. Statistical regression could account for the tremendous improvement in attitudes toward drugs exemplified by the intensive-workshop group. However, while regression might be expected to account for a shift in scores toward a more moderate level, it would not explain the change beyond even the control-group scores. Because of this crossover, statistical regression appears to be a less plausible explanation for change than either local history or treatment effects.

Summarizing the evaluation of the drug program, we have attempted to consider in a systematic fashion the likelihood that the drug abuse prevention programs initiated at School A and School B are truly responsible for the changes in drug attitudes observed from pretest to post-test. We had the advantage of comparing each treatment group with two noncomparable groups, one untreated and one receiving an alternative treatment.

Given the pattern of pretest–post test results across groups in School A, we could not discount local history, instrumentation, and maturation as possible alternative causes for the negative change in drug attitudes observed in the informational group. However, the pattern of results for School B suggested that testing effects, instrumentation, maturation, and statistical regression were unlikely explanations of the gains observed in the intensive-workshop group. Only local-history effects remained as a possible rival cause that could not be dismissed without further information.

Selection

Selection is another threat operating when the kind of people in one experimental group differs from that in another, for instance because they elected which group to be in. This effect is especially difficult to evaluate in post-test-only designs. Hormuth and Stephan (1981) were interested in the attitudinal effects of the TV series "Holocaust." Due to some external restrictions, they were able to implement a design measuring attitudes only a few days after the series was aired in the United States and in Germany. They compared people who had seen the show with others who had not. They also created an additional condition by having all subjects select which of two groups to be in: those identifying with the victims or those identifying with the group in power as related to the holocaust. The possibility that both self-selected factors interacted cannot be excluded. But Hormuth and Stephan could at least argue that such interaction of selection on both factors was very unlikely: In their study, "Holocaust" had not been watched by 108 persons; 11.1% of those said they identified with the group in power. Of the 152 interviewees who had watched the show, 11.2% identified with the group in power. The almost identical percentage made it unlikely that interactive selection was a decisive factor.

Other Quasi-experimental Design Strategies

In addition to noncomparable control groups, four other design strategies will be presented to increase interpretability in quasi-experiments. These strategies can be used alone or in combination with each other or with noncomparable control groups. In combination, such mixed quasi-experimental design strategies often provide stronger internal as well as external validity.

Multiple-pretest Observation

Combining two or more pretests into the noncomparable control-group design offers a number of advantages in interpretability. The school drug prevention program demonstrated the difficulty of determining whether noncomparable experimental groups are maturing at different rates (known as selection-maturation). Adding an additional pretest permits the researcher to check the extent to which groups change at different rates from the first to the second pretest. The rate of change for both groups should continue from the second pretest to the post-test, and any deviation from the expected growth that is exhibited by the treatment group can be attributed to treatment effects. This assumption can be tested using the control group; comparability of its change from the first to the second pretest and from the second pretest to the post-test can be determined.

Another strength associated with this combined design is its ability to detect statistical regression effects. Obtaining two estimates of the groups' means before treatment occurs provides a basis for judging the reliability of the instrument and prevents a spuriously high or low pretest score from emerging as a misleading treatment effect. An example will help to illustrate this advantage.

Cook and Straw (1981) were interested in detecting the effects of reducing the price of school lunches on pupils' participation in school lunch programs. Their task was a difficult one because they had not been able to randomly assign schools to conditions. (They had been asked to analyze the data after the data collection had taken place.) Some of the data from the study are presented in Table 5.1. For our purposes here, note first the pattern of results looking just from Pretest 2 to the post-test. After the price change was introduced, the participation rate in the treatment group rose 6.6%, a relatively large change relative to the 0.9% change in the noncomparable control group. The change does not appear quite so dramatic, however, when one takes into account the variability of the treatment-group means from Pretest 1 to Pretest 2. The second pretest mean of 71.7% seems deviantly low. While we may still conclude that reducing price increases participation, our estimates of the magnitude of the effect are likely to be revised based on the information provided by the multiple-pretest means. In this study, the availability of multiple-pretest scores prevented an overestimate of the effects of the treatment; in other instances, of course, it may prevent an underestimate from occurring.

TABLE 5.1
Mean Annual Participation Rates for Schools

	Percentage of Students Purchasing Lunch			
	Pretest 1	Pretest 2	X	Post-test
Treatment: schools with price reduction	74.3	71.7		78.3
Control: schools without price reduction	77.9	79.4		80.3

Source: Compiled by authors from data presented by Cook, T. D., & Straw, R. B. Quasi-experimentation: An introduction to its priority questions and mechanics. In T. J. Glynn & L. G. Richards (Eds.), Methodological approaches to marijuana policy research (National Institute on Drug Abuse Research Monograph No. 33, DHHS No. ADM 81-1052). Washington, D.C.: U.S. Government Printing Office, 1981.

From a cost-benefit standpoint, the added cost of administering the pretest observation is minor as related to the total cost of a study, particularly when one considers the important gains in interpreting results.

Replications

A different strategy to increase interpretability of quasi-experimental designs is to strive for replicability of experimental treatment results. This approach can take a number of forms. It may be possible to obtain multiple dependent measures for the same treatment. Instead of deciphering only one pattern of results, one would look for consistency in performance gains in the treatment group over the noncomparable control group across a number of dependent measures. In the study discussed earlier on the relative effects of geriatric day care and homemaker services, Wan and his colleagues (1980) measured the effects of the innovative programs using four assessments: (1) physical functioning, (2) contentment level, (3) mental functioning, and (4) activity level. Support for each program's effectiveness was found by looking for maintenance or gains in the treatment groups on each of these measures of functioning.

Similarly, replications of treatment effects with different groups of participants at different points in time can give more credibility to research findings. In a recent study, Ehrlich, D'Augelli, and Conter (1981) took this approach in evaluating a program to train indigenous community helpers. The program was aimed at teaching local volunteers who then solicited and taught each other to use highly specific verbal skills to respond to persons seeking help for a problem. Ehrlich, D'Augelli, and Conter sequentially implemented the program in two different rural communities, making it possible to determine whether the pretest-post test gains shown by the first group of volunteers were repeated with a different group of trainees. To the degree that the results were replicated, some assurance is provided that the initial results were not spurious.

Direct Measurement of Threats

Under some conditions it is possible to directly measure the plausibility of factors other than the intended treatment accounting for observed change. In an ingenious study of environmental conditions, Cohen, Glass, and Singer (1973) set out to show causal links between apartment noise, auditory discrimination, and reading ability in children. The study was conducted in an apartment building over a highway. Measurements showed that noise was

inversely related to the apartment floor number, with automobile noise decreasing as one went from the lower to the
higher floors. The researchers were in no position, of
course, to assign children to noisy versus less noisy
apartments or to length of time lived there. Consequently,
they were faced with a multitude of factors that might
logically be related both to children's reading ability and
to where they lived: socioeconomic status, social class,
number of other children in the home, auditory impairment,
or carbon monoxide poisoning that might be associated with
the passing automobiles.

Cohen, Glass, and Singer systematically gathered
information on these potential causal agents in order to
determine their plausibility. For instance, data were collected on fathers' and mothers' educational level as indicators of social class, and the effects of these variables
were partialed out in correlations between the floors on
which children lived and their reading ability. Air
samples were collected and tested at various floors to determine if carbon monoxide levels varied as did noise
levels (they did not). In the end, the researchers found
no explanations for the relationship between apartment floor
level and reading ability in children other than the effects of noisiness associated with living on lower floors.

Statistical Controls

Analysis of covariance using pretest scores as co-
variates is sometimes suggested as a means of adjusting
for pretest differences in experimental groups. While it is
true that covariate analysis can improve statistical sensitivity to change when used with randomized designs, the
case is not the same for quasi-experimental designs. Measurement error can lead to either an underadjustment or
an overadjustment in the analysis of noncomparable control-
group designs (Reichardt, 1979). Unless one has clear
estimates of measurement reliability, analysis of covariance
cannot be recommended as a solution. Currently, a great
deal of research is being conducted on the use of statistical analyses to control for selection a posteriori. These
include reliability-adjusted covariance analysis (compare
Reichardt, 1979), latent-factor analytic structural-equation
modeling (Jöreskog & Sörbom, 1979), and, among econometri-
cians, tobit analysis (Barnow, Cain, & Goldberger, 1980;
Heckman, 1976, 1979).

DESIGN PROBLEMS PECULIAR TO COMMUNITY PSYCHOLOGY

So far our discussion of quasi-experimental solutions has been limited to the problems of studying experimental treatments of groups of individuals in applied settings. Part of what makes community psychology unique is its additional orientation toward problems that cannot be subjected to experimental manipulation and toward large aggregate units for study. We now address some of the design problems associated with the unique features of community psychology.

Designing Studies for Nonmanipulable Treatments

Community psychologists face the challenge of designing studies for problems over which they have little or no control. We are considering here both naturally occurring events, such as disasters, and actions dictated by political, economic, or legal forces, such as factory shutdowns or school district reorganizations that might affect whole communities or segments of communities. Such phenomena rarely lend themselves to conventional methods of research. Typically, when the natural events are unanticipated, post hoc design strategies are necessary. Even when the events may be anticipated, the researcher still is constrained by the nonrandomized, typically selective choice of who receives the "treatment" and when. Other constraints may operate as well: in attempting to study the impact of the Attica prison riot on the surrounding community, Andrulis, Scherwitz, and Iscoe (1976) found the general public extremely resistant to any attempts to survey their attitudes after the riot. Ideally, community psychologists might attempt to study such phenomena by nonreactive measurements, which could provide observations both before and after the event in order to detect any change in its direction and extent (compare Webb et al., 1981). In the case of Attica, for example, one might look at differences before and after the riot in local gun sales, numbers of police officers, and published political stances of local politicians and elected officials. Such unobtrusive measures often enable us to infer social change.

When Communities Are the Unit of Analysis

Frequently a whole community or neighborhood will have to be selected as the unit of analysis. It may be necessary to do so when, for instance, members of a community communicate with each other about a treatment. Under such circumstances, treatment and no-treatment subjects cannot clearly be separated within one community. Flay and Cook (1981) discuss these problems in the context of media-based prevention campaigns. Much of what they have to say in that context applies to research in community psychology more broadly.

Many tasks of community psychology can be subsumed under the label "educating the public." These can be prevention campaigns, educational campaigns about the role and nature of mental health disorders, dissemination of information about the kinds of services available, and so on. For instance, if special services for battered wives are available, this information should be widely known, so that at the time of need victims already know or are apt to be told what options are available to them. Withholding this kind of information until need arises would defeat the very purpose of the services provided. In this example, the treatment simply consists of providing information. Access to this kind of treatment cannot be controlled as strictly as access to counseling or similar services. One can usually establish who received how much counseling or similar treatment, and control groups can be created through waiting lists. Information, on the other hand, is disseminated not only through controlled channels but also through informal, uncontrolled ones. In describing this kind of situation, Flay and Cook (1981) state that the extent of communication among individuals should be taken into account when the unit of assignment is determined. When communication among individuals is likely, it may be necessary to assign a whole community to a treatment, thereby making the community the unit of analysis, rather than the individuals who received the treatment.

One advantage of using a whole community as one single unit of analysis is that the measures obtained are particularly reliable and powerful. A composite measure based on data from many different individuals will not reflect individual idiosyncrasies to the extent that observations based on one individual could. However, there are disadvantages as well to using whole communities as units

of analysis. The statistical power of a test will be reduced because it is dependent upon the number of units.
Given a finite budget, the larger the unit size, the fewer
the number of units. This problem is not offset by the
gain in measurement reliability.

Other problems are posed: With few units per treatment, idiosyncracies of selection can confound the effects
and compromise internal validity. For example, if three
communities are studied, the researcher would probably
try to select communities which differ from each other in
some way (for example, climate, degree of industrialization,
and age distribution) and are matched on others. The
diversity would eliminate some possible threats to internal
validity. Because of the small number of communities,
however, only a few such threats can be taken into consideration. Thus, other aspects that were not part of the
sampling decision could still be responsible for observed
differences. Who would accept, for instance, that the random assignment of three cities to two conditions from among
New York, Atlanta, Chicago, Los Angeles, San Antonio, and
Houston could ever result in equivalent groupings, even
with prior stratification by city size? The most obvious
solution, that is, using a larger number of communities as
units of study, is usually not feasible because of budgetary,
time, and staffing limitations.

The decision to make communities the unit of analysis should be explicit and not made simply as a matter of
convenience or default. Frequently communities are selected
without consideration of the problems involved or with expectations that they could simply be solved by using the
individuals as units for the statistical analysis. The in-
appropriateness of this solution, if it is used as the only
level of analysis, is discussed by Burstein (1980). A
clear awareness of the reason for the decision and its consequences may allow for design alternatives at an early
stage.

One design alternative may be to compromise on the
size and number of communities involved. Using smaller
instead of larger communities may free some money and
staff for the addition of a few more communities. Using
specific, circumscribed neighborhoods within a city may
allow for sampling in an urban setting without having to
include the whole community. Some neighborhoods are, at
least in some respects, so far apart and separated even
in the same city that they can be assigned to separate

treatments. For instance, if the treatment consists of information available or steps to be taken in an emergency, the selection of neighborhood newssheets and inserts rather than city-wide newspapers and television spots may be the method of choice.

Flay and Cook (1981) discuss several methodological approaches, each of which solves some, but not all, of the problems of using communities as units of analysis. They conclude that a combination of methods, where feasible, is the most advisable. They suggest, among other alternatives, an experimental paradigm for studying communities. To employ this approach requires obtaining no-treatment control groups, a problem to which we now turn.

Obtaining Community Sites as Controls

When psychologists attempt to study change at the community level rather than the individual one, the issues of obtaining and maintaining control sites become more complex. A number of interdependent factors add to the usual difficulties of establishing suitable control groups. Our notions about comparability among units change as the unit becomes larger. This change is dependent, in part, on the inverse relationship between aggregate size and the unit under consideration and the likely number of units available. Thus, when doing research in which individuals are randomly assigned to experimental treatments, one assumes a certain comparability among units as long as a reasonable number of participants is involved. As one moves from individuals to neighborhoods, catchment areas, or entire cities, the comparability among units becomes questionable. In other words, even when one has the luxury of assigning communities to treatment groups—let us say from among all ten suburban communities surrounding a metropolitan area—the credibility of attaining some semblance of comparability in this manner is lost when some communities are wealthy, while others are low income; when some communities are predominantly black, while others are integrated; and so forth.

After having displayed the discouraging side of obtaining controls at the community level, we feel compelled to mention at least one example where such a control was obtained and added significantly to the interpretability of the design. Farquhar, Maccoby, and their associates (Farquhar, 1978; Farquhar et al., 1977; Maccoby et al., 1977) were interested in determining whether different forms of community health education would result in reduced risk of cardiovascular disease. They chose as research sites three northern California towns with comparable total populations and comparable populations for the 35–59-year-old age bracket targeted for the study. One town was designated as the control because it was more isolated from the other two communities, which shared some media. A random sample of 35–59-year-old men and women from each town was screened to determine health and behavioral factors related to cardiovascular disease, and the results were sent to participants and their physicians in all three communities. Both experimental towns experienced a mass-media health education campaign. In addition, in one experimental town, two-thirds of the individuals identified as high risk by the screening procedure were offered other, more intensive health education programs. The remaining one-third were simply exposed to the media campaign. The only "treatment" the control community received consisted of informational letters on the cardiovascular screening results.

Three factors added to the interpretability of this design. Because of the small number of communities in the sample, the results might have been open to a number of plausible alternative explanations. However, the communities were chosen on many grounds, one of which was their general similarity, including similar scores on the baseline measures of risk. The control town also provided a comparison group for judging the possible influences of historic events, national trends, and so forth, on cardiovascular health. Finally, by varying the intensity of the treatment the participants in one town received (media exposure plus intensive health care education versus media exposure alone) the researchers provided an additional probe derived from partitioning the treatment group according to the presumed intensity of their treatment. Farquhar and his colleagues possessed resources that permitted them to sample only three communities, chosen partially for convenience and feasibility. They decided to look for convergence among three probes of effect—comparisons of the pretest and post-test within communities, comparisons between the different communities, and comparisons of the intensity of the treatment within a community.

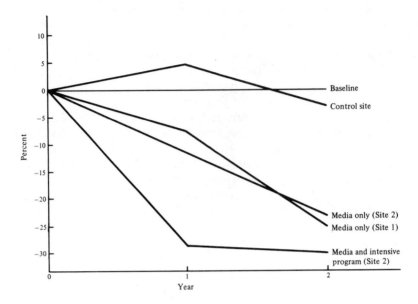

FIGURE 5.2
Percentage change from baseline (0) in risk of coronary heart
disease after one and two years of health education among participants from three communities (data for high-risk participants only). (Source: Adapted from a figure that appeared in
Farquhar, J. W., Maccoby, N., Wood, P. D., Alexander, J. K.,
Breitrose, H., Brown, B. W., Haskell, W. L., McAlister, A. L.,
Meyer, A. J., Nash, J. D., & Stern, M. P. Community education
for cardiovascular health. The Lancet, 1977, 1192–1195.

      Some of their findings are presented in Figure 5.2.
The results are reported in terms of positive and negative
changes in cardiovascular risk over the two-year duration
of the study. The decline in health risk was sizable
among both the community residents exposed to the media
campaign and those exposed both to the media campaign
and intensive health education program. The patterns of
change for the high-risk individuals exposed only to media
interventions are very similar, regardless of the experimental communities in which they lived. And, as we
would expect if the treatment and not some other coincident
was operating, the individuals receiving the combined
media campaign and intensive health education program
showed the greatest decline in risk. The control community

is particularly important for this set of results, since it suggests that regression or instrumentation effects were unlikely explanations for the degree of reduction in risk found for the experimental communities. Partitioning participants by levels of treatment provided a direct and highly sensitive test of the treatment effect.

Needing a Time Perspective on Community Change:
Interrupted Time Series

We concur with Cowen's (1977) suggestion that if one is interested in studying communities, one must be willing to take a long-range perspective. Such a perspective may be particularly necessary when studying community change. It can be essential both in detecting change and in avoiding false conclusions about the significance of observed changes.

A long-range perspective also creates some specific requirements for an appropriate design. An interrupted time-series design, in its simplest form, involves multiple observations before and after an event or "treatment" has occurred and presumably "interrupted" the normal pattern of effects. Time series is particularly appropriate when the effects of an event can be studied unobtrusively. Since effects can be expected to vary over time quite independent of the treatment event, the biggest challenge associated with time-series designs is distinguishing between spurious and treatment-related change. An example can clarify these points.

The appropriateness of interrupted time-series designs for some kinds of community psychology interests was first suggested to us by a study of the effects of crowding on prison inmates. Megargee (1977) was interested in testing the relationship between decreased physical space and incidence of disruptive behaviors among the inmates. Megargee was presented with a special opportunity to study changes in density and their consequences, since the prison was undergoing renovations that periodically reduced the amount of living space available to inmates. In addition, Megargee had the advantage that information on disruptive behavior was routinely collected by the prison on a daily basis. While Megargee (1977) used correlational analyses to suggest the relationship between density and disruptive behavior, we have tried to recast his study to match its features to the design strength offered by time series.

In Figure 5.3 we present hypothetical data to illustrate how the effects of crowding might have been studied. In actuality, the prison inmates underwent a series of space reductions, the initial one in January 1973 with the closing of one dormitory and the attendant relocation of inmates into remaining dormitories. Megargee looked at data over 36 months; we have hypothesized four years of data to illustrate our point better. Megargee was aware of, and tried to account for, the fluctuations in the prison population during the time of the study as well as temperature changes, particularly increased temperature during the summer months. Following his lead, our suggested measure of effects is the ratio of incidents of disorderly behaviors to average prison population per month. We have also built possible seasonal variations into the data. We have arbitrarily chosen six months as a reasonable estimate of the duration of an average space reduction. We should point out here that the notion of a duration of a certain time is not unusual in time series, although the more frequent case involves an abrupt event or change in policy, treatment, and so forth that is expected to continue indefinitely (see Cook & Campbell, 1976, pp. 274-284, for some interesting examples of this).

In interpreting our hypothetical results, look first at the data as if we had only a pretest and a post-test observation of the effects of reducing space at the initiation of the renovation. Comparing December 1972 with January 1973, the data would reflect a slight increase in disruptive behavior after the reduction, but it would be well within the normal monthly variability. The absolute value of none of the months from January to May 1973 exceeds occasional high monthly values during the preceding years. What is significant in this case is the alteration in seasonal patterns that seemed to occur after the reduction in space. In the previous two years, the ratio of disruptive behaviors tended to be low in winter and spring, and higher in summer and early fall (perhaps due to aggravating temperatures). During the period of renovation, the usual dip in spring was replaced by steady increases in disruptive behavior, culminating in a peak rate in June of 1973. After the renovation was completed, more normal seasonal patterns resumed. Again, however, if we

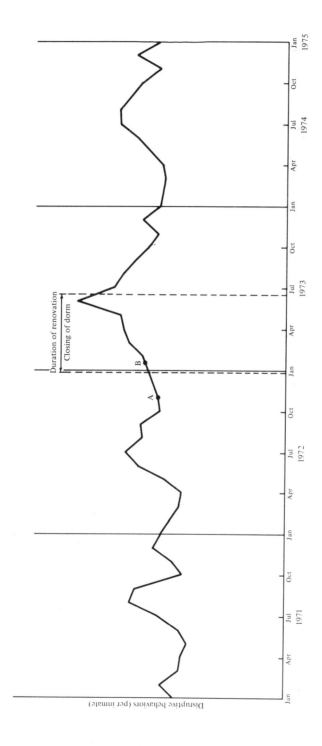

FIGURE 5.3

Time-series plot of hypothetical results of prison-crowding study. (Source: Adapted from Megargee, E. I. The association of population density, reduced space, and uncomfortable temperatures with misconduct in a prison community. American Journal of Community Psychology, 1977, 5, 289-298.

had only looked at pre-post differences to measure the effects of completion of the renovation work (that is, differences from June to July 1973) we would have overestimated the positive effects of returning to normal, since the July ratio was so extreme.

The biggest threat to a time-series design such as this is local history. A rival explanation such as an unusually hot spring could easily be checked. However, other plausible explanations are more difficult to assess. Perhaps the staff were more concerned with maintaining control during the renovation and consequently were more sensitive to minor infractions that otherwise might not have been noted as disruptive. The increased ratios during the renovation period might be an instrumentation artifact resulting from the staff's change in behavior. Or the cause might have been some third variable related to the renovation changes, such as the breakdown of inmates' daily routines, but not density or crowding per se.

The researcher would need to determine the plausibility of such local-history threats in a systematic fashion. One might identify a group of inmates as controls who, for instance, might have had their daily routines disrupted during the renovation but whose dormitory was not used for the overflow of inmates. Better still, if the renovation process involved upgrading one dormitory per year over a number of years, one might replicate the effects by using groups of inmates not affected by the relocation as controls one year and as experimental groups the next year (known as switching replication).

An example of the switching-replication interrupted time-series design is provided in a study by Hennigan, Del Rosario, Heath, Cook, Wharton, and Calder (1982). Using communities as their unit of analysis, Hennigan and associates looked at the relationship between the introduction of TV and the incidence of FBI indicators of violent crime, burglary, auto theft, and larceny.

The numbers of communities having access to TV did not steadily increase over time in the United States; rather, due to a temporary freeze by the Federal Communication Commission, this increase occurred in two stages, preferred and postfreeze, separated by a few years. If television is to be causally linked to changes in crime rates, such changes should show a consistent temporal relationship to the introduction of TV in the different communities. If, on the other hand, changes in crime rates are due to some other societal changes, they would not so coincide. Post-freeze and prefreeze communities serve thereby as their respective controls. At Time I, TV is introduced in the prefreeze communities—postfreeze communities serve as controls. At Time II, TV is introduced to postfreeze communities—now the prefreeze communities serve as controls. To further strengthen the case, Hennigan and associates also undertook an additional replication using a larger unit of analysis, namely states.

The results did not indicate significant change in violent crime, burglary, and auto theft at the time of introduction of TV. However, in each of the four tests of the effect, in four different samples (prefreeze and post-freeze, communities and states), a clear increase in the incidence of larceny was found. The multiple replication of the finding, both in communities and states, strengthens the belief in the results and allows for the exclusion of many alternative causes (other than the introduction of TV) which, as Hennigan and associates discuss, might have been associated with an increased desire for material goods among some people.

CONCLUSION

We have written this chapter with the proverbial blinders on, in the sense that we have considered community psychology inquiry only from the perspective of quasi-experimentation and what it can offer. We would be remiss if we left the reader with the impression that quasi-experimentation is more developed as a state of the art than it is. Numerous statistical problems, both in the analysis of noncomparable groups and interrupted time series, remain to be resolved (Cook & Campbell, 1979; Glass & Asher, 1980). We have tried to convey here that the strength of quasi-experimentation lies in its systematic inquiry into causality under conditions that normally do not permit strong causal inferences. We have stressed detecting causal relationships in community psychology problems and have offered quasi-experimental principles for this purpose.

We do not mean to imply that quasi-experimentation is the via regia; if feasible, randomized experimentation is to be preferred, and in other instances other designs will be feasible, appropriate, or sufficient. Finally, concern with methods should not overshadow the fact that these are mere tools. The researcher's knowledge of the issues, sensible hypotheses, or, better still, relevant theory can help make optimal use of these tools.

REFERENCES

Andrulis, D., Scherwitz, L., & Iscoe, I. Community attitudes toward the Attica prison riot--A ministudy. American Journal of Community Psychology, 1976, 4, 189-194.

Barnow, B. S., Cain, G. G., & Goldberger, A. S. Issues in the analysis of selectivity bias. In E. W. Stromsdorfer & G. Farkas (Eds.), Evaluation Studies Review Annual (Vol. 5) Beverly Hills, Calif.: Sage, 1980.

Boruch, R. F. On common contentions about randomized field experiments. In R. F. Boruch & H. W. Riecken (Eds.), Experimental testing of public policy. Boulder, Colo.: Westview Press, 1975.

Boruch, R. F. Appropriateness and feasibility of randomized tests of social programs. In L. Sechrest (Ed.), Emergency medical services: Research and methodology. Washington, D.C.: U.S. Government Printing Office, 1977.

Boruch, R. F., McSweeny, A. J., & Soderstrom, E. J. Randomized field experiments for program planning, development and evaluation. Evaluation Quarterly, 1978, 2, 655-695.

Burstein, L. The role of levels of analysis in the specification of education effects. In R. Dreeben & J. A. Thomas (Eds.), The Analysis of educational productivity, Vol.1: Issues in microanalysis. Cambridge, Mass.: Ballinger, 1980.

Campbell, D. T., & Stanley, J. C. Experimental and quasi-experimental designs for research. Chicago: Rand McNally, 1963.

Cohen, S., Glass, D. C., & Singer, J. E. Apartment noise, auditory discrimination and reading ability in children. Journal of Experimental Social Psychology, 1973, 9, 407-422.

Conner, R. F. Selecting a control group: An analysis of the randomization process in twelve social reform programs. Evaluation Quarterly, 1977, 1, 195-244.

Cook, T. D. Quasi-experimentation: Its ontology, epistemology, and methodology. In G. Morgan (Ed.), Organizational research strategies. Cambridge, Mass.: MIT Press, in press.

Cook, T. D., Appleton, H., Conner, R. F., Shaffer, A., Tamkin, G., & Weber, S. J. "Sesame Street" revisited. New York: Russell Sage Foundation, 1975.

Cook, T. D., & Campbell, D. T. The design and conduct of quasi-experiments and true experiments in field settings. In M. D. Dunette (Ed.), Handbook of industrial and organizational research. Chicago: Rand McNally, 1976.

Cook, T. D., & Campbell, D. T. Quasi-experimentation: Design and analysis issues for field settings. Chicago: Rand McNally, 1979.

Cook, T. D., & Straw, R. B. Quasi-experimentation: An introduction to its priority questions and mechanics. In T. J. Glynn & L. G. Richards (Eds.), Methodological approaches to marijuana policy research (National Institute on Drug Abuse Research Monograph No. 33, DHHS No. ADM 81-1052). Washington, D.C.: U.S. Government Printing Office, 1981.

Cowen, E. L. Social and community interventions. Annual Review of Psychology, 1973, 24, 423-472.

Cowen, E. L. Baby steps toward primary prevention. American Journal of Community Psychology, 1977, 5, 1-22.

Cowen, E. L. Some problems in community psychology evaluation research. Journal of Consulting and Clinical Psychology, 1978, 46, 782-805.

Ehrlich, R. P., D'Augelli, A. R., & Conter, K. R. Evaluation of a community-based system for training natural helpers: I. Effects on verbal helping skills. American Journal of Community Psychology, 1981, 9, 321-337.

Farquhar, J. W. The community-based model of life style intervention trials. American Journal of Epidemiology, 1978, 108, 103-111.

Farquhar, J. W., Maccoby, N., Wood, P. D., Alexander, J. K., Breitrose, H., Brown, B. W., Haskell, W. L., McAlister, A. L., Meyer, A. J., Nash, J. D., & Stern, M. P. Community education for cardiovascular health. The Lancet, 1977, 1192-1195.

Flay, B. R., & Cook, T. D. The evaluation of media-based prevention campaigns. In R. Rice & W. Paisley (Eds.), Media campaigns. Beverly Hills, Calif.: Sage, 1981.

Glass, G. V., & Asher, J. W. Causation and quasi-experimental design (Review of Cook, T. D., & Campbell, D. T. Quasi-experimentation: Design and analysis issues for field settings). Contemporary Psychology, 1980, 25, 772-775.

Heckman, J. J. The common structure of statistical models of truncation, sample selection, and limited dependent variables and a simple estimator for such models. The Annals of Economic and Social Measurement, 1976, 5, 475-492.

Heckman, J. J. Sample selection bias as a specification error. Econometrica, 1979, 47, 153-161.

Hennigan, K. M., Del Rosario, M. L., Heath, L., Cook, T. D., Wharton, J. D., & Calder, B. J. Did crime increase when television was introduced in the United States? Journal of Personality and Social Psychology, 1982, 42, 461-477.

Hormuth, S. E., & Stephan, W. G. Effects of viewing "Holocaust" on Germans and Americans: A just-world analysis. Journal of Applied Social Psychology, 1981, 11, 240-251.

Jöreskog, K. G., & Sörbom, D. Advances in factor analysis and structural equation models. Cambridge, Mass.: Abt, 1979.

Maccoby, N., Farquhar, J. W., Wood, P. D., & Alexander, J. Reducing the risk of cardiovascular disease: Effects of a community based campaign on knowledge and behavior. Journal of Community Health, 1977, 3, 100-114.

McClure, L., Cannon, D., Allen, S., Belton, E., Connor, P., D'Ascoli, C., Stone, P., Sullivan, B., & McClure, G. Community psychology concepts and research base: Promise and product. American Psychologist, 1980, 35, 1000-1011.

Megargee, E. I. The association of population density, reduced space, and uncomfortable temperatures with misconduct in a prison community. American Journal of Community Psychology, 1977, 5, 289-298.

Mullen, E. J., Chazin, R. M., & Feldstein, D. M. Services for the newly dependent: An assessment. The Social Review, 1972, 46, 309-322.

Novaco, R. W., & Monahan, J. Research in community psychology: An analysis of work published in the first six years of the American Journal of Community Psychology. American Journal of Community Psychology, 1980, 8, 131-145.

Reichardt, C. S. The statistical analysis of data from nonequivalent control group designs. In T. D. Cook & D. T. Campbell, Quasi–experimentation: Design and analysis issues for field settings. Chicago: Rand McNally, 1979.

Stoessel, R. E. A cross–modality evaluation of drug abuse prevention program effectiveness. Manhasset, New York: Methods Analysis Corporation, 1974.

Wan, T. H., Weissert, W. G., & Livieratos, B. B. Geriatric day care and homemaker services: An experimental study. Journal of Gerontology, 1980, 35, 256–274.

Webb, E. J., Campbell, D. T., Schwartz, R. D., Sechrest, L., & Grove, J. B. Nonreactive measures in the social sciences (2nd ed.). Boston: Houghton Mifflin, 1981.

6   What Ethology Is About: Some Conceptual and Methodological Implications for Community Psychology

Slobodan B. Petrovich
and Eckhard H. Hess

This chapter describes some of the elements of the biological approach to the science of behavior in an attempt to facilitate an interdisciplinary exchange among ethologists and community psychologists. The purpose is to share habits of thought on some problems and to communicate theoretical principles and methods which ethologists exploit while asking questions about behavior in its ecological setting.

At the outset, our goal is to tell what ethology is about. Then we proceed to extrapolate some of the conceptual and methodological lessons that may be of interest and of use to community psychologists. Our treatment considers exemplars of the ecological adaptation of animal and human behavior, and critically appraises the role of animal-ethological models for community research. Finally, in a concluding section, we focus from a historical perspective on some of the theoretical issues of relevance to both ethology and community psychology.

WHAT ETHOLOGY IS ABOUT: SOME CONCEPTUAL
AND METHODOLOGICAL EXTRAPOLATIONS
FROM ETHOLOGICAL STUDIES

Ethology has been described as the biology of behavior (Eibl-Eibesfeldt, 1975; Tinbergen, 1963). While ethology has a relatively long and interesting history (Jaynes, 1969) for its more recent recognition it owes much to the contribution of Lorenz (1965, 1969, 1970, 1971), Von Frisch (1967), and Tinbergen (1951, 1972). Today, the study of behavior is considered to be a new frontier in the biological sciences.

Currently, the ethological literature on various aspects of animal behavior is so voluminous and varied that it leaves one wondering about what it is that ethologists do not study. Faced with similar concerns, Tinbergen (1963) suggested that once the behavior is adequately described and operationalized, ethologists study the ontogeny or development, the immediate causation or mechanisms, the adaptive significance or function and the evolution of behavior.

At the outset, and before we proceed to enumerate various extrapolations and generalizations that can be made from the ethological approach to behavioral analyses, let us emphasize what should not be done. It would be unfortunate if one were to uncritically accept inferences and statements based on ethological findings generated from studies of infrahuman species and apply them to humans. It behooves us to conceptualize each animal as a unique preparation and to think of speciation itself as a continuous process of being and becoming unique. Thus, instead of accepting injudicious application of ethological findings to humans, it is the methodological approach of ethology that merits serious consideration as a tool for the study of human behavior.

Ethogram

Ethologists, as do other scientists, consider it important to be able to describe, define, measure, understand, predict, and control the phenomena or behaviors under investigation. The starting point consists of comprehensive and detailed descriptions of the observed behavior patterns of an individual, groups, populations or species, in the appropriate setting. Such descriptions may be labeled an ethogram.

What is the appropriate setting for the development of an ethogram? Traditionally, the preference has been for unobtrusive and obtrusive naturalistic observations. An example of the latter would include Jane von Lawick-Goodall's research (1968). She was able to integrate herself into a troop of chimpanzees and develop an ethogram that included such items as descriptive analyses of tool use, parental care, and social and asocial behaviors.

However, the development of an ethogram need not be limited only to descriptive records of animals in their naturalistic habitats. For example, we have utilized semirestricted naturalistic field observations in order to study the characteristics of the imprinting process in nature (Hess, 1973; Hess & Petrovich, 1973 a and b). This was done through very careful and detailed observation of female mallards and their offspring in natural settings, beginning with the onset of incubation and continuing through incubation, hatching, exodus from the nest, and the subsequent weeks of life. Other aspects of the research involved manipulation only to the extent that the natural situation is still left as intact as possible with experimental variation being measured in relation to the natural situation. Hence the control is always the actual natural parent-offspring relation in a feral setting. It is never a state in which animals are deprived as completely as possible and are permitted to experience only the few variables which are introduced experimentally.

Figure 6.1 depicts one of the experimental methods for studying the imprinting process in the natural setting. Sounds that are made within the next box or the nest in which the female is incubating eggs in the field are picked up by means of a concealed microphone. A speaker placed underneath the eggs permits taped sounds to be presented to the female. A thermistor probe permits the continuous recording of the nest-box temperature at the level of the eggs. Each nest box being monitored is between 300 and 700 feet away from the laboratory building which houses the tape recorders and the telethermometer.

The next step in investigating the parent-young communication in relation to hen-hatching social interaction during imprinting is to subject eggs in the laboratory incubator to the same sort of auditory stimulation and communication as is given by a real female to her own eggs. This step is illustrated by Figure 6.2. Microphones and speakers are installed in the laboratory incubator and in an actual nest where a female is incubating her eggs which have begun at the same time as those in the laboratory incubator. This two-way arrangement permits the incubator eggs to have the same auditory feedback as the female's own eggs. That is, whenever the incubator eggs emit sounds, the female can then respond to them. The vocalizations of the

FIGURE 6.1
Schematic representation of one of the experimental methods of
studying imprinting in the natural setting. The nest box in
which the female mallard is incubating eggs is an elevated
structure above the water of a large pond. The different nest
boxes in the pond are all located between 300 and 700 feet away
from the laboratory building housing the recording equipments.
This permits the observation of the natural incubation process
without the experimenter disturbing or being seen by the female
mallard. T: thermistor. M: microphone. S: speaker.

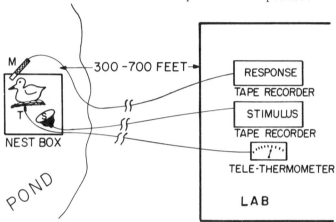

FIGURE 6.2
An experimental method of studying the effects of the parent-
young auditory communication upon hatching time and synchrony.
In this study, the nests were approximately 500 feet away from
the laboratory building housing the incubator with the eggs.
M: microphone. T.R.: tape recorder. S: speaker.

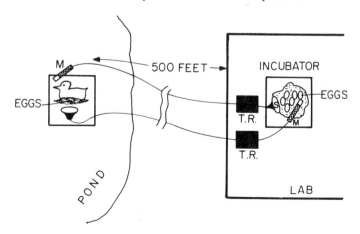

253

female can be received both by her own eggs and by the
incubator eggs.

For example, given the naturalistic observation that
clearly demonstrated some of the features of the duckling-
hen vocal interchange during the last phases of incubation,
we were in a position to design specific experiments to
test for developmental aspect of that vocal interchange and
the role it plays in imprinting and early socialization
(Hess, 1973; Hess & Petrovich, 1973b). A stimulus tape
consisting of vocalizations of a duckling while still inside
the egg was played to two groups of nesting mallard hens.
One group was tested on the first day of each week of incubation while the second group was tested daily. The results indicated that in an initial phase of incubation, the
hens do not respond at all to hatching-sound stimuli. Starting at about day 19, some of the hens are "biologically
prepared" to respond to these stimuli. Subsequently in the
last phase of incubation all of them responded. Given
these observations in nature, we were led to ask the following question: What role does a duckling-hen vocal interchange play in imprinting and the development of early
social behavior? In answer to this question, experiments
were carried out in the laboratory, and these demonstrated
that the "attachment bond" and early socialization start
to develop prenatally and that the vocal-auditory modality
is the major channel involved in communication between a
duckling and a mallard hen (Hess, 1972; Hess & Petrovich,
1973b).

Other investigators have carried out extensive observations of animals in captivity ranging from those sta-
tioned in zoos to those in drive-through wildlife parks,
while still other investigators have produced ethograms of
animals in captivity such as fish in the aquarium or pets
in the laboratory. Ethograms should include descriptions
of such behaviors as grooming, preening, signals in communication, defense of a territory, predation, care of offspring, and migration. Behaviors should also be described
in terms of their function or consequence, such as the
facilitation and establishment of sexual contact, retrieving
of offspring, or pressing a lever. Moreover, ethograms
generally include detailed accounts of the topography of
behavior such as some measures of intensity, frequency,
and patterning as well as temporal sequencing of events.
Examples include recording the pulse rate of the cricket
song, establishing pulse-rate differences among different

species, recording the fact that some species are nocturnal while others are diurnal, and relating such records to functional descriptions of behavior.

No ethologist would claim that a complete ethogram is required or necessary prior to any kind of precise, tightly controlled experimental analysis. However, the ethologist does try to persuade his professional colleagues to recognize that the real world is both the source of problems and the place where the laboratory or experimental solutions to these problems should be tested. Moreover, in the real world there exists a higher probability for detection of fitness of behavioral adaptations. The laboratory is a tool that allows for precise experimental treatment and testing of a specific hypothesis, the outcome of which should be utilized to complement and explain the puzzles of behavioral development (for example, mallard call) occurring in nature. The ethogram is the indispensible component of the healthy inductive approach to behavioral analyses.

The problems that vex community psychologists are the problems of the real world also. As is the case with ethologists, community psychologists are concerned with ecological validity of findings generated by psychological laboratories. The first "ecological assessment" stands out as the functional analogue of the first pages of an ethogram. However, an appreciation of what the ethogram is all about requires efforts beyond description or observation. Sophisticated instrumentation for the monitoring of human behavior is available. Data can be organized systematically and with discipline so as to pave the way for a more robust "testing" of a specific hypothesis.

What are some of the strengths and the limitations of sampling procedures characteristic of community psychology? What are the constraints of such an approach? Why stop there? Accountability demands that we take a holistic approach toward understanding of behavior. A human being functions in a variety of settings ranging from naturalistic to captive. These settings generate their own peculiar constraints and revelations on behavioral manifestations. For example, if a community psychologist wished to investigate the effects of clinical institutions and institutionalization on human behavior, he or she would find in the ethological literature on the behavior of wild animals in zoos and captivity many interesting hypotheses worth pursuing. More important, however, the procedural–methodological approach of ethologists, starting with an ethogram, is an invaluable investigative tool (for example, Lehner, 1979).

Social behavior and learning, for instance, are affected by the physical and social ecology of a setting and can be facilitated or limited by the manipulation of ecological factors. As used in the present context, the term ecology stands for the gross conditions of an environment that determine which events and behaviors can occur in a setting and specifically whether or not an organism can receive a stimulus or emit a response. Such physical facilitators and constraints are therefore as much setting conditions as are, for instance, deprivation-satiation operations for food stimuli. Similarly, the rules and regulations in a setting (explicit and implicit) represent social facilitators or constraints on behavior systems. Thus, ecological conditions can insulate an individual against, or cause one to be exposed to, other individuals, or their specific activities, and in that way can determine whether or not the individual can emit particular responses or seek particular ends.

The physical and social ecology of a setting can therefore impose effective constraints on behavior systems, or the ecology of a setting can also be employed to facilitate social learning of the acquisition of social skills. Thus, the occurrence of various undesirable behavior systems may be inhibited and the occurrence of various desirable behaviors may be facilitated and subsequently reinforced by conditions brought about by systematic manipulations of variables such as the available space, the type and number of materials positioned in that space, and the type and number of peers and adults in that space.

Some Lessons Stemming from
an Ecological Perspective

It is axiomatic that an organism will bring to a setting into which it is placed behavior systems that have biological-historical origins or that have been maintained by (and possibly acquired on the basis of) the stimuli in the setting from which it has come. It follows that the organism's initial behavior in response to stimuli in the new setting will be a function of the similarity of those stimuli to the stimuli that controlled its behavior in the past. If the new stimuli are markedly dissimilar from the discriminative stimuli in its former setting, the organism may infrequently respond or it may respond in a way that is quite maladaptive given the new ecological setting. When the organism does respond, its behaviors may provide the basis for new adaptive learning in connection with the stimuli available in the new setting (for example, Gewirtz, 1969).

In essence, an organism's adjustment in a new environment will depend on (1) the biological and the ecological history of that organism or that individual; (2) whether the new caregivers recognize the relevant discriminative and reinforcing stimuli controlling its responses and can provide them effectively; (3) whether stimuli in the new setting acquire discriminative and reinforcing value to maintain appropriate responses and enable the learning of new response patterns. If caregivers in the new setting are not cognizant of these factors, or are not flexibly responsive, they may fail to produce or maintain behaviors appropriate to the new setting.

Proshansky, Ittelson, and Rivlin (1970, Chaps. 3, 43), for example, attempted to facilitate the therapeutic effectiveness of psychiatric facilities by manipulating architectural-ecological design features. They proceeded to implement a change on one of the wards of a state mental institution for severely disturbed adult women. The ward consisted of one long corridor, with a nurses' station at one end near the entrance and a solarium at the other end, with bedrooms, a bathroom, and a day room in between. The psychologist observed that the solarium, though designed for relaxation and recreation, was inadequately furnished, overheated, unappealing, and exposed to an intense sunlight. The available TV was used very little. The solarium was a place for "catatonic withdrawal," one of the behavior patterns that the staff worked to change.

Redecoration of the solarium produced a marked change, but only for the solarium. Many more patients were spending their time in a "new" area using it socially and for recreation. The rate of isolated standing and withdrawal behavior drastically reduced. Unfortunately, our behavioral ecologists had succeeded in changing only the location of such behaviors, which now took place at the nurses' station. Manipulating the environmental conditions in one part of the physical environment had shifted the troubling behaviors to another location.

Another example "embellished" by Willems (1972) may illustrate the importance of subjects' biological history and ecological factors for behavioral analysis by both ethologists and community psychologists. An ornithologist affiliated with a zoo wished to add a bird called the bearded tit to the zoo's collection. Since the attempts to reproduce and maintain the bird in captivity have been unsuccessful, a great deal of effort was invested in attempting to recapitulate the naturalistic habitat of the species with appropriate manipulation of photoperiod, shrubbery, other vegetation, and landscaping. A male and a female were introduced into the new setting and by all the usual behavioral indexes available, if any birds can be said to thrive in their habitat, these two did. They sang, courted, mated, built a nest, laid eggs, hatched young, and fed them. Shortly after hatching, however, the young were found neglected outside of the nest. Parents, on the other hand, continued "thriving" in their habitat. When the new brood was hatched, the ornithologist, while carefully watching the behavior of his birds and preparing an ethogram, to his disappointment, observed the parents pushing the hatchlings out of the nest. This cycle, starting with parents doing "just fine" and ending with dead hatchlings, was repeated with regularity. Having no choice, our ornithologist went back to observe tits in the wild. The ethogram revealed that throughout the day the adults spent most of their time gathering the food for their hatchlings and, in turn, the infrequently fed hatchlings, with their gaping mouths, were continually begging for food. Finally, all inanimate objects, eggshells, beetle shells, and so forth were shoved out of the nest by "hygienic and compulsive" parents.

Now educated, our ornithologist went back to observe his captive birds. Shortly after hatching, the parents spent only a brief period of time gathering food, since it was available in abundance. In turn, after few feedings with a relatively short interfeeding interval, the satiated hatchlings fell asleep. Consequently, parent birds apparently treated them as inanimate objects and threw them out of the nest. The solution was clear. By making the food less available and less accessible, one could recapture the biological and ecological history of these species of birds. Now, the adults would devote most of their daylight hours searching for food. The hungry hatchlings were less likely to go to sleep. And, the tits proceeded to reproduce in captivity.

In a similar vein, we were faced with a problem of how to induce parental behavior in a laboratory stock of Japanese quail in light of many unsuccessful attempts by other investigators. Two hypotheses guided our attempts at solving this problem in applied ethology. The first hypothesis stemmed from observations and findings which indicated the importance, if not the necessity, of the ecologically appropriate stimuli in the induction of the biologically appropriate behavior. Thus, in order to investigate the induction of parental and filial behaviors, we had to search the original literature (especially Japanese) for descriptions of such behaviors under natural or seminatural ecological conditions and compare the outcomes with the specific behaviors (or the lack of them) generated by the deprivation or semideprivation settings characteristic of laboratory methodology.

The second hypothesis had its seeds in population genetics. It is conceivable that domestication, characterized by various forms of artificial selection, had partitioned the Japanese quail gene pool to such a degree that parental behavior was no longer a part of the repertoire of populations hatched in the laboratory. Since laboratory stocks of Japanese quail were maintained by incubation, which removes a selection factor of survival value for the species, it was hypothesized that many quail indeed lacked an appropriate genotypic substrate for the expression of parental behavior.

A special quail habitat was constructed (Figure 6.3). A covey of Japanese quail of 49 subjects (23 females and 26 males) was obtained from a special "unselected" line. The ground was covered with grasses, weeds, small shrubs, and two small cedar trees. In addition, shelters and hiding areas were constructed from pine branches. Nests and nest coverings were constructed and camouflaged by weeds, small shrubs, and pine branches. Some of the nests were structured in the form of a tunnel and others had only one end open (see Figure 6.3). The birds were exposed to the natural photoperiod (ranging from 9.3:14.7 hr to 15:9 hr light/dark) and to the natural outdoor temperatures (as low as -3° C in the winter to as high as 37° C in the summer), characteristic of Maryland's eastern shore. A thermostatically activated fan provided air circulation at temperatures above 27° C.

The quail received grit, water, and a food mixture consisting of fine cracked corn, turkey prestarter, and chick-growing mash ad lib. They were often provided with natural milo stalks from which they could pick seeds and occasionally were fed meal worms and earthworms. In addition, from spring to fall months they frequently found live food, mainly insects and earthworms, in their habitat.

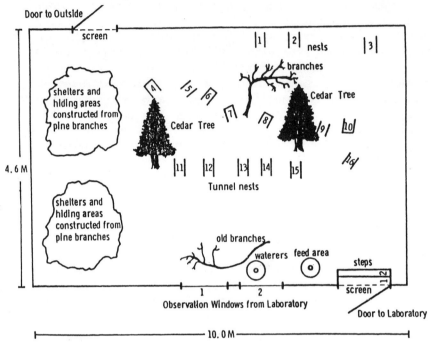

FIGURE 6.3

Quail habitat for study of the induction of parental and filial behavior of captive Japanese quail (prepared by authors).

Artificial selection was utilized to change the phenotypic composition of a population. Basically, it required choosing as parents for each generation only those individuals with the desired expression of the trait or traits in question. In our experiment, this procedure involved the selection of only the eggs or progeny of a female that had exhibited parental behavior. Subsequently, selection was terminated in order to minimize the expression of potentially deleterious traits as a result of inbreeding.

After a longitudinal study of four years, our data supported both the genetic and the ecological hypotheses and we were able to demonstrate a method for establishing a "normal" self-perpetuating population of quail (Hess, Petrovich, & Goodwin, 1976).

The last example is instructive also in the way it brings together the conceptualizations from both the genetic and traditional psychological paradigms. At the risk of overworking a distinction in order to make a point, it should be noted that a traditional psychological paradigm is often effective in manipulations when the environment plays the primary role in behavioral development. Thus, the psychological paradigm emphasizes the importance of extrinsic (environmental) factors in the etiology; the genetic paradigm emphasizes the role of intrinsic (genetic) factors for individual homeostasis. Because individuals have their own genetic makeup, for example, it follows from the genetic paradigm that each person is at specific risk.

The implications of these approaches pose a question for a reader to resolve. Should community psychology incorporate techniques of ethology, genetic counseling, psychopharmacology, and clinical and medical genetics? Or should one consider most of these approaches as best suited for molecular manipulations and microanalysis, and thus inappropriate for macrointerventions characteristic of community psychology?

Examples Illustrating the Ecological
Adaptation of Animal Behavior

All organisms must adapt to contingencies of ecological selection such as food, shelter, predation, and climatic changes. The importance of these factors in the proximal evolution of behavior can be investigated experimentally. For instance, the evolved survival value of egg pigmentation and shading is lost once the young hatch, exposing the inner white surface of the eggshell and thereby betraying a nest to potential predators. Thus, Tinbergen (1963) was able to demonstrate empirically the adaptive fitness of behaviors such as eggshell removal by gulls in the context of preserving nest camouflage. Similarly, in response to predation pressures, many species have evolved complex behavioral countermeasures, including removing cloacal droppings from the young and flying to dump them away from the nesting area.

Tinbergen (for example, 1972) and his students demonstrated convincingly the heuristic value of conceptualizations based on recognition of the importance of ecological fitness of behavior—teleonomy. Cullen's work (1957) stands out in particular. She showed that the behavioral repertoire of a cliff-nesting gull (Kittiwake) is similar to its ground-nesting gull relative, except for many behavioral patterns closely associated with the ecological peculiarity of its nesting, which takes place on narrow ledges of cliff faces. For example, the cliff-nesting gull fails to learn the identity of its own young, whereas the ground-nesting gull readily does. The cliff-nesting gull young do not wander about on the narrow cliff ledges, while the ground-nesting gull young move about and often intermingle. The learning ability involving a discrimination of its hatchlings by the ground-nesting gull seems to have evolved as a discrete unit associated with the care of the young in the context of specific adaptation to nesting habitats. In the cliff nester, there has been no selection for this sort of learning; if hatchlings are not in the nest, searching would seem unproductive.

Clinal (graduated) variations represent another clear manifestation of specialized adaptations along ecological gradients. For example, as latitude increased in the northerly or southerly direction, a number of general trends involving morphological, physiological, and behavioral adaptations became apparent: body size increases (Bergmann's rule); tails, ears, bills, and limbs become relatively short (Allen's rule); relative length of the hair increases; wings become more pointed; the relative size of the heart, pancreas, liver, kidney, stomach, and intestine increases; there is a reduction in pigments, phaeomelanins and eumelanins (Gloger's rule); relative oxygen consumption and metabolic needs decrease and general activity decreases; migratory instincts become more manifest; larger and warmer "nests" are constructed (King's rule); home ranges become larger, with territorial behavior more pronounced; and photoperiodic rhythms become more evident. As Thiessen (1972) has noted, none of these "clinal laws" could have been predicted from theoretical and empirical approaches rooted in phylogenetic sophistication. They became apparent only when climatic demands of species-specific ecological niches were considered.

Ecologically oriented research has made it possible to show that "good sleepers" are generally predators, have secure sleeping places, or both, whereas "poor sleepers" tended to be subject to predation at any time (Allison & Van Twyver, 1970). A knowledge and understanding of the behavioral repertoire of some 300 species in their natural habitats were the best predictors of their exploration and curiosity as captive animals in the zoo (Glickman & Sroges, 1966). Many investigators have attempted to study the adaptive significance of different modes of social organization that exist in nature, and at present we are witnessing comprehensive and provocative attempts at such a synthesis (Chagnon & Irons, 1979; Wilson, 1975).

The ecological-teleonomic approach has refocused comparative studies of animal learning (Bolles, 1975; Hinde & Stevenson-Hinde, 1973; Seligman, 1970; Seligman & Hager, 1972). In the last decade, a clear departure from the classical orientations has occurred. The shift from hypotheses emphasizing the principle of phylogenetic relatedness (for example, Bitterman, 1960, 1965) to those exploring ecological perspectives and biological constraints is unmistakable (Lockard, 1971; Mason & Lott, 1976). Two assumptions characterize current orientations: (1) learning is influenced by species typical constraints; and (2) because some forms of learning are particular modes of adaptation to specific ecological contingencies, based on their biological preparedness animals learn certain associations that are characteristic of the natural history of the species. For example, rats being a scavenger species will quickly learn to associate taste conditioned stimuluses (CSs) with stomach illness unconditioned stimuluses (CSs) (prepared association). In this instance, an association will occur between taste quality and the toxic agent inducing illness, even when the delay between ingestion and the aversive condition is more than an hour. More extended training is required for rats to learn to associate exteroceptive CSs with shock UCS (an example of unprepared association). In contrast, as an example of counterprepared association, rats will not learn to associate taste with shock or visual or auditory stimuli paired with the toxic agent inducing stomach illness (for example, Garcia, Ervin, & Koelling, 1966; Garcia & Koelling, 1966).

THE ECOLOGICAL DIMENSIONS OF HUMAN
BEHAVIOR: AN INTRODUCTION TO
CULTURAL MATERIALISM

The ecological perspective in psychology emphasizes proximate interdependencies, adaptations, or interrelationships involving an organism, its behavior, and environmental contingencies. It is difficult, however, to find systematic approaches in ecological psychology that deal with issues of "ultimate causation" (that is, the ecological and evolutionary contingencies selecting for specific behaviors through biological time). Perhaps the most penetrating analyses have come from the school of cultural materialism within anthropology (for example, Harris, 1966, 1974, 1977, 1979). Harris's main theoretical position contends that reproductive pressure, intensification, and environmental-ecological depletion would appear to provide a key for understanding the evolution of family and social organization, property relations, political economy, and religious beliefs including the associated dietary preferences and food taboos. The last item provides an illustrative example of Harris's illuminating thesis. Thus, Harris relates the Jewish taboo on the pig to the destruction of the Palestinian forest. In the absence of forest vegetation, swine would have to be fed with valuable grain and an expensive shelter, and water would have to be provided for the woodland-adapted, relatively hairless, and sun-sensitive animals (Harris, 1974, 1977).

But we are getting ahead of Harris's story. The forbidden flesh of pigs is familiar to most Jews, Moslems, and Christians. The god of the ancient Hebrews proclaimed the pig unclean, and about 2,000 years later, Allah gave his prophet Mohammed similar proscriptions for Islam. On the other hand, to the inhabitants of South Pacific Melanesian Islands and New Guinea, the pig is a holy animal that is sacrificed and eaten on all culturally important occasions, such as marriages, declarations of war or peace, or funerals. Why should gods exalt some human organisms to avoid pig flesh at any cost and urge others to indulge as the opportunity presents itself?

Remains of domesticated pig appear in neolithic villages of Palestine, Syria, and Anatolia almost as early as those of sheep and goats. Pigs are very efficient at converting calories of food into calories per pound of meat, much more so than cattle or chickens. It is Harris's claim, however, that when a nutritionally valuable species such as pig not only becomes ecologically expensive to maintain but in the process endangers the existing mode of substinance and ecological adaptation, then the most severe prohibitions and taboos are introduced.

When the pig was first domesticated, there were extensive forests covering regions of the Middle East. Beginning at about 7000 B.C., the spread of populations and intensification of mixed farming and herding economies converted acres of forests to grassland and agriculture. In turn, these quickly converted to desert. It is estimated that within a short period of time forests of Anatolia were reduced by about 70%. The woodlands of Judean and Samarian hills were converted to irrigated plateaus and terraces. Consequently, pigs, a free-ranging woodland species, had to be provided shelter and fed grains as dietary supplements, thereby rendering them ecologically competitive with humans from a nutritional and economic standpoint. What followed is an ecclesiastical prohibition recorded in Leviticus. To those who have claimed that a taboo against pigs stems from hygienic reasons, Harris points out that pigs are generally "quite clean" but they will wallow in their own feces and urine only when they are deprived of external sources of moisture necessary to cool their sweatless and relatively hairless bodies from the hot sun; the mud, or freshly dug humus of the forest, would be a preferable alternative. Moreover, other domesticated animals, from cattle to fowl, show no reluctance to wallow even in human excrement, yet no prohibitions were exercised against them. Furthermore, recent epidemiological studies suggest that pigs raised in hot climates seldom transmit trichinosis, whereas cattle, sheep, and goats are vectors for human diseases such as anthrax and brucellosis.

By contrast, the temperature, humidity, and vegetation are ideal for raising pigs in New Guinea and the Melanesian islands. The animals obtain their food by freely ranging over the forest floor. An unlimited growth of pig populations in absence of any predation, however, could only lead to potential deforestation and ecological competition between the human and the pig. In addition, uncontrolled increase in pig populations would endanger local gardens and agriculture. Feasting on a pig on special occasions, while worshiping it as an animal, leads to a highly adaptive behavioral tradition.

Harris extends his analysis to traditions, from the origin of the sacred cows of India to the practice of cannibalism. To an ethologist familiar with ecological dimensions of animal behavior, Harris's analyses are appealing and even persuasive. To the community psychologist, they offer a provocative challenge to their own orientation, data, and assumptions.

LEVELS OF ORGANIZATION-LEVELS OF ANALYSIS: ON THE RELATIONSHIP BETWEEN ETHOLOGICAL THEORY AND RESEARCH

Any behavioral problem can be conceived of as varying along dimensions identified as levels of analysis. Each level can be defined in terms of its position on an information continuum. The major unifying and consensually valid theme in the ethological perspective is, of course, the synthetic theory of organic evolution.

When Darwin and Wallace proposed in the 1850s their theory of evolution by natural selection of the fittest and by specific examples demonstrated how these processes could account for the evolution of organisms, they planted the seeds for the powerful scientific and intellectual conceptualization that is still unfolding. From Malthus, Darwin and Wallace knew that organisms reproduced in far greater numbers than could be sustained by a particular environmental setting. From their observations, they had evidence that populations remain relatively constant. They therefore concluded that a large proportion of the offspring must fail to survive. Moreover, they knew that animals compete for the available resources of the environment and thereby participate in an active "struggle for existence."

As Darwin indicated,

owing to this struggle for life, any variation, however slight and from whatever cause proceeding, if it be in any degree profitable to an individual of any species, in its infinitely complex relations to other organic beings and to external nature, will tend to the preservation of that individual and will generally be inherited by its offspring. The offspring, also, will thus have a better chance of surviving, for, of the many individuals of any species which are periodically born, but a small number can survive. (1859/1869, p. 61)

Thus, the principle of gradual progressive evolution by natural selection was clearly outlined. Darwin made the animal world relevant to people by arguing the mental continuity hypothesis; that is, that the animal mind and the human mind are quite similar, differing only in degree. Darwin considered behavioral characters to be just as subject to natural selection as are the physical ones; and in much of his writing, extensive consideration was given to behavioral comparisons among various species:

> So in regard to mental qualities, their transmission is manifest in our dogs, horses, and other domestic animals. Besides special tastes and habits, general intelligence, courage, bad and good temper, etc., are certainly transmitted. With man we see similar facts in almost every family; and we now know through the admirable labors of Mr. Galton that genius, which implies a wonderfully complex combination of high faculties, tends to be inherited, and, on the other hand, it is too certain that insanity and deteriorated mental powers likewise run in the same families. (1873/1971, Vol. I, pp. 106-107)

Even though it was most important for the evolutionary theory that heritable variations be present in each generation, Darwin nevertheless freely conceded his ignorance of the mechanisms of inheritance. It was not until about 1900 that Mendel was rediscovered and Hugo de Vries, working in the Netherlands, proposed his mutation theory by pointing out the likely possibility that the obvious morphological changes he observed in the evening primrose might provide the variations on which natural forces could exert selection pressure.

The major breakthrough and the beginnings of the modern synthesis surfaced in the 1930s. R. A. Fisher (1930) published The Genetical Theory of Natural Selection, Dobzhansky (1937) produced Genetics and the Origin of Species, to be followed by Oparin's (1938) The Origin of Life, Mayr's (1942) Systematics and the Origin of Species, and Huxley's (1942) Evolution: The Modern Synthesis. These published works brought together diverse areas of human knowledge and inquiry. Organic evolution began to be viewed as a by-product of the chemical evolution of matter and biophysics, biochemistry and molecular biology surfaced as the new and exciting areas of inquiry. The new neo-Darwinian synthetic theory of organic evolution made sense out of taxonomy. It explained the fossil record as well as the fitness of adaptations between organisms and their habitats. The cell theory put forward convincingly in 1839 by German microscopists Schleiden and Schwann was given a new vision: The cell is a Mendelian unit carrying the genetic code of stored variability that is crucial to evolution and, at the same time, it is a physiochemical entity obeying the laws of physics and chemistry. The bridge between particle physics and human evolution and ecology was formed. The door was left open for the new generation of Nobel laureates such as Watson and Crick who, in 1953, by their elucidation of the double-helical, physiochemical structure of the DNA molecule and its role in heredity, provided one of the major empirical validations for the new synthesis.

Unfortunately, the behavioral sciences were largely left out of the modern synthesis (Hess, 1973; Lockard, 1971; Lorenz, 1965; Wilson, 1975). The reasons were many. The pursuit of the mysteries of life focused the concerns of the biological sciences on the molecular universe, thereby leaving the behavioral territory to psychology, sociology, anthropology, and psychiatry. In turn, many professionals in these disciplines found the nativistic, materialistic, deterministic implications of the modern synthetic theory of organic evolution difficult to accept and incorporate procedurally, professionally, politically, and personally. For example, until very recently, the judicious disregard for the role of hereditary factors in behavior has been one of the hallmarks of American psychology and sociology. Thus, it is worth noting that in 1973 many behavioral scientists were surprised by the "unconventional" decision of the Nobel Foundation. It chose to award the prize for physiology and medicine to three ethologists, K. Von Frisch, K. Lorenz, and N. Tinbergen, thereby acknowledging their efforts toward bringing the study of behavior under the umbrella of the synthetic theory of organic evolution. With the subsequent advent of sociobiology (for example, Wilson, 1975) and cultural materialism (Harris, 1966, 1979), the initial surprise gave way to exchanges characteristic of a paradigm clash (for example, Kuhn, 1962; Lakatos, 1978).

At present, ethology is about four principal biological questions and concerns: What is the ontogeny, causation, function, and evolution of behavior? An explanation and understanding have required that attention be given to each of these questions and concerns and to various levels of interrelationship among them. The magnitude of the problem has required a breadth of synthesis that transcends levels of analysis from genotype to behavior and ecology-- the synthesis that transcends the extremes of levels of biological organization.

In general, we agree that organic evolution was a by-product of the chemical evolution of matter. Animal species, including Homo sapiens, are the products of natural selection. Genes chemically code for structural and behavioral traits. The natural selection favors, in terms of reproductive success, those animals whose genes through their phenotypic expressions successfully interact with the environment of the ecosystem. After stating some of these often neglected considerations, how do we relate them to levels of analysis in behavioral sciences?

As can be seen in Figure 6.4, the ethological model incorporates in a hierarchical fashion levels of organization from subatomic particles to ecosystem. No level of organization or analysis is conceived as more "important" or "adequate" than another, since a position on the information continuum is not in itself a criterion for importance or adequacy. The reduction of a behavioral problem to a neurophysiological one, or of a neurophysiological one to a biochemical one, does not in itself generate a more fundamental or a more important explanation of the original behavioral problem. Surely, we recognize that the water molecule has characteristics and properties independent of those of hydrogen and oxygen. At the same time, we must hasten to point out that knowing the characteristics of hydrogen and oxygen does provide us with some important information about water. It follows that the usefulness and appropriateness of a particular level of analysis is circumscribed by theoretical orientation, parameters of the problem under investigation, and contextual circumstances, as well as by general purposes of the discipline or the investigator. Thus, as our introductory example indicates, a student in ethology investigating the behavioral biology of the cricket song finds it necessary to acquire at least some sophistication in language and the tools of genetics, neurophysiology and neuroanatomy, quantitative behavioral analysis, systematics, ecology, and evolution.

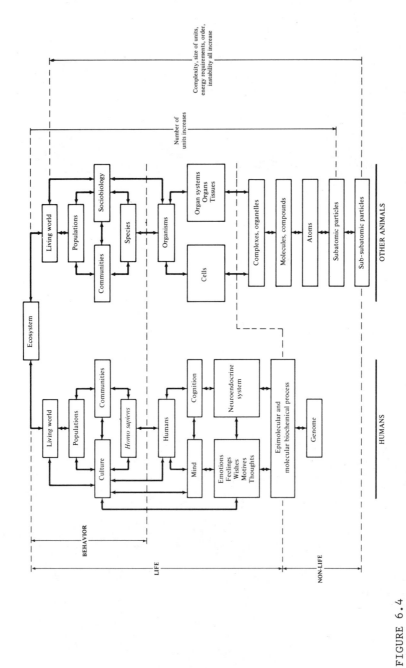

FIGURE 6.4
Schematic comparison of human and animal approaches to behavioral analyses from a biobehavioral perspective.

270

When the conceptual framework of evolution is applied to understand human emergence and existence, it is evident that two very different processes have been at work. Under the process of <u>organic</u> evolution, the human organism has evolved as have other animal species, through a creative process wherein living matter has responded to changes in its environment, based on evolutionary principles of genetic variation and systematic selective retention. In contrast, the process of <u>cultural</u> evolution has involved features very different in kind from those of organic evolution. Among these differences: (1) the mechanism of organic evolution is Mendelian, whereas the mechanism of cultural evolution is Lamarckian--in the sense that the information is passed from one individual to another and from one generation to the next via mechanisms of communication, learning, and skill acquisition rather than through genes; (2) cultural evolution is potentially much more rapid; and given language, computer language and retrieval processes, and communication modes, the storehouse of information has been retrieved and transmitted at ever-increasing speeds; (3) the basic elements of organic evolution are the genes and gene phenotypes--that is, the individual--whereas cultural evolution may include the emergence of a social unit as an entity in selection; (4) organic evolution is blind and opportunistic, whereas cultural evolution is heavily influenced by learning, tradition, foresight, and the ability to conceive of a "better way of life" for oneself and one's offspring; (5) through organic evolution, organisms respond to contingencies of survival and continue to adapt to ecological demands; in contrast, through cultural evolution, humans modify and shape the environment to fit their requirements (Campbell, 1975; Lorenz, 1969; Petrovich, 1978; Piaget, 1978).

The coevolutionary nature of the genetic and learning mechanisms is not always understood. There exists an innate storehouse of information--the gene pool. However, <u>Homo sapiens</u> is also capable of learning during ontogeny, thereby acquiring and adding new knowledge upon an ever-expanding base. Infinitely more than any other animal, by the quality of its biology, the human is a creature of socialization to a given cultural context and, as such, singularly a product of its learning (Gewirtz & Petrovich, 1982; Petrovich, 1978).

RATIONALE FOR THE USE OF ETHOLOGICAL
MODELS FOR BEHAVIORAL ANALYSIS

Animals are used extensively and productively as experimental subjects in many behavioral and medical specialties. To a student in natural sciences, the propriety of the judicious and ethical application of animals and animal-research findings toward understanding of the human organism requires no justification. However, specific concerns and issues emerge when one attempts to develop animal models of use in understanding of human behavior. The reservations with which animal behavioral data are received generally reflect the history of the dichotomy between human and brute, the methological and procedural difficulties associated with the human-infrahuman behavioral comparisons, as well as our appreciation of the uniqueness of the human species. Admittedly, the problems associated with human-infrahuman behavioral comparisons do exist. Nevertheless, there is no intrinsic reason to preclude the development of animal behavioral models that are to a large degree the functional analogues of human behavioral processes. The pertinent literature on the various aspects of the comparative analysis of behavior is so voluminous that even a limited presentation is beyond the scope of any single chapter. The following treatment is meant only to serve as an introduction to the rationale for the utility of some ethological-animal models for other behavioral sciences.

On this planet, all animals have in common the same code of life. In addition, the lower the level of intraorganismic structure and function, the greater the phylogenetic similarity (for example, comparative analyses of human and infrahuman tissues, cells, and hormones such as vesopressin). The similarity of structure and function also increases across all levels of organization as the proximity to a common ancestor increases (for example, comparative analyses of human and other primate intraorganismic and organismic processes). Furthermore, similar behavioral functions among phylogenetically unrelated or distantly related forms may result from similar selection pressures caused by similar ecological contingencies (for example, comparative analyses of territorial aggression). Thus, similar behavioral functions in different species often have identical survival value and provide us with information as to how similar selection pressures generate, through parallel or convergent evolution, similar behavioral outcomes.

Given these truisms, ethologists claim that the methodological approach of ethology, starting with the ethogram of similarities and differences among human and other experimentally appropriate infrahuman species, should be the foundation of animal models worthy of serious consideration by researchers in behavioral sciences. Each species often reveals unique patterns of behavior. What is obscure, rudimentary, or nonexistent in one species may be exaggerated to a ridiculous state in another. By cataloging dispassionately the behavioral phenomenology of different species, it is possible to filter out the significance of specific behavioral phenomena. Moreover, any behavior pattern, however deceptively expressed--ranging from obscure to exaggerated--thus stands a better chance of being objectively described and understood from both phylogenetic and ontogenetic standpoints. Classificatory models derived from data produced by the ethological approach to behavioral analysis are capable of establishing interspecies comparisons of homologous behaviors (behavioral similarities due to common descent) and of functionally analogous behaviors (behavioral similarities based on consideration of commonality of function rather than on similarities in the genotype or in the structure). Traditionally, the approach has been to emphasize the mapping of homologies. Concurrently, the recognition of the importance of ecological contingencies as a force in natural selection led to the development of comparative interspecies analysis based on analogous behavioral processes and traits. In his Nobel paper, Lorenz (1974) again reiterated that the concepts of homology and analogy are as applicable to the analysis of behavior as they are to the analysis of morphological characters, even though attempts at such behavioral demonstration pose many conceptual and methodological difficulties. At present, it is generally accepted that the demonstration of behavioral homologies and analogies is one of the major contributions of ethology.

In light of these considerations, can we have a meaningful simulation of human environments and human exo-organismic, organismic, and intraorganismic processes if, at the same time, we use nonhuman subjects? One promising if not altogether persuasive answer to that question has emerged from research designed, at least in part, to

evaluate the degree and magnitude of behavioral relatedness between the human species and nonhuman primates.
McKinney and his colleagues (Akiskal & McKinney, 1973;
McKinney, 1974), for example, have made extensive extrapolations from primate research findings, and they have presented a persuasive case for the use of animal models in
psychiatry. The salient feature of their functional-analogy
thesis rests on four basic criteria intended to compare the
degree of similarity between the human and the animal
"preparation." These four criteria include (1) contextual-
situational similarity between the human condition and the
animal preparation, (2) function and topography of behavioral responses to the situation, (3) underlying mediating
mechanisms, and (4) the nature of the subject's responses
to systematic experimental or treatment manipulation.

It should be emphasized, however, that the primates
need not be the best available preparation for the study of
a human problem. A truly sophisticated comparative approach strives for thoughtful comparison of mediating mechanisms of behavior. These mechanisms may be genetic-
biochemical, and in such cases even fruit flies as subjects
may prove to be an invaluable experimental tool. In other
cases, development and manifestation of behavior may be
mediated by neurophysiological factors (hormones, neural
maturation, diet), and the laboratory rat possesses many
functional characteristics that make it an extremely useful
research subject. Among behavioral mediating mechanisms,
we include perception, habituation, early experiences, and
learning. In this case also, a choice of the appropriate
animal model depends on the behavioral mechanism that
one is investigating. For instance, inferences about the
development of human color perception cannot be based on
experiments with our primate cousins--lemurs that lack
color vision; chicks are much better experimental subjects.

On this complex issue of the comparative approach
to the study of human behavior, let us restate one of the
axioms of ethology: Each species is a unique preparation.
Animal models allow us to test a specific hypothesis of potential relevance to our understanding of human behavior.
It behooves us to be careful when we try to explain human
behavior on the basis of data derived from such hypothesis
testing.

ETHOLOGICAL PERSPECTIVES ON THE
ROLES AND THE USE OF THEORY:
A REMINDER FOR US ALL

The development and the use of theory have been valued by researchers across disciplines and areas of inquiry. The characteristic thinking has been that theory generates research models and questions, thereby requiring that the empirical answers to those questions be referred back to evaluate merits of a particular model or if need be modify or even discard an existing theory. Disciplined empiricism requires a theory, however informal or preliminary it may be or however difficult an investigator may find testing assumptions stemming from it.

If one reviews methods and practices of adherents of community psychology, one finds a mismatch between stated objectives of the field and the contributions of its practitioners (Novaco & Monahan, 1980). Critical assessment of sources for data and theory may lead one to wonder if community psychology is a nondiscipline (Kelly, 1971; Lehmann, 1971; Reiff, 1968; Sarason, 1976). Researchers in community psychology give appearance of subscribing to methodological and theoretical approaches with which they are personally or professionally comfortable, rather than on their heuristic utility, including the degree to which they may organize many of the diverse phenomena, yield general principles, or generate new research (Novaco & Monahan, 1980). By contrast, as indicated in our previous discussion on the relationship between ethological theory and research, much of what goes on in ethology appears to reflect a self-conscious emphasis on coordinating a disciplined testing of a specific hypothesis stemming from a synthetic theory of organic evolution.

The comparison of ethology and community psychology, however, is more meaningful and encouraging if one is reminded of the early intellectual antecedents of the present-day ethology. The clash involving an emphasis on laboratory-discovered facts as contrasted to naturalistic observation culminated in the famous debates at the French Academie des Sciences around 1830, in which the naturalistic evolutionary point of view suffered a profound defeat. Baron Cuvier had laboratory facts on his side, but as we have learned subsequently, by arguing for the immutability of the species, he was wrong in principle, whereas Geoffroy-

Saint-Hilaire was right in principle without the appropriate facts (Jaynes, 1969). The debates contributed to polarization between the two camps, with Cuvier's side insisting on the laboratory analysis and founding comparative psychology, while Geoffroy-Saint-Hilaire's camp emphasized naturalistic observations and established ethology. Comparative neurophysiologist Pierre Flourens, a protégé of Cuvier, and the author of Psychologie Comparèe (1864), is credited with developing a comparative psychology that synthesized mechanistic neurophysiological approaches of human psychology of Descartes with the animal psychology of Cuvier. It is worth noting, however, that during that same year and consistent with the intellectual bias of his school, Flourens published another book, leading the attack of the French science on Darwin's Origin of Species (1859). Comparative psychology that developed in America around the turn of the century embraced the Darwinian view of the world, but it remained a laboratory science, and its failure to appreciate the importance of the ecological-naturalistic dimension of behavior contributed to its decline (for example, Lockard, 1971).

By comparison, throughout the nineteenth century the naturalistic bias was advanced by other prominent biologists. Alfred Giard emphasized ethology and E. Haeckel pushed for "oecology" (presently ecology) then and now, defined as the study of the relationships among organisms and environment. It is no accident that the more recent pioneers of ethology sought to avoid a dichotomy between the field and the laboratory research, and they succeeded in doing so under the conceptual framework of the evolutionary theory (for example, Jaynes, 1969; Lorenz, 1981).

Given the context of the early ethological history, it appears to us that community psychologists are going through a period of evaluating the merits of the laboratory and the naturalistic paradigms. On a personal level, the professionals in the field are comfortable and secure with a traditional experimental approach; at the same time, they have come to wonder about the appropriateness of many laboratory solutions when dealing with issues of relevance to community psychology.

On a theoretical level, the lessons from ethology augur the application of the systems theory. The theory has proved useful in synthesizing functional and causal explanations of animal behavior (for example, Lorenz, 1981;

Toates, 1980). The general systems approach is applicable to a wide range of problems within a particular area of inquiry and across disciplines (von Bertalanffy, 1973; Buckley, 1967; Klir, 1971; Laszlo, 1972). The reader of Miller's (1955) paper and an updated version (Miller, 1976) on the application of the systems theory in psychology will find striking parallels with levels of organization and analysis that we have identified as characteristic of ethology. Likewise, the systems approach has been invaluable in the development of a new medical model for psychiatry and medicine (for example, Balis, 1978; Engel, 1977; Weiner, 1977).

As a theoretical orientation the systems theory offers to community psychologists a conceptual framework capable of assimilating and accommodating diverse findings across levels of analysis identified with behavioral sciences. It imposes discipline with constraints on hypothesis testing, thereby fostering research on the behavioral processes about community. It is interdisciplinary, transcending and bridging the boundaries across disciplines. The prescriptions between theoretical assumption and research operations would carry with them explicit integrative features that would allow those in the field to communicate with other scientific disciplines.

Finally, community psychologists may find it refreshing to read that ethologists have had to struggle to make their approach to behavioral analyses scientifically legitimate and accepted. To date, ethologists are referred to as naturalists by some colleagues in "hard" sciences, a label for which we have developed a sincere fondness. This may forecast the concerns for respectability that community psychologists are encountering and are likely to encounter in their own ecological setting.

CONCLUDING REMARKS

In this chapter, we have described some of the elements of the ethological approach to the science of behavior. A variety of examples have been considered in order to share habits of thought and methodological approaches of ethology that may be of use to community psychology. An adherence to the general systems theory has been advocated so that the benefits of a parsimonious theoretical approach to research could be exploited and undisciplined empiricism avoided. Efficient empirical approaches have been advanced as being the ones that avoid costs resulting from the lack of fitness between theoretical conceptualization and research operations. The community psychologists are trying to map out the interrelationship between the ecological factors and human behavior with a special focus on a level of abstraction labeled community and with an emphasis on prevention and institutional modification. Though rigorous, such analyses, by definition, need not conform to the impositions of methodological approaches best suited for another level of behavioral organization or analysis.

REFERENCES

Akiskal, H. S., & McKinney, W. T., Jr. Depressive disorders: Toward a unified hypothesis. Science, 1973, 182, 20–29.

Allison, T., & Van Twyver, H. B. The evolution of sleep. Natural History, 1970, 79, 56–65.

Balis, G. U. General systems theory and biosystems: An introduction. In G. U. Balis, L. Wurmser, E. McDaniel, & R. G. Grenell (Eds.), Dimensions of behavior. Boston: Butterworth, 1978.

Bertalanffy, L. von. General system theory: Foundations, development, applications. New York: Braziller, 1973.

Bitterman, M. E. Toward a comparative psychology of learning. American Psychologist, 1960, 15, 704–712.

Bitterman, M. E. Phyletic differences in learning. American Psychologist, 1965, 20, 396–410.

Bolles, R. C. Theory of motivation. New York: Harper & Row, 1975.

Buckley, W. Modern systems research for the behavioral scientist. Chicago: Aldine, 1967.

Campbell, D. T. On conflicts between biological and social evolution and between psychology and moral tradition. American Psychologist, 1975, 30, 1103–1126.

Chagnon, N. A., & Irons, W. (Eds.). Evolutionary biology and human social behavior: An anthropological perspective. North Scituate, Mass.: Duxbury Press, 1979.

Cullen, E. Adaptations in the kittiwake to cliff-nesting. Ibis, 1957, 99, 275–302.

Darwin, C. On the origin of species by means of natural selection, or the preservation of favored races in the struggle for life. London: John Murray, 1859; New York: Appleton, 1869.

Darwin, C. The expression of the emotions in man and animals. London: John Murray, 1972.

Darwin, C. The descent of man and selection in relation to sex. London: John Murray, 1971. (Originally published, New York: Appleton, 1873.)

Dobzhansky, T. Genetics and the origin of species. New York: Columbia University Press, 1937.

Eibl-Eibesfeldt, I. Ethology: The biology of behavior. New York: Holt, Rinehart & Winston, 1975.

Engel, G. L. The need for a new medical model: A challenge for biomedicine. Science, 1977, 196, 129–136.

Fisher, R. A. The genetical theory of natural selection. Oxford: Clarendon, 1930.

Flourens, P. Psychologie Comparèe. Paris: Carnier fréres, 1864.

Garcia, J., Ervin, F., & Koelling, R. Learning with prolonged delay of reinforcement. Psychonomic Science, 1966, 5, 121–122.

Garcia, J., & Koelling, R. Relation of cue to consequence in avoidance learning. Psychonomic Science, 1966, 4, 123–124.

Gewirtz, J. L. Mechanisms of social learning: Some roles of stimulation and behavior in early human development. In D. A. Goslin (Ed.), Handbook of socialization theory and research. Chicago: Rand McNally, 1969.

Gewirtz, J. L., & Petrovich, S. B. Early social and attachment learning in the frame of organic and cultural evolution. In T. M. Field, A. Huston, H. C. Quay, L. Troll, & G. E. Finley (Eds.), Review of human development. New York: John Wiley, 1982.

Glickman, S. E., & Sroges, W. R. Curiosity in zoo animals, Behavior, 1966, 26, 151–158.

Harris, M. The cultural ecology of India's sacred cattle. Current Anthropology, 1966, 7, 51–59.

Harris, M. Cows, pigs, wars and witches: The riddles of culture. New York: Random House, 1974.

Harris, M. Cannibals and kings: The origins of culture. New York: Random House, 1977.

Harris, M. Cultural materialism: The struggle for a science of culture. New York: Vintage Books, 1979.

Hess, E. M. "Imprinting" in a natural laboratory. Scientific American, 1972, 227, 24–31,

Hess, E. H. Imprinting: Early experience and the developmental psychobiology of attachment. New York: D. Van Nostrand, 1973.

Hess, E. H., & Petrovich, S. B. The early development of parent-young interaction in nature. In J. R. Nesselroade & H. W. Reese (Eds.), Life-span developmental psychology: Methodological issues. New York: Academic Press, 1973a.

Hess, E. H., & Petrovich, S. B. Effects of prenatal and postnatal auditory stimulation on postnatal auditory discrimination and imprinting. Proceedings XIII International Ethological Conference, Washington, D.C., 1973b.

Hess, E. H., Petrovich, S. B., & Goodwin, E. B. Induction of parental behavior in Japanese quail (Coturnix coturnix japonica). Journal of Comparative and Physiological Psychology, 1976, 90, 244-251.

Hinde, R. A., & Stevenson-Hinde, J. (Eds.). Constraints on learning. New York: Academic Press, 1973.

Huxley, J. S. Evolution: The modern synthesis. London: Allen and Unwin, 1942.

Jaynes, J. The historical origins of "ethology" and "comparative psychology." Animal Behavior, 1969, 17, 601-606.

Kelly, J. G. Qualities for the community psychologist. American Psychologist, 1971, 26, 897-903.

Klir, G. (Ed.). Trends in general systems theory. New York: John Wiley, 1971.

Kuhn, T. S. The structure of scientific revolutions. Chicago: University of Chicago Press, 1962.

Lakatos, I. The methodology of scientific research programmes. Philosophical papers edited by J. Worrall & G. Currie. New York: Cambridge University Press, 1978.

Laszlo, E. The systems view of the world. New York: Braziller, 1972.

Lawick-Goodall, J. von. The behavior of free living chimpanzees in the Gombe Stream Reserve. Animal Behavior Monographs, 1968, 1, 161-311.

Lehmann, S. Community and psychology and community psychology. American Psychologist, 1971, 26, 554-560.

Lehner, P. N. Handbook of ethological methods. New York: Garland, 1979.

Lockard, R. B. Reflections on the fall of comparative psychology: Is there a message for us all? American Psychologist, 1971, 26, 168-179.

Lorenz, K. Evolution and modification of behavior. Chicago: University of Chicago Press, 1965.

Lorenz, K. Innate basis of learning. In K. Pribram (Ed.), On the biology of learning. New York: Harcourt Brace Jovanovich, 1969.

Lorenz, K. Studies in animal and human behavior (Vol. 1). Cambridge, Mass.: Harvard University Press, 1970.

Lorenz, K. Studies in animal and human behavior (Vol. 2). Cambridge, Mass.: Harvard University Press, 1971.

Lorenz, K. Analogy as a source of knowledge. Science, 1974, 185, 229-234.

Lorenz, K. Z. The foundations of ethology. New York: Springer-Verlag, 1981.

Mason, W. A., & Lott, F. D. Ethology and comparative psychology. Annual Review of Psychology, 1976, 27, 129-154.

Mayr, E. Systematics and the origin of species. New York: Columbia University Press, 1942.

McKinney, W. T., Jr. Animal models in psychiatry. Perspectives of Biological Medicine, 1974, 17, 529-541.

Miller, J. G. Towards a general theory for the behavioral sciences. American Psychologist, 1955, 10, 513-531.

Miller, J. G. The nature of living systems. Behavioral Science, 1976, 21, 295-319.

Novaco, R. W., & Monahan, J. Research in community psychology: An analysis of work published in the first six years of the American Journal of Community Psychology. American Journal of Community Psychology, 1980, 8, (2) 131-145.

Oparin, A. I., The origin of life. New York: Macmillan, 1938.

Petrovich, S. B. Adaptation and evolution of behavior. In G. U. Balis, L. Wurmser, E. McDaniel, & R. G. Grenell (Eds.), Dimensions of behavior. Boston: Butterworth, 1978.

Piaget, J. Behavior and evolution. New York: Pantheon, 1978.

Proshansky, H. M., Ittelson, W. H., & Rivlin, L. G. (Eds.). Environmental psychology. New York: Holt, Rinehart & Winston, 1970.

Reiff, R. Social intervention and the problem of psychological analysis. American Psychologist, 1968, 23, 524-531.

Sarason, S. B. Community psychology, networks, and "Mr. Everyman." American Psychologist, 1976, 31, 317-318.

Seligman, M. E. P. On the generality of laws of learning. Psychological Review, 1970, 77, 406-418.

Seligman, M. E. P., & Hager, J. L. (Eds.), Biological boundaries of learning. New York: Appleton-Century-Crofts, 1972.

Thiessen, D. D. A move toward species-specific analyses in behavior genetics. Behavior Genetics, 1972, 2, 115–126.

Tinbergen, N. The study of instinct. Oxford: Clarendon, 1951.

Tinbergen, N. On aims and methods of ethology. Zeitschrift für Tierpsychologie, 1963, 20, 410–433.

Tinbergen, N. The animal and its world. London: Allen and Unwin, 1972.

Toates, M. Animal behavior: A systems approach. New York: John Wiley, 1980.

Weiner, H. M. Psychobiology and human disease. New York: Elsevier, 1977.

Williams, E. P. Behavioral ecology and experimental analysis: Courtship is not enough. In J. R. Nesselroade & H. W. Reese (Eds.), Life span developmental psychology: Methodological issues. . New York: Academic Press, 1972.

Wilson, E. O. Sociobiology: The new synthesis. Cambridge, Mass.: Belknap-Harvard University Press, 1975.

7 The Spirit of Ecological Inquiry in Community Research

Edison J. Trickett, James G. Kelly, and Trudy A. Vincent

The promise of the field of community psychology is to maintain the highest standards of inquiry while fostering research which yields constructive community development. A major criticism and source of anxiety about the field, however, is whether, inadvertently or directly, scientific inquiry becomes a force to limit, co-opt, or lessen the development of the local community where the research takes place. Words such as elitist, ivory tower, manipulative, and hierarchical are often applied to the research investigator. On occasion, citizens have become incensed, organized, and vigilant in their efforts to extrude the researcher from their locality (for example, Nettler, 1959; Eron & Walder, 1961; Voss, 1966).

The purpose of this chapter is to illustrate how the ecological paradigm can select the topics, define the methods, and influence the processes by which community research is planned, implemented, and evaluated. While the chapter rests on the belief that community research is based in theory, method, and design, the choice of the word spirit in its title is deliberate. It is intended to convey a spirit of commitment and reciprocity vis-à-vis the community where the research occurs. The intent is one of increasing the reciprocal connections between citizens and community psychologists to maximize the local impact of research over time. To think ecologically is to consider how persons, settings, and events can become resources for the positive development of communities; to consider how these resources can be managed and conserved; and to

approach research so that the effort expended will be helpful to the preservation and enhancement of community resources.

The spirit of ecological inquiry rests on several
values. The first asserts that <u>cultural diversity</u> and
<u>pluralism</u> are valid and defining qualities of community
life. When there is more than one example of competence
which is recognized and accessible, the community is expected to have more available resources, adapt more easily
to external change, and promote more opportunities for the
development of individuals and the community at large.

The second value favors the adoption of a <u>resource
perspective</u> as a defining mindset when engaging in community research. Resources can generally be defined as
those skills, qualities, structures, or occurrences which
can be mobilized in a specific community at a particular
time in solving the community's problems or enhancing its
development. A resource perspective orients the research
staff toward the setting's potential promise rather than its
problems, the proactive rather than the reactive, and the
adaptive rather than the maladaptive.

The third value commits the research staff to the
<u>long haul</u>--to the belief that community research goes be-
yond the gathering of data in a one-shot hit-and-run operation. It involves the development of a reciprocal relationship with the host community which builds on and extends beyond the initial gathering of data. Thus, the
spirit of ecological inquiry is the spirit of commitment to
a place over time. That commitment is concretized in actions which demonstrate that community research, by being
responsive and responsible, can be a participating force
in community development.

From these statements of value comes an overarching
perspective: Community research is an intervention into
the ongoing flow of community life and should be approached
as such. While community inquiry--like all research--is designed to generate knowledge, it also can serve as a primary vehicle for the development of a setting. By its very
nature, it cannot help but have impact on the place where
it occurs. The task of the community psychologist is to
focus explicitly on the nature of this impact. It is in
that spirit that we offer the ecological paradigm as a
heuristic for the design and execution of community research.

The chapter contains two sections. Part I presents
ten principles of the ecological paradigm. They spell out

in detail how one implements the spirit of ecological inquiry in community research. One aspect of the principles
bears mention. As previously stated, the ecological paradigm involves an explicit self-consciousness in carrying
out empirical work which makes the relationship between
the research investigator and the citizens in the community
equal in import to the theoretical and measurement tasks
of the research itself. Thus, each principle contains assertions not only about the phenomena of community settings but also about the relationship of the research staff
to the community setting.

Part II takes an evolving area of research, namely,
interpersonal problem solving (IPS) as a preventive intervention, and attempts to cast it into an ecological framework. Literature is discussed within the context of ecological principles, and implications are drawn for future
ecologically oriented inquiry.

PART I: PRINCIPLES FOR AN ECOLOGICAL PARADIGM

The ecological paradigm is itself an evolving set of
ideas about the description of community settings, the
goals and values of the community researcher, and the relationship of the researcher to the community. Its earlier
statements (for example, Kelly, 1966, 1967, 1971; Trickett,
Kelly, & Todd, 1972; Trickett & Todd, 1972) focused on four
principles drawn from field biology oriented toward differing aspects of the community environment.

1. The cycling of resources principle, as applied to human
    settings, alerted the investigator to the manner in
    which resources in the setting were defined, distrib-
    uted, and developed. It focused on the evolutionary,
    the proactive, and the potential of social settings.
2. The principle of adaptation addressed the "substance"
    of the environment--those norms, values, processes,
    and demand characteristics which constrained some
    kinds of behavior while facilitating others.
3. The interdependence principle focused on the interac-
    tive nature of the system and the manner in which
    its component parts were coupled.
4. The succession principle oriented the researcher to
    the time dimension of settings, including both historical

events and persons relevant to the earlier development of the setting and the anticipatory mechanisms and processes which may be useful in promoting its future development.

Directly related to these four basic ecological principles of an earlier time, we are currently proposing ten principles which build on and particularize these more general statements. Cycling of resources emerges as three principles having to do with the nature of community resources, their conservation and management, and the importance of a proactive orientation to community resource development. Adaptation is broken down into two principles which deal with coping and adaptation as a dominant means of community change and growth and introduce the concept of systemic events which have widespread ripple effects on the community. Interdependence remains as a single principle, which, based on the assumption of reciprocal causation, emphasizes the dynamic interplay between people and the settings they occupy. Succession also remains as a single principle but is designed to relate earlier principles having to do with resource cycling to the importance of a longitudinal time perspective. Finally, three principles have been added which address directly the notion that ecological research is designed to be a preventive intervention which empowers citizens in the process of community development. The ten principles are listed in Table 7.1.

As will become apparent, the principles make little sense apart from one another. Deriving as they do from the more generally orienting ecological paradigm, they form a totality and present differing but overlapping perspectives. Therefore, the reader may discover that by reading each principle consecutively he or she will develop a fuller appreciation of the implications of each preceding principle.

Persons, Settings, and Events Are Resources
for the Development of the Community and
the Research Relationship

Our first principle is based on the value assumption that in carrying out empirical work within a community, one overarching task is for that work to serve as a model for citizens to use as they attempt to plan and initiate new services or community-based programs. If findings, new insights, and statistics are to be persuasive to citizens, the work must be embedded in a social structure. Persons who live in the setting must absorb and relate to the data, understand them in the context of their community, and adopt them within their mode of thinking.

Ten Principles Embodying the Spirit of Ecological Inquiry

Cycling of Resources
  1. Persons, settings, and events are resources for the development of the community and the research relationship.
  2. The ecological paradigm advocates the conservation, management, and creation of resources.
  3. The activating qualities of persons, settings, and events are emphasized.

Adaptation
  4. Coping and adaptation are the dominant means of growth and change.
  5. The search for systemic events illuminates the process of adaptation.

Interdependence
  6. Persons and settings are in dynamic interaction.

Succession
  7. Persons, settings, and events are assessed over time.

Research Relationship
  8. Community research and the research relationship are designed to be coupled with the host environment.
  9. Attending to the side effects of community research is a priority.
  10. Ecological inquiry is a flexible, improvisational process.

Source: Compiled by the authors.

For those persons to do so, the researcher must take time and effort to relate to the local culture and be able to respond to local community events. The task of the researcher is thus to become a knowledgeable and credible collaborator in community process. To become integrated within the local community, it is necessary to identify three broad categories of community resources: persons, settings, and events. Relationships with political leaders or other sponsors are often essential for securing funds; yet it is persons, settings, and events that define the power for making empirical connections to the community.

Persons as Resources

Persons who are considered resources include those in a position of influence, those who enjoy status within their small group, and those who themselves have access to diverse and multiple resources. The resource value of persons depends on the combination of their personal qualities, their formal and informal roles in the setting, their knowledge and particular competencies, and the content area for which they act as a resource. In some schools in which we have worked, for example, it is a secretary, janitor, or crossing guard who serves as a resource to troubled students. Similarly, support for a particular intervention may come from the PTA rather than "downtown," and the creation of a new service may activate the latent yet real skills of teachers not previously identified as having uniquely valuable competencies. Thus, a central diagnostic task of the community psychologist is the identification of such resource persons. Because communities change as the research evolves, it is a task which remains important throughout the life of the community study.

The successful identification of persons as resources has implications both for the community's ability to put research to use and for the development of the research relationship itself. Persons with access to resources can provide both necessary initial sanction for the research and ongoing advice as the research proceeds. Persons knowledgeable about the norms, processes, and traditions of the setting can serve as informants about the culture. Persons committed to the setting can support the evolution of the research relationship and provide energy for its development. For all these reasons, identifying persons with varied resource potential is one important task of community research within the ecological paradigm.

Settings as Resources

Settings represent those structural elements of the environment which mediate the research and the research relationship, including both physical context (for example, the shopping mall) and social organizations (for example, the neighborhood association). Settings as resources embrace both existing settings ongoing at the beginning of the research and potential settings whose creation may facilitate either the evolution of the setting or the development of the research relationships.

Existing settings. Existing settings can include formal structures, such as a Citizens Advisory Board whose expertise and influence can both shape and sanction community research, and informal settings, such as the teachers' lounge where conversations and daily gossip can illuminate broader school issues of import to the research. The diagnostic task for the community psychologist is to identify settings which can meld the ongoing life of the community with the events and topics of the research. The diagnosis asks which places bring people together and which settings are the sites for the celebration and validation of community values.

Potential settings. Potential settings comprise those structures which, in effect, the research group perceives are "missing," that is, those structures needed to further integrate the research with the host community. The necessity for creating such settings is readily apparent in many phases of community research. To take but one example, for research to serve as a resource for the setting, care must be given to the design of structures for the sharing of information between researchers and citizens. It is widely recognized that if research feedback is designed to aid the community in reflection, planning, or development, it is not enough to present findings only in select formal settings, interviews with the media, or in conversations with high-ranking officials. Rather, one must design settings for periodic mutual feedback involving the diverse groups participating in the research. Thus, the creation of structures embodies the intervention goals of the research.

Events as Resources

When responded to wisely, events become what we term defining resources, for they clarify the nature of the norms, processes, and values in the community and create opportunities for interchange between the research staff and persons in setting. Events can thus provide unique opportunities for connecting with the locale, for making friends, for becoming known as a person rather than a role, and for further understanding what topics, methods, and processes are congruent with the evolving life of the setting. Through all these opportunities, events can be useful in defining the research relationship between the research team and the community.

Events can be either planned or unplanned. A planned event is one that is scheduled in advance and anticipated by the research staff as well as citizens involved in the research. A case in point would be the well-publicized arrival of a federal official, whose visit may provide the occasion for a public review of the objectives and progress of the study. An unplanned event is one which is neither announced in advance nor anticipated by community residents or researchers. An instance would be the unexpected promulgation by a federal agency of a new policy which will have impact on local communities. Both planned and unplanned events can be viewed as resources that provide the research staff with opportunities to engage citizens in discussion about the meaning of the event for themselves and their locality and to explore with them how best to respond to the event.

While planned events encourage the sharing of experiences between researcher and citizen, their very nature promotes an anticipation of how the event "pulls" for certain responses and topics of conversation. Of particular interest as a resource, then, is the unplanned event, the spontaneous occurrence which gives us all an opportunity to define and express what we really believe. The unplanned event pulls us to respond, for without it our opinions and values may be uncrystallized and unexpressed. Indeed, the very experience of sharing an unplanned event may make it possible for informal exchanges to develop and deepen the working relationships. In this way, unplanned events can assume the role of catalyst for creating new resources out of spontaneous occasions.

Persons, settings, and events are interacting resources for the community. The reverberations of celebrations or catastrophes can build or destroy interpersonal ties, produce esprit or anomie, and stimulate or inhibit the development of new settings. Thus, the interplay of persons, settings, and events provides the research investigators with opportunities for integration. If such persons, settings, and events are not available, or--as is more likely the case--are not viewed as interacting resources, then the research staff has the difficult, if not insurmountable, task of artificially constructing a political constituency for research that is foreign to the life activities of the community. Without the establishment of organic connections between the community and the research staff, community research becomes yet one more example of externally imposed intellectual and professional activities that remain irrelevant or harmful as a community resource.

The Ecological Paradigm Advocates the Conservation, Management, and Creation of Resources

Our second principle, still within the framework of the cycling of resources, adopts as its fundamental value assumption the need to manage and conserve existing resources and create new ones. From this perspective, a fundamental criterion for evaluating any community research is its impact on the resources that the community requires for its current needs and its future development. Conservation of resources requires knowledge of current available resources, both those needed to maintain the current setting and those required to anticipate and plan for its future development. Management of resources requires the formulation of overall plans and procedures as well as carrying out daily operations in ways that conserve resources. Creation of resources requires the development of anticipatory problem-solving mechanisms to direct the future of the setting and ensure that resources are allocated in the service of these long-range plans. Implementing the above goals involves several orienting stances for the community researcher: (1) a commitment to assessing the environment in order to anticipate the impact of social forces on the conservation, management, and development of resources; (2) a predisposition to attend to the research program's impact on resource development in the setting (for example, the effects of bringing funds into the setting, the impact of its operation on local policies, or how the involvement of citizens influences interpersonal or interorganizational relationships among them);

and (3) a commitment to <u>the design of processes and struc-tures for feedback</u> between the researcher and citizens dealing with their respective perceptions of how resources are being conserved, managed, or created within the context of the research project.

The intrusion of research into a community brings particular opportunities to create new resources for the community. Researchers may bring new content, new ideas, into a community which, if made available, can stimulate discussion and debate. The introduction of research methods developed by psychologists can contribute new frameworks, designs, and skills in the inquiry process which community residents may use in the future in gathering information and evaluating proposals for community activities and programs. Further, the very act of appraisal and review, which is the work of the psychologist, may serve as a kind of self-analytic forum which is not available in most localities.

Affirmation of this principle, for the reasons discussed above, is essential for the evaluation of the research relationship within the spirit of ecological inquiry. The value of conserving, managing, and creating resources is embodied in any change process which emphasizes empowerment. Such a change process rests on the foundation of citizens who have the power to influence and shape the life of their communities, including the research and research relationships carried out within them.[1]

The Activating Qualities of Persons, Settings, and Events Are Emphasized

The third principle underscores the importance of identifying persons, settings, and events which stimulate activity directed toward <u>creating something new</u> which the community needs. To an extent it is, therefore, a corollary of the first principle, which stresses the importance of treating persons, settings, and events as resources. In both principles the emphasis is on the proactive rather than the reactive, the healthy rather than the pathological. The third principle simply makes this emphasis explicit.

Guided by this principle, the ecologically oriented investigator will seek to understand the ways in which naturally occurring self-correcting, self-initiating activi-

ties are generated. What specific events tend to be generative for the morale and future direction of this particular community as well as communities generally? Where
are such events apt to occur? Are there specific settings
which can be counted on to honor and encourage exploration
of needs, efforts to redress injustices, attempts to realize
positive community-building values? Who are the individuals and groups who can be counted on to provide leadership and guidance for such efforts?

To the extent the research team understands the nature of such activating behavior, knows the people involved, and understands the context within which they
function, it has the necessary data to become a meaningful
resource for the community. Within the ecological model
the research staff takes on the function of a talent expedi-
tion, looking for the settings, nutrient leadership, and the
events that identify and promote talent, and the persons
who define substantive issues and are energized by dealing
with them.

Such activating resources rarely are clearly labeled.
In addition to obviously talented, energetic, and purpose-
ful individuals, there are often caring persons who are
uncertain, awkward, or troubled about their values and
aspirations. Deep commitment to one's community may include worry and a certain amount of self-doubt. Responded
to with interest, encouragement, and support, such persons often will become valuable resources because they
care enough to go deeply into topics, devote time to think
through issues, and contribute positively to the situation.
It should be noted that such qualities are not dependent
on social status or background. For example, the history
of Head Start programs is studded with examples of poor
and relatively uneducated parents who emerged over time
as articulate advocates before congressional committees for
the need for preschool programs.

Thus, the last of the three principles dealing with
resource cycling encourages the research staff to look for
persons, settings, and events capable of pushing the community forward by virtue of energy and commitment they
can mobilize.

Coping and Adaptation Are the Dominant
Means of Growth and Change

The fourth and fifth principles of the ecological
paradigm elaborate on the general principle of adaptation.

The fourth principle asserts the importance of viewing growth and change in a community from a perspective of coping and adaptation. The fifth stresses the importance of attending to events which have widespread ripple effects within the community and even beyond.

Coping refers to the efforts of individuals and settings to respond to stress, withstand impairment, and express competence when crisis occurs. Adaptation refers to those patterned activities, structures, policies, and beliefs that individuals and settings have developed over time to maintain themselves and the integrity of their activities. Coping activities are ameliorative. Adaptations are more likely to be generative. Each involves the interaction of persons, social settings, and the broader environment over time. Each promotes the positive possibilities of both stress and crisis, for example, that stress and crisis provide opportunities for short- and long-range development or problem solving and need not be viewed merely as threats to the current level of functioning. Inherent in these concepts—and discussed more fully in Principle 7—is a longitudinal time perspective on the adaptive value of individual and institutional responses. That is, neither coping nor adaptation should be judged solely on the basis of immediate "success" but rather in terms of its preparatory value for future situations as well.

The fourth principle pays particular attention to coping and adaptation involved in the relationship between the residents of the research site and members of the research project. As in any intervention, the infusion of research into a community requires both coping and adaptation on the part of both host and interveners. The advent of empirical inquiry in a community where research has not been helpful or visible before presents residents with an unfamiliar situation and a new set of occasions for reflection, self-evaluation, and decision making. Despite possible opportunities involved, the initiation of research inevitably imposes some degree of stress. The values, traditions, and paradigms of psychology are often in marked contrast to the norms of the host environment (Billington, Washington, & Trickett, 1981). For example, citizens (including community psychologists) do not always express in daily activities a predisposition to be open, objective, rational, reflective, and probing. Rather, they (we) are likely to be closed, personal, subjective, direct, and repressive about what disturbs them (us). The intrusion of scientific help asks much from the community! Indeed, in many communities, past experience may bespeak the fact that scientific inquiry has been unhelpful at best and exploitive at worst (for example, Cottle, 1970).

The dual focuses of coping and adaptation alert the community researcher to view the research site from a perspective that emphasizes three areas: (1) how the setting has traditionally coped with and adapted to outsiders; (2) how the very notion of scientific inquiry is defined by the local culture; (3) how the entry process of the research effort is managed as a function of these understandings. Different kinds of settings impose differing kinds of adaptive requirements on the research enterprise, both initially and throughout the relationship. As we and other investigators have noted, first appearances may be deceiving. For example, it is our experience that settings providing easy initial access often encourage an appearance of participation without the deep, clear, well-defined commitment which may result from an intensely negotiated research relationship. The result of such surface agreement may be a slackening of involvement further down the line and an upsurge of previously unexpressed ambivalence should later difficulties arise. On the other hand, it is those settings where tough and candid initial negotiations are deemed a prerequisite that often deliver more long-range commitment to work in the face of adversity.

Given the cultural differences between themselves and the host environment, research staff must be able to cope with the stress experienced by community groups and be prepared to revise procedures and formats in order to achieve a condition of mutual ownership of the research enterprise. The repertoire of the research organization must include readiness to improve responses to inevitable intrusions into the research enterprise. Delays in receiving permission, refusal to participate in data collection, and requests for new topics to be studied are examples of such events. Demands from the community that the research work be temporarily put aside as the community copes with a short-term crisis, or community input which suggests a redefinition of the research problem, are all part and parcel of a research relationship where citizens are empowered in the research enterprise. Under such conditions, it is likely that even the basic criteria for methods and goals of the research will be open to redefinition. Thus, community inquiry becomes an experiment in cultural

understanding and adaptation for the research team, for
it is the research group who are outside intervenors.

The Search for Systemic Events Illuminates the Process of Adaptation

The fifth principle highlights the role of one particular kind of occurrence in providing information about
the community. <u>Systemic events are those events in the
environment whose salience causes them to have wide ripple
effects on the setting</u>. The consequences of such events
are rarely fully predictable and can trigger positive or
negative effects on both individuals and subsystems of the
community. Systemic events can include the implementation
of a controversial policy, the death of a key system member, or the winning of an athletic championship. Such
events sometimes are catalytic; they may serve to mobilize
an individual's involvement in a community activity or
cause one or more organized groups to take action in the
interest of a common cause. For example, the informal
bonds forged among teachers during a threatened school
closing may aid the research team's efforts to form a
teachers' group designed to foster parent involvement in
the classroom.
The importance of the search for systemic events lies
in the knowledge of the setting they provide the research
team and in their unique power to mobilize and, therefore,
illuminate the deeply held norms, values, and adaptive
patterns of the community. In contrast to research paradigms emphasizing detached objectivity, this principle
leads the community psychologist to become involved in
community-organizing efforts to deal with the implications
of systemic events of the community.
Implementing this principle, then, is not a traditional observer role but involves the <u>active participant</u> aspect of the participant-observer role. The expectation is
that as the community researcher uncovers facts that inform
the understanding of systemic events, there is the complementary ethical commitment to assist with the work of organizing resources so that knowledge about these effects
becomes a resource for the community.

Persons and Settings Are in Dynamic Interaction

The original statement of the general principle of interdependence focused on the interactive nature of the community as a system and the manner in which its component subsystems were coupled. The principle is restated in Principle 6 in order to direct attention to the mechanisms and processes whereby persons affect settings. The principle rests on the ecological assumption of reciprocal causation, which is believed to reflect community dynamics more accurately than the more traditional assumption of linear causality. Rarely, if ever, in the community is there a one-way, direct line of cause-effect relationship between one event and another. Rather, events interact with each other in ways which tend to create and sustain predictable configurations.

The principle of dynamic interaction directs attention to the variability and consistency in how persons behave from one setting to another. It suggests that individuals are capable of considerable variation in the patterns of behavior as well as in the skills and knowledge which they bring to bear in different types of situations. Each setting has its own demand characteristics for the individual; similarly, the individual's role expectations may differ markedly from one setting to another. Community researchers studying caste dynamics, for example, have long noted that members of minority communities who hold menial and subservient positions in the larger culture often have been outstanding and influential leaders within their own ethnic communities. By stressing the importance of tracking the generality and specificity of competencies expressed by the same individuals in contrasting settings, the principle encourages the researcher to develop the richest possible picture of the range of resources individuals are capable of contributing to their environments.

The use of the term _dynamic_ directs attention of the research staff to the ebb and flow among the various elements within a situation. Furthermore, it applies to the impact of events originating outside the immediate situation on the interrelationships between persons and settings within it. For example, in certain situations, persons and settings become coupled to combat or protect themselves from malevolent outside forces; in other situations they are coupled for the very opposite purpose of importing outside resources into their setting. The first condition, termed a <u>vigilant attitude</u>, has been noted, for example, in a school system whose members feel "burned" by an opportunistic researcher eager for an exposé. The second condition, viewed as an <u>outreach attitude</u>, is exemplified by a citizens' group which has been energized to search outside its locality to find persons with grant-writing expertise.

Such contrasting perspectives with regard to the world outside the immediate community will have equally contrasting impacts on the nature of the research relationship and the manner in which it develops over time. Faced with a vigilant attitude, the researcher will need to consider how the projected inquiry might serve as a potential resource for the <u>preservation</u> of the current integrity and viability of the community. Under the outreach condition, on the other hand, the very nature of the research enterprise can be oriented toward the purpose of becoming a resource for <u>development</u>, in which the knowledge gained will contribute to the community and strengthen its relationship with outside resources.

These contrasting attitudes within settings also carry different risks for the fate of the research in terms of whether and how well its findings are used within the community. The risk where the vigilant attitude prevails is for potentially useful research findings to be dismissed out of hand. A possibly less obvious risk where the outreach attitude prevails is for research findings to be embraced overenthusiastically and without consideration of overriding value issues or unintended consequences of suggested changes. By paying careful attention to the dynamic interaction of persons and settings within the host community, including those interactions involving its own operations, the research team attempts to minimize the contrasting risks in these different settings, thereby increasing the likelihood that the research will serve as a useful community resource.

Persons, Settings, and Events
Are Assessed over Time

The original succession principle focused on the time dimension of communities and emphasized that historical forces have shaped the nature of the current community. As reformulated in Principle 7, the principle focuses on

the time dimension as applied to persons, settings, and
events, the three resource categories discussed in Principle 1. Persons, settings, and events are subunits of communities which have existed over time and, with few ex-
ceptions, will continue to unfold as research progresses.
A focus on this history may take many complementary forms,
including engaging in discussions with old-timers, uncovering memorable systemic events, reading of archival data,
and exploring with key informants how current norms and
policies evolved. The benefits of this search are multiple.
It illuminates the history and continuity of resource utilization and development in the community; it yields a
broader contextual understanding of the community and em-
pathy about its dominant patterns and values; and it increases the likelihood of linking the research and the host
environment in a mutually beneficial way.

Various aspects of the research process may be influenced by this longitudinal perspective. For example,
the process of entry--when viewed as one instance of the
way in which the setting sizes up outsiders--may be informed by explicit attention to the history of how the setting has dealt with outsiders in the past. In another
vein, if the research team is aware of the historical context, it is in a better position to avoid jeopardizing the
credibility of the research by violating community custom
and folklore as, for example, betraying ignorance or in-
sensitivity about the history of the community when it
seeks to interpret results and feed back data which may
have implications for change in the community.

A longitudinal time perspective also engenders the
patience needed to allow events to unfold at their own
pace and in their own fashion. The researcher is thus
alerted to the perspective that persons, settings, and
events affect each other over time and that the emergence
of resources is a constantly changing process. One implication of this point of view is that different qualities of
settings may become apparent to the outside researcher at
different rates and in different forms. For example, in
one study (Kaye, Trickett, & Quinlan, 1976), the authority
structure of high school classrooms was quickly and reliably noted by outside observers, while the degree of support between teacher and student was more elusive for outsiders to grasp. This kind of finding may suggest that
some of the important forms of interpersonal support--and
the latent resources inherent in such support--may have a

subtlety which initially eludes strangers but becomes apparent only after the strangers have become more familiar with the setting and are thus able to grasp its subtleties.

An even more fundamental importance of a longitudinal time perspective derives from the fact that communities are not static entities. They exist in a dynamic equilibrium which means, among other things, that they manifest cycles of resistance or receptivity to outside influences depending on the state of balance between their internal resources and external events. For example, when in a positive phase in its cycle of development, the community might manifest a ready interest in putting to use the insights and recommendations of the research team. For some researchers, this will be the preferred condition of work. When it is on a downward cycle for whatever reason (for example, economic difficulties), people will tend to be less actively involved in the research work unless that research promises to be helpful to them in their plight. Faced with a downward cycle, the research staff must deal with the challenge of being able to invest themselves fully in the work without the rewards offered by promissory fantasies of easy success. Despite the lack of immediate gratification of short-term results and the appreciation of citizens, they must set in motion joint activities which, however limited they may seem at the outset, will--when judged over time--have the possibility of demonstrating certain clear indexes of achievement. By embracing clear, achievable, tangible goals and results which can be readily demonstrated to all concerned, the research staff can offer a useful model demonstrating how empirical fact finding and tenacity of commitment may interrupt a downward cycle and help stimulate progress toward community goals.

Implicit in this principle is the premise that sound community research must take place over a sufficient period of time. The ecological paradigm does not lend itself to quickly executed cross-sectional inquiry. The passage of time grants certain opportunities for both researcher and community which are essential to the ecological orientation. Among other things, it allows the community adequate opportunity both to test the ideas, commitment, and value orientation of the research team and to grasp the researchers' intentions and gauge their effectiveness. Given adequate mechanisms for observation, analysis, and reflection, time offers both the community and the research staff opportunities for demonstrating that people and settings are capable of change and that it is possible for citizens to define and mobilize their own resources.

Community Research and the Research Relationship Are Designed to Be Coupled with the Host Environment

The final three principles draw specific attention to the linking of the research to the community, assessing its impact on the locality and the demands which community research places on the researcher. The seven preceding principles provide a heuristic framework for this task, with each principle stressing a different aspect of the design of the research and the development of the research relationship. The broad goal, however, is not explicitly stated until the eighth principle--namely, that the research and the research relationship be coupled with, or integrated into, the host environment.

The field of psychology, with its emphasis on technique and method, can unwittingly give the impression that preventive interventions such as community research are freestanding techniques and methods which can be transported across settings and over time with minimal regard for local circumstances of history. Often both research paradigms and interventions are seen as primary, and their relation to the site of work as secondary. The ecological paradigm rejects the premise of a dichotomy between method and setting. Instead, it asserts that community research must strive to be embedded in a social setting, for it is the social setting that provides the resources, energy, and power for the research to develop into a preventive intervention. In fact, the goal of this work is to create connections between the intervention and the setting which are strong and durable enough to enable the intervention to endure over time. In our collective experience, the focus on coupling requires as much--and often more-- effort as the actual content of the research per se. It is also our experience that the richness of results, impact of the work, and interpersonal satisfactions more than vindicate the energy expended.

Successful implementation of this principle involves an assessment of both the setting and the resources necessary to implement the intervention. There are at best four complementary aspects to this process. First is the assess-

ment of the resources available to the intervention in the
host environment. Resources may include such things as
commitment on the part of key participants to support a
project, the availability of space, or policies which support the participation of local citizens in aiding in the
execution of the project. Second is the assessment of what
resources the intervention will need to have provided by
the host environment. Such resources could include access
to information, opportunities to contact key individuals or
groups, or the redefining of the roles of certain individuals for the duration of the project to facilitate its completion. Third is a focus on the resources which need to
be generated in the host environment by the researcher to
increase the likelihood of mutual accommodation between
researcher and research site. Such resources could include providing consultative or teaching skills or gathering data on an immediate problem for use by members of
the setting. These three assessments set the stage for a
coupling of the research with the host environment. Fourth
is the designing of a process whereby the host environment
can sustain the intervention. The maintaining of skills
learned by members of the host environment, the evolution
of programs or structures set up as part of the research
process, or the increased use of outside resources linked
by the research to the setting are potential indicators of
sustaining the intervention.

Thus, at its core, this principle is perhaps the
most stimulating, for it forces attention to the relationship
between technology and social settings. It is also one of
the most elusive to concretize, for at this point in time
there is little knowledge available about how to think
about the accommodation process between a technology and
the environment where it is used. At best, to implement
this principle honestly and realistically one must be oriented toward doing a "resource analysis." By learning
how to define and generate resources the researcher assumes a kind of mediating role between the research and
the setting. The complexities of this task should not be
understated. Boldly put, it is an arrogant premise to
think that any community psychologist can single-handedly
design a marriage between social setting and intervention.
The initial task is to create educational guidelines to establish goals, clarify values, define limits for accepting or
rejecting the intervention, and determine means for adapting the intervention to the needs of the host environment.

Successful implementation of these educational and consultative tasks depends on the researcher's personal commitment to a community development process. It also requires that the researcher manage the tensions inherent in working over long time periods with two autonomous yet interrelated social structures--the research project and its team on the one hand and the host environment on the other. The researcher must know what considerations and caveats are involved in sanctioning the integration of a new process, such as community research, within a social milieu. The research effort works to couple context, content, and process in the interests of a workable community prevention program. This process involves art as well as science.

Attending to the Side Effects of
Community Research Is a Priority

The second of the three principles specific to the research relationship elaborates on the principle of interdependence and the premise that community research is an intervention. It focuses on the side effects of the research process. The dominant paradigms of psychology carry an implicit notion that the important impact of research is found in its substantive findings, that is, what it contributes to the shared body of knowledge in the field. Aftereffects that may occur in persons or settings as a consequence of doing the research are often noted informally. The folklore of research in educational settings, for example, is filled with stories of researchers who, while collecting their data, left a residue of ill will in the school as a consequence of how they conducted themselves or exploited research results for their own professional ends. Yet the impact of this experience for future researchers in the same setting is not usually stressed. The ecological paradigm offers a contrasting point of view about the priorities of conducting community research; namely, that community research, being itself an intervention, sets in motion ensuing activities in the immediate setting or even the broader environment which may be as meaningful to the setting as the research findings themselves.

Thus, community research within the ecological paradigm extends beyond a concern for collaboration with citizens in the design and execution of the research. The paradigm includes the importance of those social occasions, settings, and informal, nonprescribed interactions that are created and enjoyed in the process of getting the work done. The impact of these processes may reach far beyond the overt research task itself, thus enhancing the positive side effects of the original project. For example, one of the authors conducted a project designed to survey the opinions of inner-city parents about educational alternatives for their children (Trickett and Sussman, 1976). Parents representing 14 different neighborhoods were brought together to develop a structured interview and plan for a house-to-house survey of mothers and fathers in their respective neighborhoods. The gathering of persons with common interests who were previously unknown to each other stimulated the development of social networks which continued after the project was completed and which provided energy for new efforts at improving public education in the city. In addition, project staff carried over their contacts with parents to maintain a network to provide both personal support and a basis for implementing a variety of educational projects. The project thereby provided the basis for substantial community impact in areas unrelated to its original manifest purpose.

It is clear from the above example that various kinds of side effects or ripple effects may be observed in community research. They include new forms of communication between previously unconnected resources, new plans for more efficient use of resources, new policies and procedures for relating to external resources, and new training or educational programs to manage resources more effectively. By emphasizing the importance of coupling with the host environment, the ecological paradigm places a primary value on explicit efforts to predict, discover, evaluate, and build on these side effects in order to enhance the possibility of long-lasting and useful impact of research on the setting.

The extent to which a research team is successful in detecting and capitalizing on side effects may well determine the extent to which the research has achieved its goals of becoming a preventive intervention. The research has been preventive if, through bringing persons and settings together, a more clearly adaptive community or social setting has evolved. Thus, in a seeming paradox, what were originally defined as side effects may well emerge over time as the main impacts of the research.

Finally, this principle alerts both researcher and members of the host setting to the need to assess possible <u>negative</u> side effects. To sensitize persons in the setting to be alert for negative side effects, the community researcher works to empower clients to protect themselves from potential noxious effects of the research. In so doing, the researcher must focus on the building of mutual trust in order for persons in the setting to influence the research and, thereby, control their future with respect to its possible effects.

Implementing this principle requires that the community researcher be secure and strong enough to help persons in the setting set boundaries for themselves and for the research in order to cope with and be able to exert sufficient control of the research relationship. This principle thus makes explicit the fact that in looking for and assessing side effects, the community researcher is committed to a philosophy of competence development and empowerment with the locality.[2]

Ecological Inquiry Is a Flexible,
Improvisational Process

Previous principles have focused on a preplanned, alert, self-conscious philosophy for conducting community research and for creating conditions whereby both the process and results of inquiry foster community development. The final principle asserts that while adherence to a formal set of ideas gives structure to the ecological paradigm, the spirit of ecological inquiry involves a fundamental commitment to flexibility and improvisation. Within the ecological paradigm, community research demands such flexibility because (1) it is designed to be a shared experience with the host environment; (2) it relies on an evolving understanding of what the setting is and what it is becoming; (3) it capitalizes on and responds to the ramifications of nonplanned events as they occur; and (4) it involves an ongoing interplay within the host environment among research process and findings, and interventions emanating from them. The spirit of the work generates a mode of operation relaxed and open enough to "go with the flow," to be able to see connections as they arise out of the moment and on occasion to suspend work on existing projects in order to take advantage of opportunities to learn new facts or explore new issues.

To implement this principle the community researcher needs to adopt a lifestyle which allows opportunity to experience new points of view, engage in relaxed reconnaissance of the setting, and remain open to new ideas and orientations. This orientation increases the possibility for the researcher to make connections between previously disparate elements of the environment. By contrast, concepts which are too tight, formal, and final lessen opportunities to envision and invent needed connections between persons, settings, and events.

The style and possibilities of an improvisational approach vary according to the characteristics of the community. Where persons are satisfied with current methods and concepts, opportunities for improvisation rarely develop. Under such conditions there is the possibility that community conservatism and professional orthodoxy will combine to blunt the spirit of ecological inquiry. In any event, ecologically oriented researchers should be disciplined and rigorous without becoming doctrinaire, remaining open to opportunities for designing new experiences which will enable the research to serve as a vehicle for the development of the community.

PART II: ECOLOGICAL INQUIRY AND INTERPERSONAL PROBLEM SOLVING

For the ecological paradigm to stimulate new questions and provide a general heuristic for community research, it must demonstrate its applicability to a tangible research area. This section indicates how an ecological mind set may be used to assess the research carried out in an area of particular interest to community psychology: the development of IPS (interpersonal problem-solving) skills in children.

The topic was chosen for several reasons. Deep in it is an area of expanding investigation which has captured the research energies of many psychologists interested in prevention; its content is focused proactively on nurturing coping behaviors as resources for children to use in dealing with the interpersonal aspects of their lives; it is implemented in natural settings where research and the research relationship can serve as vehicles for the development of the setting. However, the preventive potential of many of these programs is as yet unrealized because of their inability to show linkages between IPS skills and adjustment.   Thus, in our judgment, it is an area of substantive importance, well received and thoughtfully critiqued (Urbain & Kendall, 1980), and quite ripe for speculation about the missing pieces in the IPS-adjustment puzzle.

A selective overview of IPS inquiry, its logic and methods, is followed by a detailed analysis of the literature from our ecological perspective.   In preparing both these sections, we contacted the primary authors of the research reviewed and requested their feedback on our effort.   That open and responsive feedback has been particularly useful.[3]

Interpersonal Problem Solving: An Overview of Its Processes and Findings

Over the past decade several school-based models of prevention have been developed to train children in a constellation of skills known as interpersonal cognitive problem solving (ICPS), sometimes called social problem solving.   While the majority of programs have been implemented in elementary schools, there is variation in how these skills are defined and incorporated into training programs, the age of children receiving the training, and the settings in which schools are located.   In some cases, the program is implemented daily for about three months (for example, Spivack & Shure, 1974), while in others training occurs two or three times a week for approximately the same period of time (for example, Weissberg et al., 1981a, 1981b).   Despite important variations, however, all of these programs share a basic premise that teaching children basic IPS skills promotes social competency and reduces maladaptive behaviors.

The Shure and Spivack Program

The most frequently cited exemplar of IPS was developed at the Hahnemann Community Mental Health/Mental Retardation Center in Philadelphia by Shure, Spivack, and their colleagues.   Shure (1979) notes that over ten years more than 900 inner-city, predominantly black nursery and kindergarten children have been trained by 49 teachers in what this group terms ICPS (interpersonal cognitive problem-solving) skills. The program has also been extended to urban fifth graders and to mother-child dyads, among others.

The program is based on the findings of Spivack and Levine (1963) that there were important differences in the way normal and disturbed adolescents thought about and solved interpersonal problems. Adolescents who were having problems of adjustment seemed to be deficient in such skills as the ability to generate step-by-step goals or solutions in interpersonal problem situations, or to see these situations from the perspective of other involved individuals (Spivack, Platt, & Shure, 1976). Studies of other groups by Spivack, Shure, and their colleagues also yielded differences in problem-solving abilities between "normals" and clinically disturbed populations. These studies were extended to examine ten-year-olds with varying degrees of behavioral difficulties in regular schools and institutionalized dependent neglected children from ages nine to twelve. Once again, deficiencies in ICPS ability were related to poorer levels of adjustment. Further research suggested that the relationship between ICPS skills and adjustment was discernible at as early as age four (Spivack & Shure, 1974).

Based on this accumulated body of work, a constellation of skills was hypothesized as mediating adjustment: (1) The ability to conceptualize alternative solutions to interpersonal problems, (2) consequential thinking, (3) causal thinking, and (4) sensitivity to interpersonal problems (Shure, 1979). The development of such skills in nursery school and kindergarten children thus became the focus of the ICPS training program.

Specifics of the Training Program

The ICPS training program is put into practice daily for three months by the classroom teachers (or, in a more recently developed program, by mothers), with each student beginning with five minutes a day and working up to twenty. The program script is delineated quite specifically (see Spivack & Shure, 1974), and the trainers are encouraged to use the ICPS dialogue informally throughout the day.

Generally, the script is described by Shure (1979) as

> a sequenced series of lessons, in game form,
> that begin with certain language and think-
> ing skills judged to be prerequisite for

learning the major ICPS skills found to be
related to adjustment before training. . . .
Listening to people, watching them, and
discussions of ways to find out about people's feelings and desires were included.
Having learned to take emotions and preferences of others into account, children are
encouraged to think about hypothetical interpersonal problem situations, why the
problem came to be, all the things children
having the problem could do or say to solve
it, and what might happen next, if particular solutions are carried out. By extracting
from children their thoughts about the problem, and what to do about it, the children
are taught how, but not what, to think.
(Pp. 34-35) (Reprinted with permission)

Evaluative findings have been consistently promising. Trained children improved more than nonprogram controls in alternative-solution thinking, consequential thinking, and most importantly, teacher-rated classroom adjustment. Adjustment was assessed in younger children by
rating scales which clustered in such factors as impatience,
emotionality, and dominance-aggression. From these scales,
a child was judged to be either overly impulsive, overly
inhibited, or adjusted. In older children, a peer-rating
scale was also included as a measure of adjustment. Not
only were gains in ICPS skills related to improvement in
classroom adjustment ratings; those children who at pretesting were rated as less well adjusted improved most in
both ICPS skills and adjustment. Perhaps the most important aspect of these findings was that in one or two year
follow-ups, gains in reported adjustment remained intact.
Thus, Shure and Spivack's data suggest that their program
can teach ICPS skills and that children with these improved skills are perceived by teachers as better adjusted
in the classroom.

Other Research Programs

Several other large-scale prevention programs have
been implemented which share with the Spivack and Shure
group the assumption that IPS skills function as significant
mediators of healthy social adjustment (Shure & Spivack,
1979). These programs agree for the most part that the

skills mentioned above are the important components of IPS, but each program has either introduced some modifications in training methods, made the content or skill level more appropriate for older children, or both. For example, the Rochester group (Weissberg et al., 1981a, 1981b; Gesten et al., 1979) added problem-identification skills and integration of problem-solving behavior to their programs for second-grade, third-grade, and fourth-grade children, and Allen and others (1976) made similar expansions in their programs for third- and fourth-grade children.

The findings of these two groups were not as positive as those of the Hahnemann group, however. Allen and others (1976), implementing their program in a suburban Connecticut school, found that program children's gains in acquiring problem-solving skills exceeded those of controls and that the former did better than the latter on real-life structured-problem situations. However, the groups did not differ on teacher judgments of problem behavior, peer sociometric ratings, or self-report measures of self-esteem and level of aspirations. They point out that in their sample the gradient of effect for this problem-solving intervention is rather specific.

The Rochester group has introduced a number of programs for latency-age children into both inner-city and suburban schools. Thus far, their results have been mixed. One study (Weissburg et al., 1981a) found that program children in their urban sample scored <u>lower</u> on several teacher-rated adjustment measures after training, while suburban children <u>improved</u> on most of these measures. These adjustment measures include such variables as acting out, frustration tolerance, peer sociability, and adaptive assertiveness.

A modified version of this program (Weissberg et al., 1981b) found, on the other hand, that problem-solving skills and adjustment were improved for <u>both</u> suburban and urban children. Unfortunately, they found no relationship between IPS skills and adjustment gains, thus complicating the issue of IPS skills as mediators of adjustment.

Another investigation by the Rochester group (Gesten et al., 1979, 1982) of suburban second- and third-grade children employed a one-year follow-up and found somewhat more positive results. Though the postprogram evaluation found that controls generally were rated higher on adjustment than the experimental children, at a one-year follow-up experimentals performed better than controls on many of the adjustment indexes.

McClure and his colleagues (McClure et al., 1981; McCammon et al., 1977) have developed a program based on the Connecticut program which they have implemented with predominantly black, inner-city sixth graders in South Carolina. Though this program has not yet appeared in published literature, the thoughtful attention paid to eco-logical issues by these investigators in developing and reporting their program, as evident through the following pages, makes their program vital to include.[4]

Interpersonal Problem Solving: The
Persective of the Ecological Paradigm

The usefulness of a paradigm is found--at least par-tially--in its heuristic value in approaching certain kinds of problems. The task for this section of the chapter is to apply the ecological paradigm to IPS research. Certain caveats are necessary to clarify the hopes and intents of this effort.

This review does not seek to focus on the "fit" be-tween the ecological paradigm and the IPS research, since that research was generally initiated from a different per-spective. Our intent is to use the paradigm to extend ex-isting ideas about methods, define additional criteria for program success, and pose new questions which have been stimulated by investigators in this area. Thus, we view this as a generative, not replacement, activity which builds on the methods, findings, and discussions of investigators in the area.

A potential source of strain in the review results from differences between dominant canons of the profession regarding the writing of research reports and emphases of the ecological paradigm. For example, while the processes of developing and maintaining the research relationship are primary within the ecological paradigm, and would be emphasized in published articles, they are generally given only secondary emphasis in published research on IPS training.

To the degree that the emphasis on developing the research relationship is more central to the ecological orientation than to the paradigm underlying IPS research reports, this may represent a genuine paradigmatic clash. Part of it, however, may simply represent accommodations currently necessary in distilling the rich experience of community research into publishable form.

To accomplish our objective we reviewed published literature on IPS training with children and organized salient points in terms of the ten ecological principles presented earlier. We then selected the following four major topics as illustrative areas for applying the ecological paradigm to the IPS literature:

1. Cycling of resources: the process of environmental reconnaissance.
2. The interdependence of persons and settings: cultural and setting diversity and the process of adaptation.
3. Assessment over time: going for the long haul.
4. The research relationship as a developmental process.

1. The Cycling of Resources: The Process of Environmental Reconnaissance

Incorporated in Principles 1, 2, and 3 (see Table 7.1), this section focuses on the assessment of the prospective host environment to discover available or potentially available resources within the host environment and to identify needed resources which do not exist. This is the initial phase in any ecological intervention.

Well-planned reconnaissance yields at least three positive effects: (1) having acknowledged and valued the community's own resources, the researchers may gain greater acceptance from the host environment for their perceptive recognition of its positive qualities and strengths; (2) the intervention will stand a much better chance of enduring because it will be better able to draw on those strengths; (3) the research team will be better able to determine how the research relationship can serve as a resource to the community.

A. How the Setting Naturally Encourages the Development of IPS Skills

An initial step in IPS research would be to identify persons and settings which facilitate the socialization of interpersonal problem solving. While, to the best of our knowledge, there is no reported research on this issue, several authors have speculated about conditions affecting the natural evolution of problem-solving skills. Spivack, Platt, and Shure (1976) provide the most direct appraisal of how IPS skills may develop naturally. They assert that those environments, particularly learning environments which emphasize the processes of exploring the problem-solving sequences in thought (process) rather than emphasizing "correct" outcomes (content) will be most likely to promote the development of IPS skills. These authors contrast such process-oriented environments with those emphasizing power relations and authoritarian social patterns. In addition, Shure and Spivack (1978) (as cited in McKim et al., 1982) cite literature which suggests that middle-class child-rearing styles, which encourage flexible thinking and open verbal communication, are more conducive to the development of IPS skills than those based on status rules and appeals to authority. Elsewhere, Spivack and Shure (1974) suggest two additional environmental conditions which would militate against the development of IPS skills: (1) when a particular situation is so emotionally charged that normally available skills are suppressed; (2) when adults in the child's environment do not provide exposure to these skills.

These investigators suggest that some persons and settings clearly are richer resources for the development of IPS skills than others. Research based on these speculations is needed. McClure and others (1981), for example, used the classroom environment scale (Moos & Trickett, 1974; Trickett & Moos, 1973) to assess changes in the classroom as a result of an IPS intervention with sixth graders. Such a measure might be used to focus on how differing classroom environments affect the subsequent development of IPS skills in students. This kind of socialization study would yield valuable information about the types of classrooms most likely to encourage the development of problem-solving skills. By focusing on properties of naturally occurring settings which promote the development of IPS skills, we begin to document the extent to which the development of such skills is linked to local norms, values, and strategies for socialization. Such information would help subsequent research efforts be more in harmony with their host environments. A highly desirable outcome would be to extend IPS training from a person-based intervention (teaching skills to individual children) to a person-environment-based intervention which seeks to influence the interplay between children and the learning environments in which they most cope and adapt.

B. Identifying Proactive Behaviors in Persons and across Settings

Reconnaissance of the environment from a resource perspective also includes exploration of the natural distribution of proactive behaviors in persons and across settings.

IPS-related research might focus on norms governing how interpersonal problems are solved from setting to setting and over time by different kinds of children. Such explorations would highlight the range of available problem-solving options for persons in different cultural settings.

It is likely that differences in sanctioned problem-solving alternatives would be a function of person variables, such as age; cultural variables, such as ethnicity; and setting variables, such as size. If, for example, fighting is seen as adaptive in a lower-class urban neighborhood as a way of solving problems among adolescent boys and "talking things over" is seen as a sign of weakness, the available alternatives--in terms of the demand characteristics of the neighborhood setting--would be few and clearly prescribed. In other settings in the same urban area, such as an alternative high school where tolerance for diversity is encouraged, the range of options might be greater and less clearly prescribed.

A further step would be to explore the distribution of IPS behaviors among children in such contrasting environments and to discover how variations in problem-solving skills both reflect and shape their environments. As answers to such questions become available, IPS researchers will be better able to manage and conserve resources that foster desired problem-solving skills.

C. IPS Research and Environmental/Resource Reconnaissance: Examples and Implications

An IPS study which exemplifies a resource perspective was carried out by McClure and his colleagues in South Carolina (McClure et al., 1981; McCammon et al., 1977). Their assessment of the setting in which their intervention was to occur began before the program was implemented. Based on careful reconnaissance of the environment, they developed a multilevel intervention which both utilized resources and itself served as a resource at all levels of the setting.

Discussing the importance of their role as resource link in the school system, McCammon and his colleagues state that, though the IPS curriculum was not designed to influence the chaotic conditions they discovered in a school, their presence did make a difference. By involving members of the system in the project, they helped to establish links, and went on to identify and approach problems among both teaching and administrative staff. For example, their activities helped the school psychologist to be-

come more active in the school and also led to increased
involvement of sixth-grade parents. The authors go on to
include an extensive list of resources that were identified,
developed, and linked throughout the course of their program. Their discussion exemplifies an intervention flow-
ing from a resource perspective which takes into account
the interaction of setting and intervention.

While existing studies use initial scores of IPS
skills for the purpose of matching groups and as a baseline against which to measure change, there is little consideration given to the importance of these initial data,
in and of themselves. The ecological paradigm views such
data as "facts" rather than "artifacts"--that is, as evidence for naturally occurring differences among populations.

Thus far, only one study included an empirical investigation of the natural distribution of problem-solving
skills among children across environments. McKim and her
colleagues at Rochester (1982) compared the IPS skills and
adjustment ratings of suburban and urban third-grade
children and examined IPS adjustment relationships within
groups for children who had never been formally trained
in ICPS skills. They discovered that levels of cognitive
development and cultural background appear to be important factors that determine the specific skill(s) most closely linked with adjustment. Specifically, they note that it
is important to teach the skill of alternative solution
thinking to inner-city, black preschoolers whereas means-
end thinking is more functional for suburban, white third
graders. In their view less successful IPS training programs may have failed to tailor specific problem-solving/
adjustment approaches to different age and sociodemographic
groups (McKim et al., 1982).

The Rochester group (Weissberg et al., 1981b) provides an excellent example of the need to attend to persons
as resources. They mention one urban teacher who "was
excited about the program and taught it effectively; however, her pre-adjustment ratings were atypically high
(higher than all suburban classes), making it difficult to
show improvement." This passage illustrates how research
outcomes and resource development may appear to conflict.
Such an unfortunate loss of significant-change findings,
however, might be turned to the investigators' advantage
if they delved more deeply into the intriguing "atypically
high" initial adjustment ratings. If the secret of this
teacher's success were discovered, the information gained

could be incorporated into subsequent IPS interventions.
In this way the atypical teacher would become a resource
whose techniques could be used to improve scores in any
number of classrooms. Moreover, if the teacher's expertise
were acknowledged and valued by her colleagues, the ability of the researchers to recognize and respect that special
competence might gain them and their findings more acceptance by others in the setting. McClure (1981, personal
communication) cites an example of how such a teacher was
recognized by both the researchers and her colleagues as
a resource. He relates that

> one of our control teacher's problem solving
> interactions was far higher than all the
> other experimental and control teachers.
> Her CES (Classroom Environment Scale)
> scores indicate that she is low on Order
> and Organization, but high on innovation,
> and highest on increase in children's prob-
> lem solving behavior over time . . . she
> was later transferred to be the school dis-
> trict's special teacher consultant for the
> gifted student program. Thus she was (is)
> acknowledged by her network, and her
> skills as a teacher are being shared with
> others.

The Rochester experience also provides an example
of an event which could become a resource for a research
team. They note that the IPS curriculum created difficulties for the inner-city children which were not experienced
in the suburbs. In the suburbs, for example, teachers
felt that brainstorming alternatives helped children express
ideas creatively, while urban teachers found that the same
procedures produced mostly aggressive alternatives and
negatively affected class discipline. This unanticipated
consequence of the curriculum could be very useful for
clarifying the nature of the norms, processes, and values
of different settings in which the program was implemented.
In addition, such an occurrence offers an opportunity for
teachers and research staff to engage in discussion about
the values and goals of the program; this discussion provides the investigators with an opportunity to evaluate the
values and premises that have shaped their design, en-
riches their interpretation of results, and affects their

recommendations to the schools. Such discussions could also serve as a basis for a collaborative effort to shape the curriculum so as to reinforce the learning of IPS skills.

2. The Interdependence of Persons and Settings: Cultural and Setting Diversity and the Process of Adaptation

Incorporated in Principles 4, 5, and 6, this topic focuses on the concepts of adaptation and interdependence. As noted above, the adaptive requirements for survival and development differ across varying cultures, subcultures, neighborhoods, schools, and families. Adaptation involves an active role for the individual, the existence of a dynamic tension between persons and their social surroundings, and the development over time of personal qualities derived from an ongoing series of person-environment interchanges. Interdependence stresses the interrelatedness of the varied contexts where adaptation occurs. The ecological orientation to adaptation and interdependence holds several implications for research in interpersonal problem solving.

A. The Adaptive Requirements of Varied Settings Are Not Presumed to Be Similar

Many investigators of the school setting have documented how--within this one social institution--adaptive requirements for students differ in different kinds of schools. Barker, for example, in describing schools of different sizes, clearly demonstrates how size of school affects student opportunities, experience, and behavior (Barker & Gump, 1964). Kelly (1967) documented the relationship between student turnover rates and their implications for the adaptive requirements faced by students. Trickett (1978) found that the normative classroom environments in five types of schools (urban, suburban, rural, vocational, and alternative) provide different kinds of classroom settings to which students must adapt. These examples demonstrate the diversity of adaptive requirements among schools or among various settings within the same school.

The variety of adaptations a child must make extends well beyond the schools to a larger range of salient settings in which children find themselves either regularly or intermittently. The ecological paradigm advocates that IPS research explicitly focus on the varied settings of a child's life. Are IPS skills learned in the elementary school classroom equally useful on the school playground, in the neighborhood, or in the home? Do they augment the child's ability to generalize beyond the setting in which they are learned and practiced or do they present the child with conflicting norms about how to solve problems in home as opposed to school? A relevant and oft-cited example is Bronfenbrenner's (1979) work on the relationship between home and school. He discusses differences in children's behavior in the two settings and stresses the importance of assessing the relationship or interdependence among varied settings of importance to the child.

Understanding the interdependence between settings in a child's life is essential to our understanding of the adaptive nature of that child's interpersonal problem solving. Both congruent and disjunctive situations have costs and benefits to the children involved. Congruence between home and school offers the child a comfortable transition characterized by low anxiety and a sense of predictability about evolving norms governing peer relations. On the other hand, such a situation may make the child less able or willing to explore settings and relationships involving cultural diversity. The child in the disjunctive situation may experience culture conflict between home and school and suffer increased anxiety and identity issues, yet the child may learn how to cope with diverse persons and settings in the future. One implication of this example may be that a child may be unwilling to behave "appropriately" in one setting if it means losing face in others. Trickett (in press) describes one such example in which an inner-city youth avoided class attendance at his high school to preserve his "street image," yet he managed to devise a way of meeting his educational goals.

B. Interdependence, Adaptation, and IPS Research: Examples and Implications

The above perspectives on interdependence and adaptation suggest at least two ways in which the ecological paradigm can be useful. First, by emphasizing the desirability of attending to the diverse settings to which an individual must adapt in the course of even a day, the paradigm emphasizes that consideration be given to the impact that IPS training has across the child's salient settings. To the best of our knowledge, what we call "radiation of effects across settings" has rarely been systematically treated in IPS research reports. Some data are offered by Spivack and Shure. In one report, Spivack and

Shure (1974) report a discussion with a mother who cited an incident in which her child used IPS skills taught in school to persuade her mother to buy a candy bar in a supermarket. Later they cite empirical evidence from a training program developed for mothers to use in the home setting (Shure 1979). They found that children exposed to the home-based training program improved in their school behavior as rated by teachers. They further suggest that an important question—again related to the radiation of the intervention—involves the impact that a child trained in IPS skills may have on the parent.

The McClure group (McCammon et al., 1977) also has given consideration to the adaptive requirements of different settings in their multilevel IPS intervention. They state that after working with the sixth graders for one semester, they began questioning whether the messages the children received from their families were contradictory to the training. Two questions emerged: (1) What is the relevance of the strategies being taught for the child in the immediate environment? (2) How could the strategies learned in the family be built on more effectively? To answer these and more specific questions about the linkage of family to school (such as the congruence between the parents' and school's views of the role of the school) the investigators interviewed families in the home and administered the Moos family environment scale (Moos, 1974). It is relevant to our discussion to note that these researchers state that a subgoal of their inquiry was to establish a link between school and families. Awareness of the potential benefits of such "side effects" is the mark of ecological research.

Beyond the above instances, the literature has given little empirical attention to the adaptive effects of IPS training across settings. Questions which need to be explored include these: Under what conditions do family and classroom environments support the generalizability of these skills? Under what conditions do they not? Such data would both broaden an understanding of adaptation as a multifaceted phenomenon and allay concerns that IPS training only predicts conformity to classroom norms.

What about broader cultural considerations which have impact on IPS interventions as they are implemented in differing environments? The basic IPS package has been used in varied settings, from small-town Connecticut to inner-city Philadelphia. However, only the Rochester group (Weissberg et al., 1981b) has explicitly compared different settings. Their findings strongly affirm the need to consider the demand characteristics of varying environments before generalizing IPS findings and curricula. They warn that "variables such as a program's curriculum and the age and socio-demographic attributes of its targets must be better understood for IPS training to attain its objective of promoting adaptive behavioral adjustment" (Weissberg et al., 1981b). This caution is based on the results from one training program, which revealed that while suburban children improved on some measure of classroom adjustment after IPS training, urban children with the same training worsened. This finding raises some important research questions in general for the field of IPS training: Are IPS skills a necessary component in enabling the optimum adaptation in every setting and at every time? Furthermore, is this particular means of solving interpersonal problems (that is, via generation of alternatives) the preferred mode in every culture? Spivack and Shure (1974) state that lower-class children are consistently "deficient" in interpersonal problem-solving skills. Though one may label this phenomenon a deficiency, it is also possible that the skills which these children are exhibiting are more adaptive in their nonschool settings. Recall that important differences were found between urban and suburban children's reactions to the use of brainstorming as a way of generating problem-solving alternatives.

Further evidence for different cultural adaptations to the IPS curriculum (and perhaps the different cultural manifestations of those skills) is also provided by the Rochester group. The resulting curriculum revisions that the Rochester group developed as a result of urban teacher input was reported to reduce disruptive behavior in the classroom. However, another issue which might be considered is whether the change in approach was best suited to the situations and modes of response of greatest importance to the children in the broader settings in their lives, given that it seemed to discourage the children's natural response styles.

Such unexpected events can serve as heuristics for understanding more about the nonschool environments of children, the problems present in those contexts, and the model problem-solving strategies they see in their "real world." Perhaps the best test of the utility of an IPS program is whether it also increases the child's potential to adapt <u>outside</u> the school setting. This possibility, yet to be explored empirically, offers a crucial test of how the IPS approach affects adjustment.

3. Assessment over Time: Going for the Long Haul
        Incorporated in Principle 7, this topic affirms the importance of the succession principle and offers a longitudinal perspective on the impact of IPS training on children and the impact of the IPS research project itself on the host environment. Interpersonal problem-solving research shares the ecologist's basic concern with the endurance of interventions over time. Holding that interpersonal problem solving is a central competency, Spivack and Shure emphasize that to be fundamentally successful an intervention should show results that endure over time in the children who have been exposed to it (1974). It is also important to determine the impact of the IPS program on the setting where the research occurs. Change in the setting will influence the interpersonal problem-solving skills of future cohorts of children. Such effects have important implications for community development and for the preventive ideals of the ecological paradigm and IPS researchers alike.
        A. The Implications of Children's Current Adaptations for Future Adaptations
        Within the ecological paradigm it is essentially important to see if IPS skills related to current adaptations will facilitate future adaptations and whether such skills lay the groundwork for others that may be needed later.
        Research findings on the durability of IPS training in children have thus far been mixed. The Hahnemann group (Spivack and Shure, 1974) found that both IPS skills and classroom adjustment persisted over a two-year period. In contrast, the positive adjustment effects reported by Larcen (1973) were found to have dissipated after a four-month period (McClure, Chinsky, & Larcen, 1978).
        It is not yet clear why interpersonal problem-solving skills endure in some settings and not in others. However, as discussed above, the ecological paradigm suggests the need to examine certain interactional factors which might have contributed to either positive or negative outcomes, such as failure to attend to various coupling issues with the host environment or a discordance between the skills being taught in the school and those needed to cope in

other settings. Other research questions include these: Were the skills eliminated by competing socialization influences in future settings? Were they eliminated from the children's repertoire because they were rarely needed in subsequent life circumstances? Answers to such questions must come from long-range studies of the impact of the training. The results will help guide the design of future interventions based on ecological considerations of context and research relationship. This implies that the follow-up studies must focus not only on children and the setting in which the intervention was implemented but also on the many other settings with which the children subsequently came in contact.

A specific issue relating to the continuity of adaptations involves the reliance on current classroom adjustment as a primary outcome criterion for program success. It is reasonable to suppose that, depending on the circumstances, not adjusting to a current setting could have benefits in terms of either future adaptations to the setting or current or future adaptations in other settings; conversely, adjusting to a current setting could have costs in terms of future adaptations or current adaptations in other settings. For example, let us assume that in many elementary school classrooms in our society docility remains a quality socialized in young girls. The rewards received from "docile behavior" may link docility to self-esteem. Such adaptation raises questions regarding the girl's future options for coping as she matures and deals with radically different expectations of her as a woman. The intent, in this example, is not to imply that docility is not on some occasions, for some persons, the adaptive style of choice. Rather, it is simply to stress the need to view adaptation longitudinally, so as to address potential implications for how current and future adjustment may be related.

B. Implications of the Research Program for Future Adaptation of the Setting

As stated above, we assert that a meaningful "bottom line" criterion for evaluating community research is its long-term as well as immediate impact on the setting where it occurs. Each year specific children who acquire IPS skills leave school and new cadres of children enter. Meanwhile, the school changes, new problems emerge, and new opportunities arise to improve it. What is the institutional impact of the work? Does IPS training of teachers yield a different kind of classroom environment that is more helpful to students in general? Are an increasing number of teachers brought into the program over time? Does the implementation of IPS training stimulate invigorating discussions which bring teachers, administrators, and parents closer together about the nature of education they want for children?

Though much of the information on how IPS training affected settings is anecdotal, McClure and his colleagues (1981) present data on one aspect of this issue: Did training teachers in IPS skills affect the kinds of classroom environments they create? They administered the classroom environment scale (Trickett & Moos, 1973) before and after classes whose teachers were trained in interpersonal problem-solving skills. Compared to controls, trained classes showed significant changes on several dimensions of the scale at post-test, including a strong effect for system innovation. Whether similar classroom changes might occur in differing schools or with different populations of students, and whether these changes would endure, is currently unknown. Similarly, we need to study those factors which promote teachers' continued use of IPS skills after completion of training.

An example of a different type of impact of an intervention on a school setting was described by Allen and others (1976). They report that their program was adopted by the school administration only after key members of the system came to accept the notion that the implementation of preventive endeavors should be a responsibility of the system. By demonstrating that schools can contribute to the goal of preventing or reducing certain problems in children, their research had a powerful effect on climate and attitudes within the system. Unfortunately, their research design did not include empirical investigation of this impact. An important issue for future researchers to consider is not only whether the IPS program was continued in the school after the research team left but also what factors contributed to its continuation, how the program was subsequently shaped by the institution, and vice versa. Focus on such issues is consistent with the long-haul orientation characteristic of both the ecological paradigm and IPS as a preventive intervention.

The type of setting can also affect whether the program will endure in that setting. For example, the Allen and others' (1976) program was implemented in and subsequently adopted by a school in a small town described as almost totally white and predominantly Protestant. School personnel had just adopted an innovative "individually guided" program format, suggesting a preexisting willingness to accept new programs into the system. This setting can be contrasted with the school in which the McClure and others' (1981) intervention took place. Predominantly black urban children were bussed to a school with predominantly white faculty and staff in a white middle-class section of town, which led to a great deal of tension. McClure cogently cautions that because the adoption of the new style of teacher-student interaction (a result of IPS training) represented additional effort in what teachers already viewed as a stressful and unrewarding work context, it should not be assumed that teachers will maintain these behaviors. This example also reminds one that when "receptive" schools and "volunteer" teachers are used, it is possible to mask or minimize broader environmental forces which may constrain the range of settings in which a particular type of intervention may succeed.

4. The Research Relationship as a Developmental Process

The previous three illustrative areas have focused primarily on the implications of the ecological paradigm for research methods, topics, and design. This last topic, incorporated in Principles 8, 9, and 10, centers on the nature of the research relationships per se. As emphasized above, the coupling of a research effort with its host environment maximizes its chances of being a preventive intervention. Involving more than an initial entry, assessment, and reconnaissance, coupling includes (a) involvement of citizens from the host environment in the design and modification of the research, (b) sufficient flexibility to enable researchers and citizens to adapt research methods and design to changing environmental demands, and (c) attention throughout the study to developing mechanisms and means for allowing the intervention to survive. We have selected from the IPS literature two illustrative areas.

A. The Effect of the Research Relationship on the Endurance of the Intervention

What makes some interventions of enduring value to a setting and some not is a central question in intervention theory (for example, Argyris, 1970). The ecological paradigm places its bets on the relationship between researcher and setting as a critical factor. To the degree the researcher can become a resource for the setting, the impact of the work will be enhanced.

The IPS literature indicates that some interventions have clearly been more enduring than others. Speculations regarding such differences have varied. Though there are many possible explanations for the intervention not "taking," there is good reason to suppose that at least some of the variance is a function of how the research relationship developed over time. The ecological paradigm advocates a careful description of the evolution of the research relationship to understand the coupling process and the factors which may cause the intervention to endure or erode. Shure (in Munoz, Snowden, & Kelly, 1979) includes a thoughtful description of the entry process of the IPS program into the Philadelphia school system, including resistances encountered, resources offered, and the way in which the research relationship was worked out. The McClure group, as will be discussed, included an even more explicit description of these processes. It is likely that most investigators went through similar processes in implementing their programs. Our hope is that in future reporting of research, more explicit discussion of such activities will be included not only to shed more light on the program being described but also to inform future researchers of the challenges they too will face in coupling with their host environments.

B. The Research Relationship Should Promote the Investigation of Unintended Consequences

As stated earlier, the ecological paradigm focuses on side effects of the research and encourages the researcher to be ready to take into account unanticipated consequences of an intervention. Doing so requires both watchfulness and flexibility as the impact of IPS training unfolds. Such vigilance does much to inform the researchers about the natural operation of the environment because so-called side effects are often a result of the way in which a setting has adapted to the intervention. Unexpected occurrences are a means to better couple with the host environment because they clarify the nature of local norms and processes. By paying attention to unintended consequences, the flexible researcher can more accurately capture the essence of phenomena in the local setting.

In the IPS literature, instances of unintended consequences and side effects of interventions are usually presented as confounds in the research or minor disruptions rather than sources of increased understanding which can be used to improve the research process. For example,

the Rochester group (Weissberg et al., 1981b), in discussing problems with the interpretation of adjustment findings
based solely on teacher ratings of adjustment, states: "It
is difficult to separate components of rated gains that reflect actual improvements in child behavior vs. greater
(experimental) teacher acceptance of children and their
behavior" (p. 16). There are many possible implications
of this issue, including the importance of considering multiple measures of adaptation from multiple sources and the
possibility that the program had an impact on the adaptation of teachers as well as students.

    C. Attending to the Research Relationship: Some
        Implications for IPS Research

The IPS literature provides a number of examples
of how interventions have been modified in response to reactions within the host environment as adaptations to the
research project occur.

As already noted, the researcher often must impro-
vise as new research issues arise. Such improvisation occurred in the Rochester study already cited (Weissberg et
al., 1981b). When the brainstorming technique advocated
by the curriculum engendered qualitatively different student
behaviors in urban and suburban samples, the group's response was to revise the curriculum in order to limit the
generation of aggressive alternatives in urban samples.
Thus, the investigators used input from the environment as
feedback which helped shape the program.

It should be noted that this response may also have
limited the generalizability of the resultant IPS skills. By
adapting the curriculum to the setting's norms, the researchers were not necessarily adapting it to the situations and modes of response of greatest importance to the
children within the varied settings in their lives. Attending to environmental input does not necessarily lead researchers to appropriate choices about how to use that input; self-conscious researchers must be able to examine
both short- and long-term implications of the information.

Certain advantages for the research relationship of
drawing on setting resources have already been described
in the introduction to the sections on cycling of resources.
The vital nature of such coupling becomes even more apparent if we consider its potential value in helping the researcher design interventions which take into account local
needs and values. Indeed, the deliberate search for such
information is a hallmark of the ecological paradigm.

One issue to consider is whether one's intervention is not simply draining the setting of resources, without strengthening existing resources or adding new ones. IPS interventions can, and in some cases have, strengthened the resources of settings by running problem-solving workshops to deal with problems the school is facing (see for example, McClure et al., 1981).

The positive value ascribed to local resources can be affirmed at the point of initial entry into the host environment. The following description of the entry process into a South Carolina school by the McClure group (McCammon et al., 1977) captures the spirit of coupling with the host environment better than any published literature we have encountered, and it illustrates clearly the ecological values which should inform the entry process.

> Our objectives for this entry stage were not only to gain permission and support to introduce a social problem solving curriculum in a middle school; but also we aimed for an attitude of ownership and collaboration on the part of the students, parents, teachers, and school administrator. We wanted them to feel responsible for and excited about the project and we wanted them to take their rightful place in the project, as experts in the workings of their own school environment.
>
> Our method to reach these objectives can be broken down into three basic ideas: a) "go through the front door": be open about payoff, and goals and what we could offer in return; b) assess the needs and concerns of the system, in order to understand the school environment and to tailor the problem solving program to the specific needs of this school; and c) enter slowly enough to pilot methods, and be flexible enough to use feedback and reactions.

As mentioned earlier, IPS investigators also have used subjects to generate content to be used in the IPS curriculum. McClure et al. (1978) asked children in the setting to generate problems they must solve in their everyday life, and used these problems in their curriculum.

The same team also used information from teacher interviews and behavioral observations as they developed problem-solving measures.

The McClure et al. (1981) intervention also speaks to the need to attend to the management of the resources of a research setting to ensure a successful coupling. The stressful times that the school was experiencing were such that the intervention could have been seen as draining resources while providing relatively little payback. To prevent this from happening, and to encourage the development of the research relationship and a successful intervention, the researchers offered their resources in the following manner: They assessed the teachers' work environment and fed back the results to the staff as the first step in a series of problem-solving workshops. McClure (1981, personal communication) reports, "Our original motivation to shift our focus to the organizational level was a belief that the teachers were 'burned out' and that their behavior would affect the intervention and the welfare of the students. . . . The shift from training teachers to help students cope with student problems, to teachers helping themselves to cope with their own work related problem, was very informative to all concerned."

Conclusion

From the foregoing critique it should be apparent that the IPS literature is a strong body of work, which often has attended to issues addressed in the preceding section. We feel, however, that the work in this area would be strengthened even more by explicit attention to ecological considerations articulated by the ten principles both in the design and implementation of the research as well as in published reports of research outcomes and processes.

NOTES

1. There is an additional way—discussed more fully in Principles 8, 9, and 10—in which research can actively contribute as a community resource, namely, through the working relationships that can develop between the research staff and the participants. The working relation-

ship stimulated by the research staff can create occasions where the research staff can better understand the needs and aspirations of the setting and the members of the setting can increase opportunities to extend the potential contributions of the research staff.

2. The creation and maintenance of an effective citizens-based research-monitoring group is one means for community empowerment. It is, in effect, a structural means of affirming that the work of the community psychologist can be conducted in such a way as to ensure that citizens are in control of their own resources and destiny insofar as the research and its consequences are concerned.

3. In particular we wish to thank Ellis Gesten, Lawrence McClure, Myrna B. Shure, and Roger Weissberg for their prompt, extensive, and insightful comments on this section of the chapter.

4. In addition, the interpersonal problem-solving approach has, with modifications, been employed with a diverse number of populations in a wide variety of settings other than public schools. Shure (1979) cites some examples of programs for educable-retarded hyperactive children, alcoholics, and short-term inpatients. Though these programs will not be reviewed here, their broad range demonstrates the wide variety of contexts in which interpersonal problem-solving training has potential utility.

REFERENCES

Allen, G. J., Chinsky, J. M., Larcen, S. W., Lochman, J. E., & Selinger, H. V. Community psychology and the schools: A behaviorally oriented multilevel preventive approach. Hillsdale, N.J.: Erlbaum, 1976.

Argyris, C. Intervention theory and method: A behavioral science view. Reading, Mass.: Addison-Wesley, 1970.

Barker, R. G. Ecological psychology. Stanford, Calif.: Stanford University Press, 1968.

Barker, R. G., & Gump, P. V. Big school, small school. Stanford, Calif.: Stanford University Press, 1964.

Billington, R. J., Washington, L. A., & Trickett, E. J. The research relationship in community research: An inside view from public school principals. American Journal of Community Psychology, 1981, 9, 461-480.

Bronfenbrenner, U. The ecology of human development: Experiments by nature and design. Cambridge, Mass.: Harvard University Press, 1979.

Campbell, D. T., & Stanley, J. C. Experimental and quasi-experimental designs for research. Chicago: Rand McNally, 1972.

Cottle, T. J. Show me a scientist who's helped poor folks and I'll kiss her hand. Social Policy, 1970, 33–37.

Cowen, E. L., Trost, M., Izzo, L., Lorion, R., Door, D., & Issacson, R. New ways in school mental health: Early detection and prevention of school maladaptation. New York: Human Sciences Press, 1975.

Cowen, E. L. The wooing of primary prevention. American Journal of Community Psychology, 1980, 8, 258–284.

Eron, L., & Walder, L. Test-burning II. American Psychologist, 1961, 16, 237–244.

Gesten, E. L., Flores de Apodaca, R., Rains, M., Weissberg, R. P., & Cowen, E. L. Promoting peer related social competence in schools. In M. W. Kent & J. E. Rolf (Eds.), Primary prevention of psychopathology. Vol. 3: Social competence in children. Hanover, N.H.: University Press of New England, 1979.

Gesten, E. L., Rains, M. H., Rapkin, B. D., Weissberg, R. P., Flores de Apocada, R., Cowen, E.L., & Bowen, R. Training children in social problem-solving competencies. A first and second look. American Journal of Community Psychology, 1982.

Goldenberg, I. I. Build me a mountain. Cambridge, Mass.: MIT Press, 1971.

Kaye, S., Trickett, E. J., & Quinlan, D. M. Alternate methods of environmental assessment: An example. American Journal of Community Psychology, 1976, 4, 367–377.

Kelly, J. G. Ecological constraints on mental health services. American Psychologist, 1966, 21, 535–539.

Kelly, J. G. Naturalistic observations and theory confirmation: An example. Human Development, 1967, 10, 212–222.

Kelly, J. G. Qualities for the community psychologist. American Psychologist, 1971, 26, 897–903.

Kelly, J. G. 'Tain't what you do, it's the way that you do it. American Journal of Community Psychology, 1979, 7, 239–261.

Larcen, S. Training in social problem-solving: A preventive intervention in the school. Unpublished master's thesis, University of Connecticut, 1973.

McCammon, S., Fitz-Ritson, S., Felder, C., & Pratola, S. A social problem solving intervention and consultation program. In F. Medway (Chair), New directions in school mental health consultation. Symposium presented at the meeting of the Southeastern Psychological Association, Hollywood, Fla., 1977.

McClure, L. F., Chinsky, J. M., & Larcen, S. W. Enhancing social problem-solving performance in an elementary school setting. Journal of Educational Psychology, 1978, 70, 504-513.

McClure, L. F., Pratola, S., Ellis, F., Fitz-Ritson, S., McCammon, S., & Fedler, C. Enhancing social climate and social competence through social problem solving training in a public middle school. Unpublished manuscript, University of South Carolina, 1981.

McIntyre, D. Two schools, one psychologist. In F. Kaplan & S. B. Sarason (Eds.), The psycho-educational clinic. Papers and research studies. Boston: Department of Mental Health, Commonwealth of Massachusetts, 1969.

McKim, B. J., Weissberg, R. P., Cowen, E. L., Gesten, E. L., & Rapkin, B. D. A comparison of the problem-solving ability and adjustment of suburban and urban third-grade children. American Journal of Community Psychology, 1982, 10 (2), 155-169.

Moos, R. H. Family environment scale manual. Palo Alto, Calif.: Consulting Psychology Press, 1974.

Moos, R. H., & Trickett, E. J. Classroom environment scale manual. Palo Alto, Calif.: Consulting Psychology Press, 1974.

Munoz, R. J., Snowden, L. R., Kelly, J. G., & Associates. Social and psychological research in community settings. San Francisco: Jossey-Bass, 1979.

Nettler, G. Test burning in Texas. American Psychologist, 1959, 14, 682-683.

Sarason, S. B. The psychological sense of community: Toward a community psychology. San Francisco: Jossey-Bass, 1974.

Shure, M. B. Training children to solve interpersonal problems: A preventive mental health program. In R. F. Munoz, L. R. Snowden, J. G. Kelly, & Associates (Eds.), Social and psychological research in community settings. San Francisco: Jossey-Bass, 1979.

Shure, M. B., & Spivack, G. Problem-solving techniques in childrearing. San Francisco: Jossey-Bass, 1978.

Shure, M. B., & Spivack, G. Interpersonal cognitive problem-solving and primary prevention: Programming for preschool and kindergarten children. Journal of Clinical Child Psychology, 1979, 2, 89-94.

Spivack, G., & Levine, M. Self-regulation in acting out and normal adolescents. Report M-4531. Washington, D.C.: National Institute of Health, 1963.

Spivack, G., Platt, J. J., & Shure, M. B. The problem-solving approach to adjustment. San Francisco: Jossey-Bass, 1976.

Spivack, G., & Shure, M. B. Social adjustment of young children. San Francisco: Jossey-Bass, 1974.

Trickett, E. J. Toward a social ecological conception of adolescent socialization: Normative data on contrasting types of public school classrooms. Child Development, 1978, 49, 408-414.

Trickett, E. J. Toward a distinctive community psychology: An ecological metaphor for the conduct of community research and the nature of training. American Journal of Community Psychology, in press.

Trickett, E. J., Irving, J. B., & Perl, H. I. Curriculum issues in community psychology: The ecology of program development and the socialization of students. American Journal of Community Psychology, in press.

Trickett, E. J., Kelly, J. G., & Todd, D. M. The social environment of the high school: Guidelines for individual change and organizational redevelopment. In S. G. Golann & C. Eisdorfer (Eds.), Handbook of community mental health. New York: Appleton-Century-Crofts, 1972.

Trickett, E. J., & Moos, R. H. Assessment of the psychological environment of the high school classroom. Journal of Educational Psychology, 1973, 65, 93-102.

Trickett, E. J., & Sussman, R. Community survey on educational options: Final report. Yale University, New Haven, Conn., 1976.

Trickett, E. J., & Todd, D. M. The assessment of the high school culture: An ecological perspective. Theory in Practice, 1972, 11, 28-37.

Urbain, E. S., & Kendall, P. C. Review of social cognitive problem-solving interventions with children. Psychological Bulletin, 1980, 88, 109-143.

Voss, H. Pitfalls in social research: A case study. American Sociologist, 1966, 1, 136-140.

Weissberg, R. P., Gesten, E. L., Carnrike, C. L., Toro, P. A., Rapkin, B. D., Davidson, E., & Cowen, E. L. Social problem solving skills training: A competence-building intervention with 2nd-4th grade children. American Journal of Community Psychology, 1981a, 9, 411-423.

Weissberg, R. P., Gesten, E. L., Rapkin, B. D., Cowen, E. L., Davidson, E., Flores de Apodaca, R., & McKim, G. J. Evaluation of a social-problem-solving training program for suburban and inner-city third-grade children. Journal of Consulting and Clinical Psychology, 1981b, 49, 251-261.

8   Existential-Phenomenological Knowledge Building

Rolf von Eckartsberg

INTRODUCTION

In this chapter are presented three specific examples of empirical existential-phenomenological research. These methods have been developed in the psychology department of Duquesne University, one of the study centers of existential phenomenology in the United States. The concrete steps of each way of doing this type of research are illustrated in order to provide some insight into and guidelines for doing empirical existential phenomenology and its potential for social and community psychology.

THE REFLECTIVE EXISTENTIAL-PHENOMENOLOGICAL APPROACH

Existential-phenomenological philosophers and psychologists, using a general reflective approach in a non-empirical manner, have accumulated a vast storehouse of descriptions and conceptualizations which are neither well known by mainstream psychologists nor widely distributed in the professional network. One reason for this state of affairs is the complexity and esoteric quality of the language and concepts employed by phenomenologists. It is a difficult professional idiom to understand and acquire. A second and related reason is the high level of abstractness and universality in the discourse of the phenomenological approach. A third reason stems from the fact that phenomenologists look for inherent universal structures of consciousness, the essential meanings, and the most universal features of consciousness that can be articulated by the contemplation of a given phenomenon. The evidence contemplated by most phenomenologists includes personal experience, knowledge of human reality as provided by history and the arts, and the work of other philosophers. This is usually not empirical evidence based on experimentation and factual observations designed for hypothesis-testing purposes. Many psychologists consider the evidence suspect and "soft" because it is not based on the "objectivity" of measurement but on the "subjectivity" of personal experience, personal account, and story.

There are inherent difficulties in all methodological approaches, and all research is problematic in its epistemological foundations. Human life is nowhere systematically recorded or written down exactly as it is lived. The records of life are themselves man-made and incomplete. They transform original experiences into summaries and abstractions accomplished by language. Experienced life becomes life text, an account or story of existentially experienced life process which then becomes the basis for further reflections.

Phenomenologists seek to discern the essentials of meaning making by studying many stories of experienced life, looking for common themes and structures. As an existential-phenomenologist, I believe that human living is best understood in terms of the metaphor of a novel or epic. The human being is a personal existential epic in ongoing creation, a multidimensional and dramatic unfolding of human relationships and involvements. We understand ourselves and each other most basically and easily—with a degree of subtlety and sophistication as yet beyond the ken of most social-science formulation—as protagonists in stories, as "dramatis personae." Story telling tied to proper names is the foundation of common sense and everyday shared meaning making.

AN OVERVIEW: HOW ONE CONDUCTS EXISTENTIAL-PHENOMENOLOGICAL RESEARCH

There is a clear-cut progression for this type of research: We go first, from unarticulated living, or experiaction, to record or account "data"; second, from record to explication and interpretation; and finally, from interpretation to communication of findings.

The progression involves four specific steps:

1. Question formulation.
2. Data gathering.
3. Data analysis.
4. Presentation of results.

The Problem and Question Formulation—— The Phenomenon

In Step 1 the researcher delineates a focus of investigation and formulates a question, a "hypothesis." The researcher has to name the phenomenon, that is, the process to be investigated, in such a way that it is understandable to others. This is easy if the researcher names conventional and universally recognizable phenomena. It is difficult if the researcher studies phenomena that he or she has discovered and that have as yet no consensual meaning.

The Data-Generating Situation——The Protocol Life Text

In Step 2 of the existential-phenomenological approach, researchers start with descriptive narratives provided by subjects who are viewed as coresearchers. The coresearchers report their own experience in writing; the researchers query the coresearchers on their experiaction and engage in dialogue; or the researchers combine the two activities, asking for a written description first and then engaging in an "elaborative dialogue" (von Eckartsberg, 1971).

The Data Analysis——Explication and Interpretation

Once collected, the data are read and scrutinized so as to reveal their psyche-logic, that is, their structure, meaning configuration, principle of coherence, and the circumstances of their occurrence and clustering. This is Step 3. In the traditional quantitative and measurement-oriented approach, this step involves categorization and statistical treatment of group data organized in terms of sums, averages, percentages, and measures of dispersion and convergence. In the qualitative existential–phenomenological approach, emphasis is on the study of configurations of meaning in the life text involving both the structure of meaning and how it is created. This explication brings out implicit meanings by means of systematic reflection. Reflection is the return in consciousness to scrutinize a particular event via its record in memory or as a life text. It involves the tracking, scanning, and mapping of that event. Via such reflection, experiactions are able to configure themselves into meaningful psychological moves and to be revealed in relation to a discriminable "existential plot." As we reflect, we are guided by questions such as "In what way is this description revelatory of the phenomenon I am interested in?"

In order for the life text to reveal itself, we must approach it with an explicit concern expressed as a specific question. We call this the explication–guiding question because it gives focus as we question the text about its meaning. As researchers approach life text stories, they can ask at least three kinds of explication–guiding questions, those having to do with (1) situated and general structures, (2) existential process over time, and (3) social context.

1. Questions of situated and general structures. How is what I am reading revelatory of the meaning of the phenomenon in this situation? This question yields the situated structure of the phenomenon. What does the text and/or the situated structure tell me about the phenomenon in its generality and universality? What is its meaning essence? This more universalizing question yields the essential general structure of the phenomenon.

The first of the following examples, which illustrates this research approach, attempts to understand and articulate the essential meaning configuration of the phenomenon of "being anxious." The meaning of the phenomenon in each particular situation is studied as a means to arrive at its essence across situations (Fischer, 1974).

2. Questions of existential process. How does the description express the psychological movement(s) of this person over time? This experienced–meaning process becomes revealed in response to the question, How does it happen? How is the event manifested for the person? This question yields the existential process structure of the event.

The second research example on the experienced process of reconciliation illustrates this approach. It traces the unfolding of reconciliation in and through the experience of the <u>person</u>, the actor, in his or her concrete, situated existence as an <u>experienced movement and struggle over time.</u> Reconciliation is revealed as an existential process which has a certain dynamic configuration or flow and a distinctive <u>personalistic</u> flavor   (von Eckartsberg, 1978).

      3.   Questions of <u>social context.</u> The explication-guiding questions in the third approach specify the <u>social context of the experience and the account.</u> Who is in relationship to whom? Says who? With what interest in mind?

Here we take a more contextualized approach to the study of a complex social situation involving many actors and factions. We wish to determine (1) how particular historical social reality is constituted through interaction, interexperience, and mutual interpretation; and (2) how the attribution of motives reveals contradictions, vested interests, power plays, and tensions.   Kracklauer's (1960) research on drug use as a social problem (see Example 3) uses the dialectical approach and formulates its findings in terms of constellations of social relationship, communication networks, and ideologies.

The Presentation of Results--The Formulation

In the final step, Step 4, the research findings must be presented in public form for sharing and criticism. These formulations present what we have called the "essential constituents" or the structure of a phenomenon, articulating what "it really is" as a human meaning.

Two different kinds of communication networks are involved in the presentation of results: the participants in the research themselves (the subjects) and the fellow researchers.   The subjects get a "debriefing" about the experiment in everyday language; while the "fellow experts" in the researcher community, who share the professional-relevancy structure and interest in the phenomenon, are communicated to in their shared expert language or professional idiom.

EXAMPLE 1:   THE MEANING OF ANXIETY--RESEARCH
USING AN EMPIRICAL EXISTENTIAL-PHENOMENOLOGICAL
APPROACH

In this study of anxiety, subjects were asked to
write about a past experience of being anxious according to
the following instructions:

> Please discuss in detail a situation in which
> you were anxious. To the extent that' you
> can recall it, please include in your de-
> scription some characterization of how your
> anxiousness showed itself to you as well as
> some statement of how you were, that is,
> what you experienced and did when you were
> anxious. (Fischer, 1974, p. 408)

Excerpts from a detailed protocol written by one subject are
illustrative:

> I have been commuting to school by bus for
> three years now, and I hate it. I dread
> waiting for them, I detest riding on them,
> being pushed and shoved, crowded and hav-
> ing to make polite conversation about the
> weather, or the price of things these days
> with my seat-sharer when I don't feel like
> talking at all. I hate trying to stay alert
> and watching for my stop because the con-
> stant grinding noise of the motor of the bus,
> plus the squeaking of the brakes on and off,
> provide an adequate lullaby for me. I al-
> most always fall asleep while on my way to
> school or home. I become numb. But the
> worst part of the whole commuting process
> is waiting for my bus to come. . . .
>   This day was unlike the rest that I
> had known while waiting for the bus to
> come. It was a happy day. The sunlight
> was strong and brilliant. It illuminated the
> street and the pavement. The light blinded
> me for a few seconds as it bounced off the
> shiny hoods of the cars passing by. Every
> so often a cool breeze blew by not to make
> this warm light impose on and dominate the

day. The street sounds were radically and unusually hushed it seemed. I was in the middle of the city that afternoon, and yet I was in a balmy, breezy country too. Everything seemed serene and quiet and it was good.

As I was enjoying this abnormality, I was distracted by a figure that was coming closer to me from behind on my right side. The figure was that of an elderly black man. He approached me from behind, asking me, almost begging me to take his hand and hold it. At the same time he was telling me that his hand wasn't any different than mine, for me to take his hand and look at it. I was stunned and shocked for a few minutes and then retreated and thought, 'Okay, the joke is over now, please leave you old drunk.' But the joke wasn't a joke and he persisted. I became increasingly more uncomfortable and helpless as he insisted that I take his hand. I felt the easiness and happiness of the day slipping away from me when he continued to remain on that sidewalk with me. . . .

I can remember the hand coming around me from my right side, going and reaching for my hand. It was unlike any hand I had seen before. It seemed to be foreign, inhuman. The hand was yellowish brown, the skin was extremely dry and cracked so that it almost looked as if it had scales on it. The four fingers were long and fat and curved outward all in the same direction. The thumb stuck inward opposite the four fingers. All were edged with thick, whitish-yellow nails. I was repulsed by this hand, I didn't want to touch it. Every time he spoke to me and mumbled the same words, 'take my hand, its the same as yours,' I became further and further removed from him. . . .

Every time he spoke I kept hearing what different people's reactions would be when I described the situation to them. It

was realizing what their reactions would be
that held me back from acting. I wanted
to take the hand and smile and say, 'it is
like mine,' giving him the affirmation that
he wanted, but I was afraid of what he
might do once I gave him my hand. I was
also afraid of being ridiculed by any
passers-by. I could hear these strangers
to this situation saying: 'after all, a
young white girl holding an old black man's
hand, what's this world coming to?' I
knew that physically if I didn't do something, I would soon drop dead because I
felt that I was a time bomb pounding my
existence away as each second passed. But
I couldn't do anything. All the while he
mumbled, I could see myself describing this
experience to my mother, father, and aunt,
hoping to find refuge in their advice. But
my actions were restricted by their speech
and I could do nothing. I could hear my
mother saying 'You didn't take his hand did
you? God knows where his hands have been.
You didn't touch it did you? Wash your
hands immediately; don't touch anything.'
My father would say, simply and calmly,
'Well Mary, the next time that anything like
this ever happens all you have to do is . . .'
But this wasn't the next time, it was now.
I could see my aunt and she told me very
defiantly, "You should have stood up to him
and said, 'hey you, who do you think you
are? You had better get out of here.' I
didn't want to disappoint my family. I
didn't want to touch that old hand. I didn't
want to be called dirty by any stranger who
might see me as a young white girl holding
hands with an old black man. (Fischer,
1974, p. 414)

The next step was to study and "analyze" separately
each of several protocols like the above in terms of "central themes" or "meaning units" which characterize the unfolding scenes of each narrative in order to penetrate the
inner logic and sense of the total story. This step involved

a linguistic transformation from first-person singular to third-person singular, that is, a transformation from the subject's own words and perspective to that of the researcher who situated himself vis-à-vis the described phenomenon so "that it would speak to me in its own terms, so that it would show me all of its constituents" (Fischer, 1974).

The explication-guiding question that steered the reflective query activity was, What was the anxious situation that this person found herself in and what did it mean to her to live that situation anxiously? The situated structure of the protocol presented above for this subject in her unique life situation is as follows:

> Her anxious situation was one in which she found herself called upon to do that which she felt was right, but, at the same time, anticipating that if she did, others, whose opinion mattered to her, would be disappointed and might hold her up to ridicule. Being anxious in that situation meant explicitly imagining and being utterly immobilized by the expressions of ridicule and disapproval that others were expected to manifest. It meant feeling alone and inadequate in an increasing foreign world. It meant intensely experiencing an inner demand or some transforming action that would break the binding character of the situation, but feeling helpless, filled with doubts and unable to act. Finally, it meant thematically discovering different parts of her body in their affected, alien suchness. (Fischer, 1974, p. 414)

The next step was to find the universal structural meaning configuration of "being anxious" that could be culled from the various situated structures. What are the truly essential features, those without which the experience would not be one of being anxious? Proceeding in this manner, Fischer articulated a general structure of anxiety that applied to any and every particular situation described in the protocols while recognizing some subtypes or variations in the phenomenon.

As articulated by Fischer (1974),

An anxious situation is one in which a particular problematic possibility of my project to be an adequate, competent human being announces itself and solicits me to responsibly confront it; an anxious situation is one in which I am called to thematically rediscover that the who and how of my life really matter, that they are without guarantees or unquestionable justifications, and that for their realization, they may to a considerable extent depend upon my effortful commitment.

Three variations of this general characterization may be delineated: in the first the particular possibility that I am called to face and own is one that I have already been living, either directly or indirectly, as never-to-be-true-of-me; in the second, I am called to do that towards which I am already moved, but anticipating that if I do, others, whose opinions are very important to me, will disapprove of and even condemn me; in the third, I am called to explicitly face the possibility that as the project to become a certain kind of person, I may be a failure.

Initially becoming and being anxious in the above-described situation means being suddenly distracted, even torn away from my everyday, unreflective orientation towards and involvement with people, things, and possibilities of my world. No longer able to attend undividedly to whatever I was doing, I am momentarily suspended in my living: there is a kind of inarticulate confusion. Breaking through this my body, or part thereof, intrude themselves and call me to discover and immediately understand their affected, alien suchness. I find myself moved to "see" myself, to bear a critical evaluative witness to the me that is now congealed and totalized in the threatening meanings of a particular emergent possibility.

> In being anxious, I am unreflectively im-
> pelled to do something, to perform some
> self-saving act that would cut through the
> encroaching oppressiveness and would enable
> me to regain my world.
>
> Beyond this general characterization
> of being anxious, two varying modes are
> discernible: in the first, I can find nothing
> to do and further, am uncertain of my abil-
> ity to do anything; moreover, I am fearful
> that whatever I would do, it would only
> make matters worse; hence, for the moment,
> I am immobilized; ultimately I flee in the
> face of a potentially responsible confronta-
> tion with the threatening meanings of the
> problematic possibility; I refuse any genuine
> and explicit reflection upon the who and how
> of my life. In the second mode of being anx-
> ious, I ultimately speak to and affirm the
> problematic possibility as also mine; in un-
> certainty and trepidation I appropriate it and
> resolve to be myself; I thrust myself forward
> into full visibility, for others as well as for
> myself. (P. 418) (Reprinted with permission)

For the general structure, Fischer uses the first-person singular to make the characterization accessible for the reader. The "I" refers to the universal human possibility of being anxious. Empirical existential-phenomenological research tries to bridge the gap between life and thought, between existential concreteness and uniqueness and universal validity. The work of explication is directed to find, articulate, and present the most universal features—the general structure—of a phenomenon as it becomes accessible by studying unique situated events. The approach moves from account to structure in a systematic series of progressively more universal linguistic formulations. Explication is work in and through language, a multiple-level discourse.

EXAMPLE 2: THE PROCESS OF RECONCILIATION—RESEARCH USING A DIALOGAL EXISTENTIAL-HERMENEUTIC APPROACH

One of my main interests as a clinical and social psychologist is relationship building and its associated phenom-

ena. The process of "moving closer to another person" and
one of its subtypes, reconciliation, is such a phenomenon.

To begin with, I initiated a collection of stories by
asking students the following data-generating question:
Describe a situation in which you found yourself moving
closer to another person and tell what happened. I received many protocols which described initial encounters
and several which concerned themselves with reconciliation--
a moving closer, again, after a conflict. I chose one of
these protocol stories of reconciliation to illustrate my approach to the study of the existential process structure of
the phenomenon, that is, how it is an unfolding, experienced situated event for the participant.

After I obtained the story, I began the explication
and interpretation by identifying and naming chapters and
their constitutive subphases and subevents and by summarizing their contents. The explication-guiding question in
this step of the interpretation is, What are the chapters
and subphases, or episodes, that constitute the plot of
reconciliation and how can they be named?

The second step is to formulate the psychological
meaning contained in each phase of the story as an experienced existential process. The explication-guiding question of this step of the hermeneutic reflection is, What is
happening in the experience of the protagonist? What
concrete existential process is experienced by the actor in
the story in the exact sequence of its occurrence?

These questions about what happens in terms of the
protagonist's experience emphasize his or her psychological
moves sequentially over time as an existential process.
My hermeneutic work consists in articulating my view of
this unfolding process, preserving its chronological character as an unfolding plot. Table 8.1 presents the results
of this hermeneutic work.

The chaptering, subphasing, and episoding summarized in Table 8.1 reveal my own process of comprehension
and interpretation. I see the story as a long drawn-out
personal struggle by the subject, Terry, to save an important relationship, a long-standing mutually satisfying
love-mentor relationship. Their relationship had fallen
into some neglect over the years but continued underground
because it seemed an important milestone in Terry's early
development, a lasting bond of what I call inspired fellow-
ship. This is a subform of a love relationship in which
two people, one older and more experienced, mutually

TABLE 8.1
Terry's Story: A Hermeneutic Approach

Original Story	Chaptering and Subphases	Existential Process Structure
We have known each other many years—in fact she had been my teacher in junior high school. We had more than a teacher-student relationship even when I was in junior high. As I became older we shared more and more and discussed things I needed to sort out. She always had the gift to not give me direct answers to my questions and problems but rather could give me information to work with to formulate my own answers. I became close to her husband and three children also, and although I saw them infrequently, I kept in touch by letters and phone.	I From Teacher to Mentor How, over several years, the relationship between Terry and Anne, her junior high school teacher, came about and what it meant. 1. Their initial relationship: How Terry and Anne came to know each other and established a more than teacher-student relationship: discussing things Terry needed to sort out. 2. Anne's gift: Anne's gift for Terry: to help her find her own solutions. A mentorship develops. 3. Terry and Anne's family: Terry became friends with Anne's husband and three children also and stayed in contact over time.	Terry, a young girl, meets a female teacher, Anne, in junior high school with whom she establishes a personal relationship. The teacher becomes her mentor, making her feel welcome and encouraging and guiding her to always find her own solutions. Terry becomes friends with Anne's husband and three children. Terry keeps in touch with Anne over the years by occasional visits and communications and considers herself in a stable and rewarding relationship with her.

When I sent her a Christmas card a year ago, she called and told me that she had moved out of the house and was living in an apartment with another woman. I had met this woman before and Anne said enough for me to get a vague feeling for what was going on without bluntly stating it. She invited me over to the apartment. And several weeks later I did go. On the way over I had a pretty good idea of what to expect but I kept telling myself that it was just because it was easier for her to live in an apartment while going to school. After spending the day with her and Jane, there was no longer denying the fact that she had left Bill for a different lifestyle.

II Complications in the Relationship: Precipitating Event

How, a year ago, Terry realized Anne's change to a homosexual lifestyle. Serious complications arise in the relationship.

1. The news:

A year ago, news of change in Anne's life, her moving in with another woman, comes by way of an exchange of Christmas greetings. Terry writes; Anne calls.

2. The telephone call:

Terry knew the other woman and was suspicious about what was going on. Terry gets invited to visit.

3. The visit:

On the way over, what Terry expects to find and how she makes up her mind about it.

4. The realization:

After the day's visit, Terry concludes Anne is homosexual!

A crisis in the relationship occurs for Terry a year prior to the report while Terry is a junior in college. The crisis arises through a hint in a Christmas card sent by Anne indicating that she was now living with another woman whom Terry also knew. Terry suspects a homosexual bond. Terry's relationshp to Anne becomes problematic for Terry and leads to a serious struggle with herself. She experiences the emergence in herself of a social moral attitude and a stereotyped view of a homosexual lifestyle. But Terry is curious and wants to see for herself, to test out this relationship; she accepts an invitation to visit Anne in her new home several weeks later. She realizes during and after the visit that Terry is indeed living a homosexual lifestyle, and she finds herself bewildered and confused.

(continued)

Table 8.1, continued

Original Story	Chaptering and Subphases	Existential Process Structure
On the way back to the bus I found myself with half a smile on my face, thinking: "well, now you know, kid, what are you going to do about it?" I didn't honestly see anything wrong with homosexuality, but from the little bit I heard I felt obligated to find something wrong with it. So I found my point of attack in: "what about the kids?" It certainly wasn't original, but it sufficed to get me worked up enough to condemn the whole thing. The easiest thing to do is just to forget it and since I was involved in other things I managed to somewhat. But I could not deny my feelings for her. I knew I had a very dear friend and I loved and respected her.	III Crisis, Avoidance, Conflict After the visit Terry lives in conflict and avoidance of Anne and the issue for several months. 1. Terry's first thoughts: Now, you know, what are you going to do about it? 2. Feels obliged to take a stand: Terry feels socially obligated to reject and condemn homosexuality and justifies it by a stereotyped response. 3. Condemnation of Anne: Terry works herself up to condemn the whole thing. 4. Terry's avoidance: She keeps busy and forgets, almost; she avoids. 5. Terry's love for Anne surfaces again 6. Terry's hesitation: Terry reasserts her love and respect for Anne to herself, but she hesitates.	Terry is now forced into a moral dilemma and feels that she has to make a choice: for or against Anne. She cannot come to a decision in a purely rational and deliberate manner, once and for all. She becomes entangled in the conflict and resolves her ambivalence and confusion by condemning Anne, rationalizing her stance in a self-righteous but stereotyped manner. It takes months for Terry to find a way out of her pattern of projecting blame and denial. She "forgets" by keeping busy with other things and avoids the issue. Yet from time to time her continuing positive feelings for Anne and her appreciation of her as a mentor surface, and Terry cannot deny them to herself. They are in "gestation" and work "underpsychically." Yet she continues to avoid coming to terms with the relationship and with Anne.

It wasn't until the fol-
lowing summer, when dur-
ing an argument (with
mother) I blurted, "You
only love me when I live
your way," did I realize
that, that was exactly
what I was doing with
Anne. I sat down and
really thought about it
and then I wrote her a
letter. Although I
didn't say flatly what I
was trying to say, she
understood and within a
week I received a reply
from her. Her letter
sounded jubilant. She
was so happy with the
new house she and Jane
had bought, being enough
for the kids to really
enjoy and other develop-
ments in her life. But
more importantly because
she knew I had worked
through the situation
and my love for her
hadn't changed.

IV The Turning Point in Their
Relationship

Terry has the insight and re-
solves to confront and live
through her conflict and
ambivalent feelings.

1. Terry's insight:
   Last summer Terry realized
   her one-sided intolerant
   reaction regarding Anne in
   an encounter with her
   mother.

2. Contact again:
   Terry writes an explanatory letter to Anne.

3. A positive reply:
   Within a week Anne writes
   back jubilantly.

4. Good news:
   Good development; new
   house with Jane and kids.

5. Anne still her mentor:
   Anne "understood," helped
   her find her own solution
   again. Terry's love for
   her hadn't changed.

After six months of avoidance, of denial of
being anxious, and of experiencing conflict and
just letting time pass and keeping busy in
other directions, Terry finds herself confronted
with the issue of conflicting lifestyles in
another relevant social context, in a confrontation with her own mother, whom she accuses in a
spontaneous outburst of anger and frustration,
"You only love me when I live your way!" In a
moment of deep emotional agitation Terry makes
the connection to her own attitude toward Anne
and comes to an insight about her own style of
denial which had made her suppress her love for
Anne as her friend and mentor. This insight
reconfigures her understanding, and she acknowledges to herself that she had avoided the issue
by projecting the blame. Accepting responsibility for her actions from that moment of
recognition of her own self-deception and self-
justification and for denying her deepest feelings and genuine love and respect for Anne, she
makes a moral decision to respond, to face up
to her true feelings, to live authentically,
and to risk herself and her meaning-making
habits. She takes courageous action to confront
her own unknown leanings and uncertain reactions by initiating personal contact again with
Anne and to explain herself to her. She writes
a letter and receives an encouraging, understanding, and implicitly forgiving reply from
Anne within a week.

(continued)

Table 8.1, continued

Original Story	Chaptering and Subphases	Existential Process Structure
In the meantime, I read everything about homosexuality that I could get my hands on, even law books, and I was amazed that my original response was so stereotyped and narrow-minded. When I finally saw her again, I told her all the research I had done and how I felt. Somehow during the discussion we fell into a serious gaze and our hands fell into each other's. I leaned forward to her and we embraced and I began to cry silently. When we looked at each other, we were both crying but at the same time smiling gloriously. It was a special beauty in our silence and a special meaning, which language cannot begin to touch.	V. The Blessing of Reconciliation Terry overcomes her stereotyped ideas and fears, makes contact again with Anne, and a deep reconciliation and reunion ensue. 1. Homework: Terry reads up on homosexuality and gains insight into her own past narrow-mindedness. 2. Their reunion: As they meet again they have a deep personal exchange. Terry confesses her doubts. They have an emotional reconciliation in which they find themselves genuinely close and moved, and they firmly reestablish their mutual love and respect for each other, their "inspired fellowship."	Before seeing Anne again, Terry studies up on homosexuality and now fully realizes how narrow-minded, stereotyped, and defensive she has been. When they finally meet again face to face, they both experience the blessing of reconciliation after the following happened: a kind of confession of sins on Terry's part, a making speakable between them what had not been shared, and the granting of mutual forgiveness in a tender moment of mutual recognition beyond words in which both are moved to tears and embrace. Terry's loss of faith in Anne, her suspicions, erection of barriers, rejection, moral condemnation, and unjust projection of blame, is aired between them and helps to reestablish and strengthen their relationship together. And Terry realizes that Anne has been acting as her mentor all along, allowing her to come to her own insights and decisions, to make her own mistakes, and being accepting of her, concerned and always encouraging and welcoming her being without pushing her or forcing the issue. Their relationship emerges purified and strengthened through this ordeal, and both are glad over the reconciliation.

<u>Source:</u> Compiled by the author.

encourage and elevate each other in thinking, feeling, being creative, and valuing. They "bring each other out," help each other grow spiritually as persons, and even challenge each other.

A crisis in the relationship occurs for Terry through the disclosure that Anne is a homosexual. The disclosure leads Terry to a struggle with herself and her socialized moral-attitude stereotypes toward such a lifestyle. She is forced into a moral choice--for or against Anne. She cannot come to a decision in a purely rational and deliberate manner, once and for all. She becomes entangled in the conflict, and it takes a long time and some fortuitous circumstantial happenings in Terry's life for her to find a resolution which leads to reconciliation.

After a sequence of particular psychological moves (being anxious, doubting, delaying, avoiding, feeling conflict, and letting time pass), Terry is confronted with the issue in another social context, the relationship with her mother. In a moment of deep emotional agitation, she comes to the insight about herself that it has been her own warding-off style of denial which had made her repress her love for Anne as a person and mentor. Accepting responsibility for her own self-deception and denial of her deepest feelings and values, she makes an essentially moral decision to respond, live authentically, and risk herself by facing up to the conflict. She takes courageous action to confront her own unknown leanings by reestablishing personal contact with Anne, to see for herself first by letter, and then face to face, on which occasion the "blessing of reconciliation" is experienced by both. This includes a kind of confession of sins, a making speakable between them what had not been shared. The airing of Terry's loss of faith in Anne, her suspicion, erection of psychological barriers, moral condemnation, and anguish helps to reestablish and strengthen their relationship. In retrospect, Terry comes to see Anne's handling of the crisis as another instance of her concern for Terry as a mentor, thereby allowing Terry to come to her own decision.

We do not have to move very far into a meta level of theoretical understanding and discourse to account for the motives operating here. One could attempt a Freudian rendering in terms of latent homosexuality, a Jungian translation in terms of the "wise old person archetype," or a social learning interpretation in terms of the reinforcement and deconditioning of parental stereotypes. We are taking here an existentialist position, that is, the perspective of responsible personal agency which holds that people create relationships with each other through acts of moral judgment and commitment in the context of chosen value orientations.

We can add another step to our hermeneutical work in the manner of Example 1 and try to characterize the achronological configurational meaning of the phenomenon as the essential meaning structure. In this structural configurational attitude, the metastory of reconciliation turns out to be the following:

> An ongoing interpersonal relationship of intimacy and mutual importance is ruptured due to a falling out between the partners and made problematic. Ongoing face-to-face contact is disbanded and a self-righteous construal of the reasons for the break is formulated, which projects the blame for the break on the other partner. There is much denial.
>
> A precipitating event or crisis typically occurs in one of the partners which disrupts the stalemate and reminds that partner of the continuing claim of the relationship, of the living in tension, and in mutual rejection. Bringing the relationship to renewed awareness forces also a reconsideration of one's attitudes, values, and involvements. If one of the partners has a change of heart and/or insight into the situation and can dislodge his or her frozen and stereotyped perceptions and evaluations, owning up to and assuming some of the responsibility for the rupture, then movement toward renewed contact and conciliatory actions become possible, that is, imaginable and actualizable.
>
> Once initiated, the peace-making overtures must be acknowledged and reciprocated by the other so that a crucial face-to-face exchange can occur. Such an exchange involves confession of sins and stupidity, expression of regret and sorrow, and the asking

of forgiveness in so many words and gestures, in a situation and moment of great vulnerability, openness, and risk. The other, when approached, has the right and choice to refuse. The accepting response of the other seals the reconciliation in a dramatic moment of mutual recognition and ongoing shared intimacy, and cocreativity can resume its course in a strengthened relationship.

This characterization of the essential meaning structure of the experience of reconciliation is a provisional statement subject to confirmation, challenge, and modification by further work on other stories. It is subject to revision through further data and research even though there is a presumed shared consensus of meaning tied up in the very concept reconciliation. We know the verbal and experiential meaning of this word in a general way but not as a detailed psychological configuration in all its nuances. It is only by using an existential-hermeneutic approach that we can articulate both the unfolding of the existential process over time and the essential meaning structure of the phenomenon as an idea.

EXAMPLE 3: THE DRUG PROBLEM: RESEARCH USING A CONTEXTUALIZED REFLECTIVE-DIALECTICAL APPROACH TO THE STUDY OF A COMPLEX SOCIAL SITUATION

The following example of the use of an empirical existential-phenomenological approach holds great promise for the study of complex social events and community problems. Kin to much family research and insights from family therapy, it allows us to glimpse the amazing variegatedness and dynamism of social interaction within a complex social network which creates the ongoing realities of meaning and attribution in which we live and on which we act.

Kracklauer (1973) approached the study of "the drug problem" (marijuana and LSD) by focusing on three young males, identified by a professional psychologist respectively as (1) a drug abuser, (2) a drug user (recreational), and (3) an abstainer.

The "drug problem" of these individuals could not be separated from their social matrix of family members and professionals who carry out society's assigned institutional roles regarding such "problems." Inspired by the social phenomenological work of Berger and Luckmann (1966), Kracklauer realized that the drug problem is socially constituted. He set up an interview schedule with relevant professionals who perform the prototypical legal roles relating to young people's involvement with psychedelic drugs and who formulate educational and judicial policy regarding drug issues.

This combined social and professional network consisted of the following "cast of characters," as lived out in the early 1970s in America:

a state legislator	a program director
a police chief	an assistant principal
a drug attorney	a drug abstainer
a judge of juvenile court	a drug user (recreational)
a school psychologist	a drug abuser
	the parents of the drug abuser

Kracklauer noted that these people are involved in what he termed the drug-problem "language game." He interviewed an office holder in each of the role types. He chose certain guiding questions for each group. For the professionals, the questions were these: "If you believe that there is such a thing as an adolescent drug problem, how would you define it, or describe it, in other words: What is the problem?" and "Given this understanding of the drug problem, what is your role in dealing with it, in the light of your professional background?" For the users and the parents, the more general open-ended question was "How did you get involved with drugs? How do you live your relationship with drugs?" These interviews, tape recorded (with permission) and transcribed, constituted the "data" for reflection.

Regarding the professionals, Kracklauer's explication-guiding questions addressed four dimensions of the data:

1. The understanding of the problem.
2. The underlying factors.
3. The professionals' role in dealing with the problem.
4. The solution to the problem.

Reading through the data several times, Kracklauer (1973) began to discern "various contradictions, idiosyncracies, and ideological stances" which he articulated as a statement of the "contradictory perceptions of the drug problem" held by professionals.

All of these subjects tended to consistently align their perceptions of the drug problem with one or the other side of the following tendencies:

1. The drug problem is an unbounded epidemic versus situated action.
2. Drug use equals abuse versus does not equal abuse.
3. Marijuana use associates with the domino theory versus the model of alcohol.
4. The drug problem is critical versus worthy of concern.
5. Drug abuse is escape versus illness.

Kracklauer then developed the "contradictory beliefs about the solution of the problem" held by the professionals. The proposed solutions to which professionals were responding were:

1. Having recourse to the law (necessary versus irrelevant);
2. Focusing attention on getting the pusher (versus changing the system);
3. Seeking agreement (the role of education);
4. Emphasizing the role of rehabilitation (versus prevention).

The next step was to study how these contradictions were lived out and legitimated by the professionals. Kracklauer studied the institutionalization of these contradictory beliefs about the solution to the drug problem. He summarized the self-descriptions that each professional subject gave about his role in dealing with the drug problem:

a. The response of the school psychologist and assistant principal--in general, to press for the possibility of derepressing the communication between themselves as adults and the young, by assisting the young in coming to see that their problems are less indigenous to themselves than the system within which they live.
b. The response of the legislator, police chief, and judge--in general, to rationalize the behavior of the young in such a way as to render it amenable to legal technical manipulation in the name of protecting them from the menace of the drug problem.

c. The response of the program director and grant writer—in general, the same as "a" above, except that his activity tends, as does "b," to perpetuate the problem by legitimating its reality through the production of rehabilitation centers; he becomes co-opted by the system.

d. The response of the drug lawyer—to participate in both approaches to the drug problem, by working in and through the system on behalf of the people who the system might otherwise define as criminal. His understanding is informed by the perspectives of both systems; and he construes a case, within the constrained freedom of the law, that has the best chance of winning acquittal for his client in an adversary trial. The lawyer's loyalty is both to the client and to the stipulations of the law as an autonomous body of rules.

The next phase of the work was directed at understanding the impact of the institutionalized roles on the users and their self-understanding. To accomplish this, Kracklauer needed to investigate the self-perception of the young people with respect to their involvement in and relationship to psychedelic drugs. He approached the subjects with three basic questions regarding the users:

1. Understanding of drugs and relationship to drugs;
2. Self-understanding;
3. The parents' understanding of the user.

Studying the interview texts closely and using the interview questions also as the explication-guiding questions on the text, Kracklauer came to the following characterization of the meaning of the drug problem for the users:

> I came to an analysis of drug abuse, as a form of self-abuse. Whether one becomes a drug abuser is a function of how he understands drugs, which in turn is grounded in his self-understanding which itself finds its roots in the relationship he has with his parents. The subject who is most confused about himself with respect to whether his praxis is process, or, vice versa, that, whether his activity is the result of his own agency or not, is the subject most inclined

to resolve his conflicts with himself through
drug use. He tends to attribute to the effects of the drugs everything he feels inca-
pable of experiencing without drugs, i.e.
competence, community feeling, love, etc.,
while at the same time re-appropriating his
projected capacity to himself, for after all
he is the one who controls his drug use.
What eventuates, is that he progressively
tends to appraise normal experience from
the perspective of drug induced experience,
rather than into drug induced space. The
project begins to get really out of hand
when he appraises his own drug-taking from
within the reality of drug induced experience, instead of from normal experience. At
this point, his self-mystification becomes a
self perpetuating negative praxis, which systematically undermines his agency while
leading him to have an absolute faith in his
agency.

The drug-user, on the other hand,
has a solid grip on the locus of his experience and agency, and maintains this grip
by making sure that his drug induced experience remains peripheral to his normal
experience. Instead of attempting to assimilate himself into drug induced experience,
he constantly strives to assimilate drug experience back into normal experience. This,
of course, means that he does not trip very
much, and does so only when it makes sense
to him. Moreover, he also works to socialize his drug induced experience by sharing
it with others, including the parents. Although his relationship with his parents was
rocky for a while, it has returned to an
even keel. He feels that his parents were
good to and for him until his late teens,
when he began to withdraw from their values.
Although not great, his relationship to them
has been consistently less conflicted than
the drug abuser. (1973, p. 114)

This fascinating example of the application of an empirical existential-phenomenological approach is especially relevant to community psychology. It points out the dynamic nature of social attribution as it is distributed in a role-defined community setting; it explores an ecology of role configurations understood in terms of an ongoing process of linguistic communication. Kracklauer's work illustrates vividly some of the essential dimensions of the hermeneutical space of a focused social reality.

There is also a large emancipatory potential in this research. It lays bare the effective communication and attribution channels, locates points of contradiction, and identifies barriers to changes in stereotyped views. Such knowledge can help the participants arrive at a truer and more fully personal understanding of their complex placement in particular social realities. It can enable them to evolve strategies of action that would allow them to break out of false perceptions and ideological mind traps.

CONCLUSION

In this chapter, we have reviewed the empirical existential-phenomenological approach to psychology. We have also presented three representative empirical research examples.

What binds such work together is the shared concern for studying psychology from the perspective of the actor(s) consciousness. The research focus becomes the constitution of meaning, that is, the way people create and live in perceived meanings. Since the constitution of meaning is not only a personal phenomenon but also an eminently social and dialectical process, we speak of the "social construction of reality."

The existential-phenomenological approach holds great promise for community psychology. Certainly such pertinent phenomena as culture building, the creation of relationship, loyalty, mutual inspiration, value commitment, confrontation, conflict resolution, leadership, attitude change, and small-group process could be further clarified and personalized by the experiential-reflective-hermeneutic approach of existential-phenomenological psychology.

REFERENCES

Berger, P., & Luckmann, T. The social construction of reality. Garden City, N.Y.: Doubleday, 1966.

Fischer, W. On the phenomenological mode of researching "being anxious." Journal of Phenomenological Psychology, 1974, 4, 405–423.

Kracklauer, C. The drug problem. Unpublished doctoral dissertation, Duquesne University Press, 1960.

von Eckartsberg, R. On experiential methodology. In A. Giorgi, C. Fischer, & R. von Eckartsberg (Eds.), Duquesne studies in phenomenological psychology, Vol. I. Pittsburgh: Duquesne University Press, 1971.

von Eckartsberg, R. Person perception revisited. In R. Valle & M. King (Eds.), Existential–phenomenological alternatives for psychology. New York: Oxford University Press, 1978.

9   Human Stress: A Theoretical Model for the Community-oriented Investigator

Raymond W. Novaco
and Alan Vaux

A major research challenge for community psychologists is to illuminate the dynamics of community systems so as to improve the design of interventions that enhance the well-being of community members. Considerable effort has been directed toward social programs and service delivery to the neglect of research that provides insight into person-environment and group-environment relationships within community settings. In order to understand the components, processes, and outcomes associated with community functioning, we are in need of conceptual frameworks to guide research and intervention efforts. In this chapter we propose one such theoretical framework within which community psychology research can be profitably conducted.

In its nascency, community psychology predominantly was concerned with providing services. It was soon realized that environmental conditions were linked to the psychological impairments and human needs that prompted the service response. Thus, the "community orientation" was distinguished from the "clinical orientation" by virtue of its focus on social systems, environmental forces, macro-

Preparation of this chapter was supported by the Focused Research Program in Human Stress at the University of California, Irvine. We very much appreciate the helpful comments and criticisms given to us by David Altman, Ralph Catalano, David Dooley, John Glidewell, Karen Rook, and Larry Steinberg.

level change, and preventive interventions. Correspondingly, the major texts on community psychology (Heller & Monahan, 1977; Mann, 1978; Rappaport, 1977; Zax & Specter, 1974) have delineated research agenda that gave priority to these designated dimensions as the hallmarks of the community psychology perspective.

Research conducted under the banner of community psychology is considerably at variance with these characterizations of the field. In a study of the empirical articles published in the field's principal journal, Novaco and Monahan (1980) disconcertingly found that less than 13% involve prevention efforts; that the assessment of environments and of person-environment interactions was each represented in only 5% of the articles; that the highest concentration of empirical work focused on the assessment of person variables (40.5% over six years of published work and 58.1% in 1978); that despite the field's proclaimed concern with social systems, relatively little research has been conducted with regard to medical, police, and correctional settings; that there has been a steady decline across years with regard to research pertinent to primary and secondary schools (7.0% in 1978); and that the institutional setting receiving the greatest attention is the community mental health center (41.9% in 1978). Thus, if one accepts the definitions of community psychology given in the field's leading texts, which emphasize prevention, institutional change, and ecological analyses, the majority of the research published in the field's leading journal had little to do with the stated objectives of the discipline.

In large measure, this state of affairs can be attributed to the absence of overarching theoretical systems in community psychology research. Some striking findings in the Novaco and Monahan study support this assertion. Less than 30% of the empirical studies examined were directly connected to a theoretical framework. In addition, over 60% of the studies failed to specify hypotheses, either in an explicit statement of predicted outcomes or in the form of general expectations of results. This disconnectedness from theory weighs against the development of a knowledge base for community psychology and attenuates the interface of community psychology research with affiliated social science disciplines. The absence of theory was also strongly associated with nonprogrammatically conducted studies (Novaco & Monahan, 1980). Published research in our field has the look of piecemeal investigations that are conceptually and methodologically impoverished to the extent that research questions are posed in a conceptual vacuum and data are gathered by procedures that are unsubstantiated in their merit.

The emphasis here placed on theoretically directed research is based on the assumption that research questions are more meaningful when they are linked to an overarching conceptual scheme. Theories enable us to describe phenomena, to explain them, and to schematically represent interconnections between concepts. They also serve heuristic functions by prompting and guiding new research questions. Theory can also be seen to have generative potency (Gergen, 1978), in the sense that theory can challenge the fundamental beliefs of a culture and suggest alternatives for social action.[1] Progress toward a knowledge base in community psychology can be facilitated by theory-guided research, and it is also possible that inventive theories about community functioning could transform community life.

Our objective in this chapter is to encourage community psychologists to conduct theoretically directed research[2] within the conceptual framework associated with the study of human stress. The stress framework provides a conceptual system to guide research questions, a body of knowledge concerning problems of importance to community psychologists, established methodologies for conducting research, and both conceptual and procedural mechanisms for formulating intervention efforts.[3]

We will first portray the significance of stress research for the community-oriented investigator and discuss some conceptual quandaries of an elementary nature in the stress field. Upon proposing a general model for human stress, our presentation will then focus on several topic areas selected for their relevance to community psychology--namely, research in environmental demands, stressful life events, and social support. Identifying some key issues and themes across these areas of study, we will propose some priorities for research in the stress field.

PSYCHOLOGICAL STRESS AND COMMUNITY PSYCHOLOGY

Economic hardships, death of loved ones, work pressures, natural disasters, war, illness, divorce, and countless other adversities of life strain our adaptive capacities.

Whether we view communities in terms of their individual members, their social units, or as aggregate wholes, the problems of stress and coping are central to the concerns of community psychologists.

Community psychologists have done well in identifying problem manifestations at a community level and have made strides in formulating methodologies for community change. But curiously, we have abdicated to clinical psychology and to other fields the responsibility for understanding the process by which persons become distressed. We have tacitly assumed that enough is known about the development of abnormal behavior and proceed as though this area of inquiry is the business of other disciplines. Yet the task of understanding the emergence of psychological disorder, health problems, dissatisfaction with quality of life, and criminal behavior is surely an appropriate agenda item for community psychologists. As one reads the field's leading texts, which indeed vary in their views of the discipline and in their intervention perspectives, there is a conspicuous absence of theory about how community conditions lead to community problems. Research on human stress has much to offer community psychologists seeking to articulate the mechanisms or processes by which adverse environmental circumstances can result in problems at either the individual or aggregate level.

An important step in prompting community psychologists to take up the stress paradigm was made by B. S. Dohrenwend (1978). She presented a scheme for representing the activities of community psychologists in terms of psychosocial stress and prefaced the description of her model with these remarks:

> Let me start by introducing some assumptions and a bias or two. The first assumption is that community psychology is concerned with reducing the amount of psychopathology in the population at large, an assumption with which you will all agree. The second assumption is that when community psychologists tackle this problem they are guided by strong etiological hypotheses; specifically, that psychosocial stress is important in the causation of psychopathology. This assumption is, I think, also widely accepted.

What needs emphasizing here, however, is that while many community psychologists would indeed agree with Dohrenwend's second assertion, their research is not guided by that proposition. Simply observe that only one of the research publications cited by Dohrenwend (1978) was published in a community psychology journal or edited book. It is one thing to say, "Yes, stress is important," but it is quite another to conduct one's research in a way that is explicitly and actively directed by stress concepts and stress methodology.

The model offered by Dohrenwend (1978) has several basic, hypothetically sequenced components: (1) stressful life events determined in varying proportions by the environment and by the psychological characteristics of the person; (2) an immediate, transient stress reaction; (3) situational mediators (that is, supports, handicaps, values, or coping abilities); and (4) the product of the interaction of the transient reaction with the array of situational mediators (that is, psychological growth, no change, and psychopathology). Dohrenwend's model clearly has emerged from research programs in the area of stressful life events, and its principal components pertain to life crises. The model is best viewed as a heuristic scheme for identifying relevant variables, as there are many more parts than there are substantiating data. From our own perspective, the model does not adequately represent environmental determinants of stress, and by being cast in a life event framework it overemphasizes discrete, acute circumstances and underemphasizes ambient, enduring conditions. Nevertheless, Dohrenwend's model delineates stress research linkages with community intervention efforts, as she connects the schematized stress process with corrective therapies, crisis intervention, skill training, socialization, social agencies, and political action. It therefore interfaces with many community psychology concerns.

Theoretical models of stress have varying points of emphasis and applicability. While Dohrenwend's model emphasizes life crises, others emphasize coping processes (Lazarus & Launier, 1978; Pearlin & Schooler, 1978), attention overload and task performance (Cohen, 1978), controllability (Glass & Singer, 1972), person-environment congruence (Stokols, 1979), the regulation of emotion (Novaco, 1979), and physiological mechanisms and disease (Levi, 1971; Selye, 1976). There is no single, all-embracing theory of stress that adequately represents and explains the wide range of phenomena that are studied in stress research. What exist are contextually relevant theories that guide research questions and intervention efforts.

We will present a basic model of human stress that is compatible with these diverse psychological theories in terms of its central assumptions or axioms. As a preliminary step, we will first discuss some elementary issues that pertain to theorizing about stress.

CONCEPTUAL QUANDARIES IN THE STRESS FIELD

As an extensively and diversely researched topic in the social sciences and affiliated medical disciplines, stress has been conceptualized in many ways. In his landmark book, Lazarus (1966) came to the position that stress can best be understood as a field of study, a rubric under which a large body of research has been conducted. A wide assortment of target problems have been addressed, and this heterogeneity of focuses has prompted some to question whether the concept of stress is meaningful. At times it is claimed that the concept is no longer useful or that "no one knows what stress is."

The fact that stress has many empirical referents is hardly cause for advocating that its use be discontinued. It is the nature of concepts, as abstractions, to refer to many things. Psychological concepts like intelligence, motivation, aggression, dependency, and numerous others refer to heterogeneous behaviors that can be meaningfully described by the same term. Concept labels, like stress or aggression, are shorthand designations for an otherwise long story. The concept itself is a synopsis of the elaborations of ideas and observations entailed in this story.

It is perplexing to find that people puzzle over the question, "What is stress?" It is as if the definition being invoked would specify the essence of stress--so that we could always recognize it when we see it. This is an Aristotelian illusion.[4] Definitions tell us nothing about the nature of things. They inform us about rules for the use of words in a language. It can thus be seen that the real issue is not whether "stress" is a useful concept, but rather what is being communicated by the scientist when certain conditions are characterized in terms of stress.

Communication about stress does not require unanimous agreement: It does require that researchers be clear and unequivocal about how they use the concept. Investigators do not need to construe stress in identical terms. Variations in the way stress is construed are a function of the kinds of phenomena that are studied and of the research strategies used by investigators. Biologically oriented researchers utilize response-based definitions of stress, as they are interested in the organism's physiological reactions to evocative agents. Sociologically oriented investigators follow situation-based definitions, since their concern is with external circumstances that tax the adaptive capacity of persons and groups. Psychological approaches adopt interactional and transactional definitions, as they address the joint and reciprocal contribution of person factors and environmental conditions to stress outcomes (compare Appley & Trumbull, 1967; Lazarus, 1966; McGrath, 1970). The disciplinary markings of these approaches are due to the fact that research methodology is rooted in established disciplines that are geared toward the examination of problems at a particular level of analysis. Communication across these different approaches readily occurs when investigators are explicit about their perspective and its assumptions.

Despite the fact that stress refers to many things, it is often presumed that the same causal process underlies the establishment of antecedent-consequent relations for all forms of the construct ("one construct equals one developmental process"). This presupposition is embedded in the puzzlement over "What is stress?" and in hasty extrapolations of stress research performed in one context to phenomena occurring in quite different contexts. A combined illustration of these problems is Selye's (1976) effort to find the common denominator of all stress responses and his idea of the "general adaptation syndrome."[5] What may be a useful model for the physiological components and patterning of stress responses engendered by toxins and pathogens in animal laboratory experiments may not be useful for understanding stress-related person-environment and group-environment outcomes in natural life settings.

Some other illustrations may clarify this point, particularly as it bears upon material we will subsequently present. Consider the variety of stressors that impinge on the individual, and then think about the differences in the way in which a stressor in the physical environment (for example, noise, high density, or traffic congestion) will impact in contrast with how a life crisis event (for example, job loss, divorce, or death of a relative) will impact. Why assume, tacitly if not explicitly, that the process explaining somatic and affective disturbances is the same whether long-distance urban commuting or the dissolution of a marriage is the antecedent condition? Of further importance in this regard are matters concerning adaptation and coping. Once stress is conceptualized transactionally, that is, in terms of reciprocal relationships between person and environment, as we will momentarily describe, then one must view the adaptive efforts of the individual as an inherent part of the stress process. This being the case, patterns of adaptation are transparently different across stressor domains such as those mentioned above.

The one construct/one process quandary can be repeatedly observed in the stressful life events literature. We will expand on this later. Here we only note as another illustration of the general point that those occurrences labeled life events are indeed a heterogeneous lot, particularly in terms of how they are experienced by the person. A life event is not a life event. Why stipulate that the same "social readjustment" mechanism underlies the event-impairment connections for all events sharing the same arbitrary label?

To conclude this discussion on preliminary issues, we are proposing that community psychology researchers adopt the stress paradigm as exemplified by a general model that allows for a number of domain-specific explanatory processes. In the next section, we present this proposed general model. Stress research has indeed focused on the proclaimed problems of interest to community psychologists and has involved a variety of target populations, methodologies, and outcome variables. By identifying a core framework for the conduct of this research, we aim to promote a profitable utilization of it by the community-oriented investigator.

A GENERAL MODEL OF STRESS

Although rooted in laboratory experiments, stress research was extended rapidly to naturalistic settings, being concerned precisely with the environmental conditions thought to engender distress in communities. Our perspective is a psychological one, as distinguished from sociological or biological orientations. We view stress as a condition of the organism or system that signifies a state of imbalance between demands and resources. Stress, then, is a hypothetical construct, thereby not referring to any particular set of observables or being defined only in terms of organismic responses. It is a hypothetical condition defined in terms of the functional relationships between environment demands (stressors) and adverse health and behavioral consequences (stress reactions) resulting from exposure to those demands. Intertwined with these stressor-stress reaction functional connections are sequences of reciprocal relationships between environmental elements/conditions and person characteristics/behaviors which mark the process of adaptation.

The general model can be understood in terms of a set of axioms or basic postulates. These statements are the central propositions pertaining to the sources of stress, impact mechanisms, mediational factors, and transactional influence processes. We present these sequentially:

1. Stress is induced by environmental demands that exceed coping resources, thus disturbing homeostatic balance.

Environmental demands, or stressors, are elements or conditions of environmental fields that require an adaptive response from the organism or system. The demands may be biological (for example, toxins, pathogens, or injuries), psychological (for example, threat, insult, thwarting, or conflict), social (for example, prejudice, anomie, economic recession, or high-pressure work organization), or physical (noise, extreme temperature, density, or traffic congestion). The stress resulting from exposure to environmental demands is determined by a number of factors in addition to properties of the demands themselves. With regard to the environmental demands, their stress-inducing potential is a function of their potency and persistence. Potency refers to the degree of disturbance caused to homeostatic balance as resulting from a stressor's intensity and severity. Persistence refers to the temporal exposure to the stressor in terms of its frequency and duration. As objective dimensions, potency and persistence are orthogonal factors. High degrees of stress can result from high-potency, low-persistence stressors (for example, extreme physical or biological elements), as well as from relatively low potency but high-persistence stressors (for example, frustrated aspirations or recurring interpersonal conflict).

Although environmental demands operate largely through their <u>perceived</u> qualities, as stipulated below, it is not necessary that the demands be perceived as aversive nor that they be perceptually salient. Perceptual accommodation may occur with ambient stressors, such as noise or work pressures, which nonetheless continue to have stress-inducing effects.

2. <u>Stress is manifested by adverse cognitive, behavioral, and physiological consequences resulting from the exposure to environmental demands.</u>

Stress reactions consist of physiological disturbances, negative affect, and impairments to cognitive and behavioral functioning. Stress reactions vary in their <u>magnitude</u> and <u>extension</u>, which determine their severity. Magnitude refers to the degree of homeostatic disturbance and impairment to functioning. Extension refers to the temporal duration of the disturbance or impairment.

These stress reaction dimensions (magnitude and extension) parallel those named with respect to environmental demands (potency and persistence). In each regard, the intent is to specify and label parameters of severity and time. The aim here is to improve our descriptions of stress phenomena. Disagreement about what constitutes or can be referred to as stress is minimized when we are dealing with unusually harsh, intense, or prolonged circumstances or with extreme physiological or psychological disturbances. When such extreme conditions or consequences do not prevail, there is often ambiguity about whether one is observing something that is properly described as being stress. In specifying key dimensions of environmental demands and of stress reactions we thereby seek to improve how we describe and gauge stress-related events.

3. <u>Environmental demands operate in transaction with the behavior of persons or systems.</u>

Stress is viewed in terms of dynamic influence processes involving reciprocal causal relationships between persons and environments.[6] The concept of transaction (Dewey & Bentley, 1949) implies that conceptions of independently acting or interacting elements result from truncated observations of event sequences. Transaction assumes that organism and environment are interconnected components of a system in motion over time. Stress, therefore, occurs as a result of environmental demands as they operate in conjunction with various characteristics of those exposed to them and as they are shaped, selected, modified, and/or mitigated by those persons.

The transactional approach in stress research has been emphasized by Lazarus in his various research programs (Lazarus, 1966; Lazarus & Launier, 1978). The importance of this focus becomes clear when coping and adaptation are investigated. As is well known, the "interactional" models of psychological research predominantly have been restricted to "interaction" in the statistical sense.[7] However, stress research must attend to the behavior of persons and systems in response to the perturbations induced by environmental demands. The degree of stress experienced may be in large measure a product of how one copes with encountered demands. Moreover, the environmental demands to which one is exposed are to a considerable extent determined by the person's decisions, characteristics, actions, and plans. People are often the architects of their own life crises. More positively, they also strive to optimize the fit between themselves and the settings within which they must live and work (Stokols, 1977).

4. The effects of exposure to specific environmental demands are not uniform across individuals or systems but are mediated by cognitive, behavioral, and social factors.

  4.1. The cognitive representation of environmental demands and of response capabilities, on an initial and ongoing basis, is a primary determinant of stress.

The human organism primarily responds to cognitive representations of the environment, not to the environment per se (if that could be determined outside of a shared linguistic framework). Such representations influence attention to environmental demands and sensitivity to them. They consist of expectation and appraisal structures which bear upon both environmental demands and coping resources. Furthermore, cognitive processes enter into the labeling of distress, the prolongation of distress by brooding or preoccupation, and in the reconstruing of stress-related events.

The cognitive perspective has flourished in stress research, although some research areas, such as stressful life events and social support, contain a sizable quantity of work that is not guided by assumptions about cognitive mediation. However, the importance of cognitive processes has been axiomatic in most psychological approaches to stress (Appley & Trumbull, 1967; Glass & Singer, 1972; Hamilton & Warburton, 1979; Lazarus, 1966; McGrath, 1970; Novaco, 1979; Sarason & Spielberger, 1975; Stokols, 1979).

4.2. Behavioral transactions with the environment influence the probability and degree of exposure to environmental demands and the course of stress reactions.

While stressors vary in their controllability, some proportion of stressor exposure is a result of the person's behavior. In many circumstances, only if one adopts an (arbitrarily) delimited temporal frame does one see exposure to stressors as independent of the person's behavior. Events such as the death of loved ones, certain natural disasters, hereditary diseases, or societally ingrained oppression are beyond the control of the person and cannot meaningfully be attributed to one's behavior. However, as was noted earlier, various decisions and behavior patterns do lead to life circumstances that are stressful. High-pressure work environments are stressful, but people choose to be in them. The multiplicity of environmental adversities of urban life are stress inducing, but people choose to live there and accommodate to urban stressors.[8] Various frustrating conditions, interpersonal conflicts, strained relationships, and depressive circumstances are unmistakably products of the person's own activities.

The experience of stress inevitably leads to coping efforts which may be directed at the environmental circumstances or at the stress reactions resulting from them.[9] Thus, people may act to modify the demands themselves or avoid exposure to them. They may also take steps to achieve therapeutic reductions in stress manifestations, such as headaches or hypertension, or even reduce a behavioral risk factor itself, for example, Type A behavior as linked with coronary artery disease (Glass, 1977) or low-activity schedules as related to depression (Lewinsohn & Graf, 1973; Lewinsohn & Libet, 1972).

4.3. Social relationships moderate stress by reducing exposure to environmental demands, decreasing sensitivity to them, increasing resources for dealing with them, and containing subjective distress.

Supportive social relationships mitigate the impact of environmental demands. Social support insulates the

person from otherwise debilitating forces in the environment and facilitates coping with life crises. These stress-
moderating functions which serve the individual also extend
to the variety of social systems (for example, family, organization, and community) within which the social relationships are embedded. The importance of social support
is such that the loss of supportive relationships is stress
inducing.

The process by which supportive social relationships
moderate stress effects is a topic of current investigation.
The range of issues connected with social support research
are discussed later in the chapter. As with many other
areas of stress research, the specification of stress effects
requires the identification of causal pathways that are
linked to the context of behavior.

5. Stress is a product of contextually linked person–
   environment impact mechanisms which determine how
   environmental demands are experienced.

Stress arises in conjunction with clusters of situa-
tionally relevant factors. Behavior occurs in context, and
its understanding requires analysis of the ecological setting, identifying the network of variables that are functionally related to the behaving organism or system. Given
the transactional perspective, which postulates dynamic
interchanges between person and environment, one must
map the "causal texture" (Tolman & Brunswik, 1935) of the
environment and understand stress in terms of a multiplicity of interrelated factors acting in concert.[10]

The mechanisms by which stress is induced are contextually linked. In contrast to searching for isolated
causal pathways, we must study the fabric of person-
environment relationships not only with regard to some
particular setting or niche but also in terms of interconnected settings and domains (for example, home, transportation, and work; compare Stokols & Novaco, 1981). Understanding the differential vulnerability of individuals to
environmental demands can be facilitated by the identification of contextual variables.

Emphasis upon contextual variables has been integral to the field of environmental psychology, as reflected
in concepts such as behavior setting, ecological validity,
and person–environment congruence (compare Stokols, 1978).
In the field of developmental psychology, Bronfenbrenner's
(1979) ecological model of topologically nested systems is

inherently a contextual theory. With regard to Bronfen-brenner's environmental structures, our own perspective pertains primarily to his "microsystem" (particular settings) and "mesosystem" (interrelations among settings). However, the influences of the "exosystem" (institutional structures) and of the "macrosystem" (the overarching culture) are also highly relevant, such as with regard to the develop-ment of Type A behavior or the structure and function of social-support networks.

An excellent illustration of contextual influences appears in the research conducted by Folkman and Lazarus (1980). They found in their longitudinal project on stress and coping that the context of a stressful event was a pri-mary determinant of the type of coping response. Work-related episodes were associated with problem-focused cop-ing, whereas health-related episodes were associated with emotion-focused coping. Importantly, the contextual factor was found to be a much more significant determinant of the coping response than was the person involved in the coping episode.

This set of postulates represents a general model that can guide community psychology research. It is be-yond the scope of this chapter to review the literature on stress, which is indeed voluminous. We instead present some selected research areas in the stress field that are highly pertinent to community psychology and call atten-tion to three core themes that we think merit continued examination. These selected areas, which are seminal for community studies, are (1) research on environmental de-terminants, (2) stressful life events, and (3) social sup-port. As with the selection of these very areas, we will also be selective in presenting research connected with them. Our aim is to promote the use of the stress para-digm and to identify some core issues in the field.

ENVIRONMENTAL DETERMINANTS OF STRESS

Environmental forces that have an adverse impact on the well-being of communities are surely an appropriate subject for community psychology research. However, sur-prisingly little research on environmental influences is pub-lished under the banner of community psychology. What little does appear tends to be restricted to assessments of the social environment. The health consequences of social environment variables have become a prominent research topic for some time now (compare Insel & Moos, 1974), but community psychologists have yet to venture much beyond the descriptive, taxonomic analysis of settings (for example, Price & Blashfield, 1975; Trickett & Quinlan, 1979) and their effects on self-report indices of satisfaction.

One recent exception in the social climate literature is a study by Moos and Van Dort (1979) on the relationship of social climate factors to reported physical symptoms among college freshmen. Controlling for symptoms reported at the beginning of the college year, they found that the reports of physical symptoms at the end of the year were significantly related to social climate factors such as low cohesion, involvement, and emotional support. Living groups characterized by high physical symptoms also tended to be high on hostile interaction, negative affect, alcohol consumption, and use of medications.

A number of research programs have focused on particular environmental elements hypothesized to be stress inducing. Within this body of research concerned with stressors in the physical and social environment, one often finds naturalistic studies having a high degree of ecological validity.

Physical Environment Stressors

Although interest in the physical environment has grown rapidly in other areas of psychology, in both applied and basic research, very few studies on it have appeared in the American Journal of Community Psychology since its inception in 1973. Perhaps studies of the physical environment are viewed as the province of environmental psychology, not to be encroached on by those with a community orientation. But surely there is much to be learned from research on conditions such as noise, smog, traffic congestion, crowding, and temperature as stress-inducing factors that affect psychological and physical well-being.

There is an abundance of research on these elements of the physical environment as agents of stress, and there are a number of helpful reviews in the literature (Cohen et al., 1980; Rule & Nesdale, 1975; Stokols, 1978). The influence of physical environment factors on a broad range of mental health variables has also been reviewed by Monahan and Vaux (1980) with regard to the role of the community mental health professional. Rather than duplicate existing reviews, our purpose here will be to selectively present some examples of research on the physical and social environment that would seem to have heuristic value for community-oriented investigators.

One example of this genre of research is the work of Cohen, Evans, Krantz, and Stokols (1980) on the effects of aircraft noise on children. These investigators conducted a naturalistic study of elementary school children in the air corridor of Los Angeles International Airport.[11] In light of experimental laboratory findings on noise as a stressor, Cohen and his associates were concerned with the impact of routine prolonged exposure to noise on community populations. Using a matched-group design and statistically controlling for extraneous variables correlated with their criterion measures, they studied how higher noise exposure (one flight every 2.5 minutes during school hours, generating sound levels of 95 dbA) influenced cognitive, motivational, and physiological measures. They found that children in high-noise schools had higher systolic and diastolic blood pressure than did children in low-noise schools, although the group differences (7 mm systolic and 4.5 mm diastolic) attenuated over years of exposure. This finding parallels laboratory results on physiological adaptation to noise (Glass & Singer, 1972). However, with prolonged exposure to noise, children in high-noise schools were more likely to fail to solve test puzzles and were slower to solve them when solutions were achieved. These findings were interpreted as learned-helplessness effects. Also, as length of noise exposure increased (from less than two years to four years or more), children were more likely to be disturbed by auditory distractors, and this was associated with lower reading and math scores.

Community psychology researchers and practitioners ought to take note of the study by Cohen and his associates. The well-being and academic achievement of school children have been topics of long-standing interest in our field, yet we have rarely looked to factors in the macroenvironment as sources of impairment. Researchers might pursue investigations on exposure to noise in urban schools in terms of additive and interactive effects with other physical and socioenvironmental variables or with regard to noise attenuation interventions. Practitioners, armed with laboratory and naturalistic findings, might act to influence public policy decisions (compare Catalano & Monahan, 1975) so as to minimize noise in school locations.

Another example of a naturalistic study of environmental conditions associated with stress is the work of Novaco and Stokols (Novaco et al., 1979; Stokols et al., 1978) on traffic congestion. This research has concerned conditions of transportation which have a potentially stress-inducing effect on urban commuters. Exposure to traffic congestion, conceptualized as impedance, was investigated among employees of industrial firms. Stress effects were measured with regard to physiology, mood, task performance, attitude, health, and various adaptation outcomes (for example, changes in residence, job, or community mode). Travel impedance was operationalized in terms of distance and time parameters of commuting routes[12] and validated by subjective ratings of congestion, inconvenience, and dissatisfaction. Consistent with the mediational propositions of the present stress model, the effects of travel impedance were examined in conjunction with cognitive, behavioral, and social environment mediators (for example, locus of control, the Type A behavior pattern, and residential- and employment-setting factors).

Following the initial field experiments, a longitudinal follow-up was conducted which examined the continued effects of the impedance and mediational variables but which also investigated interrelationships among environmental domains (transportation, job, and residential), coping efforts, and well-being. While the preponderance of findings from the longitudinal study is forthcoming, a number of empirical trends are indicated in this series of studies. In general, the data suggest that conditions of travel impedance are associated with stress reactions (for example, elevated blood pressure, negative mood, and performance deficits), but these reactions are mediated by person variables and their reciprocal influence on environmental contexts; that dissatisfaction with commuting leads to efforts to actively alter or otherwise cope with commuting demands; that efforts to cope with commuting demands enhance perceptions of well-being, as reflected in levels of satisfaction across life domains (residential, employment, travel); and that life domains are interconnected, as dimensions of satisfaction within the residential domain prospectively influence the effects of commuting demands on satisfaction within the transportation domain (for example, perceptions of high choice in residential location are associated with lower blood pressure in high-impedance routes and with higher commuting satisfaction two years later).

There are many lines of investigation that might be pursued in the study of transportation and well-being from a stress perspective. Diverse research focuses are conceptually mapped by Stokols and Novaco (1981). In simplified form, if the manifestations of both <u>transportation conditions</u> and <u>well-being</u> are considered at the level of <u>individuals</u> and of <u>aggregates</u>, then, in a two-by-two configuration, four general research focuses emerge: (1) specific conditions faced by individual travelers as related to their experiences of and efforts to cope with those conditions; (2) transportation conditions encountered by individuals as related to organizational or community well-being; (3) communitywide conditions of transportation as related to individual well-being; and (4) communitywide conditions of transportation as related to levels of organizational or community well-being. There are many intriguing research questions in the area of transportation that emerge from the stress model.

These examples of research on noise and transportation stressors may, one hopes, alert the community-oriented investigator to the influence of physical environment conditions on the welfare of community populations. There is no reason why research on physical elements must remain the sole province of environmental psychology. The stress framework, with its inherent emphasis upon health and adjustment, serves to link research questions about the physical environment to the concerns of community psychology.

Social Environment Stressors

Stress occurs in conjunction with a number of social-context variables. Work and organizational settings press for high-performance outputs and engender stress among employees. Disruptions and strain within families tax the adaptive capacities of their members. Furthermore, lower-class families are more likely to suffer job loss, disease, accidents, premature deaths, and marital breakdown; and these adversities are even greater for lower-class blacks (Dohrenwend & Dohrenwend, 1969). Urbanization, bureaucratic thwartings, racial prejudice, and international tensions are other sources of stress entwined in the social fabric.

Research in the field of social epidemiology has demonstrated that impairments to well-being are in part a function of identifiable variations in the social environment (compare Levine & Scotch, 1970). Studies of the prevalence of psychological disorder (for example, Srole et al., 1962) and of physical illness (for example, Haynes et al., 1978) have concerned the relationship of these health disturbances to covarying demographic and psychosocial variables. The sociological characteristics (Leighton et al., 1963) and ethnic composition (Stout et al., 1964) of communities have also been examined. The large body of epidemiological research has not, however, focused on a macroenvironment element having stress-inducing potential.

An exception to this has been a growing body of research on economic change. The proposition that economic factors may have adverse effects on health and behavior can be traced to the classic work of Durkheim (1897). It was given impetus by the aggregate-level studies of economic fluctuations by Pierce (1967) and Brenner (1973), as well as the attention given to socioeconomic status as a determinant of psychological disorder by Dohrenwend and Dohrenwend (1969) and earlier by Hollingshead and Redlich (1958).[13]

Recent research by Catalano and Dooley on economic change (Catalano & Dooley, 1977, 1979; Catalano, Dooley, & Jackson, in press; Dooley & Catalano, 1979; Dooley, Catalano, & Brownell, 1980; Dooley et al., in press) combines epidemiological interests with a focus on environmental-demand elements. Their investigations have examined the longitudinal relationship between economic change of metropolitan communities[14] and the resulting effects on mood and stressful life events. Using time-series analyses of aggregate- and individual-level data, their research has examined the proposition that economic change "provokes" stress resulting in various impairments and the need for health care. The alternative to the provocation hypothesis is that well-being is not greatly affected by economic turbulence, but that previously disordered persons are "uncovered" by economic change, and thus the use of health care facilities is a function of variations in the tolerance for disorder (for example, families may no longer be willing to care for nonproductive kin).

The initial research was performed on data gathered in a National Institute of Mental Health longitudinal study in Kansas City. That study involved 1,173 interviewed respondents for whom measures of life events, depressed mood, psychiatric symptoms, and health status were obtained (compare Markush & Favero, 1974). Catalano and Dooley (1977) found that unemployment and absolute change in size and structure of the economy (see Note 14) were significantly related to depressed mood and to stressful life events when the latter two measures were lagged three months after the economic index. These findings supported the provocation hypothesis (the uncovering hypothesis was not tested) and suggested that stressful life events mediate the relationship between economic change and disorder.

In a subsequent Kansas City study (Dooley & Catalano, 1979), it was found that lower-income respondents had a more pronounced reaction to economic change than did middle-income respondents.[15] However, an attempt to replicate the Kansas City findings in a nonmetropolitan community (Washington County, Maryland) produced negative results on all hypotheses. This may have resulted from significant differences between the two communities on the distributions of demographic variables and stress measures (Dooley et al., in press).

The uncovering hypothesis requires an examination of health care utilization. Some support for "uncovering" explanations of the relationship of economic change to hospital admissions was obtained in another Kansas City study (Catalano & Dooley, 1979), as it was found that the use of inpatient facilities was not related to longitudinal variation in symptom prevalence. But more exactly, if the effect of economic change is to "uncover" disorder, then any relationship between economic change and admissions should be unaffected by controlling for variations in symptoms. Pursuing this line of reasoning, Catalano, Dooley, and Jackson (1981) in a Washington County study found that economic change was significantly associated (two-month lag) with admissions to inpatient facilities and with male outpatient case openings but that measured symptoms did not mediate these relationships. However, it was also found that economic change had a positive, synchronous association with symptoms. This suggests, first, that economic change may increase both the incidence of disorder and the use of mental health facilities, albeit through fundamentally different causal pathways and, second, that the "provocation" of symptoms and the "uncovering" of treated cases are not mutually exclusive.

Looming in the midst of this research is a question about causal mechanisms. How are the demands of the economic environment transmitted so as to affect the individual? Research based on aggregate-level measures does not inform us about such mechanisms and is subject to the ecological fallacy [16] (Robinson, 1950). Questions pertaining to impact mechanisms require a cross-level analysis. That is, variables at the macroenvironment level need to be examined with regard to their impact at the microenvironment level.

This kind of cross-level investigation was conducted by Dooley, Catalano, and Brownell (1980). They theorized that either the economy can affect symptoms (for example, depressed mood) through individually experienced life events (for example, unemployment) or that the impact of life events could be moderated by the economically related social climate. Hence they examined depressed mood outcomes as a function of economic change at the macrolevel and life events and social support at the microlevel. They found a significant interaction of economic conditions with life events as affecting depression for Kansas City males. Those who experienced undesirable life events in a declining economy were less depressed. However, this effect was not obtained in nonmetropolitan Washington County. In addition, they found that for Kansas City females and for the total Washington County sample, depression had a significant, direct relationship to life events and a significant, inverse relationship to social support. Their analyses were conducted using a covariate-adjusted panel design in which initial depression was controlled.

The causal pathways that link economic conditions to behavioral disorder are as yet to be determined and most likely vary across community subgroups. A model of the potential linkages has been proposed by Dooley & Catalano (1980), and their current research aims to elucidate the interdependencies of the aggregate- and individual-level factors.

Another epidemiological project which examined the conjoint effects of aggregate- and individual-level factors is the work of Harburg and his associates (Harburg, Blakelock, & Roeper, 1979; Harburg et al., 1973). Their studies in Detroit concerned socioecological stressor conditions, race, and personality variables with regard to their effects on blood pressure. They first examined the 382 census tracts in Detroit in terms of economic deprivation, residential instability, crime, and density so as to calibrate the social environment for chronic exposure to stressor events. This enabled them to identify four study areas: black high and low stress and white high and low stress. Approximately 175 subjects were obtained from each study area in a door-to-door procedure conducted by public health nurses.

The central focus of this investigation concerned hostility and hypertension. Respondents were presented with hypothetical scenarios of provocations (namely, police harassment, housing discrimination, and an angry boss) and asked how they would respond to the portrayed arbitrary attacks. Their coping patterns were then categorized in terms of anger suppression[17] and guilt. The cross-classifications of these personality variables with the black/white and ecological stress factors were then analyzed for their effects on diastolic blood pressure.

The initial study concerned male subjects in conjunction with the police harassment and housing discrimination situations (Harburg et al., 1973). Overall, the highest blood pressures were obtained from black, high-stress subjects. In the low-stress environments, there generally was no difference between blacks and whites. A major correlate of the blood pressure level was the coping response pattern. Anger suppression, particularly when accompanied by guilt, was associated with high blood pressure. This was especially true (mean diastolic of 94 mm) for blacks in the high-stress areas when classified according to their responses to police harassment.

A further examination of coping styles was undertaken with regard to the angry boss scenario (Harburg, Blakelock, & Roeper, 1979). In this analysis, male and female subjects were classified according to "reflective" versus "resentful" (anger) responses to an arbitrary attack by one's boss, and these coping styles were again cross-classified with the racial and stress factors. It was found that coping styles are related to sex and stress area, as reflection is more often used by women and by low-stress (middle-class) residents; "resentful" (anger suppression or expression) response subjects have higher blood pressures than "reflective" subjects; high-stress blacks who respond to the annoying boss with resentment have the highest pressure levels; and hypertension was highest for males with anger suppression responses and for females with anger expression responses.

The Detroit area studies revealed some important facts about working-class black residents. While this demographic group is known to have higher blood pressures than their white counterparts, a high majority of them do have normal blood pressure. The data indicate that psychological mechanisms involved in the response to conflict situations are important factors in determining those who are at risk for hypertension. The combination of adverse environmental conditions with an antagonistic suppressive style of responding to interpersonal conflict was associated with hypertensive pressure levels.[18] These studies by Harburg and his associates are a good illustration of how the community psychologist, guided by stress theories, can address health problems in a community population.

Conflicts arising from arbitrary and coercive behavior by one's boss are only a small part of the stress associated with work environments. Stress also arises from time pressure, responsibility, repetitiveness, role conflicts, and incongruities in person-job fit. These features of the social environment of the work setting merit the attention of community psychologists, who largely have ignored the organizational or industrial literature, except for the intervention strategies of the organization development approach (compare Heller & Monahan, 1977). Considering the large proportion of daily time spent in work settings (matched only by the amount of time spent sleeping) and recognizing the likely importance of the social network in the work organization to the person's overall life, the social environment of work is an important area of study for our field.

Physical, biological, or chemical elements in the workplace which might cause injury or impairment to the person have typically been the "occupational hazards" that health care professionals study and attempt to regulate. Psychosocial factors, which have less conspicuous points of impact, nonetheless can have equally adverse effects on well-being. The stress model serves as a framework for the identification of potentially harmful conditions and the processes by which they can be ameliorated.

Certain work environments are transparently stressful. In a well-known study of air traffic controllers, Cobb and Rose (1973) found that controllers, in comparison to pilots, had six times the incidence of hypertension, twice the prevalence of peptic ulcer, and three times the

rate of diabetes. Moreover, the occurrence of these illnesses was more pronounced in controllers working in high-
density towers. These findings are consistent with a number of stress theories that emphasize attention or information overload (Cohen, 1978; Milgram, 1970; Welford, 1973).
Overload occurs when the demands for attention exceed the
available capacity, resulting in performance deficits (Cohen,
1978) and physiological stress reactions (Frankenhaeuser
et al., 1971; Frankenhaeuser et al., 1969).

A useful classification of forms of work stress pertaining to the social environment was given by Gross (1970).
He distinguished three types: (1) organizational career
stress, such as the threat of unemployment, the career sequence, and the ultimate disengagement from the organization; (2) task stress, pertaining to job content, responsibility, supervision, and job conditions; and (3) organizational structural stress, arising from social interactions,
role conflict, and the alleged "tyranny" of organizations
over the individual. A large body of stress-related research in the organizational literature is covered by
Gross's review, and additional material can be found in
Cox (1978).

A prominent topic in the stress field related to the
work environment is the coronary-prone behavior pattern.
The behavior pattern, known as Type A behavior, is characterized by time urgency, inordinate achievement striving,
and generalized hostility (Friedman, 1969; Friedman &
Rosenman, 1974). Importantly, the behavior pattern is
thought to be engendered and elicited by the social environment, particularly that of the work setting. Considerable construct validation has been established for the
Type A construct (Glass, 1977), and it has been shown
across a large body of studies that the behavior pattern
is the strongest predictor of recurring heart attacks and
is independent of other risk factors (Jenkins, 1978).

The influence of psychosocial forces in the workplace
upon heart disease and other health impairments has been
extensively studied by French, Caplan, and Cobb and their
associates. Believing that the health of workers was determined by stressful properties of occupational environments, as well as by the more commonly recognized physical hazards, this research group at the University of
Michigan's Institute for Social Research has conducted
cross-sectional and longitudinal studies with various occupational groups.

Some of their early research with NASA employees (French & Caplan, 1970) focused on job stressors[19] that constitute risk for heart disease, either through direct action on physiological systems (for example, blood pressure and cholesterol) or by prompting other risk factors (for example, smoking). Using multivariate correlational methods, they examined the effects of particular kinds of job stressors (workload and responsibility) in conjunction with personality factors (for example, Type A behavior and need for approval) upon various cardiovascular risk outcomes. This was done across three principal occupational groups: administrators, engineers, and scientists. While there are numerous findings in this study, the most consistent results concern differences between the occupational groups. Administrators were significantly higher in smoking, blood pressure, quantitative overload, and role conflict. Furthermore, they were found to spend a high proportion (42%) of their time carrying out responsibilities for the work of others, and to be significantly higher on a set of dimensions indexing the coronary-prone personality.

Because of the correlational nature of this study, the obtained relationships between job environment variables and coronary risk factors must be viewed cautiously. However, the job stress hypothesis is bolstered by some additional findings concerning effects within the sample of administrators (French and Caplan, 1970). They found that both systolic and diastolic blood pressure was affected by the goodness of fit between the person and the organizational environment. Administrators in organizational units that were primarily administrative in mission and climate had relatively low blood pressures, whereas those in engineering or scientific units had relatively high blood pressure.

The effects of coronary-prone dispositions and job stress upon health status variables were examined in two studies, one of which capitalized on an impending shutdown of a work facility three days prior to its announced shutdown for a 23-day period (Caplan & Jones, 1975). This anticipatory period was a time of high stress, as the users of the facility worked against the approaching deadline. Caplan and Jones obtained measures of subjective work load and role ambiguity, along with an assessment of Type A personality, and examined these factors as determinants of anxiety, depression, resentment, and heart rate. Their subjects were measured as they waited for computer output and then again five months later by a mailed questionnaire. They found that work load and its changes over time were positively related to anxiety and heart rate. These relationships were especially true for Type A individuals.

The involvement of the Type A personality factor was also examined by Caplan, Cobb, and French (1975) in a study concerned with cessation of smoking. They hypothesized that quitting is greatest under low occupational stress and that it is moderated by Type A and by social support in the work environment. Type A's were assumed to be most sensitive to job stress levels and thus have a lowered ability to quit smoking when stress was high. With regard to social support, it was conjectured that those who engage in socially supportive work activities smoke as a social habit reinforced by group norms and/or as a way of maintaining physiological arousal (based on research on arousal seeking). Their data from 200 administrators, engineers, and scientists found that administrators had the lowest quitting rate. However, those in this occupational category had the highest levels of job stress (indexed by work load and responsibility for persons), Type A characteristics, and social support, which together accounted for 28% of the variation in the cessation of smoking. As predicted, quitting was least likely to occur under conditions of high job stress, high social support, and Type A personality.

The most important concept in the work of French and his associates is the notion of person–environment fit as an index of adjustment (French, Rodgers, & Cobb, 1974). This view of person–environment fit is based upon the theories of Lewin (1951) and Murray (1959) and was given impetus by Pervin's (1968) analysis of performance and satisfaction. The extension beyond earlier formulations involves the operationalization of person–environment fit concepts, their explicit link to occupational settings, and their utilization in predicting health strain. Simply put, stress is theorized to be lowest when environmental demands and supplies perfectly match the person's needs and abilities.

Basic to the person–environment fit formulation is the distinction between the objective environment and the subjective environment. This enters into the calibration of environmental supplies and demands, as well as of the person's needs and abilities. Subjective and objective indexes are separately computed, and it has been found that the perceived environment has a stronger relationship to stress measures (French & Caplan, 1970). French and Caplan (1970) put forth a set of basic equations for person-environment fit, which is generally hypothesized to have a curvilinear (inverted U) relationship to psychological strain.[20] Caplan and his associates (Caplan & Jones, 1975; Caplan et al., 1975) found the predicted U-shaped relationships for serum cholesterol as a function of person-environment fit on work load, responsibility, time pressure, and interpersonal relations. However, the clearest and most complete formulation of person-environment fit and job stress is that of Harrison (1978). He provides a crisp account of the theoretical concepts and explicitly delineates the expected relationships of person-environment fit dimensions to strain outcomes. Moreover, Harrison shows that the person-environment fit measures account for additional variation in strains beyond that accountable by separate person and environment indexes. He also elaborates on the implication of the theory for reducing job stress.

Summary

We have tried to illustrate the value of the stress perspective for community psychologists by presenting examples of research programs that are concerned with elements of the physical and social environment which affect the well-being of communities. These theoretically directed research efforts have applied experimental method to real-world problems. They can, one hopes, serve as models for how community psychologists might conduct research on environmental determinants of stress.

These studies of stress-inducing conditions in the physical and social environment have examined factors at macro and intermediate levels of analysis. That is, the studies on economic change, noise, and urban residential zones were concerned with macro-level conditions to which large numbers of persons were exposed. The studies on transportation and work settings were concerned with conditions that are relatively more circumscribed and can thus be viewed as being at an intermediate level of analysis. Each of these studies has focused on particular conditions to which aggregates of persons have been exposed.

In contrast to this aggregate-level focus, we now turn to stress research that has been conducted at the micro or individual level of analysis. Studies of stressful life events and social support focus on individually experienced stressors and on the personal resources which buffer their impact. It can be seen that the research in these areas are a special case of the study of social environmental demands.

STRESSFUL LIFE EVENTS

A Brief History

Walter B. Cannon, the pioneer of stress research, addressed the Massachusetts Medical Society in 1928 and encouraged physicians to take a "natural interest in the effects of emotional stress" upon disturbances in body functions. Interest in psychological events obviously lagged among medical practitioners. However, Adolf Meyer (1951) took special note of how life circumstances seemed to affect health and disease. As a device for organizing medical data into a dynamic biography, Meyer proposed the use of a formalized instrument, a "life chart," which would be maintained for persons receiving health care. The life chart would catalogue the sequence of life events experienced by patients, such as beginning school, graduation, job changes, residence changes, births and deaths in the family, marriage, and other circumstances having fundamental importance to the individual.

The field of psychosomatic medicine emerged during the 1930s and gave considerable attention to problems like essential hypertension and gastrointestinal ulcers. These health problems were studied with regard to personality characteristics and life crises. Some of the leading research in this area was conducted by Harold Wolff and his associates (Wolff, Wolf, & Hare, 1950) who linked bodily disease to life stress. Among the research teams was Thomas Holmes (Holmes et al., 1950) whose initial work focused on the effect of life experiences upon reactions within the nose.[21] Holmes later embarked on systematic studies of a life-chart device that was eventually to become a widely used instrument to measure stressful life events.

Using principles of magnitude estimation developed in the field of psychophysics whereby human perception could be quantified, Holmes and Rahe (1967) developed the social readjustment rating scale (SRRS). The scale was developed from a questionnaire on which subjects were asked to rate various life events for their relative degrees of required readjustment. The resulting instrument was a 43-item checklist that entailed a considerable range of personal, economic, occupational, and family events, each of which was assigned weights (life-change units) calibrated from standardization samples with regard to the degree of readjustment involved with that type of event. The scale was cross-validated with different cultural groups, and a chain of studies by a number of investigators examined the relationship between life events and health changes. Life-change events were found to have significant relationships with minor symptoms, depressive episodes, myocardial infarction, and a variety of other illnesses. These relationships were found both in epidemiological studies and in research on homogeneous populations, such as college students, naval personnel, and hospitalized patients (compare Dohrenwend & Dohrenwend, 1974). The body of research indicates that the magnitude of life change is related to the onset and severity of illness, but not the specificity of the illness (Holmes & Masuda, 1974).

Although the association between life events and health disturbances has been demonstrated convincingly and there indeed is evidence that the effects are not merely correlational (for example, Theorell, 1974), the nature of the relationship is by no means clear. The obtained empirical relationships are routinely those of correlation coefficients below .30 in magnitude, and the practical significance of such results is weakened further by the psychometric properties of the measuring instrument (SRRS), the reliability and validity of which is far from robust. An insightful review by Rabkin and Struening (1976) discussed the many problematic issues attending life-event research and offered valuable suggestions for future investigations.

Rather than engage in a thorough review, the focus here is on the theoretical underpinnings of life-events research, their relationship to stress theory, and to community research. The relevance of life-events research to community psychology derives in part from the field meth-

odologies of behavioral epidemiology, which uses sophisticated sampling and survey techniques to gather data about
the health and life experiences of community populations.
Such data have greater ecological validity than traditional
experimental work based in laboratories. However, the
ecological validity of this research has often been achieved
at the expense of empirical depth and theoretical explicitness. Research on stressful life events has reflected these
shortcomings. Specifically, life-event researchers have
been remiss in specifying hypotheses about mechanisms of
stress causation. Considering that the majority of findings reported about life events consists of relatively low
magnitude correlation coefficients, questions about causal
mechanisms are of the utmost importance.

Theoretical Issues in the Conception of Life Events

Life Change as Social Readjustment

The early research was predicated on the proposition that the social readjustment involved in life-change
events was stressful, regardless of the desirability of the
event. Implicitly, it was assumed that the required adaptation was costly to the organism. Energy or internal resources that are expended in adjusting to life change hypothetically depletes the reserve utilized in routine functioning. If demands on the organism increase, impairment may
result from the resource depletion associated with life-
change adaptation.

Increased vulnerability hypothetically results when
energy is depleted from the ongoing effort to achieve adaptive balance. But such depletion is only one possible
mechanism to account for the observed effects of life change.
As has been noted by Mechanic (1974), it may be that the
activity involved with life-change events takes time away
from protective and anticipatory coping. It is also plausible that life-change circumstances usher in new demands
ancillary to the identified life event, thus entailing new
threats or challenges. One might argue that life-change
researchers had all this in mind when they obtained the
social readjustment ratings for the life events. This may
be the case, but it nevertheless leaves the question about
causal mechanisms unanswered.

The claim that it is change per se that is stressful (Dohrenwend, 1973; Holmes & Masuda, 1974) flies in the face of both theory and the empirical generalizations that would be asserted by those who study stress from a psychological orientation. More generally, existing theory and research that are concerned with the role of situations as determinants of behavior have underlined the importance of the psychological significance of the situation for the person. Such work has emphasized variations in both the individual's perceptions of the situation and reactions to the situation (Magnusson & Ekehammar, 1975).

Desirability versus Undesirability

The change per se assumption was so inherently part of early life-events thinking that it remained untested for seven years. In fact, the very construction of the Holmes and Rahe (1967) "Schedule of Recent Experiences" precluded such testing. The first challenge to then-prevailing views on life events concerned the ambiguity of scale items,[22] specifically with regard to the issue of desirability. The change per se thesis was thus challenged, both conceptually and empirically (Gersten et al., 1974; Mueller, Edwards, & Yarvis, 1977). Using less ambiguous items, these studies have shown that undesirable life events, not desirable events, account for the adverse consequences of life change.

Dohrenwend (1978) has argued that the question of change per se versus undesirability is not a dichotomous issue, because greater change is involved with undesirable than with desirable events. Examining the list of events used in her own research and applying the Holmes and Rahe (1967) life-change scores, she found that the average amount of life change was much larger for the undesirable events than for the desirable events. This is a worthy observation. To an extent, however, it begs the question, since it assumes the validity of the life-change unit score, and the meaning of the social readjustment ratings is far from clear. We will return to this problem at several points below. Furthermore, Ross and Mirowsky (1979) have shown that when undesirable events are controlled (in regression analyses), neither desirable events nor total change (as measured by the Holmes-Rahe index) make a significant contribution to the prediction of psychiatric symptomatology. These authors conclude that "the only reason desirable events appear to predict symptomatology in the uncontrolled situation is that they are moderately positively correlated with undesirable events" (p. 172) and "the reason the Holmes-Rahe index predicts symptomatology moderately well in the uncontrolled situation is that it is highly correlated with undesirability" (p. 173). Even accepting Dohrenwend's (1978) point above, one can conclude that given the sort of events people experience, undesirable events are much better predictors than either desirable events or change per se.

Subjective Experience of Life Events

An implicit assumption in much of life-event research is that everyone experiences a given event in more or less the same fashion. This assumption underlies the use of life-change unit scores. While methodologically convenient, this assumption rubs against a large body of research in psychology in general and with regard to stress in particular.[23] As we have delineated in our own model, stress is not a direct function of external circumstances but is partly determined by contextual, cognitive, behavioral, and social mediators.

This issue surfaces, for example, in a study by Theorell (1974), who found that myocardial infarction patients, in contrast to controls matched on age, sex, and type of employment, were more likely (41% versus 17%) to have reported life change on work items for the year prior to the infarction. Aside from the obvious problem in this study of measurement reactivity, the research we have reviewed with regard to occupational environments strongly suggests that individual perceptions of work conditions are often more predictive of stress reactions than are the objective indices of the same conditions (for example, work load and responsibility). Might not more have been learned about the experiences of these coronary patients if Theorell had assessed their cognitive representations? Moreover, he might have learned still more by assessing the contribution of the person's behavior pattern to the work-related life-change events. We will take up that issue shortly.

A noteworthy alternative to the traditional scaling is the method developed by Sarason, Johnson, and Siegel (1978) which acknowledges the subjectivity of events. The Life Experiences Survey developed by these authors allows for the subjective evaluation of events as positive or negative and includes individualized weightings of event impacts. An implication of this approach is that the person's cognitive/linguistic representation of events may be more important than the event itself. This approach, to be sure, does have its drawbacks, in that the person's assessment of the event is more likely to be confounded by coping ability and psychological distress than is the mere recall of events.

Controllability of Life Events

Another implicit assumption of early life-event research is that events are beyond the person's control, that is, they "happen to" rather than are "produced by" the individual. Bruce Dohrenwend (1974) has taken issue with this assumption and presents evidence suggesting that certain classes of life events may be a consequence of, rather than an antecedent to, the person's psychological status. The PERI life-event inventory (Dohrenwend et al., 1978), therefore, was constructed with items classified as being either within or beyond the person's control.

It might be hypothesized that health impairments and/or psychological imbalances will result from events that are beyond the person's control but not from those over which the person has control, even when those events are negative. This line of reasoning would follow from theory and research concerning helplessness and exposure to uncontrollable stressors (Glass, 1977; Glass & Singer, 1972; Seligman, 1975), and it is buttressed by naturalistic research on sudden death subsequent to the loss of a loved one (Greene, Goldstein, & Moss, 1972; Parkes, Benjamin, & Fitzgerald, 1969). In a study of life events as related to coronary patients, Glass (1977) found that both coronary and noncoronary patients had significantly higher frequencies of life events classified a priori as "losses" or uncontrollable events than did healthy controls. Moreover, there were no differences between groups on negative events which did not involve losses.[24]

There is a proclivity toward viewing controllability as positive. However, as Averill (1973) has argued, the exercise of personal control does not have beneficial effects uniformly, sometimes being found to cause increased stress reactions. Thus, it may be that some negative life events are more stressful because of their controllability. Exercising control means that energy is being expended and that one is attending to circumstances which have threat potential. Perhaps the stress-inducing properties of life events are more exactly determined not by their inherent qualities of controllability, or even negativity, but instead by the process by which one attends to and responds to these events.

The Dynamics of Life Events

Viewing life events in terms of their controllability may serve to reduce ambiguity in construing them. Yet, understanding the dynamics of stressful life events requires more than classifying events according to the degree of personal control that one has over them. Controllability connotes less than our transactional axiom entails. The person can be an architect as well as a victim of stressful life experiences, and the notion of controllability does not capture the event-producing capacities of the behaving organism or system.

The very concept of life events is askew. Life events have been construed as static and discrete occurrences. To the contrary, what are designated as life events are often endpoints of temporally extended sequences. The life-event labels that are contained on questionnaires are merely a convenient shorthand. If they refer to some explicit occurrence, those occurrences are really signposts of dynamic-event chains. Marriage, divorce, retirement, jail terms, pregnancy, mortgages, and so forth are not discrete events. Even in the case of sudden death of a loved one, there are stressful sequels associated with the event which can have a major impact on the grieving person. This implies that some quantification ought to be made of the temporal parameters of life events.

There are several issues concerning the temporal aspects of life stress. First, because life events are often enduring life circumstances, part of the unexplained variance in life-event outcomes might be explained by the duration of the life stress. While improvements in life-event scales (for example, Sarason, Johnson, & Siegel, 1978) have provided for the assessment of the valence and significance of particular events, the duration of the event or, more precisely, the life circumstances, has not been measured. Since the stressful occurrences obviously vary in their period of objective exposure across individuals, it would seem worthwhile to develop measurement parameters for gauging this dimension. Admittedly, this measure would be confounded with coping ability, and these effects would need to be disentangled.

Second, in addition to the objective aspects of life events, there are the subjective aspects that we have been emphasizing. The subjective exposure dimension also varies across individuals as determined by their cognitive representations. Exposure to the stressful circumstances is to a significant extent a function of the person's cognitions. This follows from our cognitive mediational axiom. Stress may be experienced most intensely long before the "event" has actually occurred (for example, Kasl, Gore, & Cobb, 1975). However, the person can perpetuate exposure to stressful events by preoccupation. Just as events themselves may be acute or chronic, so too may be the person's cognitions about them, and acute circumstances may be prolonged by brooding. Hypothetically, the stress impact of events will vary as a function of being preoccupied with them. The degree of preoccupation will be related to the nature of the events, as well as to the individual's cognitive style and coping behaviors. While this implies a complex transactional chain, it might be useful to obtain some measurement of how often a person thinks about the stressful life circumstances.

Each of the above-raised issues suggests another related one, namely the time lag between the occurrence or onset of "events" and the manifestation of stress. Currently used lags, such as those in the Catalano and Dooley research (1977, 1979), are justified more by convention than by theoretical reasoning or by empirical evidence concerning psychological/organismic processes. In time-series research utilizing lagged-regression analyses, it would seem worthwhile to begin to speculate about the nature of the temporal interval for which one obtains the strongest regression coefficients.

Understanding the dynamics of life events will also require research on coping activities. A large proportion of life-stress research has taken a simple actuarial approach, ignoring (at least empirically) processes intervening between the activating events and the stress outcomes. Distressed individuals will vary markedly in coping skills, and coping strategies will vary with context. Recent research by Folkman and Lazarus (1980) has shown that the cognitive appraisal of events and their context of occurrence are potent determinants of coping strategies.

Some Methodological Agenda

Research on stressful life events is beset with methodological difficulties. It is no great accomplishment to point these out, and contemporary life-event researchers have been among the most persistent and vocal critics. The facts are that the scientific observations in life-event research have largely consisted of self-report markings on a questionnaire, that subjects are asked to recall events over long and varying periods, that scale reliabilities are quite low, that the content validity of scale items can be disputed, that questions about method variance are unanswered by life-event methodology, and that most studies are retrospective, correlational investigations which make the directionality of obtained effects ambiguous.

We will not dwell on the weakness of life-event scales, the discussion of which has become pedestrian. We will discuss two topic areas that beckon for advances in research methodology. The first concerns the description of life events, and we propose a set of dimensions or parameters that may improve our descriptive knowledge. The second topic concerns strategies for determining causal mechanisms, which is a theme upon which we continue to hammer. We present these not as summary appraisals of life-event methodology but as agenda that follow from our conceptual system.

Calibrating Life Events

One agenda suggested by our stress model is the identification and measurement of life-event parameters. The very description of life events is in need of improvement. Why merely describe life events through use of ordinary language labels? Surely we can improve our scientific observations of life events beyond check marks alongside the various event labels, even if our observations are limited to questionnaire self-reports. If life events were to be calibrated in terms of basic dimensions on which there is variation across individuals and circumstances, might we not learn more about their nature and effects?

While the identification of these parameters is a matter for empirical investigation and existing research has already revealed some of them, our stress model suggests what might be some relevant variable dimensions. We have conceptualized stressful life events as demands of social environments and have postulated that environmental demands vary in their potency and persistence. Existing life-event methodology addresses the potency dimension through the social readjustment ratings on life change unit scores which provide for the ranking of events on a continuum of severity. The persistence dimension, however, has not been addressed. Here, we have suggested that life events or circumstances be assessed for their duration of occurrence, in terms of both their objective and subjective presence.

Our cognitive mediation postulate indicates that stressors operate through their perceived qualities. Thus, the cognitive labeling of events becomes a relevant parameter. One approach to indexing the cognitive labeling dimension is to assess the valence or affective tone of events as either positive or negative, as certain investigators have been doing. Another approach might be to classify events according to appraisal categories. Lazarus and his associates distinguish three major types of appraisals: harm-loss, which refers to damage that has already happened; threat, which refers to anticipated harm or loss; and challenge, which refers to anticipated opportunity for mastery or gain. These appraisal categories could be usefully applied to life-event labeling, with the addition of one other category—that of gain/achievement, which would refer to an attainment that has already happened. Thus, these four appraisal categories would serve to label the valence of events and their moment (completed versus ongoing).

The behavioral mediation and the transactionality postulate point to the importance of the person's activities in the occurrence of life events and in modifying their impact once they have occurred. This suggests that whether or not an event has been potentiated by the person could be measured as a relevant parameter. Differential stress effects might be associated with events that have been activated by the person's behavior versus those occurring independently.

The same theme also suggests the dimension of impact modification. That is, it would be useful to assess whether or not the person engaged in behavior that was instrumental in attenuating the impact of the identified life circumstances. This is not a question of coping efforts. It is assumed that people will try to cope in some fashion with nearly all life events (how people cope is a separate issue). Here, the subject is the life event itself, which, as we have asserted, has a temporal extension and thereby is susceptible to change as a result of the person's activities.

The contextuality postulate stipulates that the <u>context</u> in which a stressor is embedded is a determinant of that stressor's impact. The items contained in existing life-event inventories pertain to several basic contexts: home/family, work/school, and personal health/adjustment.[25] Since we have noted that the effects of environmental demands and the coping strategies enacted are linked to variations in context, this parameter warrants systematic attention in life-event measurement.

From the stress model axioms we have thus derived a set of parameters on which stressful life events can be found to vary. In summary, these are <u>potency, persistence, cognitive labeling, potentiation, attenuation, and context</u>.[26] Three of these parameters (potency, labeling, and context) are already gauged by existing life-event instruments, although we have proposed a new way of calibrating the labeling dimension. The remaining parameters (persistence, potentiation, and attenuation) can be assessed in a relatively simple fashion. A new inventory is being developed by R. W. Novaco that incorporates these theoretically based dimensions.

Ascertaining Causal Mechanisms

The processes that transpire between the initial onset of stressful life events and the subsequent emergence of impairments to well-being are in need of identification. However, the survey questionnaire approach that has dominated life-event research has limited utility with regard to questions concerning psychological processes. The commonly used large-sample, cross-sectional methodology simply cannot inform us about the phenomenology of life events. From our perspective, an optimal strategy for the community-oriented investigator would be a combination of epidemiological and psychological methods. The cross-level analyses conducted by Dooley, Catalano, and Brownell (1980) are a step in this direction. Additional gain can be derived from an approach whereby moderate-size samples (N of 100) are assessed repeatedly in a longitudinal design so as to observe individualized reaction patterns.

The point of departure should be some explicit hypotheses about causal mechanisms. There are several ways that life-change events may operate to ultimately result in stress outcomes. We have already discussed some of the hypothesized mechanisms. The oldest view is that social readjustment depletes internal resources and thus increases vulnerability to illness. However, there are a number of alternative hypotheses. One is that responding to life-change events preempts time otherwise devoted to preventive health practices. Another possibility is that life events create cognitive overload, requiring a focused attention on primary tasks related to the event and thus interfering with routine functioning. Perhaps the most popular alternative is that negative life events induce arousal and generate emotion which interfere with functioning and are inherently linked to stress responses. Whatever the hypothesized process might be, the research protocol ought to be designed to test it. Life-event research has predominantly been concerned with correlational studies, and questions about their assumptive bases are rarely examined.

It may be the case that the stress effects of life change are explained best by more than one hypothesized causal process. Earlier we discussed the "one construct, one process" quandary that can be seen generally in the stress field, and this problem applies especially well to life-event research. It is as if calling things by one name, "stressful life events," informs us about their essential nature and dynamics (compare Notes 4 and 10). When life-change circumstances became known as "stressful life events," a common essence or homogeneity was thereby conferred on occurrences that are indeed heterogenous. A life event is not a life event. Why assume, for example, that the same causal process that may explain event impairment connections for positive events also is true for negative events? Might not the stress-engendering processes for acute events differ from that for recurring events or enduring circumstances? In light of our discussion of cognitive, behavioral, and contextual influences, as well as the preceding section on life-event description, it seems advisable to consider the operation of multiple causal mechanisms.

The unmistakable fact is that the research correlations between life events and subsequent disorders are low-magnitude coefficients. This suggests that if indeed life events are etiologically important, a number of moderator variables are operating in the causal chair, thus diminishing or obscuring the obtained effects (Johnson & Sarason,

1979; Smith, Johnson, & Sarason, 1978). To take an example of an important community problem, child abuse has been found to be associated with life-stress events. In a prospective study of the effects of life events on the caretaking behavior of primiparous, low-socioeconomic status mothers, Egeland, Breitenbucher, and Rosenberg (1980) found that mothers scoring high on life events were more likely to mistreat their children. But, as one would expect, not all high life stress mothers mistreat their children. Beyond life stress, the incidence of abuse was further determined by certain mother characteristics, baby behavior, and patterns of interaction.

As life-event research adopts more of a process-oriented focus, the existence and operation of moderating factors will become more in evidence. Increased attention to the person's active efforts to cope with life crises has led to the identification of key variables, particularly social support, which has been the most prominently studied moderator variable.

SOCIAL SUPPORT: A BRIEF NOTE

When people are faced with stressful events, the impact of these events can be moderated by the presence of supportive social conditions that protect the individual from debilitating forces. Cumulative research suggests that social support facilitates coping with life crises and that the loss of support is stress inducing. In a seminal review article, Cobb (1976) optimistically concluded that social support can protect people from a wide variety of pathological states, including low birth weight, arthritis, tuberculosis, depression, and alcoholism.

The concept of social support certainly has broad relevance to psychological and sociological research on stress. It has been a rubric for studies otherwise identified as investigations of social networks, social isolation, social integration, social participation, loss of support, and psychosocial assets. This variously labeled research has as its common denominator the concern with psychosocial factors that mitigate the consequences of stressful conditions.

Research on social support has commonly been traced to sociological and anthropological work on social network theory (e.g., Mitchell, 1979). Community psychologists might be interested to note, however, that this is ante-dated by the classic work of Thomas and Znaniecki (1920) and the social disorganization theorists of the Chicago School (for example, Shaw & McKay, 1942). Thomas and Znaniecki's Polish Peasant in Europe and America con-cerned the effects of urbanization on the migrant in terms of the move from the intimate social networks of the rural areas in Poland to the impersonal context of the American metropolis.[27] Clifford Shaw and Henry McKay, who were both raised in the rural Midwest and came to Chicago in the 1920s to do graduate work in sociology, became known for their pioneering work on juvenile delinquency. They saw the invasion of business and industry as disturbing the social cohesion of communities located in the "zone in transition."[28] In their Chicago Area Project they attempted to create community cohesion through neighborhood activi-ties and projects, so as to reinstate natural social con-trols. Their work thus serves as a precedent to social-support theory and intervention.

Several reviews of the social-support literature (Caplan, 1974; Cobb, 1976; Dean & Lin, 1977; Heller, 1979; Kaplan, Cassel, & Gore, 1977) have now led to a rapid growth of research in this area, much to the benefit of community psychology. Space constraints preclude us from dealing adequately with the topic of social support here. The interested reader is referred to a volume of recent re-search and theory edited by Sarason (in press).

PRIORITIES FOR STRESS RESEARCH
IN COMMUNITY PSYCHOLOGY

The relevance of stress research for community psy-chology derives in part from the manner in which that re-search has been conducted over the last two decades. The previous emphasis on experimental laboratory methodology has given way to a blossoming of research in quasi-experi-mental field studies and in behavioral epidemiology. These approaches have a number of advantages for the community psychologist. Research conducted in the community implies greater ecological validity than laboratory research. The environmental-demand literature, for instance, concerns "naturally occurring" community conditions, such as air-craft noise, traffic congestion, and economic change. True experiments are typically unsuited for studying such variables, but carefully conducted quasi-experimental designs can be profitably utilized. Correspondingly, the literature on life change and social support features methodologies from behavioral epidemiology. By means of sophisticated sampling and survey techniques, information is gathered about the diverse aspects of the lives of community populations. The interrelationships among life history, environmental forces, well-being, social relationships, and efforts at adaptation are indeed complex and require methodologies which rely on multivariate analyses and conceptualizations.

Yet the advantages of the community-oriented research strategies are accompanied by certain liabilities. The broad scope of this research has sometimes been achieved at the expense of depth and explicitness. In a sense, research has identified physical environment and social environment inputs into a black box and linked those inputs to various outcomes which emerge over time. In particular, macro-level analyses of life change and social support, while valuable in their attention to important community problems, nevertheless require more micro-level analyses if we are to disentangle the intervening processes and specify how such generally conceptualized events have their specific effects.

A shift in emphasis has already begun, though it is far from complete. Early life-stress research rested on a number of assumptions, only some of which have even now been made explicit. We have discussed the engaging issues pertaining to the nature and dynamics of life events and have formulated a set of descriptive parameters that are suggested by our stress model. Increased specification of life events can lead to fresh conceptualizations and empirical advances. Such specification is surely necessary if we are to disentangle the effects of life change from other confounding variables. "An increase in arguments with spouse" may not only reflect life stress but may be etiologically significant with regard to the loss of social support.

An implicit assumption in the life-event literature which we did not discuss is that the inventories contain a reasonably representative sample of the universe of life events. Yet it is clear that these samples are not a matter of consensus. Happily, there is a clear trend to address this issue, with scales becoming longer and explicitly representative of different areas of life. For instance, the PERI life-event inventory (Dohrenwend et al., 1978) contains items regarding education, work, love and marriage, family life, crime and legal matters, finances, social activities, and health. Such developments are a welcomed advance in the specification of events and their context.

Another issue concerns the independence of life events and outcome variables. While life-change inventories are often used to predict health or psychological outcomes, they also contain items relating to these outcomes. With this in mind, Bruce Dohrenwend (1973) recommended that life events confounded with health be excluded when a relationship between life change and health is tested. Yet this strategy blocks the testing of an eminently valid hypothesis that ill health is in part a function of life stress generated by previous ill health. Such positive feedback loops, characterized by Maruyama (1963) as "deviation-amplifying mutual causal processes," are characteristic of many systems and surely apply to human interaction systems. Life-event research has emphasized a simple actuarial approach to the conceptualization of life stress. This treatment of life events has certain advantages, but there must be some explicit recognition of the transactional nature of person-environment relationships. Thus far, we have made little progress in specifying what is stressful about life change, in what context, and by which mechanisms.

Research on social support seems immediately relevant and very attractive to community psychologists. A persistent ideal of the community approach has been to emphasize "resources" and "competencies" as opposed to a sole focus on deficits. The early literature on social relationships was not explicitly concerned with "support" as a resource leading to health and well-being, and certainly not as some immunization or antidote for stress. But epidemiologists recognized that social resources can counteract the demands of life change, concerning which research was blossoming. Yet from the perspective of community psychology, the epidemiological level of analysis has been a mixed blessing. On the one hand, it allowed a rich construct to be researched within the context of the community. On the other hand, epidemiological methodology has been somewhat of a constraint on the construct. The macro-level analyses emphasizing roles and morphology need to be supplemented by research focusing on the actual social-support processes.[29]

The concept of stress is, at the most general level of abstraction, understood as a condition of imbalance between demands and resources. We have pointed to some recent work on physical and social environments which has special significance for community psychologists. This research has been conducted at the macro level of analysis in some instances and at intermediate levels in others. While detailed measurements are often made on individuals, it is nonetheless the case that there has been little specification of the behavioral or otherwise psychological processes that mediate the obtained relationships between environmental demands and well-being. That is, how does exposure to conditions such as noise, traffic congestion, density, and economic change translate its impacts on psychological functioning and health? What are the mechanisms which underlie stressor → stress reaction relationships? There is a need for more precise understanding of how macro-level conditions transmit their effects to individuals and how adaptation efforts by individuals enter the process that results in stress outcomes. The answers to these questions can best be obtained from multivariate longitudinal studies.

To summarize, there are exciting prospects for research in community psychology to go beyond the "mental health care" or "service delivery" mold that has been its main thrust. An empirical examination of research in our field has shown that improvements must be made in the theoretical and methodological character of the existing body of research. In this chapter we have presented a model of human stress as a framework within which the community-oriented researcher might profitably address the scientific agenda of our discipline. The model views stress as a hypothetical condition of demand/resource imbalance, emphasizes the transactional and contextually determined nature of person-environment relationships, and stipulates that cognitive, behavioral, and social processes mediate the effects of environmental demands on stress reaction outcomes. Various research programs have been presented to illustrate the relevance of this area of study for community psychology and to engage the reader with regard to unresolved issues in the field.

NOTES

1. Gergen's (1978) concept of the generative potency of a theory is to be distinguished from the more commonly recognized concept of heuristic value. The generative potency of a theory refers to its potential for transforming social reality by challenging cultural assumptions and serving to reorder social conduct. In contrast, a theory's heuristic capacity refers to its ability to generate new research or problem solutions.

2. This valuation of theory-based research is not to say or imply that research conducted outside of an explicit theoretical framework cannot be worthwhile, nor does it assume that theoretically directed investigations should follow the classical positivistic work. Hypothesis testing is not central to a number of nontraditional research paradigms that have distinct utility for community psychology, such as ecological analyses (Hawley, 1950) and systems theory (Buckley, 1968), nor to other potentially valuable approaches, such as applied behavioral analysis (Nietzel et al., 1977).

3. These four characteristics might be useful criteria for judging any proposed community research paradigm.

4. Aristotle, in his Metaphysics, asserted that we know a thing by knowing its essence. Definitions, accordingly, must provide an exhaustive description of a thing's essence. An elegant and rather caustic criticism of Aristotle's essentialism can be found in Popper's (1957) The Open Society and Its Enemies. Popper argues with vituperative flair that Aristotle's method of definitions has been an inexhaustible source of confusion and stands in contrast to the methods of modern science. For Aristotle, definitions point to the essence of something and describe it by means of a defining formula. According to Popper, scientific use of definitions is nominalistic. That is, symbols or labels are introduced in order to simplify otherwise complicated sets of information, "to cut a long story short." Aristotle's essentialist definitions are thought to contain our knowledge. Scientific nominalist definitions contain no knowledge whatsoever; they merely introduce a convenient shorthand.

5. Selye's (1976) view of stress is that it is a nonspecific response to any demand. His stress model can be seen to have a spatial dimension consisting of a tri-component physiological-response cluster (adrenal cortex

enlargement, shrinkage of lymphatic structures, and gastro-intestinal disturbances) and a temporal dimension consisting of a tristage developmental sequence (alarm reaction, stage of resistance, and exhaustion). The "general adaptation syndrome" refers to this latter dimension, although Selye equivocates about the occurrence of all three stages (compare 1976, p. 79). There is incredibly little evidence that all stress responses consist of these physiological re-actions exclusively. Furthermore, the nonspecificity thesis has been challenged by Mason (1971). We do, however, recognize Selye's seminal contributions to the stress field in the 1950s and should also note that it was he who pushed for conceptual clarity in differentiating stress, a condition of the organism, from stressor, an agent or de-mand.

6. The principle of reciprocal causality is an in-herent part of systems theory (compare Buckley, 1968; Katz & Kahn, 1966), particularly open systems concepts, such as negative entropy and differentiation (von Bertalanffy, 1950), and Maruyama's (1963) concept of deviation–amplifi-cation. Reciprocal determination has also been proposed by Bandura (1977) as a basic analytical principle for un-derstanding self-regulatory processes in psychosocial func-tioning.

7. Experimental laboratory methodology in psychol-ogy has primarily involved stressors that are easily manipu-lated and the subject samples have well-known limitations. The stress situations in laboratory investigations are not the sort that impinge on people over extended periods of time and result in various pathological states. Such is the recognized trade-off between internal and external validity. But in addition, the stimulus-response frame-works of such experimentation, characterized by unidirec-tional causal models, have truncated the observational process. That is, the experiment ends when the subject has responded to the array of stimulus conditions. This precludes the study of interaction in the phenomenological sense.

8. Urban dwellers indeed adapt to the adversities of the metropolis. Dubos (1965) and others have main-tained that these adaptations have associated costs. Milgram (1970), following the work of early urban sociologists George Simmel and Louis Wirth, views adaptation to urban life in terms of overload. Milgram identifies a range of six adap-tive responses to overload which consists of (1) allocation

of less time to inputs, (2) disregard of low-priority inputs, (3) shifts in burdens of responsibility, (4) blocking
and screening of social contacts, (5) filtering of inputs to
diminish their intensity, and (6) the creation of special institutions to absorb demanding inputs.

9. The very concept of coping embodies the transactional axiom and the behavioral mediation axiom. Pearlin
and Schooler (1978), for example, state, "By coping we
refer to the things that people do to avoid being harmed
by life strains. At the very heart of this concept is the
fundamental assumption that people are actively responsive
to forces that impinge upon them" (p. 2). Further exemplification can be found in the work of Folkman and Lazarus
(1980).

10. Lewin (1935, 1936) in proscribing principles
for a dynamic psychology, argued that the transition from
Aristotelian to Galilean concepts demands that we should
seek explanations for events not in the nature of the isolated object but rather in terms of the relationship between an object and its surroundings. Lewin's contrast
of Aristotelian and Galilean modes of thought exemplifies
the reciprocal causality postulate, as well as that concerning contextual determinants.

11. This project followed from laboratory research
on the stress effects of noise exposure (Glass & Singer,
1972; Krantz, Glass, & Snyder, 1974) and from other field
experiments extending from that laboratory work (Cohen,
Glass, & Singer, 1973).

12. Subjects were classified as low, medium, or
high impedance on the basis of the frequency distributions for distance and time of commuting obtained from a
larger sample of employees in the two companies in the
study (compare Novaco et al., 1979, or Stokols et al.,
1978, for details concerning selection criteria).

13. A thorough and insightful review of this field
of research, with which community psychologists ought to be
acquainted, can be found in Dooley and Catalano (1980).

14. Catalano and Dooley have used two basic measures to characterize the economic environment: the unemployment rate and a computed index of change in the size
and structure of the work force. They consider the unemployment rate as a measure of perceived economic performance, since it is widely publicized and is not designed
to index the ability of an economy to provide jobs. Unemployment rates are computed in terms of the available work

force; thus the unemployment rate can increase (decrease) even though the number of jobs provided has increased (decreased). To measure actual economic performance, these investigators use employment data which tap the amount and direction of change in the work force. While previous investigations have used political areas as units of analysis (for example, the state of New York), Catalano and Dooley conduct their analyses on economically defined communities by using as a unit of analysis the "standard metropolitan statistical area."

15. The inflation rate was found to be unrelated to life events or symptoms for the total sample and across demographic subgroups.

16. The fallacy refers to inferences concerning correlations obtained between independent and dependent variables in cross-sectional aggregate analyses. The inclination is to infer that the individuals who exhibit the dependent variable (for example, some stress reaction) are the ones who experience the independent variable (for example, the environmental demand).

17. Numerous studies and clinical reports have implicated suppressed anger in the etiology of essential hypertension. Among such studies is the work of Funkenstein, King, and Drolette (1957), who developed a response-mode classification of "anger-in" versus "anger-out" in their laboratory experimentation which was utilized by Harburg and his associates in the Detroit studies.

18. A cognitive-behavioral analysis of anger that accounts for environmental conditions and links anger to chronic-stress reactions can be found in Novaco (1979).

19. The stress terminology of this research group (for example, French et al., 1974) varies from our own. For them, stress refers to characteristics of the job environment which pose a threat to the person, and it also refers to a misfit between person and environment. Their use of the term strain parallels what we refer to as stress reactions. Their term stress involves an unnecessary equivocation, particularly since it confounds operational variables with a hypothetical construct.

20. There are actually three types of possible relationships (monotonic, asymptotic, and curvilinear) between dimensions of fit and strain, which are best delineated by Harrison (1978). The functions are alternatively mapped for fit as operationalized in terms of either a supply versus motive dimension or a demand versus

ability dimension. In all cases, high strain is associated with either deficient supplies (vis-à-vis motives) or deficient abilities (vis-à-vis demands). Strain decreases monotonically as perfect fit is approached. After the point of balance, the function then takes divergent shapes. Monotonic relationships are expected when excess supplies are either preservable or exchangeable (for example, money or tokens) and, in the case of the demand/ability dimension, when excess abilities can be used to serve other motives (for example, having extra time to socialize or recreate). Asymptotic relationships are expected when excess supplies are not exchangeable for other motives (for example, having extra food or having more opportunities than one can use) or when excess abilities have no bearing on other motives (for example, knowing more mathematics than the job demands). The curvilinear function occurs when the presence of excess supplies for one motive results in deficient supplies for another motive (for example, having too much privacy reduces affiliation) and when excess abilities reflect insufficient supplies for other motives (for example, having more competence than the job requires can negatively affect self-esteem). Thus, as supplies or abilities increase (plotted on the abscissa), strain (plotted on the ordinate) can continue to decrease, level off, or increase.

21. The nose knows. Holmes indeed began his research on life events with studies of inflammations in nasal passages.

22. Some examples of scale items are "change in health of family member," "change in financial state," "change in living conditions," "change in recreation," "revision of personal habits," "change in number of arguments with spouse," and "change in eating habits."

23. This conceptual attack on the life-change-unit construct might properly be complemented by an empirical one. The life-change construct was ascribed validity from findings indicating consensus among different groups regarding the magnitude of social readjustment associated with the events. These included differing ethnic and socioeconomic status groups (Holmes & Rahe, 1967) and differing cultural and national groups (Masuda & Holmes, 1967; Rahe, 1969). However, Askenasy, Dohrenwend, and Dohrenwend (1977) have criticized these studies for using samples of convenience (often of professionals belonging to a "cosmopolitan" culture). Using a systematic New York City sample stratified by social class, ethnicity, and sex, Askenasy,

Dohrenwend, and Dohrenwend (1977) found greater variation than usual in judgments of life-change magnitude, though there was still considerable agreement.

More critical than intergroup consensus regarding life change, however, is the effectiveness of these social-readjustment weightings in predicting psychological distress. Despite the variety of methods for weighting life events, many studies fail to demonstrate any superiority of weighted scores over simple unit scores (that is, number of events experienced) in predicting distress. The most recent, explicit, and comprehensive test of this issue is a study by Ross and Mirowsky (1979). In this study 23 different methods of weighting life events were compared regarding their power in predicting psychiatric symptomatology. The authors conclude that the most predictive and efficient index consists of simply summing events classified as undesirable. This simple score was just as good as several weighted undesirability scores and better than unweighted or weighted desirable change, or overall change, scores. The only weighting system which improved on the predictive power of this simple unit-weighted sum score was a complex procedure developed by the authors. This procedure involved regressing symptomatology on all of the individual life events and using the resulting regression coefficients as weights for the respective items. Nonetheless, the general predictive effectiveness of unweighted life-event scores vis-à-vis fairly complex weighting systems represents a serious empirical challenge to the concept of social readjustment.

24. Not all of Glass's (1977) "loss" events were uncontrollable, as he himself notes. While items concerning death of loved ones or financial declines are largely uncontrollable events, divorce and separation are more generally controllable. The negative-events index (nonloss items) entailed events such as "trouble with boss," "detention in jail," "mortgage foreclosure," "sexual difficulties," and "in-law troubles."

25. It is worth noting that nearly all life events on existing inventories are occurrences in what Stokols (1976) calls "primary environments," in contrast to "secondary environments." Primary environments are those in which one spends a high proportion of time, relations with others are personal, and personally important activities occur. Secondary environments are those in which encounters with others are transitory, anonymous, and inconse-

quential. Stokols distinguishes these two classes of environments on the basis of the continuity of social encounters, the psychological centrality of goals, and the character of interpersonal relations.

26. It might be noticed that controllability is not among the set of parameters. Analyses of the cognitive mediation of stress have often utilized the concept of control, and semantic difficulties have resulted from the various conceptualizations (compare Novaco, 1979). The confusion is evident when the term control is used to specify some class of cognitive processes. The notion of control, least equivocally, refers to a relationship between persons and environmental elements or events. Perceptions of control can be more explicitly described in terms of expectations and appraisals, which are more generic terms for describing cognitive activity. With regard to the parameters of life events, once cognitive labeling, potentiation, and attenuation have been ascertained, the person's "perceived control" over events is superfluous (and irrelevant). Also, the notion of control with regard to life events is often confused as a result of viewing life events as discrete occurrences. The onset of an event may not be controlled, in the sense of causing the event to happen, but the issue of control may still be relevant to how the event is experienced over time. Thus, events that are classified as uncontrollable, by either researchers or subjects, may very well have controllable sequellae.

27. Social disorganization theorists believed that societal norms are transmitted through primary groups, such as the family and neighborhood. Urban industrialization and patterns of in-migration and out-migration were thought to erode or disturb social cohesion and thus disrupt traditional norms of conduct. For Thomas and Znaniecki, the Polish peasant was a convenient and fortuitous subject, as this population was in transition from an old form of social organization, having been stable for centuries, to a modern society to which they brought their attitudes and values. Shaw and McKay (1942) viewed delinquency in terms of a breakdown of social controls in communities.

28. "Zone maps" were one kind of mapping done by Chicago School sociologists, such as Shaw and McKay. "Spot maps," "rate maps," and "radial maps" were also constructed. The zones consisted of concentric areas mapped at certain intervals from the city center, otherwise known

as the central business district (CBD). The "zone in transition" was the area surrounding the CBD and was occupied
by new migrants to the city. Land use in this area consisted of that by factories forced out of the CBD by increasing rents and that of low-rent housing which was
either in the process of decay in anticipation of purchase
by industry or was a high-density tenement.

29. This is consistent with behavioral theories of
depression which view the affective disorder as resulting
from low-activity schedules and associated reductions in
positive reinforcement (Lewinsohn & Graf, 1973; Lewinsohn
& Libet, 1972).

REFERENCES

Appley, M. H., & Trumbull, R. (Eds.). Psychological
stress. New York: Appleton-Century-Crofts, 1967.
Askenasy, A. R., Dohrenwend, B. P., & Dohrenwend, B. S.
Some effects of social class and ethnic group member-
ship on judgments of the magnitude of stressful life
events: A research note. Journal of Health and
Social Behavior, 1977, 18, 432-439.
Averill, J. Personal control over aversive stimuli and its
relationship to stress. Psychological Bulletin, 1973,
80, 286-303.
Bandura, A. Social learning theory. Englewood Cliffs,
N.J.: Prentice-Hall, 1977.
Bertalanffy, L. von. The theory of open systems in phy-
sics and biology. Science, 1950, 111, 23-29.
Brenner, M. H. Mental illness and the economy. Cam-
bridge, Mass.: Harvard University Press, 1973.
Bronfenbrenner, U. The origins of alienation. Scientific
American, 1974, 231, 53-61.
Bronfenbrenner, U. The ecology of human development.
Cambridge, Mass.: Harvard University Press, 1979.
Buckley, W. Modern systems research for the behavioral
scientist. Chicago: Aldine, 1968.
Caplan, G. Support systems and community mental health.
New York: Behavioral Publications, 1974.
Caplan, R. D., & Jones, K. W. Effects of workload, role
ambiguity, and Type A personality on anxiety, depres-
sion, and heart rate. Journal of Applied Psychology,
1975, 60, 713-719.

Caplan, R. D., Cobb, S., & French, J. Relationships of cessation of smoking with job stress, personality, and social support. Journal of Applied Psychology, 1975, 60, 211-219.

Catalano, R., & Dooley, D. Economic predictors of depressed mood and stressful life events. Journal of Health and Social Behavior, 1977, 18, 292-307.

Catalano, R., & Dooley, D. Does economic change provoke or uncover behavior disorder: A preliminary test. In L. Ferman & J. Gordus (Eds.), Mental health and the economy. Kalamazoo, Mich.: Upjohn Foundation, 1979.

Catalano, R., Dooley, D., & Jackson, R. Economic predictors of admissions to mental health facilities in a non-metropolitan community. Journal of Health and Social Behavior, in press.

Catalano, R., & Monahan, J. The community psychologist as social planner: Designing optimal environments. American Journal of Community Psychology, 1975, 3, 327-334.

Cobb, S. Social support as a moderator of life stress. Psychosomatic Medicine, 1976, 38, 300-314.

Cohen, S. Environmental load and the allocation of attention. In A. Baum, J. E. Singer, & S. Valins (Eds.), Advances in environmental psychology (Vol. 1). Hillsdale, N.J.: Erlbaum, 1978.

Cohen, S., Evans, G. W., Krantz, D. S., & Stokols, D. Physiological, motivational, and cognitive effects of aircraft noise on children. American Psychologist, 1980, 35 (3), 231-243.

Cohen, S., Glass, D. C., & Singer, G. E. Apartment noise, auditory discrimination, and reading ability in children. Journal of Experimental Social Psychology, 1973, 9, 607-622.

Cox, T. Stress. Baltimore: University Park Press, 1978.

Dean, A., & Lin, N. The stress-buffering role of social support. Journal of Nervous and Mental Disease, 1977, 165, 403-471.

Dewey, J., & Bentley, A. Knowing and the known. Boston: Beacon Press, 1949.

Dohrenwend, B. S. Life events as stressors: A methodological inquiry. Journal of Health and Social Behavior, 1973, 14, 167-175.

Dohrenwend, B. S. Problems in defining and sampling the relevant population of stressful life events. In B. S.

Dohrenwend & B. P. Dohrenwend (Eds.), Stressful life events: Their nature and effects. New York: Wiley, 1974.

Dohrenwend, B. S. Social stress and community psychology. American Journal of Community Psychology, 1978, 6, 1-15.

Dohrenwend, B. P., & Dohrenwend, B. S. Social status and psychological disorder: A causal inquiry. New York: John Wiley, 1969.

Dohrenwend, B. S., & Dohrenwend, B. P. Stressful life events: Their nature and effects. New York: John Wiley, 1974.

Dohrenwend, B. S., Krasnoff, L., Askenasy, A. R., & Dohrenwend, B. P. Exemplification of a method for scaling life events: The PERI life events scale. Journal of Health and Social Behavior, 1978, 19, 205-229.

Dooley, D., & Catalano, R. Money and mental disorder: Toward a behavioral cost accounting for primary prevention. American Journal of Community Psychology, 1977, 5(2), 217-227.

Dooley, D., & Catalano, R. Economic, life, and disorder changes: Time-series analyses. American Journal of Community Psychology, 1979, 7, 381-396.

Dooley, D., & Catalano, R. Economic change as a cause of behavioral disorder. Psychological Bulletin, 1980, 87, 450-468.

Dooley, D., Catalano, R., & Brownell, A. The relation of economic conditions, social support, and individual life change to depression cross-level analysis of behavioral disorder. Paper submitted for publication, 1980.

Dooley, D., Catalano, R., Jackson, R., & Brownell, A. Economic, life, and symptom changes in a non-metropolitan community. Journal of Health and Social Behavior, in press.

Dubos, R. Man adapting. New Haven, Conn.: Yale University Press, 1965.

Durkheim, E. Suicide. Paris: Alcan, 1897.

Eden, Dov, et al. Kibbutz as support system. In C. D. Spielberger & I. G. Sarason (Eds.), Stress and anxiety (Vol. 4). Washington, D.C.: Hemisphere Press, 1977.

Egeland, B., Breitenbucher, M., & Rosenberg, D. Prospective study of the significance of life stress in the etiology of child abuse. Journal of Consulting and Clinical Psychology, 1980, 48, 195-205.

Folkman, S., & Lazarus, R. An analysis of coping in a middle-aged community sample. Journal of Health and Social Behavior, 1980, 21, 219-239.

Frankenhaeuser, M., Nordheden, B., Myrsten, A-L, & Post, B. Psychophysiological reactions to understimulation and overstimulation. Acta Psychologica, 1971, 35, 298-304.

Frankenhaeuser, M., Post, B., Nordheden, B., & Sjoberg, H. Physiological and subjective reactions to different physical work loads. Perceptual and Motor Skills, 1969, 28, 343-348.

French, J., & Caplan, R. Psychosocial factors in coronary heart disease. Industrial Medicine, 1970, 39, 383-397.

French, J., Rodgers, W., & Cobb, S. Adjustment as person-environment fit. In G. Coelho, D. Hamburg, & J. Adams (Eds.), Coping and adaptation. New York: Basic Books, 1974.

Friedman, M. Pathogenesis of coronary artery disease. New York: McGraw-Hill, 1969.

Friedman, M., & Rowenman, R. Type A behavior and your heart. Greenwich, Conn.: Fawcett, 1974.

Funkenstein, D. H., King, S. H., & Drolette, M. E. Mastery of stress. Cambridge, Mass.: Harvard University Press, 1957.

Gergen, K. J. Toward generative theory. Journal of Personality and Social Psychology, 1978, 36, 1346-1360.

Gersten, G. C., Langner, T. S., Eisenberg, G. G., & Orzeck, L. Child behavior and life events. In B. S. Dohrenwend & B. P. Dohrenwend (Eds.), Stressful life events: Their nature and effects. New York: John Wiley, 1974.

Glass, D. C. Behavior patterns, stress and coronary disease. New York: John Wiley, 1977.

Glass, D. C., & Singer, J. E. Urban stress. New York: Academic Press, 1972.

Greene, W. A., Goldstein, S., & Moss, A. J. Psychosocial aspects of sudden death. Archives of Internal Medicine, 1972, 129, 725-731.

Gross, E. Work, organization, and stress. In S. Levine & N. Scotch (Eds.), Social stress. Chicago: Aldine, 1970.

Hamilton, V., & Warburton, D. Human stress and cognition: An information processing approach. Chichester, England: John Wiley, 1979.

Harburg, E., Blakelock, E. H., & Roeper, P. Resentful and reflective coping with arbitrary authority and blood pressure: Detroit. Psychosomatic Medicine, 1979, 41, 189-202.

Harburg, E., Erfurt, J., Hauenstein, L., Chape, C., Schull, W., & Schork, M. Socio-ecological stress, suppressed hostility, skin color, and black-white male blood pressure: Detroit. Psychosomatic Medicine, 1973, 35, 276-296.

Harrison, R. V. Person-environment fit and job stress. In C. L. Cooper & R Payne (Eds.), Stress at work. New York: John Wiley, 1978.

Hawley, A. Human ecology: A theory of community structure. New York: Ronald Press, 1950.

Haynes, E. G., Levine, S., Scotch, N., Feinleib, M., & Kannel, W. B. The relationship of psychosocial factors to coronary heart disease in the Framingham Study. American Journal of Epidemiology, 1978, 107, 362-383.

Heller, K. The effects of social support: Prevention and treatment implications. In A. V. Goldstein & F. H. Kanfer (Eds.), Maximising treatment gains: Transfer enhancement in psychotherapy. New York: Academic Press, 1979.

Heller, K., & Monahan, J. Psychology and community change. Homewood, Ill.: Dorsey Press, 1977.

Hollingshead, A. B., & Redlich, F. L. Social class and mental illness. New York: John Wiley, 1958.

Holmes, T. H., Goodell, H., Wolf, S., & Wolff, H. G. The nose. An experimental study of reactions within the nose in human subjects during varying life experiences. Springfield, Ill.: Chas C.Thomas, 1950.

Holmes, T. H., & Masuda, M. Life change and illness susceptibility. In B. S. Dohrenwend & B. P. Dohrenwend (Eds.), Stressful life events: Their nature and effects. New York: John Wiley, 1974, 45-72.

Holmes, T., & Rahe, R. The social readjustment rating scale. Journal of Psychosomatic Research, 1967, 11, 213-218.

Insel, P. M., & Moos, R. (Eds.). Health and the social environment. Lexington, Mass.: Heath, 1974.

Jenkins, C. D. Behavioral risk factors and coronary artery disease. Annual Review of Medicine, 1978, 29, 543-562.

Johnson, J. H., & Sarason, I. G. Moderator variables in life stress research. In I. G. Sarason & B. D. Spielberger (Eds.), Stress and anxiety (Vol. 6). Washington, D.C.: Hemisphere Press, 1979.

Kaplan, B. J., Cassel, J. C., & Gore, S. Social support and health. Medical Care, 1977, 15(5) Supplement, 47–58.

Kasl, S. V., Cobb, S., & Brooks, G. W. Changes in serum uric acid and cholesterol levels in men undergoing job loss. Journal of the American Medical Association, 1968, 206, 1500–1507.

Kasl, S. V., Gore, S., & Cobb, S. The experience of losing a job: Reported changes in health, symptoms, and illness behavior. Psychosomatic Medicine, 1975, 3, 106–123.

Katz, D., & Kahn, R. L. The social psychology of organizations. New York: John Wiley, 1966.

Krantz, D. S., Glass, D. C., & Snyder, M. L. Helplessness, stress level, and the coronary prone behavior pattern. Journal of Experimental Social Psychology, 1974, 10, 284–300.

Lazarus, R. L. Psychological stress and the coping process. New York: McGraw-Hill, 1966.

Lazarus, R. L., & Launier, R. Stress-related transactions between person and environment. In L. A. Pervin & M. Lewis (Eds.), Perspectives in interactional psychology. New York: Plenum, 1978.

Leighton, D. C., Harding, J. S., Macklin, D. B., MacMillan, A. M., & Leighton, A. H. The character of danger. New York: Basic Books, 1963.

Levi, L. Society, stress, and disease: The psychosocial environment and psychosomatic diseases. London: Oxford University Press, 1971.

Levine, S., & Scotch, N. Social stress. Chicago: Aldine, 1970.

Lewin, K. A dynamic theory of personality. New York: McGraw-Hill, 1935.

Lewin, K. Principles of topological psychology. New York: McGraw-Hill, 1936.

Lewin, K. Field theory in social science. New York: Harper & Row, 1951.

Lewinsohn, P., & Graf, M. Pleasant activities and depression. Journal of Consulting and Clinical Psychology, 1973, 41, 261–268.

Lewinsohn, P., & Libet, J. Pleasant events, activity schedules, and depression. Journal of Abnormal Psychology, 1972, 79, 291–295.

Magnusson, D., & Ekehammar, B. Perceptions of and reactions to stressful situations. Journal of Personality
and Social Psychology, 1975, 31, 1147-1154.

Mann, P. Community psychology. New York: Free Press,
1978.

Markush, R. E., & Favero, R. V. Epidemiologic assessment
of stressful life events, depressed mood, and psychophysiological symptoms--A preliminary report. In
B. S. Dohrenwend & B. P. Dohrenwend (Eds.), Stressful life events: Their nature and effects. New York:
John Wiley, 1974.

Maruyama, M. The second cybernetics: Deviation-amplifying mutual causal processes. American Scientist, 1963,
51, 164-179.

Mason, J. W. A reevaluation of the concept of "nonspecificity" in stress theory. Journal of Psychiatric
Research, 1971, 8, 323-333.

Masuda, M., & Holmes, T. H. The social readjustment
rating scale: A cross-cultural study of Japanese and
Americans. Journal of Psychosomatic Research, 1967,
11, 227-237.

McGrath, J. E. (Ed.). Social and psychological factors in
stress. New York: Holt, Rinehart & Winston, 1970.

Mechanic, D. Discussion of research programs on relations
between stressful life events and episodes of physical
illness. In B. S. Dohrenwend & B. P. Dohrenwend
(Eds.), Stressful life events: Their nature and effects. New York: John Wiley, 1974.

Meyer, A. The life chart and the obligation of specifying
positive data in psychopathological diagnosis. In
E. E. Winters (Ed.), The collected papers of Adolf
Meyer (Vol. 3). Baltimore: Johns Hopkins Press,
1951.

Milgram, S. The experience of living in cities. Science,
1970, 167, 1461-1468.

Mitchell, J. C. (Ed.). Social networks in urban situations:
Analyses of personal relationships in Central African
towns. Manchester, England: Manchester University
Press, 1979.

Monahan, J., & Vaux, A. The macroenvironment and community mental health. Community Mental Health Journal, 1980, 16, 14-26.

Moos, R., & Van Dort, B. Student physical symptoms and
the social climate of college living groups. American
Journal of Community Psychology, 1979, 7, 31-43.

Mueller, D., Edwards, D., & Yarvis, R. Stressful life events and psychiatric symptomatology: Change or undesirability? Journal of Health & Social Behavior, 1977, 18, 307-317.

Murray, H. A. Preparations for the scaffold of a comprehensive system. In S. Koch (Ed.), Psychology: A study of a science (Vol. 3). New York: McGraw-Hill, 1959.

Nietzel, M. T., Winett, R. A., MacDonald, M. L., & Davidson, W. S. Behavioral approaches to community psychology. New York: Pergamon Press, 1977.

Novaco, R. W. The cognitive regulation of anger and stress. In P. Kendall & S. Hollon (Eds.), Cognitive Behavioral Interventions. New York: Academic Press, 1979.

Novaco, R. W., & Monahan, J. Research in community psychology: An analysis of work published in the first six years of the American Journal of Community Psychology. American Journal of Community Psychology, 1980, 8(2), 131-145.

Novaco, R. W., Stokols, D., Campbell, G., & Stokols, G. Transportation, stress, and community psychology. American Journal of Community Psychology, 1979, 7, 361-380.

Parkes, C. M., Benjamin, B., and Fitzgerald, R. G. Broken heart: A statistical study of increased mortality among widowers. British Medical Journal, 1969, 1, 740-743.

Pearlin, L. I., & Schooler, C. The structure of coping. Journal of Health and Social Behavior, 1978, 19, 2-21.

Pervin, L. A. Performance and satisfaction as a function of individual-environment fit. Psychological Bulletin, 1968, 69, 56-68.

Petrinovich, L. Probabilistic functionalism: A conception of research methods. American Psychologist, 1979, 34, 373-390.

Pierce, A. The economic cycle and the social suicides rate. American Sociological Review, 1967, 32, 457-462.

Popper, K. The open society and its enemies (Vol. 2). London: Routledge & Kegan Paul, 1957.

Price, R. H., & Blashfield, R. K. Explorations in the taxonomy of behavior settings: Analysis of dimensions and classifications of settings. American Journal of Community Psychology, 1975, 3, 335-351.

Rabkin, J. G., & Struening, E. L. Life events, stress and illness. Science, 1976, 194, 1013–1020.

Rahe, R. H. Multi-cultural correlations of life change scaling: America, Japan, Denmark and Sweden. Journal of Psychosomatic Research, 1969, 13, 191–195.

Rappaport, J. Community psychology: Values, research and action. New York: Holt, Rinehart & Winston, 1977.

Robinson, W. S. Ecological correlations and the behavior of individuals. American Sociological Review, 1950, 15, 352–357.

Ross, C. E., & Mirowsky, J. A comparison of life-event-weighting schemes: Change, undesirability, and effect-proportional indices. Journal of Health and Social Behavior, 1979, 20, 166–177.

Rule, B., & Nesdale, A. Environmental stressors, emotional arousal, and aggression. In I. G. Sarason & C. D. Spielberger (Eds.), Stress and anxiety (Vol. 2). Washington, D.C.: Hemisphere Press, 1975.

Sarason, I. G. Test anxiety, stress, and social support. Journal of Personality, in press.

Sarason, I. G., Johnson, J. H., & Siegel, J. M. Assessing the impact of life changes: Development of the Life Experiences Survey. Journal of Consulting and Clinical Psychology, 1978, 46, 932–946.

Sarason, I. G., & Spielberger, C. D. (Eds.). Stress and anxiety (Vol. 2). Washington, D.C.: Hemisphere Press, 1975.

Segal, B. E., Weiss, R. J., & Sokol, R. Emotional adjustment, social organization and psychiatric treatment rates. American Sociological Review, 1965, 30, 548–556.

Seligman, M. Helplessness: On depression, development, and death. San Francisco: W. H. Freeman, 1975.

Selye, H. The stress of life. New York: McGraw-Hill, 1976.

Shaw, C., & McKay, H. Juvenile delinquency and urban areas. Chicago: University of Chicago Press, 1942.

Smith, R. E., Johnson, S. H., & Sarason, I. G. Life change, the sensation seeking motive and psychological distress. Journal of Consulting and Clinical Psychology, 1978, 46, 348–349.

Srole, L., Langner, T. S., Michael, S. T., Opler, M. K., & Rennie, T. A. C. Mental health in the metropolis. New York: McGraw-Hill, 1962.

Stokols, D. The experience of crowding in primary and secondary environments. Environment and Behavior, 1976, 8, 49–85.

Stokols, D. Origins and directions of environment-behavioral research. In D. Stokols (Ed.), Perspectives on environment and behavior: Theory, research, and applications. New York: Plenum, 1977.

Stokols, D. Environmental psychology. Annual Review of Psychology, 1978, 29, 253-295.

Stokols, D. A congruence analysis of human stress. In I. G. Sarason & C. D. Spielberger (Eds.), Stress and anxiety (Vol. 6). Washington, D.C.: Hemisphere Press, 1979.

Stokols, D., & Novaco, R. W. Transportation and well-being: An ecological perspective. In I. Altman, J. Wohlwill, & P. Everett (Eds.), Human behavior and environment: Advances in theory and research, Vol. 5: Transportation environments. New York: Plenum, 1981.

Stokols, D., Novaco, R. W., Stokols, J., & Campbell, G. Traffic congestion, Type-A behavior, and stress. Journal of Applied Psychology, 1978, 63, 467-480.

Stout, C., Morrow, H., Brandt, E., & Wolf, S. Unusually low incidence of death from myocardial infarction in an Italian-American community in Pennsylvania. Journal of the American Medical Association, 1964, 188, 845-849.

Theorell, T. Life events before and after the onset of a premature myocardial infarction. In B. S. Dohrenwend & B. P. Dohrenwend (Eds.), Stressful life events: Their nature and effects. New York: John Wiley, 1974.

Thomas, W., & Znaniecki, F. The Polish peasant in Europe and America (Vol. 2). New York: Knopf, 1920.

Tolman, E. C., & Brunswik, E. The organism and the causal texture of the environment. Psychological Review, 1935, 42, 43-77.

Trickett, E. J., & Quinlan, D. M. Three domains of classroom environment: Factor analysis of the classroom scale. American Journal of Community Psychology, 1979, 7, 279-291.

Vinokur, R., & Selzer, M. L. Desirable versus undesirable life events: Their relationship to stress and mental distress. Journal of Personality and Social Psychology, 1975, 32, 329-337.

Welford, A. T. Stress and performance. Ergonomics, 1973, 16, 567-575.

Wolff, H. G., Wolf, S., & Hare, C. C. Life stress and bodily disease. Baltimore: Williams & Wilkins, 1950.

Zax, M., & Specter, G. A. An introduction to community psychology. New York: John Wiley, 1974.

10 Seven Approaches for the Study of Community Phenomena

Thomas D'Aunno, Donald C. Klein, and Edwin C. Susskind

This chapter briefly surveys seven approaches for community inquiry developed by social researchers from various disciplines. The seven include action research, community self-survey, case study, participant observation, simulation, epidemiology, and social indicators. These diverse approaches and techniques share in common the fact that they offer useful, often ingenious means for addressing the study of community phenomena.

Unlike other chapters in this volume, which are intended to deepen understanding of single research methods, this chapter surveys a variety of approaches: some of these have been treated elsewhere in texts on community psychology (that is, epidemiology and social indicators); some may be considered qualitative orientations rather than distinct research technologies (that is, case study, participant observation); some represent attempts to integrate inquiry and action that for the most part have contributed more to action than to research (that is, action research, community self-survey); and one can serve as a useful research tool within various approaches to community study (that is, simulation). Because it is impossible within the scope of this volume to examine them in detail, we discuss each approach briefly and supply references for those who wish to delve more deeply.

The approaches are by no means separate and distinct from one another. Participant observation, for example, lends itself to the development of case studies of cultures and complex systems; and community self-survey might well be included as part of an action-research project which assesses community needs and resources. The approaches are presented in order along a continuum which roughly reflects the degree of researcher involvement in efforts to change the phenomenon under study. At one end are approaches in which the researcher is engaged collaboratively with subjects and offers feedback from the inquiry process in order to alter the phenomenon being studied (for example, action research); at the other end are methods in which the researcher remains an observer-analyst who neither has personal contact with subjects nor attempts to change the phenomena via feedback or other means (for example, social indicators).

The discussion of each approach is divided into three major sections: (1) a general overview which provides a brief historical perspective, a general description of the approach, and a discussion of its defining and distinctive features; (2) a concrete example from the literature which offers a moderately detailed demonstration of how the approach was utilized; and (3) a critical appraisal of the approach's pitfalls and potentials.

ACTION RESEARCH

Though the concept of using inquiry to facilitate social change had emerged within adult education and social reform circles prior to World War II, the term action research appears to have been introduced by Lewin (1946) and elaborated further by other social and organizational psychologists (for example, Chein, Cook, & Harding, 1948; French & Bell, 1973; Price & Cherniss, 1977; Sanford, 1970).[1] Action research integrates theory building and social intervention. Its basic premise is that in order to gain insight into the dynamics of a social process, one should attempt to change it (Marrow, 1969). Action research is thus distinguished from other approaches to inquiry in three ways: (1) it attempts to change the behavior of individuals, groups, and organizations in order to advance knowledge of general behavioral principles; (2) it is conducted in a naturalistic setting; and (3) it combines knowledge building with the aim of engaging members of the setting in gathering and interpreting data in order to be of practical help to them.

It is its explicit commitment to knowledge building which distinguishes action research from other types of social intervention. Action researchers are in a particularly advantageous position to use their knowledge of social science theory to enhance the process of community change. Moreover, theory, even as it guides the course of action, may be developed or revised continuously as a consequence of its application to a social problem.

Action research is further distinguished from certain other approaches to inquiry by its commitment to collaboration between researchers and clients, or "subjects," of the inquiry. Community members work with action researchers to identify needs and to carry out ameliorative or preventive interventions. When clients are participants in research rather than "subjects," they are more likely to contribute to the design of the overall project, be familiar with the practical problems of implementation, utilize the findings of the research, and contribute to the understanding of implications of the findings for both action and theory.

The Cycle of Action Research

The process of action research, guided by both client and researcher, moves through several stages.

1. Diagnosis. Subsequent to an initial exploratory client-researcher contact, both parties engage in a general diagnosis or analysis of the setting. They use the data at hand to design an intervention or action program to meet the client's needs. The client's input is essential as the specific goals and components of the intervention are outlined. The researcher uses specific theoretical concepts to understand the client's situation and to develop the intervention. Tentative hypotheses, derived from established theories or findings, are also generated at this time.

2. Preintervention data collection. Data are collected and analyzed to identify needed changes and to design the means for achieving them. Preintervention data serve three purposes: first, to provide baseline measures by which to determine the success of the intervention; next, to serve as an initial data base for use following the intervention as a means of verifying theoretically based hypotheses generated at the outset of the inquiry; finally,

to check out assumptions about the individuals and social setting for whom the intervention is designed in order to determine whether the projected action plan is appropriate.

3. Data gathering during the action phase. Data typically are collected at multiple predesignated points during the intervention phase. These data serve two main purposes: they provide insights into participants' responses to change and their ways of coping with it, thereby enriching knowledge and theory about the social processes involved; and they help the researchers assess the efficacy of their efforts and identify needed modifications either of means or goals.

Far from waiting for final results of an intervention or completion of the analysis of outcome data, the action-researcher becomes immersed from the outset in the dynamics of the phenomena being studied and typically engages in creative reflection on the data as they become available. New concepts are formulated and hypotheses generated as possible "explanations" for what is being observed at each point, only to be discarded or modified in the light of subsequent observations. Data are usually shared with clients both as a means of enlisting their help in interpreting findings and as a way of helping them understand and cope more effectively with the phenomena. Over the years a number of ingenious and impactful methods have been designed within the action-research orientation for feedback of data to the coparticipants (Mann, 1957). Such gathering and feedback of survey and other data have become a powerful part of the basic tool kit of organization development consultants and other applied researchers (Bowers, 1973).

4. Postintervention data collection and evaluation. Postintervention measures usually include both those used during the second stage as well as others which have suggested themselves during the course of the intervention. Outcome data are intended to accomplish two main purposes: first, to indicate the extent to which change objectives have been realized and, thus, to determine whether further intervention is indicated; and second, to provide additional clues as to the usefulness of concepts and hypotheses on which the intervention was based, thereby contributing to refinement of theory. It is in this fashion that during the course of each loop or cycle of action research, theories are tested even as social change is initiated to

meet community needs. Wherever possible, additional outcome data are collected at one or more intervals subsequent
to the intervention.

    5. The cycle continues. If the intervention proves
to be less than fully successful, another cycle of intervention (data collection, evaluation, analysis) may be initiated,
depending on the combined judgment of researchers and
clients. The cycle ideally continues until key objectives
for both action and research are realized or abandoned in
favor of more achievable alternatives.

    The fact that action research builds in iterative
loops uniquely suits it for examining long-term processes
of systemic change. The flexible stages outlined above
may be employed in the study of a wide variety of community phenomena having to do with how fundamental social
processes (for example, distribution of resources, management of differences, and leadership-followership dynamics)
unfold over time in real-life situations.

An Example of Action Research

    Saltman (1975) provides an example of action re-
search on racial discrimination in housing which further
clarified factors affecting compliance with legislation. A
community group was concerned about the apparent failure
of realtors to comply with antidiscrimination legislation.

    1. Diagnosis. An initial analysis of the community
in question suggested that there were widespread violations
of open housing legislation. Saltman sought to ameliorate
this problem and to test the hypothesis that federal laws
regulating realtors' behavior were not sufficient in and of
themselves to decrease discrimination in housing. Saltman
based his hypothesis on the theoretical principle that behavior is most strongly influenced by contingencies operating in a specific social setting. That principle implies
that legislation is ineffective unless violations are made
public and punished. Thus, although real estate companies
might be aware of open housing legislation, they would
continue to discriminate against minorities so long as the
contingencies of the law were not being enforced.

    2. Preintervention data collection. One means to
document the existence of discrimination was to collect

data through "audits" of local realtors. The first audit included two phases: in one phase, trained volunteers from the community interviewed real estate executives to determine their overall awareness of open housing laws and practices. In phase two, six pairs of black and white volunteers were matched by age, family composition, and income level. They contacted 13 real estate companies for housing assistance and recorded their behavior on several criteria: locations offered, forms required, access to units, access to listings, price differentials, courtesy, and racial remarks.

An evaluation of the data collected during phases one and two revealed consistent, systematic discrimination by 12 of 13 companies. The results also showed that 76% of the companies had specific knowledge and awareness of open housing laws. The data thus supported the initial hypothesis that legislation alone is not sufficient to bring about social change.

3. Intervention. On the basis of the data and the original hypothesis a series of interventions were planned and implemented to (a) present the findings to the public at a community meeting (b) notify real estate companies of the findings, and (c) present the data to the U.S. Department of Justice for possible legal action.

4. Postintervention data collection and evaluation. As a result, the justice department began an investigation into housing discrimination. The local board of realtors initiated action to inform realtors of open housing laws and met with representatives of the community on the issue.

5. The cycle continued. Subsequently, two similar audits assessed discrimination in apartment leasing. Resulting interventions effected significant reductions in patterns of discrimination.

The action research thus decreased discrimination in housing and furthered understanding of the relationship between legislation and social change by demonstrating that to reduce discrimination in housing, it was necessary to enforce legislation and to publicize that enforcement, thereby bringing about changes in the contingencies governing realtors' behavior.[2]

Pitfalls and Prospects

The action-research paradigm, more than 30 years old, has so far failed to fulfill the great promise that

Lewin and others have envisioned. Indeed, we were not able to find an example for this chapter of a project which would exemplify an ideal interweaving of applied intervention with an in-depth exploration of a major theoretical question. According to Lewin's model, it should be possible for this interweaving to occur in two ways. First, action research asserts that the concepts and hypothesized relationships of psychological theorists can offer practical implications relevant to the solution of real-world in vivo problems. These implications can be used to guide an interventionist, influencing the change agents' conceptualization of the problem and their choice of strategies for dealing with it. Let us label this "the principle of intervention guided by theory."

Second, action research asserts that the act of intervention can, in turn, lead to the development of theory. The setting in which the research occurs becomes a context for testing the theory and its corollaries. The outcome of the attempted change (recorded in both formal and informal observations) either confirms a particular theoretical position or calls for its modification. Let us label this "the principle of theory modified by intervention."

One can argue that both these principles are only minimally demonstrated or fulfilled in the Saltman example. Saltman's study is an example of how action research has been used as a tool for social change, which is grounded in what might be called a theory of social engineering to which it makes a modest contribution. By modest we mean that the theoretical proposition explored by Saltman appears to have drawn more on common sense than on established theoretical constructs. With regard to the principle of intervention guided by theory, one can readily imagine that a change agent, with no theoretical background in social science, might have proposed the same set of interventions. Similarly, with regard to the principle of theory modified by intervention, one is hard pressed to see how the findings of the study led to a sizable confirmation, rejection, or modification of theory.

How does one explain the apparent discrepancy between the presumed potential of action research for contributing to theory building by becoming involved in social change, on the one hand, and the paucity of powerful examples, on the other? Should one reject the model as impractical and unrealizable? We have three points to make about these questions.

First, we are not prepared to dismiss action research. The problem is not that action research has been attempted and has failed but rather that it has rarely been attempted. The fact is that serious attempts to use the approach in a theoretically grounded fashion are virtually absent from the literature. This fact leads us to revise our questions and ask, "Why have there been so few implementations of action research?"

Second, in reply, we note the possibility that the approach may well be appropriate for only a small number of researchers who, like Lewin, are capable of actualizing its potential. There are some psychologists who have the predilection and skill to generate new, impactful interventions. There are others who are brilliant in generating theories which capture our imagination and help make sense of our experience. However, there are relatively few who innovate brilliantly—or even comfortably—in both spheres. That combination, in fact, was the rare genius of Lewin.

Third, it may also be possible that the problem derives neither from an inherent impracticality of the action-research model nor from individuals' difficulties in gaining simultaneous expertise in intervention and theory building. Rather, it may be that the fault lies in our current approaches to theory building. On the one hand, we generate psychological theories that deal primarily with the micro-level behavior of individuals, behavior that is readily amenable to analog testing in the laboratory. On the other hand, we abdicate attempts to generate psychological theories which have concrete, immediate implications for macro-level social phenomena because such phenomena are not readily amenable for study within our traditional research settings, that is, the undergraduate subject pool in the campus laboratory.

A second potential problem emerges from the method's reliance on feedback of data to participants while a study is in progress. Such feedback introduces serious questions about possible contamination of the phenomena because of the nature of the inquiry process itself. Given the traditional emphasis on the importance of avoiding such contamination by maintaining separation of researcher and subject, it is possible that more than one generation of researchers has decided that such possibilities are too big a price to pay for the potential gain—however great—of a more dynamic analysis of complex social processes.

In a different context of what constitutes acceptable inquiry, however, researchers might well conclude just the opposite--namely, that the possible failure to understand the subtleties of real-life complex social processes resulting from the failure to use action is too great a price to pay for the acknowledged gain in objectivity and precision which results from using more traditional but less revealing methods. Traditional methods have favored precision of measurement and purity of design over richness of data and involvement in changing social processes. This bias (or choice) has been attributed largely to the dichotomy between action and research in the social sciences and their training programs (Price & Cherniss, 1977; Sanford, 1970).

The separation of research and practice begins in graduate school, where students are taught conceptions of each that are largely incompatible. "Control groups, analyses of variance, and other tools of research as they are taught even today are simply inconsistent with practice which largely involves intensive contact with individuals for long periods of time" (Price & Cherniss, 1977; p. 223). This dichotomy has been dictated in part by the historical demand that social sciences be as "pure" as natural sciences. The thrust toward division of labor in society at large has further widened the gulf between researchers and practitioners.

Yet another barrier to basing action research on theoretical concepts is that many current theories of social behavior have been developed and studied in laboratory rather than natural settings. As a result, they lend themselves neither to description nor prediction of community phenomena as they naturally occur.

Several graduate-training programs in community psychology are addressing such problems by creating curricula which integrate action and research (see Rappaport, 1977; Price & Cherniss, 1977). Joining these disparate camps may prove difficult. The separation between action and research is well established. For the pure social researcher, action research represents a radical departure from the traditional separation of researcher and subject which has exemplified, though not always enriched, scientific inquiry in psychology. The action-research orientation itself has been preempted by social practitioners within the field of organization development. For them, the involvement of clients in data gathering and analysis is both ideologically sound and practically effective. The approach works because it helps them meet their objectives as agents of change.

The case studies and theoretical formulations which emerge from the efforts of such organizational change agents bear little or no resemblance to the conceptual frameworks offered within the mainstream of social psychology. The data with which they deal rarely resemble the less complex data from the laboratory. They study changes which have real-life consequences for those with whom they are working; their populations are by no means hypothetical. Moreover, they are not able to omit from their purview phenomena which cannot fit neatly into a priori formulations or controlled observations.

The implications of action research for community inquiry are clear from the work of practitioners in social change. If the gulf can be bridged, then action research may be able to meet its promise of adding to knowledge and theory about complex, real-life events which have significant consequences for community life, events which can be fully understood and appreciated only by well-conceived, in-depth in vivo studies. If so, it will become a major tool for theory building and knowledge development for use in coming to grips with many of the complex social phenomena of greatest interest to community psychology.

COMMUNITY SELF-SURVEY

Over the years researchers have learned much about the life of communities by collaborating with community members to organize fact-finding investigations termed community self-surveys (Hunter, Schaffer, & Sheps, 1956; Warren, 1965).[3] In a community self-survey, citizens work with researchers to design and conduct an inquiry concerning some facet of community life (for example, racial or religious discrimination and health needs). Community self-surveys differ from other surveys in that community members are involved as inquirers. The premise for involving community members is that when citizens advance proposals based on their own assessment of unmet needs, those proposals for change will be more apt to carry widespread support. Thus, one goal of involving community members is to mobilize them for action to meet the needs identified by the survey research (Kimball, 1955).

Community self-surveys originated in the late 1940s and 1950s with work done by the Commission on Community Interrelations (CCI), a group organized by Kurt Lewin (Cook, 1949). The CCI was concerned with racial discrimination in community life and, hence, they used the term community self-survey exclusively to refer to research concerning interracial relations. Since that time the term has been used to refer to survey research concerning a wide range of community phenomena, most particularly having to do with the availability of health services and citizens' satisfaction with them (Hunter, Schaffer, & Sheps, 1956).

The term survey has many meanings. It can denote a study of the strengths and weaknesses of a large community, involving several staff persons for several months, or it can refer to a brief study of the conditions of a particular organization (Warren, 1965). Three dimensions along which surveys vary are discussed below.

Dimensions of Surveys

Goal: Information versus Action

Surveys can be designed primarily for information gathering or as a first step toward an intervention or action program. Researchers as well as community members may be interested in learning more about social processes or conditions for theoretical reasons or simply to better inform themselves. In practice, however, community self-surveys are usually the first phase of action projects and are often followed by planning and social intervention. Surveys set the characteristic cycle of action rsearch into motion.

Breadth: Range of Issues Examined

Surveys vary according to the scope or number of areas they attempt to sample (for example, welfare, health, education, recreation, economics). If one were interested in a distinct aspect of the community such as education, a more intensive survey might be possible. Surveys can be specifically designed to assess a community's need for a particular service or facility (for example, day-care center).[4] Surveys of larger scope are almost always more superficial in nature. Nevertheless, they can be helpful to a community group which seeks to establish priorities as it responds to a wide range of competing needs, interests, and concerns.

Leadership: Volunteer and Professional Involvement

Though community self-surveys have been conducted without professional guidance, professionals typically are involved. Community psychologists or other applied researchers provide technical assistance (in such areas as helping citizens clarify questions and define them in measurable terms) and train volunteers to gather and analyze data.

Client-Inquirer Collaboration

As noted above, the community self-survey approach is characterized by extensive collaboration between professional researchers and community members. In fact, community members, or clients, determine much of the nature of the research, often deciding the content areas of the survey, the sample size, and how results will be utilized. Three aspects of client-inquirer collaboration are discussed briefly in this section.

Community Sponsorship

Community self-surveys usually have been initiated by social or business organizations including, for example, service clubs, chambers of commerce, churches, women's clubs, and farm bureaus. Community sponsorship of a survey is important: it lends prestige to the inquiry and gives it some standing in the community. If an "outsider" researcher initiates a study, he or she should attempt to work with a community sponsor. At the same time, however, not all community groups are suitable sponsors. Choosing a sponsor involves careful planning:

> Is the organizaton considered to represent only one particular economic group? Is it considered to prefer its own selfish interests to those of the larger community? If this organization is sponsor, will large segments of the community feel alienated? Can this organization act as sponsor without "taking

over" the survey and using it merely for
its own aggrandizement or to promote the
special economic interests of its members?
(Warren, 1965, p. 303)

If no existing organization can act as sponsor, it may be
necessary to organize a council or committee, which should
be both representative of the community and familiar with
the aspect of the community under study (Warren, 1965).

Technical Assistance

Though the clients often determine the goals of the
survey, the researcher must provide technical assistance
to help them meet their goals. In many instances, the
experts apply their knowledge of research procedures to
facilitate the work of community leaders.

Follow-Up

Client-inquirer collaboration continues at least until
the results of the survey are presented to the community.
Presenting the results is important regardless of whether
they will be used to formulate interventions. At the very
least, reporting the results of information-gathering surveys contributes to building awareness of community
strengths and weaknesses. Further, it is both considerate
and politic to provide recognition for individuals and
organizations who helped conduct the survey.

If the survey is intended to provide a data base
for remedial action, inquirers typically work with clients
to establish priorities for the needs expressed in the survey, plan interventions, and make recommendations to
other service organizations in the community.

An Example of Community Self-Survey

The Pittsburgh Neighborhood Atlas project is an instructive example of a community self-survey (Ahlbrandt,
Charny, & Cunningham, 1977). One of the problems confronting neighborhood leaders, city planners, and elected
officials is a lack of information about neighborhoods. In
many cases they need data to monitor changes in neighborhoods, identify neighborhood problems, assess citizens'
attitudes toward public services, and plan for the delivery

of services. Members of the Pittsburgh Neighborhood Association, a coalition of several neighborhood groups, decided to conduct a city-wide survey in order to identify
the boundaries of Pittsburgh's neighborhoods and to develop an information system to aid decisionmakers. Social
scientists and city planners were invited to work along
with neighborhood leaders.

Method

The first task was to identify neighborhood boundaries throughout the city. Community volunteers met with
residents from 40 areas of the city in order to determine
their perceptions of neighborhood boundaries. At meetings
held in schools and churches, residents were asked to
draw maps indicating the boundaries of their neighborhoods.
In addition, a mail survey (sent to 10,000 residents) was
used to gather data on citizens' perceptions of boundaries.
Social scientists contributed to this phase of the project by
developing a data management system which stored the results of the survey on computers. The outcome was a city-
wide map comprised of 78 neighborhods, ranging in size
from a few hundred citizens to nearly 30,000.

The next phase of the project involved gathering
data on economic, demographic, and quality-of-life characteristics of each neighborhood. Included in the economic
indicators, for example, were measures of neighborhood
income, demand and supply of mortgage and home improvement loans, and residential real estate prices. Demographic
data included measures of family size and racial composition. Among the quality-of-life indicators were ratings of
satisfaction with public services, identification of neighborhood problems, and reasons for dissatisfaction with services. Once again researchers worked with neighborhood
leaders to collect data, using both a mail survey and
archival data. The result or product of the survey was
an "atlas" containing a wide range of information for each
neighborhood.

Utilization

The information was disseminated throughout the
city in a variety of ways. The Pittsburgh Neighborhood
Alliance, for example, held workshops to explain how to
interpret atlas data. Two hundred and fifty atlases were
printed and distributed to residents, neighborhood groups,

and human service providers. Within one month there were more than 200 additional requests for atlases. In addition, a computer terminal was purchased for use by community members. Technicians assisted the community members in using the terminal to gain further access to the survey data.

Though there has not been an evaluation of the impact of the data on community decision making, it is clear that the project itself prompted diverse segments of the community to work together. When coupled with adequate survey data, such partnerships provide a strong foundation for action to improve community life.

Pitfalls and Prospects

As with action research, the fact is that community self-survey has not been widely employed as a basic research tool for adding to our understanding of social process. From the outset it has been used primarily as a practical means of motivating people to initiate and support community change. To quote one of its major theoreticians and protagonists, "The basic hypothesis is that a self-survey as compared with surveys of other types is more likely to be followed by changes in the social practices of the community" (Cook, 1949, p. 2). Though no controlled study has been done to compare the effectiveness of self-surveys and other methods for introducing social change, the self-survey method appears to have certain potential advantages:

1. It is a comparatively low-cost means of generating needed information about an area of community concern.
2. The information, because it is generated and shared by a highly committed group of citizens, becomes a community resource.
3. Residents who have been involved in the self-survey process are apt to be highly motivated to become involved in actions to meet community needs revealed by the inquiry itself.
4. The knowledge, skills, and understanding gained by citizens because of their participation in the self-survey are available to the community when future needs and issues arise.

5. The involvement of local residents enables researchers to gain a more vivid and realistic awareness of a community's strengths and weaknesses as well as a more intimate understanding of less readily observable dynamics.

By its very nature the community self-survey approach recognizes the inherently political nature of virtually all community inquiry. Traditional community inquiry has been based on a relationship between researcher and subject which tends to enrich the former, who gain knowledge, reputation, position, and income, without any guarantee of equal return to the latter, who often has no way of translating research findings into community practice. A number of social scientists, notably Margaret Mead, have questioned both the appropriateness and ultimate value of basing community inquiry on such an uneven exchange (Mead, 1969). In recent years an alliance of radical social interventionists and adult educators has translated these gnawing concerns into a model for participatory research in which the researcher becomes both ally and advocate of heretofore disempowered groups (Hall & Gillette, 1978). The international movement for participatory research combines the action-research, applied anthropology, and community self-study traditions within the framework of a radical orientation designed to foster the dignity, independence, and ability of oppressed peoples to take control of their lives (Hall & Gillette, 1978). Participatory research advocates question traditional community research on several grounds:

1. Insistence on quantitative methods results in superficial and inaccurate understanding of complex reality.
2. Casting individuals and community groups in the role of passive objects to be studied runs counter to the democratic-humanistic ideal of participative citizenship.
3. Separating knowledge production from matters of practical application results in large segments of inquiry which are useless as a knowledge base for dealing with urgent and complicated areas of social concern.
4. Those served by traditional social researchers are more often administrators or policymakers rather than those citizens from whom information is gathered and who are ultimately affected by policies and procedures which they have not directly participated in establishing.

5. Research which treats respondents merely as sources of information fails to create an environment which actively supports desired changes stemming from inquiry.

The term <u>participatory research</u> refers to efforts in both developing and developed countries to involve those who are traditionally the "researched" in the formulation of the inquiry, data collection, and interpretation of findings. Guidelines for participatory research have emerged from exchanges between about 80 researchers in several countries (Hall and Gillette, 1978). They include the following principles:

1. A research process can be of immediate and direct benefit to a community.
2. A community gains both from the results of the research and the research process itself if its members are as much involved as the researcher in the process of discussion, investigation, and analysis.
3. Rather than grounding research in theory brought or developed by the researcher, the community goes through a process of developing its own theories and solutions about itself.
4. The research process involves "a dialogue over time," not a static focus on one point in time.
5. The aim of research is to liberate creative potentials within the community and thereby mobilize human resources for the solution of community problems.
6. There is a need to examine the ideological implications of any community research process because knowledge placed at the disposal of one set of clients gives them increased potential for powerful political action.

Apart from considerations of values having to do with democratic participation and empowerment of oppressed groups, participatory research advocates hold that participative orientations are essential to successful knowledge building in the community. They point out that "community" is at one and the same time an objective phenomenon which exists and has continuity apart from its specific residents and a subjective phenomenon which can be understood only in terms of the viewpoints and values of those residents. According to Freire (1974), "concrete reality is the connection between subjectivity and objectivity; never objectivity isolated from subjectivity" (p. 134).

Fundamental community processes become understandable only by addressing the connections between subjectivity and objectivity. Traditional research eliminates the subjective and is not, therefore, capable of focusing on those connections. Whether grounded in an ameliorative or more radical model of social change, the community self-survey process is one means whereby community researchers can contribute to a more vigorous political and problem-solving process.

From the outset of a self-survey the research team is confronted by political considerations. These have to do with such essential questions as "which citizens will be encouraged to participate?" and "at what level of influence and power?" A heterogeneous group of community sponsors reduces the likelihood that one particular segment of the community will gain control of the research and thereby attain the power to unduly influence its outcome. On the other hand, the very heterogeneity of sponsorship tends to ensure that the research process will not produce a fundamental shift in the power dynamics of the locale. A coalition of previously low-power groups as sponsors of the research may represent a step in the direction of increased influence of those groups in the community; it also may mean that important aspects of the community will be less accessible to study and that the chances of implementing needed change will be reduced because high-power groups have not been included in the process.

The very selection of the focus for the research is a political act. Representatives from one section of a city, for example, may undertake a self-survey to "demonstrate" the need for a new hospital in their area as opposed to other areas. Survey data often have implications for public policy decisions. The survey process itself influences the extent to which various stakeholders will become involved in the decision-making process. Depending on how they are used and who is involved, community self-surveys may contribute to community cohesiveness or dissension as various individuals and groups seek to gain or maintain power in the interests of advancing economic or other interests, achieving their version of social justice, or attaining other ends. Those involved in the self-survey process are often drawn together in a continuing network; hitherto diverse elements of the community often achieve a level of mutual respect and trust never before possible; collaborative interaction of such groups may help the

community achieve a degree of consensus on priorities which
will provide the foundation for mutual efforts for some time
in the future.

The self-survey process requires considerable commitment on the part of the researcher to citizen participation
and control as well as skill in bringing it about. The
patience, persistence, and energy required to mobilize
citizen interest, build a viable collaborative effort, train
and supervise interviewers and data analysts, and involve
citizens in the interpretation of findings represent a high
level of investment for the researcher. The question which
any community researcher must confront is whether a sufficient depth of understanding and insight into community
phenomena can be gained in any less demanding way.
The fact that self-surveys have not been extensively used
for basic community inquiry suggests that so far community
psychologists and other researchers have not known how to
go about the process or have not expected the results to be
worth the effort. We believe that the self-survey method
will become increasingly attractive and will be used more
extensively as community psychologists turn increasingly to
studying fundamental community processes. As noted elsewhere in this book, community researchers have all too
often studied micro-level rather than macro-level events
(for example, the adjustment of individual children in a
classroom rather than how the interplay between different
segments of a community ultimately affects what goes on in
all classrooms). As they address macro-level phenomena,
community psychologists may well join the ranks of those
radicalized scientists and educators who hold that community research without full participation of those being
studied is counterproductive both for democracy and sound
research.

CASE STUDY

As we use it here, the term case study refers to an
in-depth, qualitative description and analysis of the behavior either of a single individual, group, organization,
or community or of a collection of individuals or collectiv-
ities which are dealing with a specific type of event or
situation. The case study method is one of the best ways
of organizing social data so as to preserve the unitary

character of the social object being studied while illuminating events and processes over time.

In-depth case studies usually offer multifaceted views of the phenomena being presented, including careful description of events and aspects of the situation, a historical component, and an emphasis on the experiencer(s) of the phenomena. They require involvement of subjects as allies of the researcher, an alliance which often is achieved only by greatly reduced distance between researcher and researched. Levinson (1978, p. 47) describes the tone of the case study interview as "one of the consultant and interviewee working together . . . so that the consultant will know as well as possible what this person's work experiences are and what they mean to him."

Most readers are aware that the case study method is used by historians, for example, to provide biographical accounts of cultural, political, and religious leaders (Neale & Liebert, 1973). They are also aware that the case study method is used in a wide range of disciplines including medicine, clinical psychology, law, business administration, sociology, and anthropology (Bennis, 1968). Indeed, there are few disciplines having to do with human affairs which have not made meaningful use of the case study method in one form or another. A variety of approaches to case study have developed over the years. We have chosen to divide them into three basic categories. The first category has typically involved a "clinical" intervention in which the researcher gains information from an individual client or client system in exchange for helping the client. In the classic clinical case study the physician enlists the patient as an observer of his or her body's response to a succession of treatments. Psychoanalytic and other in-depth clinical approaches to treatment of psychiatric problems represent an extension of the clinical case study approach to the psychological and psychosomatic realms. Indeed, Freud's most significant contribution to the field of personology may well have been his creation of a new form of clinical laboratory in which the tools of free association, analysis of the transference, and dream analysis could be used to great advantage in the in-depth study of personality development.

A second major category of case studies has adapted the clinical model in order to study more complex human systems, such as communities and organizations. In such cases, social researchers have gained access to complex social organizations on an ongoing basis by offering in exchange their consulting, training, and action-research skills in the interests of systemic problem solving. Much of the theory and practice within the field of organization development has been derived from such in-depth case studies developed by systemic change agents. A major outlet for such material has been the Journal of Applied Behavioral Science, most issues of which contain at least one case study of a particular system, type of organization, or social process.

A third category departs from the clinical-interventionist model and is more purely descriptive in nature. That is, the case study is conducted without the framework of a help-seeking or help-giving relationship.

Such nonclinical descriptive case studies can be either retrospective, current, or prospective in nature. Retrospective studies make use of informants to recreate the sequence of events, critical incidents, and significant social processes which characterized the phenomenon being studied. Examples include several revealing case studies of community decision making (for example, Martin et al., 1961) which revealed the tendency for different configurations of influentials to be involved in such disparate decisions as the building of a community hospital, the modernization of an airport, or the initiation of a major downtown renewal program.

Current case studies are cross-sectional in nature; they are concerned with phenomena which do not unfold over time. An example is the existential phenomenological study of reconciliation described by von Eckartsberg in his chapter in this volume. Another instance is the classic study of the role of the school superintendent based on Gross's probing interviews with a large sample of current school superintendents in Massachusetts (Gross et al., 1958).

Prospective case studies are designed to track a set of phenomena or the life trajectories of one or more persons over a specified time period. For example, Karsk (1977) engaged the services of a small number of adolescents who shared with him over a year's time their experiences within the physical and social milieu of the new town of Columbia, Maryland.

A variety of research tools are available to supplement information gained from case study interviews with the principal actor or actors. Having talked with and

observed one's patient or client (in the clinical-interventionist model) or one's coresearcher or informant (in the
nonclinical descriptive model), the inquirer may search
out information from at least three other major sources:
(1) secondary actors, whose interactions with the primary
actor(s) may serve as significant sources of understanding
about the latter's transactions with his or her relevant
environment; (2) observing informants, whose observations
may shed further light on the perceptions and behaviors
of the actors; and (3) nonobtrusive sources of information
which can be gathered without any need to interact with
one's subjects, for example, news reports and other public
records; diaries and letters; systematic time-sample observations; indicators of use, such as wear and tear on
floor surfaces in public places; and photographs, movies,
and videotapes.

Karsk's study of patterns of adolescent involvement
in the new town, for instance, combined weekly logs maintained by his informants with periodic interviews, questionnaires administered to samples of teenagers and their
parents, participant observation in activities involving
young people, casual observations of teenage behaviors
within public places such as the shopping mall, as well
as informal conversations with storekeepers, law enforcement officials, human service workers, and others with
whom teenagers come in contact.

An intriguing question for anyone using the case
study approach has to do with the scope of the inquiry.
It is usually desirable to incorporate, where possible, the
experiences and perspectives of all major actors within
the setting being studied. Where feasible, it is also often
desirable to enlist the help of observing informants who
are in a position to comment knowledgeably on what they
believe is happening or has already occurred. In situations involving controversy, it is wise to recognize that
the eye of the beholder views the same events from different and often opposing perspectives, depending on whether
the beholder is a bystander or advocate, and if the latter,
depending on with which side he or she is aligned. And
yet there are practical limitations having to do with time,
funding, and ease of access to phenomena which will influence where boundaries are set for any inquiry.

Case studies are partial in nature; they must abstract for our view only the highlights, and even those
highlights are illuminated via the colorations and intensities

of one's informants. In the case study there is no ultimate truth; there is only the experience of those involved
filtered through the conceptual lenses and empathic capacities of those conducting the study.

Apart from the scope of one's inquiry or the techniques used for developing a case study, at the heart of
the method is one's willingness to become immersed in the
perceptions, events, and contexts of the people involved.
Cottle (1977) has coined the term observant participation
for such immersion, in which one is basically interested in
recounting the essence of those lives which are the raw
materials of one's inquiry. At the heart of any case
study is the artistry of the inquirer. The test of that
artistry is whether the finished product evokes strong
feelings of recognition, surprise, wonder, and appreciation
from its readers.

Distinctive Characteristics

There are four distinctive characteristics of the
case study method:

1. Small number of subjects. Researchers select
no more than a few subjects; it is simply too expensive
and time consuming to gather detailed data on a large
number of cases.
2. Longitudinal time span. The approach is
longitudinal in nature. The subject of a case study is a
set of naturally occurring phenomena involving a series of
events which occur outside of a laboratory and which are
not manipulated by inquirers. Such phenomena usually
extend over a period of weeks, months, or even years.
Consider, for example, a community's decision to build a
new library. Deliberations by various decisionmakers--
including library board, city officials, and community
members--may delay the building of a facility for months
or even years.
3. Generation of hypotheses: Within the case study
approach, researchers typically begin to collect data with
more tentative, less detailed hypotheses than in experimental research. Rather than attempting to test hypotheses,
researchers using the case study approach are more concerned with providing a thorough, rigorous description of
the phenomena. To be sure, inquirers will rely on

"hunches" to guide initial data collection, but these loosely defined hypotheses are often revised during the course of the study.

4. Induction--generalizing from the particular. The approach is primarily inductive in nature. That is, one attempts to develop general principles based on analyses of particular situations or events. Researchers using the approach are, therefore, careful to observe the ways in which their subjects differ from and resemble other individuals, groups, organizations, or communities. Inquiry into the life of Paris, Missouri, for instance, is likely to shed only a limited amount of light on life in Paris, France. Thus, one must be particularly careful to delimit the population to which results may be generalized.

Methodological Considerations

Relying on self-report data from interviews, journals, or other sources poses a number of possible disadvantages well known to social researchers. Self-reports can often be inaccurate. Subjects anxious to present themselves in a favorable light, for example, may respond to interview questions with what they think they "should" say; that is, their responses are influenced by their perceptions of social desirability (Stern, 1979, p. 75). Similarly, when the researcher asks questions about events which happened in the past, respondents' memories are inevitably influenced by the well-known processes whereby recollections become simplified, elaborated, and otherwise distorted.

To compensate for errors introduced by such subjective procedures, it is desirable to use a multimethod approach to data gathering within a single case study and to base theory development on the careful analysis of a series of cases. It is possible to establish the convergence of findings arrived at via various data-gathering techniques, each of which has different "built-in" strengths and weaknesses.

As noted above, in addition to using interviews, questionnaires, and surveys, researchers can employ unobtrusive measures, that is, measures that do not require the cooperation of respondents and are obtained without their knowledge (Webb et al., 1966). There are three classes of unobtrusive measures: (1) archival records, (2) physical traces, and (3) observation.

Archival Records

Archival records are data periodically compiled for purposes other than the specific research project but which can be exploited for that project. For example, library withdrawals were used to demonstrate the effect of the introduction of television into a community. Fiction titles dropped; nonfiction titles were unaffected (Webb et al., 1966).

Physical Traces

There are two types of physical traces: erosion and accretion. Erosion involves selective wear on some material. The floor tiles around the hatching-chick exhibit at Chicago's Museum of Science and Industry, for example, must be replaced every six weeks. Tiles in other parts of the museum need not be replaced for years. The selective erosion of tiles, indexed by replacement rates, is a measure of the relative popularity of the exhibits. Accretion is the addition or deposit of a material. For example, one investigator wanted to learn the level of whiskey consumption in a town that was officially "dry." He did so by counting empty bottles in trash cans (Webb et al., 1966).

Observation

In observation, researchers have no control over the behavior in question and play an unobserved, passive, and nonintrusive role in a setting. For example, changes in patterns of clustering of black and white students in classrooms were observed as a measure of interracial relations at two colleges (Campbell, Kruskal, & Wallace, 1966).

An Example of the Case Study Method

A comparatively early application of the case study approach in community psychology is found in Klein and Ross's (1960) research on the impact of school entry on the family. It was hypothesized that kindergarten entry is an emotionally hazardous experience (that is, a period of quick transition marked by observable tensions within the family group) and that the transition period is marked by a regularly occurring sequence of phases (for example, initially heightened apprehension followed by a sense of loss and grief) over a limited time period.

Method

Participants in the study were parents of prekinder-gartners, recruited at general meetings held by parent-teacher groups in two middle-class communities. Forty-five mothers and nine fathers, representing 46 families, volunteered to participate.

A group interview technique was used to collect data. It involved weekly meetings of approximately two hours duration with six to ten parents per group. Each group also included a nonparticipant observer and a leader who facilitated group discussion (both were members of the research team). Participants were encouraged to pool information and observations regarding the behavior and reactions of the kindergartners, other siblings, and the parents themselves.

Variables Studied

The data included these variables: "(a) verbatim records of group discussions for each meeting; (b) observer notes on sequence of topics, as well as initiators and participants for each topic area; (c) observer ratings of group tension level and degree of involvement at intervals of approximately 5 to 10 minutes throughout each meeting" (Klein & Ross, 1960, p. 63).

At the conclusion of group meetings, each pair of leader-observers prepared a meeting-by-meeting summary of major themes, attempting to identify possible sequences in content and affect areas. Each group summary (which was conducted independently of analyses of every other group) was then compared to determine the degree to which sequences of content and affect were similar from group to group. In addition, a separate analysis was conducted on the verbatim records, and tabulations were made for reports of child behavior reflecting the following: increased tension; increased independence, responsibility, sociability, and other indications of maturity; parents' concerns about school entry; and factors facilitating or hindering adjustment to school, as judged by parents (Klein & Ross, 1960).

Results

The results supported the research hypotheses. Parents noted indicators of increased stress (for example, loss of appetite, fatigue, and upset stomach) and increased maturity (for example, cooperative play at home) in their children in the weeks immediately following kindergarten entry. Parents reacted to kindergarten entry with varying degrees of tension before the first day of school, feelings of loss, value conflicts (for example, desire to have the child learn how to conform to the group versus strong emphasis on the importance of maintaining individuality), and irritability associated with change in parental role (for example, annoyance with child for holding teacher as authority). These data suggest that interventions at the point of kindergarten entry may be useful to prevent school adjustment problems by helping families deal with the stress induced by role transition in ways which strengthen school-home collaboration.

Results also showed a consistent four-phase sequence of parental responses extending over approximately four to five weeks following school entry: first, a period of high tension prior to the first day of school; next, relief coupled with some depression once the child had successfully begun school; then attempts to redefine parental role and reconstruct meaningful parent-child ties; and, finally, reduction of tension and establishment of a new pattern of parent-child interactions that takes into account the role of the school. It was not until the final phase of the transition period, for example, that parents felt entirely comfortable visiting their children's kindergarten rooms.

Pitfalls and Prospects

Critics of the case study method claim that it lacks both internal and external validity. The Klein and Ross study, for example, presents problems of internal validity. It attempted to demonstrate a causal relationship between kindergarten entry and increases in stress. Except for the fact that several groups supplied data independent of one another in two different years, it is not possible to partial out the researchers' expectations or the parents' attempts, unconscious or otherwise, to satisfy those expectations. As noted above, to increase the internal validity of case study data, a collection of methods should be used where possible. Rarely should subjects' self-reports be the sole source of data collected in a case study. The Klein and Ross inquiry presents meaningful and plausible first findings which can be profitably pursued further using a multimethod approach.

Questions also remain about the extent to which the relationship between variables in the kindergarten entry study can be generalized to and across populations of persons, settings, and times. Subjects were volunteers recruited from one middle-class community by a mental health center. There was no way of assessing possible biases introduced by the nature of the participants in the study. Would the findings hold true for families from higher or lower socioeconomic classes? For nonvolunteers as well as willing participants? For those responding to nonmental health related researchers as well as those clearly identified with a mental health program? Problems of external validity arise in case studies because one can rarely choose subjects randomly so that they are truly representative of a particular population. Although not always economically or operationally feasible, it is desirable to increase external validity by conducting a series of case studies within a single problem area. A series of studies on school entry, for example, could vary across cities, be conducted by schools and other agencies as well as mental health centers, include nonvolunteers, and make use of observations made by school personnel or other independent observers as well as by parents. Taken together, the results of a set of such case studies would demonstrate the range of generalizability of the findings.

There are several advantages to using the case study method which derive from the distinctive features cited above. Two such advantages accrue because the method involves the description of naturally occurring community phenomena over extended periods of time. First, the method provides in-depth and detailed understanding of how processes unfold over time. Second, it allows the researcher to keep existing theory and technology open to change and refinement. It does so by virtue of the fact that with each case study the investigator is applying theory-related hypotheses to an in vivo situation in order to determine goodness of fit between theory and fact as revealed by the case and, where necessary, to modify theory in light of the case study. Theories originally developed in laboratory contexts are apt to be enriched when applied via case study method to complex natural settings. Similarly, the efficacy of techniques for both community interventions and inquiry may be judged on the basis of their use in case studies (Walton, 1972).

A third advantage of the case study results from its inductive nature. It is possible to draw general conclusions, however tentative, about how all or certain types of communities operate from the in-depth study of particular instances. The case study method has served as an important vehicle for the development of seminal new theories of community behavior. Some of the most generative hypotheses about community processes have emanated from case studies. An outstanding instance was Hunter's study (1953) of the power structure in a large city, which so energized the field that it resulted in a series of creative inquiries by a number of other investigators into the nature of community power.

Case studies also provide a unique opportunity to gain access to the perceptions and perspectives of those being studied. Understanding differences in participation and interpretation is essential to certain case studies (for example, of situations involving intergroup conflict); such richness in perspective is always desirable.

A final advantage derives from its insistence that the investigator pay careful attention to detailed and rigorous description. Such delineations of crucial phenomena are ideally suited to provide illustrations of prototypical behavior and/or unusual phenomena (Neale & Liebert, 1973).

Any community researcher addressing an aspect of community life which has not heretofore been investigated in depth would do well to begin with in-depth case studies. The case study method is a sine qua non for gaining an understanding in vivo of the natural history of a complex community phenomenon, including an appreciation of how the phenomenon unfolds over time, the critical issues to be faced by those involved, adaptive and maladaptive coping patterns, the involvement of relevant groups and institutions, and the meaning of the phenomenon to those caught up in it.

PARTICIPANT OBSERVATION

As noted above, the case study offers a means for approaching complex phenomena from a variety of perspectives, thereby enabling one to compare, for example, the views of an insider or participant with those of an outsider or observer. Within the field of social anthropology a tradition evolved which recognized that as one immerses oneself over time in the phenomena of a culture, inevitably one becomes drawn into the lives of those who are being studied. In effect, one becomes a participant as well as an observer. This threat to objectivity was at first viewed as an undesirable complication. However, once rigorously conceptualized, the inevitable combination of participation and observation, with its inherent subjectivity, offers one of the most profitable approaches to inquiry available to the community researcher (Bruyn, 1966).

Known as participant observation, the method enables researchers to both systematically observe and participate in the day-to-day life of the communities, organizations, and other social milieus being studied. The distinctive feature of participant observation is the degree of the researchers' involvement with those who, in other research contexts, would be considered the subjects of the inquiry (Selltiz, Wrightsman, & Cook, 1976). Participant observers seek to maintain face-to-face relationships with those whose lives they wish to understand. They are prepared to share in the daily experiences and to immerse themselves in the lives of the people being studied. By doing so, investigators are better able to understand a social phenomenon from the perspective of a person who is experiencing it. By participating in the phenomena under study, researchers also minimize certain barriers which typically exist between researcher and subject, such as sociocultural and linguistic dissimilarities. The researchers are thereby in a better position to gain a more intimate, accurate, and qualitatively rich understanding of complex social phenomena.

A full appreciation of the participant-observation approach requires that we examine the sociopolitical context within which it evolved. One leading anthropologist has noted that anthropology evolved in the context of an exploitative relationship between English imperialists and non-English colonies.

"Anthropology is the outcome of a historical process which has made the larger part of mankind subservient to the other, and during which millions of innocent human beings have had their institutions and beliefs destroyed, whilst they themselves were ruthlessly killed, thrown into bondage, and contaminated by diseases they were unable to resist. Anthropology is the daughter of this era of violence. Its capacity to assess more objectively the facts pertaining to the human condition reflects . . . the state of affairs in which one part of mankind treated the other as objects" [italics ours] (Levi-Strauss, 1966, p. 126).

Participant observation became an essential response for the anthropologist to avoid treating colonial peoples as objects, thereby perpetuating colonialist abuses. Anthropologists' concerns with the political/exploitative implication of a chosen research methodology is echoed in the values of a number of contemporary social researchers. Note, for example, the ecological position voiced by Trickett, Kelley, and Vincent in Chapter 7 of this book, concerning the collaborative relationship between researcher and the participant-subjects, as well as material in this chapter regarding the ideology of participatory research. Community psychology may do well to learn from anthropology's experience, namely, that the methodology of participant-observation fosters a disciplined, but nonexploitative, approach to knowledge building. Margaret Mead (1969), describing the field-study model used by her and her colleagues, writes:

"Anthropological research does not have subjects. We work with informants in an atmosphere of trust and mutual respect. . . . It stresses not only the importance of the relationship between a research worker and those among whom he seeks new knowledge, but also the possibility of substituting voluntary participation for 'informed consent' as a precondition of ethical research work" (p. 361).

Apart from anthropological field research, participant observation has long occupied a strategic place in the methodological tool box of community-oriented inquiry (Bell & Newby, 1972). In some instances, it has enabled researchers to study phenomena not otherwise accessible. For example, the behavior of street gangs and religious cults has been opened to social scientists who became members of such groups (for example, Festinger, Riecken, & Schachter, 1956). Along with the case study approach, participant observation shares the advantages of being able to contribute to the inductive development of theory, the refinement of hypotheses, and in-depth descriptions of complex community processes.

Methodological Considerations

This section discusses three areas of concern for participant observers: (1) formulation of hypotheses and delimiting field settings, (2) entry into field settings, and (3) the relationship between data collection and analysis.

Formulation of Hypotheseses and Delimiting Field Settings

Participant observation typically begins with only loosely defined or detailed hypotheses and imprecise delineation of the geographic area or other location in which data are to be collected (that is, the field setting). By virtue of such initial ambiguity, participant observers are able to take fullest possible advantage of their first-hand experience of the phenomena being studied. They are typically free both to develop, revise, and test hypotheses in view of their observations and to modify their definition of the physical boundaries within which they need to work as they learn more about the nature of the setting itself.

For example, in a study of a state institution for the profoundly retarded, a researcher "entered the setting with the intention of studying residents' perspectives on the institution only to find that many residents were non-verbal and many others were reluctant to speak openly about the institution. He then shifted his attention to attendants' perspectives, which proved to be a fruitful line of inquiry" (Bogdan & Taylor, 1975, p. 27).

Entry into Field Settings

The most fundamental entry question facing participant observers has to do with whether or not to reveal their identity as researchers to the members of a group or community. The implications and consequences of two alternative strategies are discussed briefly below (see also Gold, 1958, and Junker, 1960).

Covert Participation. In the strategy euphemistically termed "complete participation," observers entirely conceal their identity as researchers as they attempt to become full-fledged members of the group under study. A classic example of this approach is the study of a small group of persons who predicted the destruction of the world (Festinger, Riecken, & Schachter, 1956). "The nature of the group led the authors to believe that if they presented themselves as sociologists, entry would be denied, so they posed as persons genuinely interested in the unusual predictions of the group and soon were able to penetrate its boundaries and become full-fledged members" (Denzin, 1978, p. 186).

The covert approach enjoys the major advantage of enabling inquirers to gain access to settings where they would not be accepted as "social scientists." On the other hand, there are three problems with the approach. First, it is difficult for observers to conceal their lack of experience in or commitment to the setting. In the research described above, for example, an observer was asked to lead a group meeting—an action for which he was ill-equipped and which he handled rather awkwardly.

Second, it is difficult to enter fully and whole-heartedly as a participant in the life of a group, to be able to respond authentically to others' expectations and overtures and, at the same time, maintain the degree of apartness needed to conduct systematic observations.

Third, the ethics of covert participation are questionable. Some social scientists reject covert research, that is, research conducted without explicit consent of subjects (for example, Erikson, 1967), holding that such practice violates both the subjects' rights to privacy and the democratic spirit of open inquiry. Indeed, one could argue that the term complete participation is a misnomer, that might be replaced by a more appropriate term such as covert participation or infiltration. On the other hand, others claim that the benefits of covertness justify its continuation. There is no consensus on this matter among researchers or within the society at large. However, we believe that community researchers who understand the possible negative consequences and implications of covert research will choose to tell the truth about their intentions and to opt for the second strategy, participant as observer.

Participant as Observer. In the approach termed "participant as observer," observers make known their presence as inquirers and attempt to form relationships with members of a setting. Because of the problems of covert participation, the second approach is more commonly used for entering field settings, particularly in community studies (Denzin, 1978, p. 188). The following description (Janes, 1961) exemplifies the approach:

> Field work was begun by visiting town,
> county and school officials, and the news-
> paper editor to explain the purpose of the
> study and to ask their cooperation. Court-

house and school records and newspaper
files were checked and interviews begun with
officials and leading citizens. In time social interaction was initiated by attending
church, joining a veteran's organization,
returning visits of neighbors, and later
spending social evenings with the families
of several of the younger businessmen of the
community (p. 447).

One of the crucial tasks facing observers who reveal
their identity is minimizing the effects of their presence
on a community's usual behavior and social processes.
This can be accomplished by becoming "one of the crowd,"
that is, by participating in social events and by adopting
the language and dress of a group. The observers, however, must strike a balance between too little participation
and too much:

The researcher who remains passive and aloof
will find that subjects are reluctant to share
information. At the same time, the observer
must remember that his or her primary purpose is to collect data. . . . We know an
observer who, on his first day in the field
at a teachers' lunchroom, overheard his subjects express a desire to have a sensitivity
training workshop. Since he had previously
led a number of such workshops, he immediately offered to help. Needless to say,
he was forced to abandon his role as a researcher (Bogdan & Taylor, 1975, p. 51).

Observers may rely initially on one or two subjects
to help them enter a setting. "In settings such as prisons
that are characterized by distrust or danger, for example,
it may be necessary for observers to have a key figure
vouch for them before they can be trusted by others"
(Bogdan & Taylor, 1975, p. 48). Nonetheless, observers
must quickly develop and maintain a variety of relationships with community members so that the data they collect
are representative of an entire setting.
Participants as observers also find that subjects
attempt to place constraints on when, whom, or what they

shall observe. Participants as observers must therefore carefully resist being forced into relationships, modes of dress, and patterns of behavior that are not conducive to their research.

Data Collection and Analysis

In participant observation, as in action research, data collection and data analysis go hand-in-hand (Lofland, 1971). Observers typically examine their field notes on a daily basis to identify themes, revise hypotheses, and plan for further data gathering. Examination of the meaning and implications of data occurs on an ongoing basis.

In addition, participant observers' accounts of their own behavior, emotional reactions, thoughts, and plans are an important source of data. The following excerpt is from an observer's notes in a study of a state institution: "Although I don't show it, I tense up when residents approach me when they are covered with food or excrement. Maybe this is what the attendants feel and why they often treat the residents as lepers" (Bogdan & Taylor, 1975, p. 67).

As in any other case study approach, data collection techniques, in addition to observation, are frequently used to supplement the data collected by participant observers.

An Example of Participant-Observation Research

Middletown (Lynd & Lynd, 1929) is a classic participant-observation study which influenced a generation of community inquirers (Bell & Newby, 1972, p. 34). The goals of the study were ambitious: first, to attempt to describe the life of Middletown as a whole, that is, "to study synchronously the interwoven trends that are the life of a small American city" (Lynd & Lynd, 1929, p. 4); and second, to attempt to determine what social changes, if any, had occurred in Middletown since 1890.

Procedure

Pre-Field Work. Before entering the field setting, the observers established neither specific hypotheses nor a detailed plan for data collection. Their only plan was to

use a sixfold classification scheme to organize their observations of behavior: "Whether in an Arunta village in
Central Australia or in our own seemingly intricate institutional life . . . human behavior appears to consist in
variations upon a few major lines of activity: getting a
living, making a home, training the young, using leisure
in various forms of play, art, and so on, engaging in religious practices and engaging in community activities"
(Lynd & Lynd, 1929, p. 4).

Entering the Setting. The five-person research team became members of the community for 18 months, using the
participant as observer strategy to gain access to a variety of social settings (for example, court sessions, labor
meetings, civic club luncheons, and churches). The team
rented space in a local office building; and whenever they
were questioned about their activities, they responded that
their purpose was to "study the growth of the city," thus
projecting a positive image while revealing little about the
nature of their work.

Narrowing the Scope of the Study. After the observers had
lived in Middletown for a few months, they began to narrow the scope of the inquiry by identifying phenomena of
interest within each of the six areas of their classification
scheme. Consider, for example, the area of making a living. Based on observation and an analysis of employment
records, the observers categorized a diverse number of occupations into two groups: a working class (for example,
factory workers) and a business class (for example,
merchants).

> As one prowls Middletown streets about six
> o'clock of a winter morning one notes two
> kinds of homes: the dark ones where peo-
> ple still sleep, and the ones with a light in
> the kitchen where adults of the household
> may be seen moving about, starting the
> business of the day. For the seven out of
> every ten of those gainfully employed who
> constitute the working class, getting a liv-
> ing means being at work in the morning
> anywhere between six-fifteen and seven-
> thirty o'clock, chiefly seven. For the other
> three in ten, the business class, being at

work in the morning means seven forty-five,
eight or eight-thirty, or even nine o'clock,
but chiefly eight-thirty (Lynd & Lynd, 1929,
p. 54).

Later in the study, the working/business class distinction proved significant in gaining insight into a community decision concerning daylight savings time. On the
one hand, the working class wanted Middletown to remain
on standard time because their homes remained warm in
the summer until after midnight; they needed the cool
early morning hours for sleep. On the other hand, the
businessmen wanted to adopt daylight savings time because
standard time was a disadvantage in conducting business
with companies in the East.

Data Collection. An impressive feature of data collection
in Middletown was the successful use of a variety of techniques. For example, four methods converged to provide
the researchers with a multifaceted picture of the impact of
unemployment among working-class men on the men themselves and on other aspects of community life. At an
observation of a Middletown Advertising Club luncheon it
was noted that the Club was asked to use its influence to
stop out-of-town factories from printing "want ads" in the
Middletown Times, the concern being that such advertising
would lure unemployed machinists away from the town.
Interviews with the wife of an unemployed factory worker
and the wife of a prominent businessman revealed diametri-
cally opposite perspectives on the seriousness of the situation and the motivation of unemployed men to seek work.
Archival records (in this case, figures regarding factory
employment in the community) showed that between 1923
and 1924 the total number of full-time employees had
plunged from 802 to 205. Finally, a survey of 122 housewives concerning their families' responses to unemployment
revealed that 68 had made changes in routine habits of
living, including reduced expenditures on clothing, food,
housing, and telephones, failure to pay insurance premiums,
taking substitute part-time or full-time work, and requiring
high school age children to leave school in order to supplement the family income. The simultaneous use of a variety
of data gathering methods provided a far richer and more
meaningful appraisal of the severity of the unemployment
problem and varied ways in which different individuals
and groups were responding to it.

Results

The study generated a wealth of data (which the Lynds condensed into a 450-page book) that are difficult to summarize. Generally, however, the data suggested three conclusions concerning the rate and impact of social and technological change on life in Middletown.

First, the rate of change differed among the six areas of life activity. The means of making a living in Middletown had changed the most since 1890 as a result of the technological advances made in industry. For example, the number of factory employees and the specialization of their tasks were greatly increased. The use of leisure time also changed considerably as a result of the introduction of the automobile and motion pictures. The activities of homemaking, education, and community involvement (for example, social clubs) changed less rapidly; and there was little change in formal religious activity.

Second, change in life activities was more prevalent among members of the business class, who, for example, were more likely to own an automobile.

Third, social change in Middletown was primarily the result of technological innovation:

> New tools and inventions have been the most
> prolific breeders of change. They have
> entered Middletown's industrial life more
> rapidly than new business and management
> devices. Bathrooms and electricity have
> pervaded the homes of the city more rapidly
> than innovations in the personal adjustments
> between husband and wife or between parents
> and children (Lynd & Lynd, 1929, p. 445).

The study also raised significant questions for further inquiry: What effect does change have on the emotional adjustment of various groups within the community (for example, groups classified by social class, sex, or age)? What factors influence the acceptance of social change and innovation? What effect does the differential rate of change among social institutions have on individual well-being?

Pitfalls and Prospects

A serious problem with participant observation is that while it produces changes in the behavior of the community under study, the specific effects that observers have on a community are difficult to determine. Such effects may well fluctuate over time as participant observers interact with community members in various situations. To reduce the severity of this problem, it is generally agreed that data should be collected only after there has been enough time for the researcher to develop a relatively stable relationship with the setting. In any case, observers should be continuously sensitive to the effects of their presence on community life as they shift over time. Field notes, for example, should include the observers' perceptions of how their actions are affecting the behavior of others.

Critics of the approach also note that the low level of structure provided to participant observers poses certain dangers. One danger is that participation in a setting may unduly affect the observers' ability to develop and test hypotheses. For example, a researcher attempting to study the relationship between city government and a neighborhood with unemployment problems may become so involved with the plight of residents that "city hall" becomes an enemy. The term going native has been coined to refer to observers who abandon their role as researchers to become members of the settings they have been studying (Gold, 1958). Bodgan and Taylor (1975) provide an extended discussion of the problem.

Critics also claim that observers' data are subject to selective perception. That is, observers tend to focus on behaviors they want or expect to see, often disregarding unexpected aspects of a situation or behavior and sometimes overlooking the obvious. Further, the observer's behavior as a participant in community affairs may influence a sequence of events to occur "as predicted."

There are several ways to deal with these problems of bias and subjectivity. One is to use more than one observer in order to determine interobserver reliability. Another is to use more than one data-gathering technique.

The convergence of data can be established using a multi-method approach.

Finally, one may begin with an unstructured pilot study to generate a more structured set of hypotheses and variables to be pursued in the next phase of inquiry. One advantage of an unstructured approach is that it increases the likelihood that observers will perceive phenomena that otherwise might have been filtered out by their a priori hypotheses.

SIMULATION

Simulations are <u>operating models</u> of social systems. They reproduce the essential characteristics of systems as they change over time. The goal is to reproduce a social system <u>in action</u>, enabling inquirers and participants to experience "a sequence of outcomes that strongly resembles the original" (Duke, 1964, p. iii). The use of simulation in social science research has increased considerably since its original use in the 1940s. By 1965 simulation had become a widely used methodology in several disciplines (Dutton & Starbuck, 1971). Today it is viewed as a method of choice for <u>within laboratory</u> study of complex multivariate phenomena which cannot readily be observed or manipulated <u>in vivo</u>.

Approaches to Simulation

One can distinguish three types of simulation according to the extent of their reliance on human actors: (1) all-person simulations; (2) person-computer combinations, and (3) all-computer simulations. <u>All-person</u> simulations rely solely on human actors, who, operating within certain predetermined role definitions and rules, participate in a multifaceted role play to clarify what processual regularities are involved in the system being studied. The best-known example of such all-person simulations in psychology is the Prisoners' Dilemma game (Rapoport & Orwant, 1965), which was developed to explore the conditions under which interpersonal negotiation will become competitive or collaborative. The game is based on the following scenario:

> Two suspects are taken into custody and sep-
> arated. The district attorney is certain that
> they have been partners in committing a
> specific crime, but he does not have adequate
> evidence to convict them. He points out to
> each prisoner that he has two alternatives:
> to confess to the crime the police know he
> and his partner are guilty of, or to deny it.
> If neither confesses, then the district attor-
> ney states he will book them on some minor
> charge, such as petty larceny and illegal
> possession of a weapon, and they will both
> receive some minor punishment; if they both
> confess, they will be prosecuted, but he
> will recommend less than the most severe
> sentence; if, however, one confesses and the
> other does not, then the confessor will be
> treated very leniently for turning state's
> evidence, whereas the other will have the
> "book" thrown at him (Raser, 1969, p. 87).

Each prisoner can thus gain most by "double-crossing" the other--but only if the other prisoner does not do the same. If both double-cross, both lose. If both cooperate, both win something, but less than either would have won had he or she double-crossed the other and "got away with it." The scenario has been translated into a simple two-party game in which the positive or negative payoffs for each are determined by the independent selections both parties make from the two available alternatives.

The most striking finding from numerous Prisoner's Dilemma studies is that given the differential payoffs pre-sented, there is surprisingly little cooperation among the parties, even though both stand to gain from a collabora-tive trusting stance. Rarely does the total rate of coopera-tion exceed 50% (Nemeth, 1970). Though the game itself is quite simple, it has been deemed to capture "the essential feature of much social interaction: the simple fact that by being cooperative, one exposes oneself to exploitation" (Schneider, 1976, p. 421).

A second set of simulations is built around a combi-nation of human participants and computers. The former are decisionmakers; the computers respond to the humans' decisions from a predetermined data base and track the quantitative tabulations resulting from those decisions.

A widely known example of the person–computer approach is the InterNation Simulation (INS) developed by Guetzkow to explore the dynamics of international conflict management (Guetzkow et al., 1963). The INS has many of the features of national and international politics, including three or more "nations," each with its voters, national resources, military capability, polls, channels of communication, advisors, trade, and elections. The players act as chiefs of state, diplomats, and cabinet members. Relationships among some components of the model are expressed mathematically and programmed into the computer. For example, if players decided to increase the military capability of their nation, the computer is programmed to indicate a decrease in certain national resources. As the model operates, changes in one component produce changes in others according to previously established equations.

The players are typically given few rules. Their task is to determine their nation's goals and to decide how to allocate resources to meet them. They may negotiate, form coalitions, bargain, threaten, trade, wage war, and try to carry out elaborate plans, most of which involve resource allocations. The consequences of these decisions are periodically fed back to the players and their decision possibilities are partially based on the outcomes of earlier activities. The advantage of the computer to INS is its ability to monitor interplay among numerous variables, involving rapid calculations that would be prohibitive for humans.

Researchers have adapted Guetzkow's original INS model to explore a variety of international situations. Raser (1969), for example, studied the impact of nuclear weapons invulnerability on the international system:

> In general, we found that when one nation
> in the system achieved nuclear invulnerabil-
> ity, it was seen as stronger and more threat-
> ening, it was less apt to precipitate acci-
> dental war, and it lost interest in arms
> control agreements, even though the interest
> in arms control of other nations increased.
> Alliances tended to shift and opponents of
> the invulnerable nation were more deterred,
> but wars occurred with greater frequency
> than when no nation was invulnerable
> (Raser, 1969, p. 97).

In the third type, all-computer simulations, researchers program computers with equations expressing relationships among several variables. The values of certain
variables are then systematically changed, without involving decisions by human actors who are central to the
person-computer approach. The result is a series of outcomes or configurations which are useful to inquirers attempting to understand the dynamics of a system. For example, all-computer simulations have been used to gain
insight into the economic problems of developing countries
(for example, Holland, 1972). Computers were first programmed with formulas relating variables such as prices
and wages, rates of inflation, consumer demand, import
and export levels, and capital investment. A series of
computer "runs" was then completed in which different
values were assigned to the variables. It was then possible to analyze the impact of economic-policy decisions (for
example, lowering capital investment) on a number of indicators (for example, rates of inflation). The computer
simulation enabled Holland to examine interactions among
aspects of an economy that are typically studied in isolation from each other. He noted that, in the past, such
isolated inquiry has led to erroneous conclusions.

As knowledge increases about any specific set of
interrelated variables, the logical progression of simulation gaming would be from a preponderance of all-person
or person-computer versions to an increasing reliance on
all-computer approaches. The limiting factor is whether
relationships among variables are sufficiently understood
to be expressed in quantitative terms and fed into the computer. At present, few relationships are so well analyzed;
thus the bulk of simulations must rely on a combination of
human actors and computer technology.

An Example of the Use of Simulation

Klein (1975) has developed a simulation for community inquiry in which community members' knowledge of
real-world conditions plays an important part.[5] An important characteristic of his Community Action Simulation (CAS)
is that it is based on the work of actual community groups
which are attempting to achieve specific objectives (for
example, a coalition of Spanish-speaking groups seeking
bilingual education in the public schools of their city).

The community or action group helps to create the simulation by identifying other relevant groups—-allies, opponents, or significant neutrals. Such groups become part of the simulation and interact with the action group as it attempts to achieve its objective. For example, "in a simulation involving the attempt of a community mental health center to form a coalition to work on the problem of drug abuse, public representatives included an adolescent drug user, a suburban parent, an ex-addict, and a non-drug-user senior high school student" (Klein, 1975, p. 362).

Conditions for Interaction

The CAS attends to three social-psychological variables which are presumed to influence interactions among community groups and which are used to affect the nature of interaction among players in the simulation: trust, social distance, and power. Ratings on all three variables are used to define the ground rules for interaction in the simulation.

Trust refers to the extent to which one group feels that another group's motives are beneficent and its agreements will be honored. Each group rates the others on a scale from 0 to 9. A rating of 0, for example, implies that no trust exists; in that case the ground rules would allow only restricted communication between the groups.

Social distance refers to the ease with which community groups can contact each other. "In real life opportunities for direct contact between groups vary according to such factors as socioeconomic status of group members, location of leaders' and members' residences, extent of memberships in overlapping social groups, and political and social values" (Klein, 1975, p. 361). Ratings of social distance between groups are used to determine how many contact points a group must use in order to make contact with any other group. Since each group has only a limited number of contact points at the beginning of each period of play, groups must consider carefully the relative cost of attempting to interact with other groups.

Power in CAS is defined "as the ability of a group to realize its will in a communal action despite resistance from others participating in the situation" (Klein, 1975, p. 362). Power points are awarded each group by a monitor on the basis of each group's ratings of itself and all other groups, taking into account discrepancies between ratings as well as absolute levels. The formula by which power points are assigned each group is not made known; neither is any group told the number of power points it possesses. Instead, as in real life, groups are left to operate as best they can on the basis of their own judgments about their ability to influence others.

Action and Review Periods

Thirty-minute action periods are followed by review sessions during which participants, no longer in role, are debriefed. Questionnaire data are processed immediately after each action period and fed back to participants during the review sessions. The information includes ratings reflecting intergroup trust, perceived power, and social distance, and outcome ratings having to do with the extent to which participants believe group goals are being achieved and how satisfied they are with "the general well-being of the simulated community." During the review sessions comparisons with "real life" are encouraged because they help participants and inquirers understand the phenomena being simulated.

Guidelines

Klein explains that, as in the INS discussed above, participants are given few rules:

> Participants are asked to enact roles as
> realistically as they know how within their
> own understanding of what is expected of
> such people in real life. They are instructed
> to remain open to influence during the simu-
> lation insofar as they believe the actual
> role incumbents would be; they are expected
> to respond spontaneously to the kinds of in-
> fluence attempts they experience from others.
> They also are asked to improvise and use
> their imaginations freely within the con-
> straints of CAS ground rules. . . . Within
> those constraints, groups are free to develop
> their own strategies. (1975, p. 363)

Use of CAS

The CAS has been used successfully as a means of consulting with and training a variety of action groups including, for example, community mental health center outreach teams, a school/community council, and a group ministry working on race relations in a suburban county (Klein, 1975). Participants' postsimulation evaluations of the method have been highly favorable. By involving actual community groups, the CAS has a unique advantage: the results it generates can be compared to real-world outcomes to determine whether and how realistically it represented the essential characteristics of a community.

Pitfalls and Prospects

The critical test for a simulation is how well it reproduces real-world conditions; that is, does the simulation enable one to make valid generalizations to social phenomena? Most directors of community simulations are convinced that participants' behavior in simulations is an authentic reflection of what would happen in real life (see Shepard, 1970; Gamson, 1969). However, there is a clear risk of making invalid generalizations to real social phenomena. Researchers and participants may be drawn into playing the game for its own sake, creating a mass of data having to do with that game but possibly little else in the real world. Consider, for example, the finding in Prisoner's Dilemma studies that there is little cooperation among the participants. Nemeth (1970) makes an excellent case for the hypothesis that such generalizations are, to a large extent, due to the nature of the simulation itself. The players typically "play against persons whom they do not know and whose motives are ambiguous. They are instructed to consider their own welfare and play for imaginary money without the aid of communication. Available evidence in the areas of reciprocity and help giving . . . suggests that all these variables reduce reciprocity and altruism" (Nemeth, 1970, p. 397).

Devising a good simulation is like devising a "good" portrait. How do we know whether the portrait is a good likeness of the subject? The answer lies in the agreement of those who know the subject best. Similarly, it has been suggested that in community simulation, "the crucial tests

. . . are evaluations of professionals whose competence includes the phenomena that are being modeled. They are likely to know the most about the working of the real world" (Meier, 1964, p. iii). The test of "knowing" can also be extended to include a variety of other participants in that real world of which the simulation is, at best, an analogue--namely, community leaders, representatives of various constituencies, and government officials. The CAS is an example of a simulation which increases its validity by involving community members.

What are some of the advantages to be gained from simulation? Simulation gaming involving human actors with or without computers seems especially well suited to community inquiry. Because of the community's multisystemic nature, it is difficult--and usually impossible--to carry out direct observation of the multiple and often simultaneous phenomena involved in any sequence of events deemed worthy of study. One available substitute for direct observation of or participation in actual phenomena is a simulated version.

Advantages of the approach for study of community complexities include the following five areas: (1) Economy: running a model is usually far less expensive in terms of time, energy, and money than studying the "real thing." Complex space and extended time can be collapsed into manageable packages, sometimes involving little else but game boards (for example, Community Land Use Game, Feldt, 1966), other times involving one or more rooms full of charts and diagrams, players' locations, and reams of printout material from well-fed computers (for example, Metropolis by Duke & Meier, 1966). (2) Safety: "laboratory analogues" of dangerous phenomena protect the health and safety of human participants. (3)Staging the future: researchers can explore hypothetical events within a future that has not yet transpired and can generate alternative responses. (4) Studying processes in ways that nature prohibits: it is possible to explore conditions that rarely occur (for example, wars and riots), to replicate events that occur only once in nature (for example, a specific international situation), and to stop or start events at will. (5) Accessibility: inquirers can gain access to events that occur "behind closed doors" (for example, military strategy meetings and political decision making).

EPIDEMIOLOGY

In general terms, epidemiology is the study of the distribution of the occurrence of physical and mental health disorders within and between specified populations over given rates of time. As an important tool of public health, it seeks to understand the factors associated with the occurrence of such disorders so that preventive measures can be taken to control or eliminate the disease. Epidemiologists count the cases of specific disorders or disabilities within specified population groups. They do so to determine the rates of occurrence of those disorders within those groups under ordinary conditions and special circumstances. Subgroups found to manifest unusually high rates of a disorder are considered "high risk" or "at risk."

Epidemiologic analysis attempts to single out particular biophysical, psychological, sociocultural, demographic, or physical environment conditions that contribute to the development of specified disorders in high-risk groups. Epidemiologists in the mental health field have shown consistently, for example, that there is a higher rate of schizophrenia among members of lower socioeconomic classes (for example, Hollingshead & Redlich, 1958).[6]

Epidemiologic methods were originally developed by medical scientists in the mid-nineteenth century to understand and control epidemic diseases such as typhoid and cholera. In the early twentieth century social scientists borrowed the method to study phenomena other than infectious diseases, including, for example, accidents and behavioral disorders.[7]

Methodological Considerations

As noted above, a typical sequence of epidemiologic inquiry consists of two phases: first, determining the frequency of a disorder in a population (that is, descriptive epidemiology); second, isolating variables which contribute to the development of that disorder (that is, analytic epidemiology). We discuss each phase briefly in this section.

Descriptive Epidemiology

There are two commonly used approaches to counting cases of disorder in a population: incidence and prevalence.

Incidence is the number of new occurrences of a disorder within a specified interval of time. "New occurrences" are defined as the first occurrence of a disorder within an individual's lifetime (Zax & Specter, 1974). The interval under study can vary from a day, week, or month to a year or longer. Meaningful comparisons between populations or communities which vary in size are made possible by expressing incidence as a rate per 1,000 or 100,000 persons. Hence, incidence rate is the ratio of the number of cases found in a specified interval to the number of people in the population under study, multiplied by a constant (which we shall label K). Consider, for example, the incidence rate of mental health disorders in the United States for the year 1979–80. In that year approximately 2.5 million Americans were hospitalized for the first time with mental disorders; thus, using a constant, or K = 1,000, the incidence rate is expressed as

$$\frac{(\text{New cases in 1979–80}) \ (K)}{\text{U.S. Population in 1979–80}} = \frac{(2.5 \text{ million}) \ (1,000)}{220 \text{ million}}$$

Thus the incidence rate equals 11.36 per thousand. Note that K is an indexing constant which simply converts our percentage figure to a rate, which in this case is "rate per thousand." The numerator and denominator of a rate must, of course, be defined in the same terms: if the numerator refers to a specific age, sex, or racial group, the same must hold true for the denominator.

Prevalence, on the other hand, is the total number of cases of a disorder in a population at a given point in time. Consider, for example, the prevalence rate of broken legs among students at X university for the month of September 1980. The prevalence rate is expressed as

$$\frac{(\text{Known cases in Sept. 1980}) \ (K)}{(\text{University students in Sept. 1980})} = \frac{(30) \ (K)}{(30,000)}$$

where K equals 1,000. Thus the prevalence rate equals 1.0 per thousand.

The number of cases of a disorder at any given point in time (that is, the numerator of a prevalence rate) is dependent on two factors: (1) the number of new cases that develop during the time interval under study <u>plus</u> (2) the number of cases that exist at the time the interval under study begins. In the example above five students may have broken a leg in August 1980. Since their legs were not fully healed in September, they are counted as cases along with the 25 new cases that occur in September itself.

Thus, the significant difference between prevalence and incidence is that the former is a more inclusive measure. Prevalence is usually easier to calculate than incidence: prevalence rates can be obtained by simply counting all cases of a disorder within a population <u>at a</u> <u>given point in time</u> and dividing that figure by the total number of people; in contrast, to determine incidence one must know when a case became symptomatic in order to classify it as either an "old" or "new" case.

There is a disadvantage, however, to using prevalence rates. They are difficult to interpret because they reflect both the rate of occurrence of new cases (incidence) and duration of a disorder (Zax & Specter, 1974; Davison & Neale, 1978). Consider, for example, research involving the relationship between social class and schizophrenia. Suppose we determine from prevalence data that there is an inverse correlation between social class and rates of schizophrenia. One would then need to ask, Is there a higher prevalence rate of the disorder among lower social classes because they tend to recover less rapidly from schizophrenia (and therefore there are <u>more existing cases</u> <u>when a study begins</u>)? Or does the correlation reflect the <u>occurrence of a greater number of new cases</u> of schizophrenia during the interval under study? Using prevalence data alone, one cannot answer such questions. When one is studying phenomena whose duration may vary considerably (for example, as a function of social-class status), it is necessary to calculate incidence as well as prevalence.

Analytic Epidemiology

Once prevalence and/or incidence rates for a disorder have been determined, epidemiologists attempt to <u>isolate</u> variables which contribute to the development of the disorder. To achieve this, they compare socioeconomic or demographic groups which are similar to each other with respect to many significant characteristics but differ with respect to one characteristic under study. Consider a simplified example concerning the relationship between

gender and mental illness. If one wanted to learn if
gender contributed to the onset of mental disorder, one
could compare the incidences of disorder in 30-year-old
white females and 30-year-old white males from a middle-
class background. If gender is related to the occurrence
of mental disorder, one group would show a significantly
higher rate of disorder. A series of such comparisons enables epidemiologists to presume a relationship between a
variable and the occurrence of a disorder.

Examples of Epidemiological Research

In this section we discuss chronologically three
classic studies which contributed to the development of
epidemiological research in the area of mental health and
illness: Faris and Dunham, 1939; Hollingshead and Redlich,
1958; and Srole et al., 1962.
One of the first epidemiological studies of mental
health concerned the differential rate of severe behavioral
disorder in various geographic areas of Chicago (Faris &
Dunham, 1939). The inquirers divided Chicago into seven
geographic zones, extending from the inner city to the
suburbs. Prevalence rates were calculated for each zone
by counting the total number of people admitted to hospitals with diagnoses of mental disorder.
The results suggested that prevalence rates increased
regularly as one moved toward the center of the city.
Moreover, specific types of disorder were associated with
particular geographic locations. Many cases of paranoid
schizophrenia, for example, were found in the rooming
house districts of the city. Faris and Dunham (1939) suggested that the disorder was caused by the conditions of
social isolation that characterize such settings. It is
possible, of course, to challenge their interpretation by
proposing an alternative explanation, namely, that individuals were clustered together in particular locations as
a result of their disorders; that is, individuals drifted to
single-room boarding houses after the onset of schizophrenia.
The study nonetheless established epidemiology as a useful
tool for studying social and physical conditions associated
with the etiology of mental health disorder.
After World War II, Hollingshead and Redlich (1958)
began epidemiologic inquiry into the role of social class
in both the etiology and treatment of behavioral disorders.

They hypothesized that social-class status was associated with both rates of various disorders and types of treatment individuals received. Using clinical records from private and public practitioners in New Haven, Connecticut, they calculated prevalence rates for five social classes.

Among their findings were the following: The preponderance of cases were from the lower social classes. Higher-class patients tended to be labeled neurotic and to receive individual psychotherapy from private practitioners. In contrast, lower-class patients tended to be hospitalized as schizophrenics and to receive somatic treatment rather than psychotherapy. The study made two significant contributions. First, it gave empirical support to the notion that environmental conditions, such as social class, contribute to the development of disorder. Second, it pointed out that an individual's social-class status influenced the type of treatment that he or she received.

The Midtown Manhattan study (Srole et al., 1962) was innovative in that it included assessment of the mental health status of "untreated" individuals, that is, those who were not receiving treatment for behavioral disorder. Previous epidemiological research had calculated incidence and prevalence rates only by counting cases of disorder recorded by private and public mental health practitioners. Thus, individuals who had mental health problems but were not receiving professional treatment had not been included in calculations of rates of disorder. To improve the technique of case finding, the study incorporated a random sample of 1,660 untreated community residents who were given a standard mental health interview and later diagnosed. Another important feature of the study was its inclusion of a broad range of demographic factors.

The results indicated that nearly 60% of adults studied manifested subclinical symptoms, 20% displayed severe symptoms, and only 20% were symptom free. Analyses demonstrated no sex-related mental health differences, but older individuals and those from lower socioeconomic groups were more impaired than younger individuals and those from higher socioeconomic groups. The Midtown study is significant because it demonstrated the importance of establishing a community-wide prevalence rate, that is, a prevalence rate which includes individuals not receiving professional treatment. Prevalence rates which do not represent untreated individuals are likely to be inaccurate.

At the same time, the study indicated that human services were reaching only a small percentage of the people who could benefit from them. Despite the high prevalence rate among the untreated sample, less than 2% of the population was receiving treatment of any kind (Lin & Stanley, 1962; Langner & Michael, 1963).

Pitfalls and Prospects

The Problem of Reliability

A major difficulty in conducting epidemiological research is to obtain reliable estimates of prevalence and incidence. At first glance, it might seem simple to record frequencies of disorder from existing records of treated cases kept by private and public human service agencies. But, "such a technique of case finding would ignore all the cultural, social, economic and situational factors affecting the distribution and utilization of psychological treatment" (Heller & Monahan, 1977, p. 99). The Midtown Manhattan study demonstrated that many individuals with behavioral problems never receive professional treatment. To overcome the selection factors that operate in bringing persons to treatment, a community-wide prevalence rate must be established.

Though this community-wide method of case counting is a significant improvement, it is difficult to reliably measure psychological disorder in individuals who are not receiving treatment. That is, interviews and tests given to assess psychological well-being do not consistently identify individuals with disorders. As a result, 40 to 50 epidemiological studies of mental disorder have calculated prevalence rates which vary from less than 1% to a high of 64% (Heller & Monahan, 1977, p. 100).[8] The problem of reliable diagnoses is not, of course, unique to epidemiological research. Clinicians face the task of reliably recognizing cases of disorder when they encounter them. Further research to develop more reliable diagnostic tools is needed to improve the accuracy of counts of disorder.

Defining Onset of a Disorder

A difficult dilemma for incidence determination in epidemiological studies in community mental health involves the matter of establishing precisely when a "case" of a mental disorder can be presumed to have occurred. The typical onset of a neurotic or psychotic pathology is gradual in nature. It is rarely possible to establish precisely when a case becomes bona fide. Faced with this apparently insoluble dilemma, most investigations have been restricted to treated cases. In such studies a case operationally becomes so when the person is diagnosed. It is obvious that our ability to apply the concept of incidence in the study of mental disorders is severely limited by the inability to specify time of onset for many, if not most, untreated cases. Thus, for prevalence purposes it is usually possible to agree on criteria for labeling a person as psychologically disabled; however, it is far more difficult—if not impossible—to establish when that person's disorder began, information which is essential for determining whether this case is to be labeled new or old.

Correlational Nature of the Data

Epidemiological findings are usually correlational in nature; that is, the types of variables examined are usually ones over which the epidemiologist has little or no direct control (for example, social class, residence, gender, and prevalence of a disorder). As a result, it is often difficult to assert the direction or directions of causal relationships. Note, we say directions rather than direction because of the fact that causal relationships involving psychological and social phenomena are nearly always multidirectional. In the Faris and Dunham (1939) study cited earlier, for example, the researchers themselves attributed the findings primarily to the effects of less than optimal physical and social environments of the inner city, which generate stress and a higher incidence of emotional disorder. The findings, however, may also be due to the effects on the social and physical environment of marginal people drifting to the inner city. At the same time, it may be that the high incidence of emotional disorder among inner-city residents contributes to the crime and violence which create a less than optimal social environment. Finally, the availability of low-cost housing in the inner city is probably a further factor in attracting marginal individuals.

To cope with the problem of determining the strength of differing pathways and effects, epidemiologists use a range of innovative statistical analyses (see, for example,

Blalock, 1973), and quasi-experimental designs (see, for example, Chapter 5 in this volume.)

Four Advantages

Despite problems of reliability, case identification, and directionality of causal relationships, epidemiological inquiry can provide vital information for community planners, practitioners, and researchers.

First, it can improve planning for delivery of services by providing an estimate of the nature, severity, and distribution of problems in a given community. That is, descriptive epidemiology provides data on the frequency of various types of disorders that enable decisionmakers to plan accordingly: "Geriatric services are not emphasized in a 'new town' composed largely of young married persons, nor does one open a day-care center in a retirement village" (Heller & Monahan, 1977, p. 101).

In addition, epidemiological inquiry can be used to study complex phenomena which cannot be assigned in the laboratory (for example, the relationship between social class and psychological disorder). As Heller and Monahan put it, "One cannot randomly assign children to a certain social class and then raise them in a controlled 'laboratory analogue' of society" (1977, p. 103). Analytic epidemiology does nothing to disturb the usual behavior of a community. It enables inquirers to establish correlations among factors involved in the etiology of a phenomenon.

Further, descriptive epidemiological surveys can provide outcome measures demonstrating the effects of services in preventing and/or reducing the frequency and severity of disorders.

Finally, it should also be possible to apply the epidemiological model and technology to the study of rates of occurrence of desirable psychological and sociological phenomena within the populations of entire communities or subcommunities. Manifestations of leadership, creativity, contentment, sense of community, and similar phenomena would lend themselves to incidence and prevalence studies. To our knowledge, however, no one has yet done so.

SOCIAL INDICATORS

In the twentieth century the United States and other countries have developed increasingly inclusive and sophisticated measures relating to material and economic aspects of life. These economic indicators have served as guides to the current status of the nation; they have afforded some basis for prediction of future developments in such areas as employment and cost of living; and they have contributed to recommendations for public policy, economic legislation, and the like made by the President's Council of Economic Advisors. By now, it is generally accepted that statistics regarding per capita income, expenditures for consumer goods, savings, and production of goods and services offer useful indications of the present and future economic well-being of the nation. Complex indexes, such as the gross national product and the consumer price index, have become part of the decision-making fabric of the society, influencing not only public governmental actions but also the individual actions of investors and the calculation of salaries within the framework of labor-management contracts.

This influential and pervasive system of economic indicators was born following the report of the Commission on Social Trends established by President Hoover. That report, published in 1933, called for a system of economic indicators, which became linked to the Council of Economic Advisors.

During the years 1949-69 the United States enjoyed steady economic growth. Its gross national product doubled, as did the median income of American families. But at the same time there was an explosion of social turmoil, including increases in crime rates, racial unrest, demonstrations, and other manifestations of urban crisis. These conditions reinforced doubts among both social scientists and legislators that economic growth and social progress were equivalent (Parke & Seidman, 1978). The result was an upsurge of interest in gathering and interpreting data on social well-being, both expressed and further encouraged by publication of the influential volume Social Indicators edited by social psychologist Raymond Bauer (1966). This key publication brought together early work and gave substance to the fledgling social indicators movement which had as its objective developing ways to monitor the status of the population in such areas as health, education, employment, law enforcement, and political participation.

In 1967 the Department of Health, Education, and Welfare (HEW) published a report comparable to that of the Hoover Commission, calling for a system of social indicators, parallel to those in the economic arena, which would yield an annual social report to the nation (1967). The concept of social indicators has generated considerable attention among both social scientists and public-policy makers; it has led to a considerable body of theoretical and empirical work, which can be usefully applied to studies of public well-being both at local and national levels.

In 1973 the first of a series of triennial reports on social conditions and trends in the United States was prepared by the social indicators staff of the Bureau of the Census. Subsequent reports were published in 1976 and 1980. Each presents "a comprehensive variety of statistical information selected and organized to depict important aspects of our current social situation and their underlying historical trends and developments" (Weitzman and staff, 1980, p. xix). The most recent publication covered 11 subject areas:

1. Population and the Family.
2. Health and Nutrition.
3. Housing and the Environment.
4. Transportation.
5. Public Safety.
6. Education and Training.
7. Work.
8. Social Security and Welfare.
9. Income and Productivity.
10. Social Participation.
11. Culture, Leisure, and Use of Time.

Each of the 11 sections includes three types of material: (1) selected topics of broad social significance, (2) selected statistics or measures describing the status of the population in the subject area, and (3) time-series information where available.

The early aims and aspirations of the social indicators movement were described in the mid-1970s by Angus Campbell during an invited address at the annual meeting of the American Psychological Association:

> The gross national product, important as it undoubtedly is, is clearly not the ultimate touchstone against which the quantum of happiness in this country can be assessed. Realization of this fact has given rise in

recent years to an energetic search . . . for
a broader and more sensitive set of measures
that will provide a fuller description of
people's lives. (1976, pp. 117-118)

Methodological Considerations

Integrating Objective and Subjective Measures

Early work in the field paid attention primarily to
objective measures of social well-being, ones which could be
readily derived from census and other publicly available
data: for example, education level, adequacy of health
care, quality of housing. Such measures were labeled sur-
rogate indicators (Campbell, 1976, p. 118) because while
they presumably related to the experience of life, they only
indirectly and imperfectly reflected it.

A number of investigators, among them Campbell and
his colleagues, were stimulated by the social indicators
movement to turn to the task of developing measures which
would get more directly at the subjective life experience of
large numbers of people. In his address Campbell summarized data having to do with the relationship between objective indicators and measures of individual happiness.
He stated that "if we are primarily concerned with describing the quality of the life experience of the population,
we will need measures different from those that are used
to describe the objective circumstances in which people
live" (1976, p. 118).

He noted that in the few available population
studies, correlations between affluence and happiness were
close to zero or, in some cases, even negative. His survey of the literature led him to conclude that there was a
need to develop "an archive of measurements of psychological well-being to set alongside the more familiar economic and social indexes" (p. 119).

Measuring Subjective Well-Being

Approaches to measuring subjective well-being on a
large scale have, for the most part, developed along three
lines: (1) the measurement of cognitive expectations,
(2) reports of affective well-being, and (3) surveys of
stress-related symptoms.

Cognitive expectations involve measures of satisfaction-dissatisfaction based on individuals' comparisons of their present situations with those situations which they expected, desired, or felt they deserved. An outstanding example of this approach is Cantril's comparison of the aspirations and satisfactions of citizens of 13 countries (Cantril, 1965). Other examples are to be found in the many studies of job satisfaction or marital satisfaction.

Affective well-being involves reliance on individuals' own reports of mood states or more sophisticated techniques for getting at emotional well-being. For example, Bradburn (1969) studied avowed happiness by counting the number of positive and negative events in people's lives in the recent past. Some indication of the complexities to be faced is found in the fact that the positive and negative affect measures turned out to be unrelated to each other! Bradburn's approach was subsequently used in a study of a nationwide sample (Andrews & Withey, 1976). One thing is clear from these studies and those of other investigators—happiness, like intelligence, is multifactorial in nature.

Surveys of stress-related symptoms involve a variety of techniques for estimating prevalence of psychological and related types of disorder in communities. The Midtown Manhattan study, mentioned earlier in the section on epidemiology, is an example. Another well-known investigation by Alexander Leighton and his colleagues carried out prevalence studies in a single Canadian county, which compared rates of individual malaise and indexes of social disorganization in two villages (Hughes, 1960). Symptomatic surveys have used a variety of means to determine the presence or absence of psychological disorder, among them symptom checklists, experts' ratings of psychopathology based on interview protocols, and the use of explicit criteria for assessing the degree of impairment of functioning in relation to work and other areas.

The feasibility of integrating these three approaches was demonstrated by Campbell and his colleagues, who carried out a national survey involving 75-minute interviews with 2,164 persons aged 18 and older (Campbell, 1976). The structured interviews assessed individuals' life experiences in 15 separate domains and inquired into their general reactions to life as a whole. Their work yielded three general indexes of life experience: (1) a satisfaction-with-life index based on a composite of data from the satisfaction scores in ten domains; (2) a general affect index having to do with the experience of pleasantness-unpleasantness, derived from responses to paired adjectives (for example, interesting-boring, lonely-friendly, and enjoyable-miserable); (3) a perceived stress index based both on questions having to do with feelings of time, money, and other pressures and on two paired adjectives (easy-hard and free-tied). The first two indexes correlated .57 with each other; the third index correlated about .40 with each of the other two. Note that these correlations, showing the degree of consistency and convergence among the three measures, compare quite favorably to those of other standard measures in psychology (for example, the intercorrelations between different measures of personality).

The Campbell team also was interested in exploring empirically the relationship between their three subjective indexes and objective indicators upon which the field has placed considerable reliance. From their interviews they were able to describe ten characteristics of each individual's situation: urbanicity, age, race, job status, family income, occupation of head of household, education, religion, sex, and a measure called life cycle (age coupled with marriage and children). They found that the ten variables accounted for no more than 17% of the variance of the three indexes. Therefore, it would appear that the objective and subjective measures do not measure the same phenomenon or, perhaps, the same aspects of well-being. At present, we do not know how to account for this difference or discrepancy. We would conclude, then, that any study of well-being needs to include both objective and subjective measures.

The Bureau of the Census reports on social indicators reflect the work of Campbell and his associates. Three types of indicators are included, two of them based on analyses of available statistics, one of them grounded in the subjective feelings of respondents.

The first type of indicator--system performance-- juxtaposes data having to do with the presumed relationship between certain inputs into an aspect of the society (for example, public expenditures for education during the year in question) and quantifiable outputs within the same sector (for example, the number of M.D.s produced by the nation's medical schools).

The second type--well-being--provides data regarding rates of occurrence of phenomena believed to reflect the manner and degree to which the society is coping with meeting the needs of its members. Current rates, changes, and long-term trends are provided in such areas as inflation, crime, and infant mortality.

The third type—public perceptions—summarizes people's subjective feelings about certain aspects of their current condition, including satisfaction with family life, perceived influence of organized religion in American life, peace of mind, and perceived level of national well-being.

In January 1981 an issue of The Annals of the American Academy of Political and Social Science was devoted to interpretive essays based on the statistical data provided in Social Indicators III. The issue also includes an extensive bibliography on social indicators, including references to social indicators reports for states and local areas within the United States.

A promising approach by community psychologists to integrate subjective and objective indicators was offered by Newbrough and his colleagues at the Urban Observatory in Nashville, Tennessee. They formulated a fourfold approach for using social indicators as a basis for monitoring the effects of preventive programming in five mental health catchment areas (Newbrough, 1974). Whereas most researchers using social indicators have required national samples in their designs, Newbrough proposed that these indicators can be used by individual community psychologists whose study is limited to a single, specific metropolitan area. The approach included the following:

1. Use of census data for two purposes: (a) to develop indicators of so-called stressful events for each of the areas, using information regarding the number of births, deaths, marriages, divorces, graduates from high school, children about to enter school, persons 65 years of age or older, and households changing residence; (b) to identify populations considered to be at special risk, among them persons living alone; divorced, widowed, and separated persons; unemployed, teenagers; female-headed households; and families below the poverty level.
2. Use of data gathered from community mental health centers, social agencies, and local hospitals regarding demands for service, defined as contacts for help at the agencies and rates of utilization of the hospitals' emergency wards.

3. Bimonthly household surveys involving individual interviews with representative cohorts from the population having to do with individuals' moods, feelings of alienation, felt needs, and encounters with stressful life events.

4. Use of both qualitative and quantitative information to be gathered from a series of community goal-setting meetings to be conducted by the metropolitan government as part of a projected series of community development activities.

Funding for this ambitious and costly effort in Tennessee was not forthcoming, and ultimately all the proposed Urban Observatories went the way of the Great Society. Nevertheless, the plan gives some indication of the methodological challenges which must be confronted if social indicators are ever to be used to keep track of human needs in a locality and to determine how well those needs are being met. No doubt it will be possible, once we have had decades of experience with the workings of a multifaceted approach, to reduce the number of indicators and to simplify the process considerably. For the present, however, any serious use of the indicators approach is bound to be costly in both time and money.

The Need for a Multivariate Model of Relationships

Single, isolated statistics will not contribute much to our understanding of social well-being. Consider, for example, the statistic that the percentage of all adult women in the U.S. labor force has changed from 30% in 1940 to over 50% in the 1970s (Land & Spilerman, 1975). What effects has the movement of millions of women into the labor force had--on the women themselves, their families, and their communities? What changes have been introduced into the work setting? What effects, if any, have there been on the quality of work life, attitudes about sexual stereotyping and occupations, and the relationship between women's salary levels and those of men?

To answer such questions we must analyze relationships among a number of social indicators (Land & Spilerman, 1975). We must also develop a model which allows us to select from among the vast range of possible indicators those aspects of the society or specific types of social systems that are important for psychological well-being. The

importance of an integrative model is stressed in the following definition by Land, which appeared in 1971:

> I propose that the term social indicators re-
> fer to social statistics that (1) are compo-
> nents in a social system model (including
> sociopsychological, economic, demographic and
> ecological) or of some particular segment or
> process thereof, (2) can be collected and
> analyzed at various times and accumulated
> into a time series, and (3) can be aggregated
> or disaggregated to levels appropriate to the
> specifications of the model. Social system
> model means conceptions of social processes,
> whether formulated verbally, logically, math-
> ematically, or in computer simulation form.
> The important point is that the criterion for
> classifying a social statistic as a social in-
> dicator is its informative value which de-
> rives from its empirically verified nexus in
> a conceptualization of a social process.
> (P. 323)

Suppose, for example, that we are interested in the relationship between citizens' involvement in community activities and their level of well-being. We might hypothesize
that higher levels of participation in various activities
are associated with a higher level of happiness, satisfaction, or freedom from disabling stress. One could develop
measures of individuals' involvement in and satisfaction
from community activities, such as volunteer work, participation in voluntary associations, and involvement in
religious organizations, political parties, or other value-
oriented organization. In effect, one would be developing
a model of social participation which would provide a
meaningful context or framework in which to view the relationship between participation and well-being. After
careful analyses of the interrelationships among several
measures of participation and well-being, one could have
informative objective indicators which reflect subjective
levels of well-being.

A promising approach is reflected in the systems
performance type of indicator being used by the Bureau of
the Census. Suggested by Fleming (1972) it orients the
social indicators process around an open systems model,

involving "the monitoring in energy terms of the adaptation of a population to its habitat through time" (p. 16). Within such a model indicators might focus both on social output data (for example, reduced infant mortality rates) and social input data (for example, increased funding for prenatal care). Though each indicator taken alone might be descriptive of improvement in the well-being of a population, the input-output model permits an emphasis on interrelationships between expenditure of resources (inputs) and resulting altered conditions (outputs).

To arrive at the point where social indicators can serve as a truly useful basis for social accounting, it is imperative that work continue to develop and test models which can relate indicators in a meaningful manner. However, we do not advocate that researchers wait for the ultimate social theory which explicates interrelationships among social indicators before they conduct empirical studies. Quite the contrary! "Indeed, a comprehensive theory may never exist unless attempts are made to approximate it by making the most of available data" (Heller & Monahan, 1977, p. 94).

An Example of the Use of Social Indicators

As noted above, one important application of social indicators is to monitor the need for human services. In this section we describe the National Health Examination Survey (Roberts & Baird, 1972), which attempted to assess the needs of school children ages 6 through 17. Though not strictly speaking a social indicators study because it was limited to measuring social indicators at one point in time (rather than at regular intervals on an ongoing basis), the survey does provide some indication of the uses to which population-oriented data can be put.

Method

The school teachers of a national sample of children were requested (in a questionnaire) to (a) identify those needs of children which were unmet, that is, those for which there was no available service program, and (b) to estimate the number of children who could benefit from additional resources. Data for two age groups of children (6–11 and 12–17) were collected in separate surveys conducted in 1963–65 and 1966–70.

TABLE 10.1
Children for Whom Needed Teacher-recommended Special Resources
Are Unavailable, 1976 (estimated populations)

	Age of Children		
	6-11	12-17	Total
Type of Problem	(by thousands of children)		
Hard of hearing	110.3	20.1	130.4
Sight saving	150.6	5.5	156.1
Speech therapy	442.0	71.3	513.3
Orthopedic handicap	21.1	4.5	25.6
Gifted	556.7	51.7	608.4
Slow learner	1,590.9	282.8	1,873.7
Mentally retarded	48.4	32.4	80.8
Emotionally disturbed	399.8	88.3	488.1
Other	434.6	152.9	587.5
Remedial reading	--	270.5	--
Remedial training	--	229.5	--

Source: Compiled by authors.

Table 10.1 translates the sample data into population estimates for 1976. It assumes that the teachers' evaluations and the students' needs have remained the same since the data were collected. It is possible, of course, that data collected in 1963 do not accurately reflect the needs of children in 1976. This possibility underscores the need to measure social indicators at regular time intervals so as to monitor changes over time and to provide data on current conditions.

Nonetheless, the data indicate that the needs of thousands of school children are going unmet. The data also indicate that there is a wide variety of unmet needs among children: gifted children as well as slow learners need additional resources. Teachers report that the unmet needs of children decrease during the ages 12-17. It is difficult to interpret this finding. Does the uniform decline result because teachers of older children are less sensitive to their needs? Have earlier problems been "corrected" by service programs? Or have the problems disappeared with maturity?

In addition, the study indicated that "more boys are perceived as having needs requiring attention than girls. A larger proportion of girls than boys are thought to be gifted, and smaller proportions of girls are perceived as slow learners, as mentally retarded, as emotionally disturbed, as needing speech therapy, etc., than boys" (Ferriss, 1978, p. 159).

The study demonstrates the importance of obtaining measures of well-being beyond those typically gathered by the census. The data give human service providers some idea of the need for services among a large segment of the population. Given the severity of problems identified by the survey, a follow-up study is warranted to update the information and to answer questions concerning the decline in the perceived needs of older children. It would also be important to link these measures to other relevant indicators, for example, the family background of children believed to need services. Such inquiry would enable a more meaningful interpretation of the data (Ferriss, 1978).

Pitfalls and Prospects

As noted above, many of the early reports on the development of social indicators shared an interest in providing data which could be used in public policy making (Parke & Seidman, 1978). For example, Bauer's early and definitive volume featured social scientists who were interested in generating data which could be used to evaluate social programs and to set national goals and priorities for social well-being. Other proposals have focused on the use of social indicators to monitor the impact of large-scale social change on the "quality of life" (see Campbell, Converse, & Rodgers, 1976). Closely allied to the social change objective has been a social-reporting rationale which has emphasized the importance of annual systematic reports on general social conditions (possibly as a means both of predicting future well-being and helping to shape it).

The social indicators movement has from its inception been unabashedly ameliorative in nature and, therefore, grounded in value judgments about what constitutes social well-being. In his address to the American Psychological Association, Campbell presents a quote by Sir John Sinclair, who in 1798 in his Statistical Account of Scotland described statistics as follows: "The idea I annex to the term is an inquiry into the state of a country, for the purpose of ascertaining the quantity of happiness enjoyed by its inhabitants, and the means of its future improvement [italics ours]." Essentially the same values appear in the widely quoted definition of social indicators in the HEW document Toward a Social Report: "A social indicator . . . may be defined to be a statistic of direct normative interest which facilitates concise, comprehensive and balanced judgments about the conditions of major aspects of a society. It is in all cases a direct measure of welfare and is subject to the interpretation that, if it changes in the 'right' direction, while other things remain equal, things have gotten better, or people are 'better off'" (p. 7).

No doubt the processes whereby consensus is arrived at regarding what constitutes the "right direction" and the criteria to be used to determine when people are "better off" will be as much political as scientific. This is as it should be. For if and when a nation implements an ongoing system of social indicators coupled with social reports to the opinion leaders, legislators, and population at large, it will have inaugurated a system of value definitions which, in and of themselves, will increasingly be taken for granted as part of the givens of that society. The system of social indicators will become a kind of lens through which, however imperfectly, changing community conditions, population needs, and impacts of public policies will be viewed and evaluated.

Clearly, then, the definition of well-being involves the social indicators researcher in a political act, as well as a scientific undertaking. In regard to setting social goals and priorities, for example, some have cautioned that "indicators must be regarded as inputs into a complex political mosaic" (Sheldon & Freeman, 1970, p. 169). Though potentially useful in contributing to decisions about social-program planning and development, they will remain subject to important political considerations which decisionmakers must take into account.

Campbell (1976) notes the interaction between the politics and science of social indicators research in which they mutually shape each other: "Indicator research is not experimental research and its utility is not likely to be as immediate or as explicit" (p. 123). However, he goes on to make the point that in the long run it may become even more important because it will provide a general context of information "that restructures the decision maker's cognitive and affective map of society" (p. 123). It should be clear by now that like any other sociotechnical invention, the social indicators approach applied systematically on a nationwide basis would both shape and be shaped by the society of which it is a part.

It is still too early to determine the extent to which social indicators will contribute to the evaluation of specific public or agency programs. Far more basic research is needed on the nature and validity of both objective and subjective measures before we will know whether any set of general indicators of well-being applied to the population as a whole will be sensitive enough to reflect the impact of particular interventions or changes in public policy. In the meantime, the multifaceted indicators orientation adopted by groups such as the Nashville Urban Observatory (Newbrough, 1974) is worth considering for use in evaluating local programs over time.

Given the above caveats on the utility of indicators for public policy making, it should be acknowledged that the social indicator movement is still in its infancy and its full promise is yet to be determined. In the meanwhile, it continues to offer the means for developing, however imperfectly, a balance sheet or system of social accounts which, as it is monitored and improved over time, might well make a useful contribution to establishing social goals and priorities. To begin to take steps in that direction, social indicators can be immediately useful in three areas: (1) improving descriptive reporting; (2) analyzing social change; and (3) predicting social events and the well-being of the population according to certain criteria. "The three tasks of course are interdependent. Adequate descriptive reporting is essential for the development of improved investigations of social change and correspondingly increased understanding of past social changes is required for better prediction of future events" (Sheldon & Freeman, 1970, p. 172).

CONCLUSION

We believe this chapter demonstrates that there is a wide range of options available to those of us who seek to study the phenomena of the community. Our chapter is a microcosm of this book, in its assertion that we do not have to chain ourselves to a single model of research. There is a range of disciplined, rigorous approaches, many of which permit both _in vivo_ study of actual, rather than analogue, phenomena, as well as a more personal and involved relationship between the researchers and the community.

It is also clear to us that each of the approaches we have presented contains pitfalls and requires further development. Most of all, each approach requires committed researchers willing to refine and forge it into a tool of demonstrated efficacy. We have not been able to show the way to the top of the mountain. However, we have identified paths, clearly trod by our predecessors, that should lead closer to the summit if we are willing to further clear the brush and mount the inclines.

NOTES

1. French and Bell (1973) trace the origin of the term action research to John Collier as well as to Lewin. Collier served as United States Commissioner of Indian Affairs from 1935 to 1945.

2. The research also contributed to developing a general method to combat discrimination. Soon after the results of the intervention in Akron were published, other communities (for example, Columbus and Cleveland) requested information about the methods which were employed (Saltman, 1975).

3. Much of this portion of the chapter is based on Warren's outstanding handbook on community inquiry Studying Your Community (1965).

4. The term needs assessment is often used to refer to survey research whose goal is to determine a community's need for human service programs (see Coursey, 1979).

5. We have chosen to discuss this particular simulation because it is one we have used ourselves to enhance our understanding of the dynamics of community action. However, a limitation is that the method has been used primarily for purposes of training rather than formal research.

6. It should be noted that these findings are based on so-called treated cases, that is, those reported by mental institutions and individual practitioners. This method of case counting is probably biased in that it underestimates rates among affluent individuals who are more readily cared for at home or in more confidential settings.

7. See MacMahon and Pugh (1970) for a comprehensive discussion of the development of epidemiology and its contemporary applications.

8. Some but not all of this variation in prevalence rates is due to the fact that different studies used differing target populations as well as differing methods and criteria for assessing psychopathology.

REFERENCES

Ahlbrandt, R. S., Jr., Charny, M. K., & Cunningham, J. V. Citizen perceptions of their neighborhoods. Journal of Housing, 1977, 7, 338–341.

Andrews, F., & Withey, S. Social indicators of well-being: Americans' perception of life quality. New York: Plenum, 1976.

Bauer, R. S. (Ed.). Social indicators. Cambridge, Mass.: MIT Press, 1966.

Bell, C., & Newby, H. Community studies. New York: Praeger, 1972.

Bennis, W. G. The case study. Journal of Applied Behavioral Science, 1968, 4(2), 227–231.

Blalock, H. M., Jr. Causal inference in non-experimental research. New York: W. W. Norton, 1973.

Bogdan, R., & Taylor, S. J. Introduction to qualitative research methods: A phenomenological approach to the social sciences. New York: John Wiley, 1975.

Bowers, D. G. Organization development techniques and their results in 26 organizations: The Michigan ICL study. Journal of Applied Behavioral Science, 1973, 9, 21–43.

Bradburn, N. M. The structure of psychological well-being. Chicago: Aldine, 1969.

Bruyn, S. Human perspective in sociology: The methodology of participant observation. Englewood Cliffs, N.J.: Prentice-Hall, 1966.

Campbell, A. Subjective measures of well being. American Psychologist, February 1976, 117–124.

Campbell, A., Converse, P. E., & Rodgers, W. L. The quality of American life: Perceptions, evaluations and satisfactions. New York: Russell Sage Foundation, 1976.

Campbell, D. T., Kruskal, W. H., & Wallace, W. P. Seating segregation as an index of attitude. Sociometry, 1966, 29, 1–15.

Cantril, H. The pattern of human concern. New Brunswick, N.J.: Rutgers University Press, 1965.

Chein, I., Cook, S. W., & Harding, J. The field of action research. American Psychologist, 1948, 3, 43-50.

Cohen, W. J. Social indicators: Statistics for public policy. The American Statistician, 1968, 22, 14-16.

Cook, S. W. Introduction. In M. H. Wormser & C. Selltiz (Eds.), Community self-survey: Principles and practice. Journal of Social Issues, 1949, 7, 330-361.

Cottle, T. Private lives and public accounts. New York: Watts, 1977.

Coursey, R. D. (Ed.). Program evaluation for mental health. New York: Grune & Stratton, 1979.

Davison, G. C., & Neale, J. M. Abnormal psychology: An experimental clinical approach. New York: John Wiley, 1978.

Department of Health, Education, and Welfare. Toward a social report. Washington, D.C.: U.S. Government Printing Office, 1967.

Denzin, N. K. The research act: A theoretical introduction to sociological methods. New York: McGraw-Hill, 1978.

Duke, R. Gaming simulation in urban research. Institute for Community Development Services, Michigan State University, 1964.

Duke, R., & Meier, R. Gaming simulation for urban planning. Journal of the American Institute of Planners, 1966, 32, 3-17.

Dutton, J. M., & Starbuck, W. H. (Eds.). Computer simulation of human behavior. New York: John Wiley, 1971.

Erikson, K. T. A comment on disguised observation in sociology. Social Problems, 1967, 14, 366-373.

Faris, R. E., & Dunham, H. W. Mental disorders in urban areas: An ecological study of schizophrenia and other psychoses. Chicago: Chicago University Press, 1939.

Feldt, A. Operational gaming in planning education. Journal of the American Institute of Planners, 1966, 32, 17-23.

Ferriss, A. L. Trends in education and training. In C. Taeuber (Ed.), America in the seventies: Some social indicators. Philadelphia: The American Academy of Political and Social Science, 1978.

Festinger, L., Riecken, H. W., & Schachter, S. When prophecy fails. Minneapolis: University of Minnesota Press, 1956.

Fleming, K. H. Toward social reporting in Milwaukee. Final Phase 1 Report, Milwaukee Urban Observatory Social Indicators Project, January 1972.

Freire, P. Research methods. Literacy discussion. Teheran: The International Institute for Adult Literacy, Spring 1974.

French, W. L., & Bell, C. H. Organization development. Englewood Cliffs, N.J.: Prentice-Hall, 1973.

Gamson, W. A. SIMSOC: Simulated society, instructor's Manual. New York: Free Press, 1969.

Gold, R. L. Roles in sociological field observations. Social Forces, 1958, 36, 217-222.

Gross, B. (Ed.). Social goals and indicators for American society. Annals of the American Academy of Political and Social Science, May 1967.

Gross, N., Mason, W., & McEachem, A. Explorations in role analysis: Studies of the school superintendency role. New York: John Wiley, 1958.

Guetzkow, H., Alger, C. F., Brody, R. A., Noel, R. C., & Snyder, R. C. Simulation in international relations: Developments for research and teaching. Englewood Cliffs, N.J.: Prentice-Hall, 1963.

Hall, B., & Gillette, A. (Eds.). Creating knowledge: A monopoly. Toronto: International Council for Adult Education and International Institute for Adult Literacy Methods, 1978.

Heller, K., & Monahan, J. Psychology and community change. Homewood, Ill.: Dorsey Press, 1977.

Holland, E. P. Simulation of an economy with development and trade problems. In H. Guetzkow, P. Kotler, & R. L. Schultz (Eds.), Simulation in social and administrative science. Englewood Cliffs, N.J.: Prentice-Hall, 1972.

Hollingshead, A. B., & Redlich, F. C. Social class and mental illness. New York: John Wiley, 1958.

Hughes, C. C. People of Cove and Woodlot. New York: Basic Books, 1960.

Hunter, F. Community power structure: A study of decision makers. Chapel Hill: University of North Carolina Press, 1953.

Hunter, F., Schaffer, R., & Sheps, C. Community organization: Action and inaction. Chapel Hill: University of North Carolina Press, 1956.

Janes, R. A note on the phases of the community role of the participant observer. American Sociological Review, 1961, 26, 446-450.

Junker, B. H. Field work: An introduction to the social schemas. Chicago: Chicago University Press, 1960.

Karsk, R. Teenagers in the next America. Columbia, Md.: New Community Press, 1977.

Kimball, S. T. An Alabama town surveys its health needs. In B. D. Paul (Ed.), Health, culture and community: Case studies of public reactions to health programs. New York: Russell Sage Foundation, 1955.

Klein, D. C. Macrosystem simulation for community research and problem-solving. American Journal of Community Psychology, 1975, 3, 353-366.

Klein, D. C., & Ross, A. Kindergarten entry: A study of role transition. Orthopsychiatry and the school, 1960, 60-69.

Land, K. C. On the definition of social indicators. American Sociologist, 1971, 322-325.

Land, K. C., & Spilerman, S. (Eds). Social indicator models. New York: Russell Sage Foundation, 1975.

Langer, T., & Michael, S. Life stress and mental illness. New York: Free Press, 1963.

Levinson, D. The seasons of a man's life. New York: Knopf, 1978.

Levi-Strauss, C. Anthropology: Its achievements and its future. Current Anthropology, 1966, No. 2.

Lewin, K. Action research and minority problems. Journal of Social Issues, 1946, 2, 34-46.

Lin, T., & Stanley, C. The scope of epidemiology in psychiatry. Geneva: World Health Organization, 1962.

Lofland, J. Analyzing social settings: A guide to qualitative observation and analysis. Belmont, Calif.: Wadsworth, 1971.

Lynd, R. S., & Lynd, H. M. Middletown: A study in modern American culture. New York: Harcourt, Brace & World, 1929.

MacMahon, B., & Pugh, T. Epidemiology: Principles and methods. Boston: Little, Brown, 1970.

Mann, F. Studying and creating change: A means to understanding social organization. Research in Industrial Human Relations, Industrial Research Association Publication No. 17, 1957.

Marrow, A. J. The practical theorist: The life and work of Kurt Lewin. New York: Teachers College Press, 1969.

Martin, R. C., et al. Decisions in Syracuse. Bloomington: Indiana University Press, 1961.

Mead, M.   Research with human beings: A model derived from anthropological field practice.   Daedalus, 1969, 98(2).

Meier, R.   Preface.   In R. Duke, Gaming simulation in urban research.   Institute for Community Development and Services, Michigan State University, 1964.

National Commission on Technology, Automation, and Economic Progress.   Technology and the American Economy. Washington, D.C.:   U.S. Government Printing Office, 1966.

Neale, J. M., & Liebert, R. M.   Science and behavior: An introduction to methods of research.   Englewood Cliffs, N.J.:   Prentice-Hall, 1973.

Nemeth, C.   Bargaining and reciprocity.   Psychological Bulletin, 1970, 74, 297-308.

Newbrough, J. R.   Needs assessment for preventive programming from a social indicators system.   Paper presented at Symposium on Primary Prevention: Models and Action.   American Psychological Association, September 1974.

Parke, R., & Seidman, D.   Social indicators and social reporting.   In C. Taeuber (Ed.), America in the seventies: Some social indicators.   Philadelphia: The American Academy of Political and Social Science, 1978.

Price, R. H., & Cherniss, C.   Training for a new profession: Research as social action.   Professional Psychology, 1977 (May), 8(2), 222-231.

Rapoport, A., & Orwant, C. J.   Prisoner's dilemma: A study in conflict and cooperation.   Ann Arbor: University of Michigan Press, 1965.

Rappaport, J.   Community psychology: Values, research and action.   New York: Holt, Rinehart & Winston, 1977.

Raser, J.   Simulation and society: An exploration of scientific gaming.   Boston: Allyn & Bacon, 1969.

Roberts, J., & Baird, J. T., Jr.   Behavior patterns in school children.   Rockville, Md.:   National Center for Health Statistics, Health Services, and Mental Health Administration, 1972.

Saltman, J.   Implementing open housing laws through social action.   Journal of Applied Behavioral Science, 1975, 11, 39-61.

Sanford, N.   Whatever happened to action research?   Journal of Social Issues, 1970, 26, 3-23.

Schneider, D. J.   Social psychology.   Reading, Mass.: Addison-Wesley, 1976.

Selltiz, C., Wrightsman, L., & Cook, S. Research methods in social relations. New York: Holt, Rinehart & Winston, 1976.

Sheldon, E. B., & Freeman, H. E. Notes on social indicators: Promises and potential. Policy Sciences, 1970, 1, 97–111.

Sheldon, E. B., & Parke, R. Social indicators. Science, 1975, 693–699.

Shepard, C. Simulation games: Potential sociological utilization. Unpublished paper, University of Cincinnati, 1970.

Srole, L., Langner, T. S., Michael, S. T., Opler, M. K., & Rennie, T. A. Mental health in the metropolis: The midtown Manhattan study. New York: McGraw-Hill, 1962.

Stern, P. C. Evaluating social science research. New York: Oxford University Press, 1979.

Walton, R. E. Advantages and attributes of the case study. Journal of Applied Behavioral Science, 1972, 8, 73–78.

Warren, R. Studying your community. New York: Free Press, 1965.

Webb, E. J., Campbell, D. T., Schwartz, R. D., & Sechrest, L. Unobtrusive measures: Non-reactive research in social science. Chicago: Rand McNally, 1966.

Weitzman, M. and staff. Social Indicators III: Selected data on social conditions and trends in the United States. Washington, D.C.: U.S. Department of Commerce, Bureau of the Census, 1980.

Zax, M., & Specter, G. A. An introduction to community psychology. New York: John Wiley, 1974.

Afterword

Donald C. Klein

In its most fundamental sense this book is about knowledge building. Its several contributors have described a variety of procedures and perspectives to guide scientific investigators as they go about the business of adding to the store of useful knowledge about community life.

It may be apparent to even the casual reader that, taken as a whole, these presentations convey the important idea that <u>there is no one best way of going about community research</u>. At the same time, however, anyone who has studied this book carefully will have noted that some of its contributors have strong convictions about the correctness of the paths to community understanding which they describe. These paths, moreover, are by no means the same and sometimes appear to be contradictory or even mutually exclusive. How can we reconcile these differing perspectives? Is there, in fact, a best way to conduct community inquiry? Or is the overall theme of the volume correct when it implies that each of these approaches, however irreconcilable it and others may seem to be, has merit?

The key lies in a simple yet important principle: <u>the method of inquiry must be suited to the nature of the knowledge or understanding being sought</u>. The best approach to a community study is to use that method or combination of methods which, with the least expenditure of time, energy, and money, will be most likely to yield the knowledge or understanding that is desired. In most cases, as several of the authors in this book have emphasized, a <u>combination of converging methods</u> is indicated.

This principle can be illustrated by using the obvious example of a territory that has just been opened to exploration, the aims of which will dictate the methods to be used. To gain an overview of the topography of the land as well as an indication of its vegetation, mineral resources, and similar characteristics, one could carry out aerial surveys using the latest in sophisticated photographic technology. To determine more precisely the number and distribution of plants, animals, birds, insects, and other creatures, one

497

could conduct a carefully planned on-site census. To
understand how these various species are interrelated
ecologically, one could carry out over time a number of
detailed observations tracking the movements of specific
animals at various times of day and through seasonal
changes. These and numerous other methodologies would
be appropriate, depending in each instance on the purpose
of the inquiry. Even the phenomenological approach described in this volume by von Eckartsberg might be called
upon should the territory turn out to be inhabited!

The phenomena in which most community researchers
are interested are surely as complex and multifaceted as
the ones to be found in an unexplored territory. It is
best to view them from a variety of perspectives using
tools that are best suited to one's research purposes. No
single approach, however rigorous or precisely controlled,
can do the job by itself. Each of the research methods
and perspectives described in this book has a part to
play. No one is better than another.

The relationship between the aims and methods of
research is a reciprocal one. Though most psychologists
and other social researchers would agree with the principle that research methods should fit the aims of an inquiry, they are equally aware that investigation in psychology and social science, as in science generally, must
be tailored to fit the methods that are available. Just as
it was impossible, for example, for Western scientists to
study microorganisms before the microscope was invented,
so it became truly possible for community researchers to
inquire into the dynamics of subcultures in industrialized
societies only after anthropologists had devised the disciplined method of participant observation.

In practice, however, the reciprocity often is ignored. Many investigators approach every research problem by using that One Best Method which, in their minds,
is the only path to true research. For example, in the
mid-1900s there were numerous attempts to determine experimentally whether or not repression did, in fact, exist.
Freud's psychoanalytic method of inquiry was perfectly
suited for discovering the phenomenon which he termed repression. From the perspective of the One Best Method,
however, the existence of phenomena such as repression
could be accepted by some experimentally minded psychologists only after they had devised ingenious--and always
artificial--ways to reduce them to the status of dependent

variables. As a result a good deal of time and effort was wasted in the laboratory to "prove" the existence of a phenomenon which had already been amply demonstrated by the psychoanalytic method.

There is also the tendency for some researchers to become so fascinated with a particular method that they focus solely on exploring the various uses to which it can be put. An example of this tendency is the outpouring of research that occurred after the Prisoner's Dilemma game (described in Chapter 10 in the section on simulation) had been devised. Give human beings a beguiling tool—whether it be a computer or a less tangible device such as Prisoner's Dilemma—and they are apt to use it in as many ways and apply it to as many situations as they can think of.

There is nothing necessarily wrong with this tendency. The virtually unlimited fascination to be found in exploring the possible applications of computers has led to the useful word processor on which this afterword is being composed. Similarly, in social research, exploring the potential of new methods often leads to important revelations.

However, this natural tendency to explore can easily turn into the Infatuation with Method Syndrome in which favored techniques are employed even though other approaches would have been better suited. An example is the use of a computer to balance one's checkbook despite the generally acknowledged fact that it is actually more efficient to do it by hand.

As scientists, we readily acknowledge that, despite meticulous efforts to adhere to rigorous conceptual and methodological safeguards, research is a highly fallible undertaking. We know, for example, that a century from now much of the data, many of the methods, and almost all of the theories that are now taken as givens in the field of community research will have been discarded. Indeed, the entire mind-set of the scientist is to seek to modify, discredit, and ultimately overthrow today's "truth" in favor of descriptions that are more accurate and more elegant in their simplicity. Nevertheless, most of us give up our theories and our methodological convictions with considerable difficulty, especially when they are ideas or methods we ourselves have created or with which we have become identified.

An experimentally minded community psychologist is not apt to place much stock in research findings grounded

in phenomenology. Similarly, a phenomenologist is not
likely to be predisposed to find much value in data revealed by experimentation. In each case there are egos
at work, belief systems at the ready, and deeply held
values to be defended.

One is especially grateful when respected colleagues
and teachers are able to transcend their egos and question
their scientific investments. As a graduate student at the
University of California, for example, I was deeply moved
to hear the noted learning theorist Edward Chace Tolman,
close to the end of his distinguished career, frankly acknowledge that he had begun to question whether his concentration on animal research had made the best use of
his time and talents.

The concept of paradigm shift comes up repeatedly
in this volume. The very diversity of this book may itself
reflect the fact that we are in the midst of a paradigmatic
transition in community research from the cause-effect orientation of the experimental model to the no-cause orientation of ecology and phenomenology.

By a no-cause orientation I am referring to the
point of view that community phenomena are not usefully
viewed as dependent variables resulting from the action of
a small number of independent variables. Rather, it is
more fruitful to conceive of such phenomena in terms of
variables that function in a mutually interdependent way.

Shippee's chapter on the true experiment and the
chapter on quasi-experimental methods by Hormuth, Fitzgerald, and Cook, on the one hand, are firmly grounded
in the cause-effect paradigm which holds that true understanding of any phenomenon exists only when we have discovered what factors cause it to occur. Von Eckartsberg
in his exposition of existential-phenomenological inquiry,
on the other hand, presents a perspective which says that
true understanding of human experience is to be found in
the meaning that the experience holds for those who live it.
Cause-effect figures not at all in this view, except when
it is found phenomenologically in the world view of those
who share their life experiences with the researcher.

Trickett, Kelly, and Vincent in their presentation of
an ecological orientation to community research also come
close to saying that there is no such thing as cause-effect.
From the ecological viewpoint, every element must be in
place for any situation to exist as we observe it. No
single element from the constellation of interrelationships

can be singled out as the "cause" of what is occurring. If we extend the concept of cause-effect to its extreme by maintaining that every element is "causing" the situation to exist as it is, we are not being inaccurate. We are, however, distorting the cause-effect idea to the point at which it is neither precise nor particularly useful.

We are probably close to a time when many of the phenomena of psychology, including those associated with the complexity of community, will be recast in terms of a no-cause paradigm. If and when that occurs, Western psychology will have taken a paradigmatic leap in the direction of Eastern disciplines that have articulated the principle of no-cause for centuries. Cause-effect thinking, however, will not have been discarded. It will continue to have value in explaining those phenomena to which it is best suited, just as Newtonian physics retains great utility in these days of Einsteinian relativity.

In closing, something remains to be said about the spirit of community inquiry. It is by now a truism to say that the very act of observing a phenomenon alters it. There is, as we know, no such thing as a totally detached observer. When we study community phenomena, we cannot avoid intruding ourselves into the life of a place and its people. In the pursuit of understanding, it is not always easy to avoid being like intrepid explorers hacking our way through virtually impenetrable thickets with little or no regard to those who call that habitat "home."

One of the most exciting discoveries for me in these chapters was that the contributors, despite the fact that they adhere to quite dissimilar methodologies, come together on one fundamental principle: it is the participatory spirit of the research enterprise that carries it forward toward significant discovery, useful theory, and appropriate application.

Shippee says, for example, "The experimental social innovator must actively encourage and solicit, through the democratic participation of professionals, lay persons, and problem population representatives, the involvement and input of all concerned persons in the community prior to the conduct of a research."

Von Eckartsberg speaks of the "large emancipatory potential" in the existential-phenomenological approach. For him, those being studied are "participants" who can be helped to "arrive at a truer and more fully personal understanding of their complex placement in particular social realities."

Trickett and his colleagues associate ecological inquiry with a "spirit of commitment and reciprocity vis-à-vis the community where the research occurs." Their chapter is grounded in an approach to research that is "helpful to the preservation and enhancement of community resources."

The spirit of commitment and reciprocity also is reflected repeatedly in the sections of Chapter 10 devoted to action research, participant observation, community self-study, and participatory research.

The traditional spirit of research is one of detachment, in which the guiding principle is the pursuit of pure knowledge, encumbered neither by considerations of applicability nor by value questions regarding what knowledge should be pursued. Judging by the chapters in this book, in the field of community research that spirit has been replaced by two others.

The first has to do with gaining an understanding of phenomena in order to bring them under control so that those who are in a position to do so can improve community life and create environments that are more conducive to healthy physical, mental, and spiritual growth. The second has to do with grasping the essence of community, so as to discover and share the underlying guiding principles that enable human beings to create a positive sense of community in whatever settings they find themselves.

It is clear that the spirit of inquiry that shapes the methods, paradigms, and applications in this book is one of deep dedication to the improvement of human community. It is the spirit which spurred us, its editors, to finish the volume despite many difficulties and long delays. We are confident that those who use this book will appreciate its spirit as well as its substance.

INDEX